The Red and the White

The Red and the White

A HISTORY OF WINE IN FRANCE AND ITALY IN THE NINETEENTH CENTURY

BY LEO A. LOUBÈRE

Drawings by Mark Blanton and Philip Loubère

State University of New York Press • Albany 1978

First published in 1978 by
State University of New York Press
© 1978 State University of New York
All rights reserved
Made and printed in the United States of America

Library of Congress Cataloging in Publication Data

Loubère, Leo A
The red and the white.

Bibliography: p.
Includes index.
1. Wine and wine making—France—History.   2. Wine
and wine making—Italy—History.   I. Title.
HD9385.F8L68 1978   338.4'7'663200944   78-2304
ISBN 0-87395-370-3

This book is dedicated to the memory of

MARVIN FELDMAN

Contents

Figures

Tables

Maps

Graphs

List of Equivalents

1 HECTARE = 2.47 ACRES

1 LITER = 1.05 QUARTS

1 HECTOLITER = 100 LITERS = 26.4 GALLONS

1 FRANC = 100 CENTIMES

1 LIRA = 100 CENTÈSIMI

Preface

This book has its origins in an odyssey from politics to wine. From 1959 to 1970 I studied a group of politicians known in France as the Radicals, whose name I capitalize to differentiate them as a political party from the garden variety left-wingers often collectively referred to as radicals. About midway during these years I discovered that one of their strongholds until 1910 lay in the huge vineyard of the Mediterranean coast. Indeed it became evident that their southern contingent were the spokesmen for a multitude of small wine producers. At this point I became interested in wine as a political force and began a search for the element in grape- and wine-growing which could have an impact on governmental affairs. The year was 1968, *l'année terrible*, as anyone will discover when consulting a vintage chart for France. During the summer I began to study the reports of the current grape crop, reports so discouraging as to make me aware of the deeper problems of the wine industry, above all of its technical and human dimensions. I became equally aware of my deep ignorance concerning its many aspects. Happily, ignorance can always be conquered, and to do so I decided to become a true devotee of Bacchus, not merely as a drinker—which I had long been—but also as a producer. After persuading my good friend Marvin Feldman to join me, I borrowed a rusty fruit press, bought several bushels of both New York and California grapes, hurriedly read Taylor and Vine's manual, and succeeded in turning out the most vile liquid ever to emerge from man's efforts—and this after both Marvin and I had wrenched our backs turning the press. Small wonder that I did not abandon both the grape and the book at this point.

My only encouragement was that I liked to drink good wine, enjoyed living in regions where it was produced, and recognized that its history in recent times was unexplored. There were many historical studies about its fabrication in antiquity and the middle ages, but historians' interest flagged as they approached recent times. Besides, my first experience making wine had aroused my curiosity, as it had Marvin's, with the result that we read more extensively in the technical literature, tried again, and concocted a beverage that proved at least drinkable, thanks to the better quality of our grapes. Then in 1971 I undertook the first of several extended journeys to the winelands of France and Italy, where I studied both the art of viniculture, as distinct from the science of enology, and the history of its development. The present book is the end result of that most pleasant labor of love.

Labors, like love, is more pleasurable when it is shared. And numerous people have shared their knowledge and their love of wine with me. Especial thanks go to Charles Warner and Orville Murphy, who read "the whole thing," and their suggestions saved me from some egregious errors. I am equally grateful to Murray Brown and George Strauss, who read and helped me revise chapter seven, Bert Hall whose knowledge of technology helped me to improve chapter six, Georg Iggers and Richard Brace who suggested improvements of chapter eight, Ira Glazier for chapters seven and eleven, and Nelson Shaulis for all the material on grapes. Needless to say I alone am responsible for the data and conclusions of the entire manuscript, and my Bacchic smile has persevered despite the occasional knowing frowns of my colleagues regarding several sections that I could not bring myself to change.

I am equally grateful to the following persons who aided my search for documents. In France: M. François Bonal of the Comité Interprofessionel du Vin de Champagne; Mme de Maigret and M. Marcel Hiltzer of Moët and Chandon; M. Louis Marc d'Harcourt of Veuve Clicquot; M.J. Nollevalle of the Syndicat Général des Vignerons de la Champagne; MM. J.M. Courteau and de Traversay of the Conseil Interprofessionnel du Vin de Bordeaux, Professor Georges Dupeux and Mlle Marianne Dupeux, Professors Charles Higounet, Robert Pijassou, Georges Clause, Emmanuel Leroy Ladurie, the staff of the Library of the Chamber of Commerce of Bordeaux, M. A. Manoncourt of Saint Emilion, and Louise Tilly. I also wish to acknowledge the aid of MM. Gustave Petit and Régis Rochoux *vignerons avisés*. In Italy, I am grateful to the enologist Signore Renato Ratti; Signori Luciano Garretti and Ercole Garrone of the Consorzio dell'Asti Spumante; Signora Isa Ricci of the state archives in Turin, and Professors Angelo Moioli and Mario Romani. My readers will thank Margaret Mirabelli whose editing greatly improved the literary style of this book.

I also gratefully acknowledge my debt to the Research Foundation of the State University of New York for two grants, which enabled me to carry out research in Italy and France in 1971 and 1972, and to my departmental head, Clifton Yearley, and Provost Arthur Butler who arranged my leave during 1973–74.

Before going into the story I must acknowledge that the sections dealing with France are more extensive and detailed than those on Italy. This is not because of any Gallic prejudice. Rather it is the result of the sparsity of available or accurate information about grape and wine production in the peninsula. Italians, although they have written extensively about their vineyards and fermented beverages, have not published for their viticultural regions the detailed and sophisticated monographs that can be found for several areas of France, nor were their local libraries, archives, chambers of commerce, and enological institutes as rich in data as those of France. Undoubtedly there are sources that I did not discover. Perhaps luck was against me; I began research in Italy in 1972, precisely when the "Italian miracle" in economic growth came to an end. Important libraries closed at 2 P.M. and archives were open only for three hours on weekdays. This situation simply did not leave me with sufficient time to find—if it is there at all—the information I needed on vintages, economics of production, and the human element. In addition, much of the pamphlet literatuare in the National Library at Florence was lost in the recent flood. I offer this book, therefore, as the first serious effort to study the wine industry in recent times; it is a pioneering work, and may the paths it opens encourage others to enter as road builders.

Buffalo, N.Y.
1977

Introduction

In this book I attempt to describe the heartland of the world of wine during the nineteenth century. This world, as even the most casual reader knows, did not begin in 1800, for by this arbitrary date its history was already an old one, and like the story of man, obscure in its beginnings, hesitant in its growth, and uncertain of its conquests and future. What is known about its earliest centuries has often derived as much from myth and poetic imagination as from fact; it seems likely that man happened upon the fermented juice of grapes long before he learned how to note down either his pleasure of it or his stupor. If the deliberate making of wine—whenever that occurred—cannot claim to be the oldest profession, it must still have been one of man's most ancient means of solace against the natural harshness of life. Only as man ascended to the higher levels of civilization did he come to look upon wine as more than a consolation and perceive it as a creation worthy of his advanced culture. This attitude was the heritage of nineteenth-century enophiles who preserved the imagery and inspiration of earlier times. In consequence, the most rational and hard-headed of growers continually sought to convince his skeptical fellows that his wine was a work of art, a gift of the gods, indeed their own nectar, a symbol of ecstasy. Neither Dionysus nor Bacchus died with the ancient civilizations of Greece and Rome; their songs, their revels lived on, their cups were bottomless, their rites without end.

But since ancient times the world of wine has also displayed its down-to-earth, realistic side: the growing of grapes, the making of wine from their juice, and the selling of the finished product in order to earn a living. These more mundane activities brought both despair and joy to each grower, for while there were years of poor and years of great vintages, wine-making always demanded back-breaking labors, heavy outlays of time and capital, the acquisition of technological knowledge, and infinite patience—all unknown to most of the reveling gods of man's imagination.

This book concentrates less on the poetry and more on the social, technological and economic aspects of wine. And it concentrates on the period 1800–1914, because this was the century of profound innovation in all three aspects. In the preceding century, man knew hardly more about cultivating vines and making wine than did his distant predecessors. The seventeen centuries of the Christian era, although they consecrated wine as a holy beverage and included it as a divine symbol of Jesus' blood, hardly encompassed any major transformation of its manufacture, save the use of wooden vessels for its storage and maturation. Nonetheless Christian culture preserved it, and Christ's devotees eventually did more than this: from the Middle Ages, and most especially from the late seventeenth and eighteenth centuries on, they provided the monastic savoir faire and financial resources needed to enhance wine's quality, although without greatly altering its technology. So that only about the mid-1700s did there occur on a wide scale a truly notable wine industry, with a life, a history, a destiny of its own. That man had always made wine does not alter the argument that chiefly after 1800 did wine make man, that is, offer him an industry and commerce and new wealth undreamt of before.

This general assertion is not intended to deny the importance of wine in the lives of men living, loving, and drinking before the rather arbitrary date of 1800. After all, the competition between the nectars of Burgundy and Champagne in the seventeenth century—when the best of the latter was still red or reddish and nonsparkling—inspired a host of poets, all creating rhymes to prove that one was superior to the other. In several privileged regions, such as these two, plus Bordeaux, Barolo, and Tuscany, the beverage of the gods was an economic and therefore cultural basis of life. And in numerous monastic sculptures grape clusters stand out as motifs; everyone who could afford to cultivate grapes enjoyed eating them and drowning his sorrows in their fermented beverage. And yet the fact remains that until the late 1700s the wine industry, although quite widespread geographically, was carried out on a small scale, turned out a product consumed by a minute part of the population, save on festive occasions, and consequently was hardly an important economic force. Indeed, the vineyard as such hardly existed, except in the above privileged areas, for vine rows were laid out—when they were laid out—among other crops. More often than not vines were hung on live trees, and the wine made from their grapes demanded both the absence of a delicate palate and a stomach steeled against acidity.

Before I begin this history of the wine industry, it is necessary to describe briefly the wine-making process that existed during the last decades of the eighteenth century. Let us begin by trying to empathize with the local folk, with their expectation and hope at that season of the year—September and October—when the grapes mature and numerous pickers go into the vineyards to harvest the fruit. Full of gaiety, and also fatigue, they pick the ripest clusters, and sturdy men carry full-loaded baskets of them to the winery. There a special crew takes over the day's harvest for crushing, an operation consisting of men—never women—walking or stomping over the clusters to break the grape skins and liberate the juice from the pulp. In the case of white wine, the crushed grapes are immediately placed in a hand-manipulated press for the extraction of their juice, which flows into wooden barrels for the primary fermentation. For the next week or so the working of natural yeasts transforms the grape juice into alcohol, carbonic acid, glycerin, and other chemical substances, and during this interval the juice becomes wine. To make red wine, the grapes are first crushed and then dumped into large wooden vats, and the juice oozing from them, known as "must," is not separated but fermented with the skins and pulp from which it draws color, tannic acid, and other chemical products necessary to its maturation. After this primary or alcoholic fermentation the new wine is drained from the sediment and put into barrels. The remaining solids and the additional wine, gushing out from the great heap of skins and pulp under pressure, is either added to the barrels or placed in separate containers, since many vintagers believe that the liquid derived from pressing is inferior in quality to the free-run wine oozing from crushed grapes in the vat. Oftentimes this pressed wine is reserved for the necessary operations of the cellar.

These operations, once the seemingly miraculous change of grape juice into wine has taken place, are part of a process of maturation. Most important is racking, the removal of clear wine from its dregs by the pouring of it into clean barrels. After two or three rackings the wine is ready for shipping. Before the late eighteenth century most wine had to be sent out well before the summer heat, lest it turn sour in the cellars of its makers, rather than in those of its buyers. To safeguard the precious liquid from souring, usually a result of exposure to oxygen, it is also necessary to top the barrels, that is, to pour in extra wine, often that resulting from pressing, to keep barrels filled right up to their bung holes, thereby eliminating any airspace in them. Probably most of the defects of wine resulted from ignorance or disregard of routine cellar work: the use of unclean barrels; failure to rack, so that the wine picked up, by autolysis, the tastes of dead yeasts in the sediment; and failure to top, leaving too much oxygen in the barrel, so that the liquid became overly acid. Until relatively recent times, the wine industry involved great risks and remained rather a small-scale enterprise.

By the late eighteenth and early nineteenth centuries, however, an increasing number of grape-growers and wine-makers, among whom were many merchants with heavy investments in their stocks, gradually acquired greater knowledge of the total vinicultural process and several areas began to distinguish themselves for the high quality of their beverages. It is these areas that we are now ready to visit. But first a word of caution. The grapes and their wines of the late eighteenth and early nineteenth centuries belonged to a viticulture that exists no more, having been laid waste by a deadly aphid called the phylloxera. Its invasion in the 1870s literally devastated the vineyards of France and Italy and replanting altered so drastically the cultivation of grapes that we may appropriately refer to the earlier viticulture as that before phylloxera and the more recent as that after phylloxera.

Finally, one note on terminology; viticulture denotes the growing of grape vines; viniculture is the knowledge of making wine; and vinification is the process of transforming grape juice into wine.

PART ONE

Geography of Wine

CHAPTER ONE

France's Mediterranean Vineyard

The vineyards of France and Italy were already of great age when the nineteenth century opened with the battle sounds of Napoleon's incessant wars. Under his rule the French were to become masters of Europe, but only for a brief moment in history. Far more enduring were the later conquests of the *vignerons*, the vine-growers, who would cover Europe with armies of casks and bottles. For the moment, however, many of them were soldiers spread over the war-torn fields of Europe. Willingly or not they became part of the great and terrible upsurge that was the Revolution and Empire, and they too helped to topple thrones and to raise new states. We can only imagine their derision when the most skilled among them descended the Alps into Italy and found vines hung upon trees, resembling the long tails of monkeys who had not yet come down from the branches to become earthbound creatures. Napoleon's armies conquered this land just as French vines and viticulture would conquer it three or four generations later. These conquests were almost the reverse of history: two millenia in the past the Romans had conquered Gaul, the cradle of France, bringing new rulers and a vast knowledge of vine culture. Now, in the 1790s the French came into Italy, bringing new rulers and a knowledge of vines based, in large part, on skills their ancient Roman conquerors had brought them and in lesser part on popular lore most Italians had forgotten after the fall of Rome.

The French invaders were more immediately innovative in politics than in agriculture. They overturned thrones, but not the rule of the hoe, sickle, and pruning knife, the simple tools used since antiquity. When the imperial armies collapsed before a European coalition in 1814, the peasants and vine growers among them returned to their lands; they had not changed agriculture abroad because they had not even changed it at home. Yet the viticultural maps of France and Italy in 1815 reveal a long process by which vines were adapted to soil and local climate. And the techniques that formed part of this process enabled growers to produce wines highly regarded for their qualities, indeed, the best wines in the world. But they also made some of the worst, and these too, must be sketched into the map. So as we set out to visit the vineyards first of France, then of Italy, we shall make our way unbothered by an exclusive concern for high quality and go to all the significant regions of production.

But first a word of caution about the accuracy of information. No one will deny the high quality of wines made in certain areas of Bordeaux, Burgundy, Champagne, or in Piedmont and Tuscany. The consensus of taste has repeatedly confirmed this phenomenon. What has never been confirmed, however, was the amount of wine produced or even its annual price. In the early nineteenth century, administrative and fiscal offices of national governments lacked the numerical data to draw up a precise map of agricultural production. Underway in France was a vast survey (*cadastre*) of the hectares devoted to various crops, but this project was costly and therefore slow; it went on for a generation or longer and was partly out of date when completed. The same was true for most of the Italian states. The peasant, who worked the land as small owner, as part owner-part laborer, or as crop sharer, was firmly resistant to the cultivation of one crop to the exclusion of others. However revolutionary and violent he might have been when acquiring land in the 1790s or in conquering Europe, he was a fanatic traditionalist when he planned the cultivation of his beloved hectares. He clung to the old system of planting several crops, not in separate fields, but in the same field. He was determined to produce enough food for his own needs first, only then would he sell his surplus in the market. He was subsistence-minded rather than market-minded. With a sense of confidence he planted two or three rows of vegetables, two or three of corn, several of cereals, and, interspersed among them he laid out several rows of vines. Since this system was fairly widespread in the areas of ordinary wines, it has been nearly impossible to measure accurately the surface given over to viticulture. Moreover this peasant-vigneron—for he was not a true vinegrower, as we shall see later—was most reluctant to offer information about his vines from fear that the declared value of his holding would be raised by fiscal agents and his land tax increased. This type of person was omnipresent in France and his contribution to the wine market varied.

Considering only areas that heavily supplied the market, both qualitatively and quantitatively, it becomes apparent that the significant vineyards of France formed an imperfect square, three sides of which paralleled her national borders. At first glance, one is tempted to say that the wine vine entered long ago like a foreign invader unable to penetrate the central keep of the fortress, for central France is a land of mountains and deep valleys where the vine could not flourish and where transport to distant markets was unavailable. Vineyards need not only ideal soils and climate, they also require ease of shipment and access to the broader world. Only the outer rim of France provided all of these factors.

Starting our tour in the south, we can set out from the ancient city of Toulouse and the department of Haute-Garonne. Here begins a viticultural region that stretches into the Mediterranean coastal plain of Roussillon and Languedoc and then on to the lower Rhône Valley and ends in Provence, just east of the naval port of Toulon. Vines were planted here in ancient times by Greek and Roman settlers and have thrived ever since in the typical Mediterranean climate. Moderate winters and long, sunny summers allow grapes to mature fully and early. The entire area produced chiefly three types of wines: ordinary reds, sold in local markets; undrinkable reds distilled into alcohol; and sweet wines both red and white. Several communities were famous for these last since they sold as aperitif and desert wines in both the national as well as an international market.

Roussillon was, and still is, famous for its sweet wine. Particularly attractive was the old town of Banyuls and its environs, for here blended the ancient traditions and language of Catalonia and the innovative spirit of modern France. The landscape has always enchanted and challenged winemen, who required centuries to adapt the vine to the steep hills reaching from the Pyrenees to the sea. The grape was the Grenache, a fruit of high quality, neither truly noble nor plebeian, but rather an upper-class commoner worthy of the great effort its cultivation required.

Over centuries growers had cut terraces in the hillsides and built low stone walls to support them. Unlike other parts of France, stone was easily available in Roussillon, where bedrock lay under a few inches of soil. The problem was rather with planting. Fortunately local inventiveness had rather recently discovered the dibble, or long iron bar, with which the worker pounded a narrow hole into the bedrock to a depth of about fifteen inches. He then inserted a vine cutting and filled the hole with soil. But here his ingenuity ended, for he rarely added fertilizer or water, with the result that at least half the cuttings died. Those that survived were hearty indeed because they had to sink roots deep into rock crevices in search of food and moisture in order to survive the dry hot summer. The great advantages of this method were that vines were laid out in rows and enjoyed a monopoly of the terrain, since no other crops would grow under such conditions. The *cru* (growth) of Banyuls, therefore, claimed a special character, different from those areas around

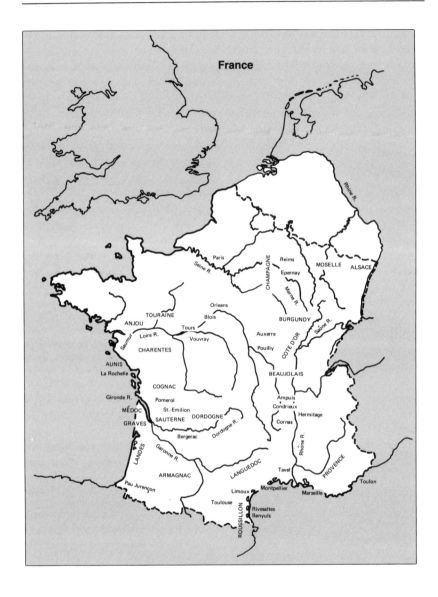

France

MAP 1: *Wine Areas of France*

Rivesaltes, Frontignan, and Lunel, where vineyards enjoyed deeper soils and the Muscat grape predominated.

Vine culture in Roussillon and Languedoc was probably well suited to the arid terrain, but local growers rarely seemed aware of improved techniques. The southerner persisted in pruning his vines excessively short and even clung to the old-fashioned *serpe* (knife) rather than use the newly invented *sécateur* (shears). It is perhaps laudable that he rarely used fertilizer (there was none readily available anyhow) and that he followed the old practice of carrying back up the slopes the soil that winter rains had washed down. Although sound, this practice was exhausting, because the vigneron carried his soil in baskets borne on his own back. During the year, however, he turned the earth only twice and left his vines very much to themselves. He provided no *echalas* (wood supports) and let the branches and shoots grow at will. Costs of production were undoubtedly among the lowest in France.

Viniculture, the process of making wine, had evolved with the needs of an area that relied on sweet wine for income. The sweetness resulted in part from the qualities of the grapes (although both the Grenache and Muscat were also used to make dry wines), the long hot summers when fruit ripened fully, and low rainfall in July and August that limited the moisture available to the grapes and therefore concentrated their sugar content. In order to add to the sugar content, growers delayed the *vendage* (picking) until late September or early October and then allowed the picked grapes to lie in the sun for several hours each day to further reduce the water in the juice.

After a week of basking, the grapes were crushed with bare feet. They were not stemmed because growers had learned from experience that the acids contained in the stems were a desirable component in the future wine, helping to preserve it and adding that barely perceptible bitterness that gave it character. The must or juice crushed out of the grapes went into large casks and fermented for a month or more. This must was commonly known as the *vin de goutte*, or free-run wine. The skins, when they were finally removed, were pressed for more liquid, but this, the *vin de presse*, was not blended with the *vin de goutte*, because it was considered inferior and was consumed at home or sold in a different market. The first wine was rather thick, highly colored, and quite *capiteux* (alcoholic), rising to 15 degrees or more in hot years. In cool years the alcoholic content could not reach this degree, so growers added a local brandy called three-sixth. When well made and aged in cask for eight to ten years, this wine acquired great durability and, like good sherries and ports, could live for a century.

Wines of this quality were produced for distant markets. Their largest sales after 1815 were in the Paris basin and Bordeaux, where wholesale merchants either sold them as dessert wines or blended them with good wines weak in alcohol. Shipped out of Port Vendres and Sète (formerly Cette), they also made their way to Italy, central Europe, the Low Countries, Denmark (where the cold climate encouraged the drinking of alcoholic wine), and to the United States, where they were sold as liqueurs. In the 1820s this trade was active and profitable. Wine-makers whose vineyards lay in the flat areas where yields were high earned up to 30 percent of invested capital, while those in the hills, where yields were low but the wine superior, earned 13 percent, an indication that quantity rather than quality determined profits.

This characteristically high income of the 1820s did not persist. Two decades of declining profits ensued and the small owners, the true vignerons, suffered economic hardship. Where there were many of them, as in Banyuls, they sought to increase yield to compensate for lower prices, and when their efforts produced weaker, less colored wine, they sought to disguise its defects by adulteration. The result was loss of confidence among buyers and decaying markets. This propensity of the small owner to seek quantity at the expense of quality, to which large owners were by no means immune, will be explored later in this book. For the present we must continue our tour.

The lower South was not yet either the wine barrel of France—as the cereal-growing North was her breadbasket—nor the almost exclusive producer of wine for rapid consumption, a dubious distinction it acquired later. In the Plain of Roussillon, lying between Banyuls and Rivesaltes, large growers made a red dry wine using the Grenache for mellowness, the Carignane for color, and the Mataro for quantity. The result was a full-bodied, deeply colored, and spirited beverage sold either as table wine or for blending with weaker wines. It was a good *ordinaire*, stocked chiefly in local markets.

A white wine enjoying a largely local reputation was the blanquette of Limoux, produced in the upper Aude Valley.* Local growers used the Blanquette grapes that, incidentally, made a dry still wine in Rivesaltes. The vinification process was typical of the time: crushing with the bare feet, the early separation of skins from must, and fermentation in barrels. To remove impurities the makers filtered the must through cloth rather frequently, for once the wine cleared they could bottle it as early

---

* Throughout this study I use lower case for the names of wines and capitals for the names of wine districts and grapes.

as March, when a slight fermentation was still going on and producing just enough carbonic acid gas to give it a sparkle. According to one of its ardent champions, the blanquette of Limoux was well known in the sixteenth century, which would make it the oldest of French sparkling wines.[1] Unfortunately we do not know whether the blanquette was a sparkling wine at so early a date, and given the enormous difficulties even as late as the nineteenth century of finding bottles to withstand pressure, there is reason to doubt that it was. Nonetheless local growers have stubbornly acclaimed it as the champagne of the South. For outsiders, however, it rarely equaled its reputation, and several of the famous enologists preferred the reds of the area, made by blending the Carignane, Teret *noir*, and Picpoule grapes in varying quantities. Jules Guyot, visiting Limoux in the 1850s, found the best of them equal to an ordinary, solid beaujolais. There was also an above average dry red made in Saint Georges d'Orques near Montpellier. It had finesse, bouquet, a lively ruby color, and sufficient alcohol to endure traveling. These were the exceptional *crus* and their average production was quite limited. The Limoux district rarely turned out more than 10,000 hectoliters of reds and 3,000 of blanquettes, while Saint Georges, 510 hectares in size, placed only 9–10,000 hectoliters on the market.

There were other common wines made from many grapes, including the Espar, and strictly for local consumption. But at least three-fourths or more of these were intended for distillation, and Hérault department was the major source of three-sixth, a cheap alcohol. Thanks to distillation, an immense quantity of bad wine was removed from the market, at least until after midcentury.

Mediterranean Provence was far less planted in vines than Languedoc, for reasons that have as much to do with topography as tradition. Over many decades the rural economy had oriented itself to serve the important urban markets of Marseille and Toulon, where city people required grains and other staples. Indeed, before 1789 and after 1815 the Bourbon monarchy encouraged a policy designed to keep urban populations well supplied with bread lest they resort to riots. The main vineyards also lay around these cities, but their wine was a crude liquid intended mainly for the lower classes. It was hardly worthy of note save in this social context and to illustrate how traditional agriculture persisted into the nineteenth century and dominated viticulture. Everywhere in Provence vines were part of a polyculture; they were planted in fields with other crops or even used as luxuriant fences around fields. Cereals and vegetables stole their nutriment; olive and fruit trees deprived them of sun. They were treated, as Jules Guyot put it, with "a liberty, equality and

vegetarian fraternity that destroyed three-fourths of their vigor and fecundity." [2] This condition was called *culture à la Provençale*, a curious
misnomer, since it was quite characteristic of much of France south of
the Loire River, and, as we shall see, of Italy, as well as of Spain. It was
prevalent where subsistence farming, necessarily general, had a strong
hold, or where steep slopes had to be terraced, very few peasants under-
taking such an arduous task merely for vines. Since they made wine of
such low quality, the price they received for it hardly encouraged
monoculture.

What the entire southern peasant population lacked was professional
leadership and education. Until the 1840s most peasants, even if they
could write their names, were functionally illiterate. They could sign
their marriage certificates, but they could not read the already growing
body of literature on vine-dressing and wine-making. The educated and
well-to-do middle class and local nobles, the organizers and leaders of
departmental agricultural societies, were not often interested directly in
wine and new techniques. These societies were primarily concerned
with food crops, an attitude revealed in their periodicals. Few were the
articles on wine and the instructions given in them clearly indicated the
primitive notions of their literate authors. One has only to look through
the *Journal d'agriculture pratique* to become aware of this deplorable
situation.

Of course the most advanced enology could not create, save by a
miracle, a fine wine out of the grapes grown in the soils of the lower
South. The heavy deposits of the coastal plain, the gentle hills stretching
away from the sea, barren and lovely all at once, were not suited to fine
vines. To find a more appropriate setting, one must go inland, following
the great river valleys. [3]

CHAPTER TWO

France: Riparian Winelands

Rhône Valley

The lower Rhône Valley is a flat sweeping landscape, too dry or too swampy for fine vines, and most of the vineyards there produce the mediocre beverages of the seacoast. Not until one reaches the area located near the Pont-du-Gard do there appear the soft rising hills capable of producing superior wines. In the communes of Tavel, Lirac, and Chusclan, on the west bank, highly reputed, light, fruity, dry wines, as well as a sweet "very agreeable" wine were made and sold for the modest price of 18 francs per hectoliter in the 1850s. Elsewhere along the river, and opposite on the east bank, peasant growers made a good ordinary wine from the Mourvèdre grape, called Espar in Languedoc and Mataro in Roussillon.

The only other lower Rhône vineyard worthy of special consideration—and it was most worthy—was Châteauneuf-du-Pape, a region, as its name denotes, that had once belonged to the Papacy. By 1815 all 500 to 600 hectares of it were in lay hands, some noble, others middle class, and a few in the rough work hands of the peasants. Given its size and diverse ownership, its wines varied in quality. The soil, covered with small rounded rocks which the sun heated, and human skills combined to transform middling and better grapes into a superior product. The grapes were those used elsewhere: Grenache, Mourvêdre, Cinsaut, and Clairette. The best wine came from the vineyard of La Nerthe (16 hectares) spread over a hill high above the valley floor. Its owner, the Marquis de Villefranche, had added to its fame by serving its wine during his celebrated dinners in Paris. Until 1840 its wine was never sold until four or five years old, and it fetched the remarkably high price of 88 francs per hectoliter in good years. Domaines of similar quality were Fortia, Château de Vaudieu, and Condorcet where the Petite Syrah grape was widely used. These, plus the lesser estate of Jacquinotte, marketed only a modest amount of all the wine bearing the district's name because most of it came from the grapes of medium and small owners, simple vignerons on the whole, whose produce was about one or two degrees above the better *ordinaires*. Yet they learned some of the new techniques from the richer growers and were more devoted to making quality wines than most peasants in the South.

Vinification in Châteauneuf included several refinements. Many owners abandoned crushing with bare feet. Instead they stemmed their grapes by using a *fourchette* or large wooden pitchfork and then passed them through a newly invented, hand-operated crusher. Small growers, unable to purchase this device, rented it from their well-to-do neighbors. All growers then followed the best procedures, described in chapter six. A notable advance limited to upper-class producers was the aging of wine for three years in wood before bottling. Smaller peasant owners sold their wine young to brokers who in turn shipped it to Burgundy, and there, because of its high alcoholic content, wholesalers blended it into weaker wines of the area. This lesser wine sometimes sold for 45 francs, as in 1843, a good price considering the minimum care given to vines even in this special region. More often this young product went for half that sum, since the little winemen could not go for two or three years without a cash income. For this reason hardly any ordinary Châteauneuf appeared on the open market; it had become a blending wine.

Moving northward we pass into the Ardèche and Drôme departments and enter the heartland of the Côtes-du-Rhône region. Our entry, however, could be somewhat deceptive for we shall not find grand vineyards widespread over the banks nor myriads of skillful vine tenders. Descriptive literature of the earlier nineteenth century hardly mentions the common vines and wines of these districts or, if it does, makes no effort to hide a note of scorn. To find great wine the voyager must know where to look, because the distinguished vineyards were—and still are—quite small. On the west bank Saint-Péray was the largest, with a mere 172 hectares, all on slopes with an eastern exposure. Grapes were the small and large Roussette that produced two white wines, a sparkling one made in the champagne method and a still wine of sweet taste. The sweetness was retained by a process well developed in Banyuls: frequent rackings (transfer of wine from one container to another) prevented a full fermentation and therefore some of the natural sugar was not transformed into alcohol. The sparkling was particularly good; Rendu referred to it as "the champagne of the Midi." It was exported to England, Germany, Russia, Holland, and Belgium and the finest sold for 75 francs in the 1850s and 1860s compared to 60 in the 1820s.

Very good reds were made in Cornas (100 hectares) and St. Joseph (6.5 hectares). The grapes were Picpoule and Syrah, with the latter predominant in St. Joseph whose produce sold for 50 to 75 francs. These same prices prevailed in the 1820s according to Cavoleau. When considering such high prices, it is necessary to remember that the costs rose to 500 francs per hectare in these small vineyards, owned by well-to-do men who hired vignerons to care for the vines and to make the wine. These vines were part of a viticultural world quite distinct from that of the *ordinaires*. They belonged in fact to a hierarchy even more rigid than that of French society, for a grape at the bottom of it could never rise to the top. The Aramon could never become a Syrah, even by grafting, a form of viticultural misalliance. Nor could the Syrah become a Pinot *noir* or a Cabernet. It was nonetheless a part of the noble rank, and for Guyot it produced "the king of healthy and nourishing wines."

It was certainly king on the east bank, where the only vineyard of great distinction rose several hundred feet above the mass of common vines. Here was Hermitage, located in the commune of Tain. It derived its name from a hermitage founded in 1225 by Gaspard de Sterimberg, a knight of the court of Queen Blanche of Castille. By the nineteenth century the old buildings had disappeared, along with the forest that once crowned the slopes. These slopes or *côtes* had become divided into three sections, called *mas*: that of Bessas consisted of granite soil; *mas* of M'eal was the upper part of the alluvial slope, and *mas* of Greffieux the lower part. They totaled 140 hectares. Each section produced a distinctive wine and a subtle blend of all three created the best, the first *cru*. Here reigned the little Syrah for reds and the Roussane for whites. The large Syrah, a mere commoner, was relegated to the plains.

The vines were cultivated with skill and care. Although Jules Guyot, during his visit in the 1850s, complained that vines were planted too deeply and weakened as a result and that layering (burying a branch of one vine to create another vine) further limited their energy, he and other knowledgeable visitors were full of praise for the long trim used and the sturdy support given the vines. Vegetation in the Rhône Valley was subjected to the terrible and maddening blasts of the *mistral*, a north wind that frequently followed the valley as a corridor in its drive to the sea. Most of the vines of Hermitage were partially sheltered by the high hill and by their southerly exposure, but they and other quality vines in the Rhône area had to be supported by trellises built in the shape of pyramids. The single pole support was not strong enough, especially since the vines grew rather tall. Inasmuch as they were not fertilized, save for the use of horse manure when they were layered, adequate support and careful dressing were apparently sufficient to maintain healthy stock. Yields were moderate but adequate for quality, about 24 hectoliters, and costs were high, about 900 francs per hectare in mid-century. The price of land was equally high; in the 1850s the finest reached 60,000 francs per hectare and that of third quality 36,000 francs. As far as peasants were concerned these slopes were untouchable.

Vinification was also carried on at a level several steps above that of the peasant vigneron. As in Châteauneuf the progressive growers used mechanical crushers and filled their fermenting vats rapidly with fresh grapes to obtain uniform fermentation. However most winemakers in the Côtes-du-Rhône continued the old method of crushing the grapes with bare feet twice daily for a week and then only once daily for the next few days. These hardheaded vignerons argued that the human foot, since it was soft and arched, could never crush the grape seeds and release an oil injurious to wine. No argument could convince them that the mechanical crusher was equally safe and, perhaps, cleaner.

Tradition also persisted in the practice of a long primary fermentation lasting from fifteen to twenty days, sometimes a month, in order to obtain a deep red color from the grape skins. Undoubtedly the persistence of this antiquated practice resulted from an active market for the best Hermitage wines in Bordeaux, where merchants blended them with high-quality but weak local wines destined for overseas markets. As a result the product sold under the Hermitage label in retail trade was generally of second quality or less. Yet all the *crus* sold for high prices. Superior wines fetched about 166 francs per hl. in the 1820s, up to 200 in the 1850s, and between 250 and 300 a decade later. However costs were also quite high, especially for the new cooperage rinsed in brandy. Consequently income amounted to only about 1.5 percent of the capital invested in the finest vineyards. Apparently the rich put their money here not for the sake of high returns but for prestige, *la gloire*.

In addition to Hermitage, Drône boasted several more notable vineyards in the immediate area: Crozes, Larmage, and Mercurol. The most esteemed was Crozes, immediately north of Hermitage. Over a century ago its wine resembled a fourth-growth Hermitage and unscrupulous sellers were never reluctant to pass it off as an authentic beverage from the famous slopes. Under its own label it sold normally for 40 to 50 francs in the 1850s, and the best quality could rise to 150 francs in good years.

Much eastward, really in the Alpine foothills, there was a white sparkling wine originating in the small town of Die and made of the Clairette grape, hence its label, clairette de Die. The natives of Die regarded their clairette as highly as those of Limoux regarded their blanquette. In mid-century both Rendu and Guyot, who made the trip inland to taste it, tendered it moderate praise; however, Cavaleau, writing in the 1820s, thought less of it and was perturbed by the villagers who compared it favorably to champagne. Perhaps he should have remembered that there were numerous grades of champagne.

Such local enthusiasm was by no means rare in the Rhône Valley, and with boisterous pride small growers produced a rather large quantity of ordinary wine. Vignerons, using above-average grapes and skills they acquired from well-to-do owners, turned out solid wines for the markets of Grenoble and Lyon. These were the *ordinaires* consumed by the rapidly growing lower middle class; neither cheap nor dear, they expressed the rising expectations of this social stratum.

Well above the pocketbooks and, perhaps, even the expectations of the lower middle class—except when they splurged for festive occasions—were the splendid wines in the southern tip of the Rhône department. Here lay the vineyard of Condrieux (35 hectares) and of Ampuis, site of the Côtes Roties (Roasted Slopes, 35 hectares). They formed the northern limits of the Côtes-du-Rhône region. The grape reigning here was not the Syrah, which distinguished the midsection of that region, but the Sérine *noire* for reds and the Viognier (or Vionnier) for the few whites. The Sérine occupied about the same social status as the Syrah and produced an equally distinguished wine.

The whites of Condrieux, at their best when young, were above average with their freshness and slight sparkle. Their chief market was Paris where they arrived early and sold quickly. The more distinguished reds of the Côtes Roties were, like those of Hermitage, made from privileged fruit grown on slopes with a southwest exposure and a thirty degree inclination. The best of these reds resulted from blends of Sérine and Viognier grapes, the latter in a small dosage to add softness and finesse. According to local taste and tradition the dosage varied. In that section called Côte Brune (Brown Slope) more Sérine produced a rich deep tone; in the other section, Côte Blonde (Blond Slope), more Viognier lightened the color, giving the wine a translucent appearance. Today much is made of this distinction, but in the nineteenth century wholesalers were not greatly concerned with it, being content to preserve the superiority of both Côtes to other famous slopes and *crus* of the vicinity: Côte Turque, Grande-Vigne, Grosse-Roche, Grande-Plantéc, Claperanne, and Poyette.

Vinification was similar to that of Hermitage, save that the violent fermentation was short, eight to ten days, and the red wine kept in barrels for the exceptionally long time of six years. In the seventh year it attained the highest stage of its development. The average yield was 25 hectoliters per hectare, and it sold in the 1850s for about 80 francs, although in good years that price might ascend to 200 francs. The net profit, roughly 900 francs per hectare, and return on capital were the same as in Hermitage.

Thus far we have concentrated on small, quality vineyards, standing like islands in a long river of vines. The term "river" is quite appropriate for the vineyards of the Rhône. Although the valley is quite broad in its southern part, it narrows considerably in its upper reaches, and this characteristic continues as we leave the Rhône and ascend the Saône Valley. In fact, not only were the vineyards long and narrow, typical of a riparian area, they were all on the west bank. From Châteauneuf-du-Pape to Dijon at the northern end of the Burgundian vineyard all the major wine districts were, and still are, on the western banks of river valleys, Hermitage being the one exception. Soil conditions accounted for this in part, but so did the desire to obtain an eastern and if possible southeastern exposure and protection from north winds that could freeze the vines in winter.[1]

Burgundy

Having advanced beyond the Rhône, we have also escaped the bitter chill of the mistral. And not long after passing Lyon with its great silk industry and insatiable thirst for wine, the district of Beaujolais stretches northward into Burgundy. It is one of the most attractive wine districts of France, far more green and lush than the barren South, whose beauty emerges in the stark lines of rocky hills, and more graceful than Champagne. Only Saint-Emilion, Asti, and Chianti rival it, all displaying the steep and rolling hills, the sudden rise of a terraced slope, the seeming velvet softness of a land everywhere covered by vines.

We now enter the true realm of the Gamay grape. As with the Syrah, there were two major types, similar to the *petit* and the *gros*. But what counted heavily was the soil in which each vine sank its roots. In the granitic soil of upper (northern) Beaujolais, the Gamay acquired the chemical components required to produce a fine wine, whereas in the heavier, clay soils of lower Beaujolais and elsewhere it produced a coarse wine, a low-grade *ordinaire*. At its best its wine was, if we believe the enologists of over a century ago, a *"grand ordinaire."* The wines of Morgon and Moulin-à-Vent could claim equality with the finest Côtes du

Rhône; higher than that they could never aspire. They were best when young. As L. Rougier aptly put it, "Beaujolais is the table wine par excellence, it is agreeable, fresh, fruity and can be consumed in a certain quantity—in normal limits—with impunity so to say." [2] After four or five years, however, they degenerated into an undrinkable liquid of an oily consistency.

In addition to the two types of Gamay mentioned above, the Gamay *teinturier* gave a deep red-colored juice from which came a wine that was lacking in finesse, that was, frankly, coarse and harsh. The finer grape gave a clear colored juice and the color of the wine was derived from its fermentation with the skins; it was suave and delicate. The *teinturier* dominated the Lyonnais market, at least until Lyon was invaded by cheap southern wines after 1850. Some was also exported to Switzerland. The finer Gamay was dominant in the rolling hills of Beaujeu and Belleville cantons. The entire district covered over 17,000 hectares in 1824 and about 20,000 in the early 1850s. The good years of the next decade encouraged planting in 7,000 more hectares, an almost sacriligious act, because vines now extended into areas quite unsuited to them and turned out a truly low-grade beverage.

Within this large area there were only a few thousand hectares of fine *crus*. Villié and Morgon produced the longest-lived wines of the beaujolais family, although those of Chénas also had staying power: they were generous, had a fine bouquet, and were not at their best for five or six years, an age when most other beaujolais had faded. Those of Brouilly were full-bodied, velvety, alcoholic, and rich in color. There were, in addition, the excellent vineyards of Moulin-à-Vent, Chiroubles, Juliénas, Sainte-Etienne-la-Varenne, Regnié, and Durette.

In the earlier decades of the century, before the massive expansion that came after 1850, vines were well tended, even in the ordinary vineyards. The vignerons had a more professional orientation and depended more heavily on income from wine than peasant growers of other regions. Nearly all of them were local men who had learned their trade as young boys from their fathers and whose operations were controlled by the local landowners. They were part of a very old system of crop-sharing known as *vigneronnage*, which we shall study in detail later. For our present needs, a brief sketch will do. The vigneron cultivated two or three hectares of vines belonging to a large or medium owner and received each year about half the wine, his main source of income. Since viticulture here tended toward monoculture, both owner and worker had a personal interest in making a salable product for the markets of Lyon, Paris, the North, and Switzerland. The proprietors usually resided in or near the area—absentee ownership was not widespread—and they were active in the departmental agricultural society, informed of the newest techniques, and sought to induce their vignerons to adopt them. As local notables they could set the style even for the small independent owners who made wine for their own benefit. This situation was by no means exclusive to Beaujolais—it existed to a certain extent everywhere—but it was of particular importance there and certainly helps to explain why the region turned out some of the best table wines of Europe.

In the better vineyards planting was carefully undertaken: workers laid out vines in rows rather than in the traditional bunches, a daring innovation that facilitated cultivation and lowered costs somewhat. Expenses, however, remained high, because these vineyards made widespread use of wood supports and highly sophisticated pruning. The local population seems to have put greater effort into viticulture than into viniculture; their methods, even for fine wine, were simple in the extreme and rarely included the use of mechanical crushers. Innovation by some growers was not altogether absent: devices to keep skins and stems submerged in the fermenting juice were tried, as was shortening the time of primary fermentation. Since the upper-class owner rather than his vignerons usually made the wine, the conditions of the cellar were cleaner than those of peasant growers. There was adequate and properly prepared cooperage, and most important, a below-ground cellar for storage so that temperature remained fairly constant. Much common wine turned sour because the above-ground sheds were cool by night and hot by day, contained damp straw and, at times, animals with foul smells that infected the wine. On the other hand the owner's cellar was usually clean and odorless and adequately ventilated. Of course procedures were not perfect even in the better cellars. Several visiting enologists were shocked upon discovering the widespread use of wooden buckets in racking, for it exposed the wine to air and increased the chances of oxidation or souring.[3]

Conditions were hardly different in the department of Saône-et-Loire, located just to the north. We are now fully in the old province of Burgundy, a name so famous that even wine grown elsewhere often became an "adopted" offspring in order to acquire distinction and a higher price. To the old question, "What's in a name?" the answer is, "A considerably higher price." However wine from Burgundy was rarely sold as such in the early nineteenth century. Most of it came from the vines around Mâcon and Châlons and went under various labels. In fact consumers could not have found much to distinguish the mâconnais from an ordinary beaujolais before the denomination came in the twentieth century. Producers of mâconnais also had the system of *vigneronnage*, having adopted it during the sixteenth and seventeenth centuries when well-to-do bourgeois of Mâcon invested heavily in vines and settled vignerons on the land to make wine on a large commercial scale. The Gamay dominated in both Mâcon and Châlons and was trimmed in the same manner, a practice with notable advantages for merchants who took advantage of this similarity; when the market for mâconnais was more active they simply bought beaujolais to sell under that label and vice versa.

All the superior wines of Saône-et-Loire were grown on its borders. The best gamay reds came from the communes of Romanèche and Thorins, today a part of the Moulin-à-Vent district, and from Chapelle de Guinchay, today a part of Chénas. The famous whites, made of the Chardonnay grape, were from the vineyards of Pouilly, Fuissé, and Solutré on the western border of the upper Loire Valley. Some excellent reds were found in the communes of Mercurey and Touches in the north, where Gamays mingled with Pinots.

These border wines, the *grands ordinaires*, sold for 50 to 55 francs in the 1820s. The truly ordinary wine of the Mâconnais and Châlonnais brought in 35 francs and the lowest type, from bottom land, went for 14 francs. Of course these statuses were not unchanging. A superior wine was made early in the century in Mercurey, but later declined in quality, with the result that merchants from Beaune in Côte d'Or, who had bought wines in Mercurey to mix with the great Volnay in order to enhance its vinosity, later abandoned this practice when both producers and local sellers reduced quality in their search for greater quantity. Producers were also tempted by that old demon color. To obtain it they prolonged the primary fermentation, coarsening the wine they put on the market, and they found compensation for the decline in price by the rising volume of sales. As in numerous other wine areas, the 1850s began a period of rising prices, increased yields, and wine prosperity. A horde of little vignerons began buying lands on credit and planted them in big Gamays. This was the age of viticultural imperialism, when lesser vines took over rich lands once denied them. The Gamay reached a peak of glory unknown in earlier times, when it had been scorned, even referred to as "disloyal" by several kings who believed that lesser quality was traitorous. Now it became boldly expansionist, not hesitating to invade the land of the Pinot.

The department of Côte d'Or, where for centuries growers had stressed quality, followed this same trend. Vineyards had never been extensive, earlier averaging only 2 percent of the national vine areas, and earning a mere 2.8 percent of all income from wine. The entire department had only about 25,000 hectares in 1789, 26,400 in 1830, and nearly 28,000 in 1854. This increase came to about 7 percent in forty years. But after 1850 came a jump to 36,914 hectares, reached in 1878, on the eve of the phylloxera, a rise of 41 percent in just eighty-nine years. Then came a sharp drop and this high point was never reached again.[4]

What truly distinguished the Côte d'Or was not the rising tide of ordinary but rather the quality wine produced there almost exclusively from the Pinot *noir* grape and from vines located along a ridge called the Côte, which extended from the southern border of the department to Fixin, just south of Dijon. It was divided into three sections: Dijon to the north, Nuits in the center, and Beaune in the south. Beaune was the largest in extent and the most devoted to vines as a monoculture, so that in 1800 about 46 percent of its revenue came from the sale of the wine. Nuits came next with 35 percent and then Dijon with 14 percent.[5] The golden ridge was one extensive stretch of vines, and yet this territory comprised only about 3,000 hectares of the departmental total and could be crossed by foot from east to west in about thirty minutes or less, from north to south in a day. Côte d'Or therefore conforms to the vineyard pattern of Burgundy and most of eastern France: vineyards of exiguous size. In addition, the areas that could meet all the circumstances for the production of fine vines were more limited.

Even the Côte did not offer all the best conditions. The soil was not sufficiently different from other vine areas to explain the high quality of its grapes. The climate was not the best. Burgundy, after all, was fairly close to the northern limits of the viticultural belt, at least for the growing of excellent red wines, and there were fairly numerous spring frosts which, by causing the flowers to drop in late May or early June could reduce the crop of grapes. Fortunately the major vineyards were protected fairly well from the chill of the northwest winds, but not those of the northeast. The sharp angle of the Côte, while certainly important, was perhaps not decisive. Some of the most renowned vineyards, Clos de Vougeot for example, were located partly on the steeper slope, partly on the nearly level ground at its base, and the most distinguished wine was made by blending that of the steeper sections with that of more level parts. None from the really flat plain of the river valley (the *pays bas*) was included in this blend.

These geographic features were important, but also, and perhaps more so, was the harmonious marriage between them and the grape: the several Pinot varieties, chiefly the black and the white. There was a definite hierarchy of grapes, a result of the connection over centuries past between class-conscious nobles and viticulture. During the Middle Ages and the early modern period the lay nobles and many wine-producing churchmen of aristocratic background came to equate the excellent wine of the Pinot with their own exalted station in society and its breeding with their belief that they were bred of pure racial stock. So the Pinot acquired noble status. The Gamay, on the other hand, when some land-owners with less concern for quality sought to plant it extensively, came to be looked upon as inferior, as ignoble, subversive of the reputation already enjoyed by the fine wine of Nuits and Beaune. Since then the Gamay has acquired what we might call "bourgeois" status. The little Syrah, as noted above, would also fall into this strata. At the bottom of our social pyramid would come the grosser vines, such as the Aramon and Terret Bouschet, the low peasant and proletarian varieties, which lacked good breeding and excellence.

Yields per hectare were further evidence of the hierarchy of quality. The Aramon, at the bottom as regards quality, was highest in quantity of juice, well over fifty hectoliters on the average. The little Syrah and the better Gamay varieties averaged from 25 to 30 hectoliters, while the best Pinot rarely exceeded 20, and in the finer vineyards the yield was kept under 15 hectoliters. In consequence the amount of great wine from the Côte was rarely more than 15 percent of the total departmental pro-duction earlier in the century and fine vines occupied only about 15 to 20 percent of the entire vine area of the department. Its price, however, was four or more times those of the lowest ordinary, called *passe-tout-grain*.

Since the time of the Gauls, Gamay and Pinot have fought for acreage. In reality this was a struggle between rich owners, who wished to enjoy a monopoly of fine wines, and peasants, who were devoted to the ordinary grape. Before the Revolution of 1789 various royal ordi-nances and decrees had sought either to prohibit or to limit the planting of Gamays. They do not seem to have had any effect on peasant grow-ers, given their skill in frustrating royal wishes and in buying small plots before 1789, and their "silent revolution" won confirmation when liberal revolutionaries, in the name of liberty, cast away all the restrictions that remained. Liberty also hastened the purchase of land by peasants. They could never afford the great vineyards, but they did acquire lands higher in altitude in the Arrière-Côte (behind slope) and in the plain, and they rapidly planted Gamay—even of the grossest variety—in order to obtain as much juice as possible. After midcentury the great expansion of vine-yards was more than a purely viticultural factor; it was the means by which vignerons ascended the social scale from laborers to owners, at least until about 1878, when the phylloxera destroyed their vineyards and checked their social advance. During the 1850s and 1860s, however, they were the ambitious, the aggressive, expansionists, and the Gamay was their weapon. Writers such as Victor Rendu argued in favor of the better Gamay varieties, chiefly the Gamay Nicholas which, planted in the Arrière-Côte, produced a wine combining savor, softness, and color, and which had the distinct advantage of bringing a good income while remaining cheap enough for the lower classes to buy. It represented a democratization not only of production but also of consumption.

Its greater quantity notwithstanding, the Golden Slope was not famous for these lesser beverages. The great wines were the source of its renown and around them a kind of exclusive folklore had grown up, narrated in palaces rather than peasant huts, which told of their medicinal qualities that could restore the failing health of princes and kings. Of course, the partisans of champagne poked fun at such childish notions that burgundy of any *cru*, be it a vougeot or a conti, could improve a sovereign's health—only champagne could do that. There are other stories that tell of *bons vivants* genuflecting before bottles of chambertin, of army officers commanding their soldiers to present arms as they marched by the vineyard of Richebourg, and so on. We are not prepared to contest these assertions; on the contrary, a good wine can be as beneficial as a visit to a physician, or to a psychologist, and probably not more expensive. Psychologically a properly aged bottle of vosne can be as curative of ills as a visit to Lourdes—and about as expensive.

Clearly Burgundian fine wine producers, many of whom were of noble origin, had publicized their product to the point that it was universally admired. They were aided by wine merchants and it was chiefly these merchants who divided the vineyards according to their standards. It was generally agreed that there were five grades of wine:

> The *Testes de cuvées* consisted of wines renown for their exalted quality and balance. Included were the red wine vineyards such as La Romanée, Conti, Vosne, Le Chambertin, Richebourg, Vougeot, La Tâche, Saint-Georges, and Corton d'Aloxe. Then came the *premières cuvées:* their qualities rival those of the above, but lack their balance. These were still great wines and some very skilled tasters even divided this group into two parts, a division not universally accepted. These vineyards were found in the communes of Nuits, Prémeaux, Chambolle, Volney, Pommard, Beaune, Morey, Savigny and Mersault.
> Below them were the *Bonnes cuvées*, the *cuvées rondes* from the higher and lower areas of the Côte, and the *passe-tout-grain*. The Pinot still

figured largely in these wines, but their quality was weakened by poor exposure, or less suitable soil. In the *passe-tout-grain*, there was a blend of Gamay and Pinot or pure Gamay.[6]

The whites were also given a hierarchical status, and the best and the medium quality came from the communes of Puligny and Meursault. The grape used in most vineyards were chiefly the Chardonnay and Pinot *blanc*, so the exposure and the soil often accounted for the differences in quality.

Differences were also determined by the method of cultivating vines. Great care was taken in the fine vineyards. As regards planting throughout the department—and in much of Burgundy—the vines were clustered *"en foules,"* literally, in a crowd. Rather than being planted in rows, the vines grew in bunches, so to speak, without orderly ranks. This method undoubtedly resulted from the widespread use of layering.

Most writers on wine, when they deal with the Côte d'Or, exclaim at the small size of the vineyards. Echézeaux and Romanée-Conti had only two hectares each; Clos de la Perrière in Fixin had just under 4 hectares and Richebourg just under 5 hectares. Moreover these diminutive properties often belonged to several people. Robert Laurent, our guide in these matters, emphasized that the size of a property must be viewed in its context. For cereal production, four or five hectares would be small indeed, hardly sufficient for a livelihood. In southern vineyards, six hectares approached medium-size property. But in Burgundy, and especially in the Côte, two hectares was of medium size and six a fairly large property. Most large vineyards, therefore, were to be found where the Pinot was grown almost exclusively. In the slope of Beaune, for example, where vignerons were hired on the half shares (*mi-fruits*) system, a fine property of six hectares needed the services of three families, a total of at least six adults and about twelve youngsters of varying ages for numerous tasks, a total of eighteen. In the slopes of Nuits and Dijon where both the wage and shares systems were used, a slightly smaller number could be employed permanently and people were hired as needed to do several short jobs. Therefore where the Pinot dominated, about two-thirds of the holdings can be classed as large; where Gamay dominated, small property, under two hectares, was widespread. Although large and small properties were close to one another, truly peasant property was rather rare in the high-priced Côte, but was extensive in the Arrière-Côte, where the small owners planted Gamay, tilled their own vines, and sought higher yields as a way of living. As might be expected, the larger properties of the Côte were owned by well-to-do bourgeois or nobles, most of whom, even if they did not reside on the land, were local residents living in Dijon, Beaune, or Mâcon (about 80 percent were "propriétaires du pays"). The others lived chiefly in Paris. An example of a large property, exceptionally large, really resembling a Bordeaux estate rather than a Burgundian vineyard was Clos Vougeot, over 50 hectares, all of which belonged to Monsieur Ouvrard, who bought it in 1818 and paid the then fabulous price of a half million francs. He owned, in addition, Romanee-Conti and several other fine vineyards.[7] His wealth, parenthetically, came from shady speculations during Napoleon's Empire.

Methods of cultivating vines were centuries old and their practitioners were convinced that they were the best—a conviction that was probably correct. In the 1860s it cost about 600 francs per hectare to cultivate an average vineyard and more in the fine vineyards. So exacting was the work that one vigneron and his family could not attend to more than two hectares. The aim was a quality grape, and the shorter trim, by limiting yield, produced superior juice. Peasants, seeking quantity, used the longer trim to increase productivity, relied on the coarser Gamay d'Arcenant, and used some fertilizer to enhance yields. A major deficiency was the excessive number of vines planted per hectare, with a lesser property containing as many as 40,000, a superior one not less than 20,000. Such numbers, the highest in France, resulted from layering without restraint.[8]

Traditionalism predominated from the smallest grower upward. New techniques were scorned by rich owners who were convinced of the high quality of their wines. When the viticultural reformer, Dr. Jules Guyot, came in the 1850s urging fewer vines per hectare, longer pruning, moderate use of fertilizer, and planting in rows, he encountered polite, but strong opposition. No change came until the blight of the phylloxera struck in the 1880s, and then it came out of necessity.

Little of the fine wine was consumed locally because of its high price, from 150 to 220 francs per hectoliter. Only wine at this price was suitable for export, being able to cover the high costs of transport. The vineyards of Burgundy were not on the coast, as those of Gironde, and their wines had to travel over land and over rivers and canals toward the north and east, where their major buyers were. River transport, while cheaper than overland, was still expensive because canals were costly to build and the boats were both slow and cumbersome. Tolls remained high and time ran on during which the casks were exposed to variations of temperature as well as the thirst of the boatmen. Little wine was shipped in bottle until later in the century, when improved means lowered the price of inland transport and new glass-blowing techniques reduced the prices of bottles. The exception, of course, was sparkling wine, necessarily sent out in bottles.

The wines of Chablis and Auxerre, on the route toward the Loire Valley, were the products of the district of lower Burgundy. The enthusiasts of "dry" were here the masters of the field, or rather, of the vineyard. The whites of Chablis were (and still are) reputed the driest wines in the world. Made of the Chardonnay, often called the Pinot *blanc*, they enjoyed a reputation far beyond the confines of their limited area of rolling hills lying between the valleys of the Yonne and Armaçon rivers. More directly in the Yonne Valley were the vineyards that once produced a highly reputed red wine, made of the Pinot *noir*, whose first growth sold for 125 francs per hectoliter, while the second growths went for 90 francs. These prices were greater than those of the better known chablis, that sold for 98 francs. All of the expensive growths were the products of exiguous vineyards, 138 hectares for the finest auxerre and a mere 55 for the best chablis. A considerable quantity of ordinary wine also came onto the market, was classed as burgundy, and by the 1860s made up one-third of all Burgundian wine.[9]

Alsace

Traveling to the northeast extremity of France we arrive in the Moselle and Rhine valleys, specifically in the Moselle and Alsace vineyards where white wines reigned. The former produced only a small amount of good wine, chiefly around Metz and Thionville, having merely 6,000 hectares of vineyards from the 1820s to the 1860s. Alsace, on the other hand, combining the departments of Haut and Bas-Rhin, had about 23,000 hectares. Because of cold northern winds, severe winters, and persistent frosts, red grapes could not thrive, and even whites survived only in carefully selected areas with slopes protected from northern winds. Before 1789 the most suitable sites had been taken by Benedictine and Chartreux monks, and the grape, formerly called Gentil Aromatique, was well adapted by them to local conditions, and produced a fine wine. After 1789, when church vineyards were divided among peasants, quality declined and emphasis was put on quantity. More productive vines appeared, and in the 1860s Guyot wrote of average yields of fifty hectoliters, quite remarkable for such a northerly area. Their wine, however, was acid and hard, and since the French did not like it—they had sufficient amounts of acid wines from other parts of the country—the local population consumed it, although they sold some of it to Switzerland and Germany, where merchants probably sweetened it.

There persisted, however, pockets of traditional viti-viniculture. Around Ribeauville, Riquewihr, Unawihr, Guebwiller, Turckheim, and Thann, the Traminer and Riesling grapes produced a truly notable beverage, fresh, piquant, and fruity. Vines were trimmed long and their branches were tied to stakes six to nine feet high. Vignerons were encouraged to cultivate them carefully either because of promising market conditions if they were independent peasant growers or because owners were bent upon growing a quality product. Only great energy combined with skill made it possible to turn out a fine wine that could penetrate European markets. However costs were extremely high, with the result that makers of lesser wines could actually net more income than makers of fine wines. So naturally there was the ever present temptation to cultivate inferior grapes, especially after the 1860s when prices for all these wines went up drastically. But the Franco-German war of 1870–71 resulted in the loss of Alsace to Germany, leaving only the small Moselle vineyard, barely a drop in the vast ocean of French wine.[10]

Champagne

Moving south and west from Alsace we come to another great wine district, Champagne, a territory invaded by the Germans and Russians in 1814–15, but saved from annexation to the German Confederation by the balance-of-power principle that divided France's enemies. Here, as with Burgundy, we must distinguish between the old provincial boundaries and the borders of the wine area (*Champagne viticole*). This is even more desirable because we have entered the northern reaches of fine vine cultivation and therefore vineyards become increasingly scarce—far more so than anywhere in Burgundy—and only the production of quality grapes commanding a high price made commercial viticulture worthwhile. The heartland of this special area was the department of Marne, but only its western section between the towns of Reims and Epernay (See map 6).

In Champagne we are still in the land of the Pinot, but a Pinot adapted to the chalky soil and the more rigorous northern winter. It was, therefore, not identical to that of its homeland Burgundy, albeit of the same family. Unlike some other varieties of Pinot it was certainly not a poor relation. It was rather proud, independent, and equally famous, and in its two local variants was called the Doré d'Ay (also the Franc

Pinot) and the Vert-Doré. Their principal area of cultivation was in the stretch of hilly land running southeast of Reims, called the Montagne de Reims. Only about ten to twelve miles long and four to six wide, it contains the major villages whose vineyards produced grapes for the finest wines, the "*têtes de crus*": Beaumont-sur-Veste, Verzeny, Mailly, and Sillery, and the next finest, the "*premiers crus*": Verzy, Ludes, Chigny, and Rilly. Just at the southern tip of the mountain were the *tête de crus* villages of Ambonnay, Louvois, Tours-sur-Marne, and Bouzy, with Trépail as the only *premier cru*. Another major district followed the north or right bank of the Marne River: Ay was the only *tête de cru*, with Mareuil-sur-Ay, Dizy, Avenay, Champillon, Hautvillers, and finally Pierry on the left bank as the *premiers crus*.

Most of these vineyards produced red grapes and until the nineteenth century they had provided a famous red wine. For centuries, however, some local producers pressed their grapes early in order to obtain an off-color wine, often referred to as tawny or of the tint of a partridge's eye (*oeil de perdrix*). This wine had adequate body, strength, and force and was widely consumed until sparkling champagne appeared. By this time, the eighteenth century, producers learned how to get a perfectly white juice from red grapes, and it made up about three-fourths or more of the blend for the finest beverages. The natural white wine, made from white grapes and formerly too weak to travel, was made of the Epinette, a variety of Pinot *blanc*. It was grown in the Côtes des Blanc, a chain of hills stretching southward of Epernay. The *têtes de crus* were to be found in the villages of Cramant and Avize, the only *premier cru* was Oger. These whites made up about one-fourth to one-eighth of the blends. Such a blend was intended to balance the greater body, generosity, and strength of the red grape with the finesse, lightness, and transparency of the white. The more perfect the balance, the more prized the finished wine. In their search for wines, however, merchants used those from the southeastern part of Aisne and from small areas of Aube department around Bar-sur-Aube, Bar-sur-Seine, and Troyes, the ancient capital of the province of Champagne.

The end result, therefore, was always a blend of two or more juices, which was true of most great wines, the fine burgundies excepted. Really skillful blending probably began with the famous monk Dom Pierre Pérignon, in the late seventeenth century. He was undoubtedly the most ingenious vintner of his time. As the cellar master of the monastery at Hautvillers he had the remarkable skill of blending grapes before they were pressed, which he could do because the monastery possessed vineyards spread over a wide area. Enjoying such a wide choice, he could overcome the weaknesses of grapes from one vineyard by employing the strengths of grapes from others. This practice, however, was not continued by later champagne-makers; they often bought wines rather than grapes and blended these liquids in large vats and, like Dom Pérignon, guarded jealously the secrets of their concoctions.[11]

Of course the quality of the finished product depended only in part on the blender's sense of taste and other skills. A great wine depends on the quality of the grapes and this holds true whether it is sparkling or still (and there was more still wine produced than sparkling in Champagne until about mid-nineteenth century). The man who could make a fine wine from a poor or mediocre grape would not be an enologist, he would be a magician. So in one sense the rigor of the climate of northeastern France made the production of lesser wines unprofitable and encouraged the cultivation of quality grapes, chiefly in the chalky soils which, useless for other crops, were splendid for Pinots. The Revolution led to considerable division of this soil, so that the average grower worked only about one or two hectares. Since vines were his chief source of revenue, he lavished attention upon them with the result that champagne firms could procure the finest of raw materials.

The province of Champagne devoted only a small acreage of its vast surface to vines, for they could be grown with success in only a limited area, about 18,000 hectares in Marne department in 1886, 8,000 in Aisne, and 22,000 in Aube. Not all of these vineyards produced grapes for champagne; outside of Marne only a few thousand hectares did so, the rest being devoted to production for home or purely local consumption. And this acreage shrank after the prosperous sixties came to an end. In the Reims and Epernay districts the vines enjoyed a yield of about thirty hectoliters per hectare. Vines were so precious that the punishment meted out to thieves was terribly harsh. A man caught for stealing three bunches of vine shoots risked exposure for three days in the stocks, branding, and nine years in the galleys! [12]

The making of champagne began to be a sizable industry in the eighteenth century. The monks of Hautvillers had sold their champagne; in fact, thanks to Dom Pérignon, they were able to sell it for 200 to 300 *livres* higher than other producers. But the greatness and world fame of champagne were more a result of laymen, at first usually individual entrepreneurs, who set up companies to sell it on the international markets. Before their appearance sparkling champagne, as distinct from still, had been sold or given by its owners—whether clerical, noble, or bourgeois—chiefly to friends. Whatever remained might be sold in bulk to brokers (*courtiers de vin*), who sold it in other parts of France.

The rising demand for champagne did not lead to a notable extension of vineyards. On the contrary, acreage declined in "Champagne viticole," the exclusive area growing the grapes most commonly used for fine wine. In 1818 there were about 17,000 hectares, by 1868 there were only 14,000, and by 1913 just over 11,400. There was not a decrease in production, however, for vintners could draw on a limited number of grape vines in Aube and in Aisne, to the north and south. As the volume of wine increased, so did the value of vineyards, especially between 1850 and 1880. In the latter year, in the district of Ay and Dizy, a hectare was valued at 40,000 to 45,000 francs, in Hautvillers at 20,000 to 22,000 francs, and these were the highest and lowest valuations. Values had quadrupled over this thirty-year period and had been preceded by a continuous fragmentation of land. There were about 16,000 owners for roughly 16,000 hectares of vines over the century, which meant an average vineyard of one hectare. A livelihood therefore could be maintained only by the production of high quality grapes and first-class wine. During most of the nineteenth century a majority of growers crushed their grapes and fermented the juice which they later sold to the big champagne companies, where those basic wines were blended and made into the sparkling beverage. The price of the finished product had to be high to cover all the costs from those of the grape grower up to those of the merchant, and indeed it was high for all the quality wines of the area.

Quality wines included not only the sparkling type, but also white still wines as well as red. However both of these gradually disappeared, probably around midcentury. Until then, still wines sold well and competed with sparkling, but as the price of sparkling rose sharply after midcentury, it became less profitable to make still wines, hence their near demise. The victory of sparkling and the disappearance of the once-famous red wines was probably inevitable. After all, red and white still wine, while good, had to compete against all the other wines of similar quality in France. But the white sparkling, with which people came to associate the word champagne, was unique—or nearly so—and competition has never been serious for the quality brands. Early in their histories the major houses adopted a policy of quality control and maintenance which helped them to expand their markets just as Europe was entering its earlier stages of economic innovation and the massive creation of wealth for a rapidly growing population. Expanding commerce, industry, finance, and agriculture not only brought forth riches, they brought forth a new wealthy class that reinforced and combined with the older upper classes, thereby enlarging the market. Without this economic growth it hardly seems possible that the champagne industry could have expanded as it did. After all, it grew from about 300,000 bottles sold in 1785 to 39 million in 1909, an astronomic rate of growth.

To profit from this trade new companies emerged as naturally as flowers in the rain, the rain of sparkling drink. The champagne industry therefore was thoroughly established and prosperous when the Italian *spumante* industry was first getting underway. In a sense both industries came to symbolize the economic rise of Europe and both its old and new wealth. Far more so than the less expensive *spumante*, champagne was the drink of aristocrats as well as of *parvenus*. In the 1830s a bottle of Moët-Chandon sold for five or six francs, or more than twice the average daily wage of French factory workers. In the 1890s it sold for ten or eleven francs, still far beyond lower-class budgets. It was above all the drink of English gentlemen at their clubs and elegant restaurants and of Russian nobles at their *salons* and festive balls; that is, it was often consumed by those who were the recipients rather than the creators of wealth.

For the Russians champagne-makers prepared an especially sweet beverage to be consumed with dessert. Most other Europeans, including the French, demanded a moderately sweet sparkling wine, which they consumed with dessert or simply to celebrate special occasions; the popping of corks gave a note of gaiety to the assembly, as did the first spray to gush out of the bottle. This attitude led the defenders of still wine, who referred contemptuously to sparkling as "*saute bouchon*" or cork popper, to look upon it as a ladies' drink or a plaything at best. But the English took champagne seriously, so much so that they constituted its largest single market. They were equally instrumental in the large sale of dry champagne, called *brut*.

According to Forbes, in 1848 a Mr. Burnes, wine merchant in London, requested the Perrier-Jouët firm to send him some unsugared champagne.[13] He had tasted some during a visit to Epernay. The producers were undoubtedly taken aback, for probably since the time of Dom Pérignon a *dosage* of sweetened wine or brandy had been added to each bottle before shipment. A goodly dose was added for Continental buyers, less for the English. But there was no truly dry champagne, perhaps because sugar helped to disguise the acid taste of wine put early on the market to avoid the costs of aging. Burnes argued that sweet champagne, drunk chiefly as a dessert wine, had to compete with port, and the English were firmly attached to their port, as they were to sweet sherry and madeira. If the English could be induced to drink dry champagne as a table wine, sales would rise considerably.

Perrier-Jouët acceded, sending Burnes some of their 1846 vintage. The enterprising merchant tried out his "dry" on members of a military club—at a time when the English military were extremely opposed to change. The soldiers were outraged and returned the dry. After this, for over a quarter of a century, no champagne companies would risk their reputation on such a venture. At best they reduced the *dosage*, but not until the remarkable wine of 1874 was ready were the makers prepared to export a truly unsugared wine. And from then on Englishmen had a choice between various degrees of dry and sweet. Naturally "schools" appeared, with the defenders of dry scornfully condemning sweet as "chorus girl's mixture," and champions of sweet replying in turn.[14]

Loire Valley

Entering the Loire Valley, we encounter one of the better vineyards of France. As in the Rhône and Saône valleys, transport was easy and wine producers were encouraged to strive for a product they could sell in the national and international markets. For centuries vines were grown along the low green slopes of the Loire and its tributaries: the Cher, Loir, Indre, and Layon rivers. Most of the vineyards were planted near the river because of the ease of transport, with the unfortunate result that more preferable slopes were relegated to other crops if they were not close to water. This pattern of planting continued even after the construction of railroads and the large modern barges (*péniches*) could not use the treacherous river because of ever-shifting sand and banks.

Like the Rhône, the Loire valley was not everywhere suited to vines, and distinguished plantings were severely limited to a few areas. For whites, Sancerre in the upper valley, just across the river from Pouilly-sur-Loire, used the Sauvignon grape called Blanc *fumé*, blended up to one-third with either the Chasselas *doré* or the Meslier. Since its wine resembled that of Pouilly, merchants could sell it as such. Both were good table wines selling for 30 to 40 francs in the 1850s.

The central valley, after turning westward toward the Atlantic, spreads out into a broad plain, rolling, and covered with forests and cleared fields. From Blois to Saumur the Renaissance period had been one of notable creativity. The châteaux-building and cultural interests of the rich aristocrats and royalty of France were accompanied by high living and an active concern for fine cuisine as well as matching wine. Noble vine owners were desirous of producing a delicate beverage for their feasts and spared neither effort nor money; hence not only distant markets, but even the local market, stimulated improved wine-making. A monoculture appeared, especially around the cities of Orleans and

Blois. But by the late eighteenth century the Blésois and Orleannais had fallen from their Renaissance splendor. When the royal court abandoned their châteaux in these two districts for Paris and then Versailles, the quality of wines declined. The lure of markets abroad was not yet strong enough to overcome the numerous obstacles, such as tolls on river traffic, which hindered transport. In consequence the price of land also went down and peasants began to buy it; seeking quantity rather than quality, they turned out a gross beverage for the Paris market. The further division of land following the Revolution of 1789 encouraged this tendency, for during the Revolution and Empire wines of the central Loire were not affected by the English blockade, since they were more easily shipped to the capital. In fact, there was a rapid expansion of vineyards north and south of the river, where the dominant grape for reds was the Cot, blended with the Meunier or Gascon or Gamay, while the whites combined the Arbois, Blancheton, Romorantin, and Chasselas. After the fall of Napoleon in 1815 wine production became excessive and low prices until 1840 caused the trade to stagnate. But then came a revival that continued until the 1870s, partly stimulated by railroads and by prices that at midcentury rose to 15 or 20 francs, a good average for *ordinaires*. Unfortunately for the middle Loire growers, railroads also brought Midi wine to Paris so those who could not lower their prices had to find new markets. This they did, locally. Peasants, notably those in the cereal lands of the Beauce just to the north, had improved their living standard and consumed more wine, as did the populations of Orleans and Blois. By the 1870s peasant producers acquired a true winegrowers' mentality, some of them making superior wines by greater use of the Gamay and even the Pinots, both red and white.

However we do not enter the area of superior wine until we reach the vineyards of Indre-et-Loire, the former province of Touraine. East of Tours lies the Vouvray district including Rochecorbon. Excellent sparkling and still whites were made of the Pinot *gris*, locally called the Malvoisie. When white Meunier was added in small amounts, a fine wine emerged that was ready in two years, albeit not capable of long life. In 1854 such wine sold for about 30 francs a hectoliter and up to 40–45 and higher for the finer variety from grapes of steep slopes, where vignerons carefully and patiently carried out the cultivation of vines and undertook wine-making with equal care, a tradition of Touraine. Vouvray was (and still is) the land of fine whites: the grapes were often not picked until late in the season, from about mid-October to early November, so as to encourage higher sugar concentration, and were pressed at once, without crushing, and then fermented in wood. At first the must was heavy and sweet, then, as fermentation continued, the resulting wine became dry and highly alcoholic; it acquired durability, solidity, and a "salutary" character according to Guyot.[15] Storage cellars were simply enlarged caverns found in the chalky cliffs of the valley, caves made by nature and used by the medieval monks who were the first to plant vines in the Vouvray and to lay down the principles of vine culture. An important and early innovation, however, was the alignment of vines in rows and the use of wooden plows drawn by horses.

Sparkling vouvray did not appear regularly because it was not made consciously until about 1840. Before this time high sugar content caused the wines to ferment slowly until winter's cold put them to sleep; they reawakened naturally in the spring when warm weather returned. With the control and regularization of this process, learned from the champagne-makers, Vouvray growers called their product by various titles: "vouvray *mousseux*," "touraine *mousseaux*," "vouvray champagne." In 1843 a merchant of Rochecorbon labelled his wine simply "champagne." Because this practice spread, the Veuve Cliquot company of Reims brought a suit against him and was successful in this early effort to prohibit use of the word "champagne" for wines not produced from the grapes of that region. In 1880 Albert Fleury put on the market a sparkling wine called "vouvray monopole" and found himself promptly hauled into court by Heidsieck, whose principal champagne was called "monopole." However Fleury won his case and by 1890 had many imitators. By this time sparkling vouvray was well established and it improved when M. Koenigswarter, owner of the Montcontour vineyards, hired a wine-maker from Champagne. Due to these efforts vouvray competed successfully with the lesser champagnes amongst middle-class drinkers, who could not afford the exorbitant price of the best sparkling beverages. In fact it was not uncommon for dishonest champagne merchants to buy still vouvray, blend it with their local wine and ship it to Paris as a lower-grade champagne. As we shall see, this practice caused serious disturbances among the Champenois vignerons after 1900.

While Vouvray produced the best white of the Loire Valley, the Bourgueil and Chinon districts grew the best red table wine of the district. Here the grape was the Cabernet *franc*, locally called the Breton. That of Chinon was ready for consumption early, but the Bourgueil was a solid wine, deeply colored, and demanded three years or longer before it gave off its fine aroma and full taste. Here vignerons crushed the grapes with their feet and fermented the must in open vats. When the skins floated to the surface, they pushed them down into the bubbling liquid once or twice a day during the primary fermentation, that could last up to fifteen days. Finally they stored the wine in new casks in cool, clean cellars. The finer of this wine did not fetch a price commensurate with its quality, about 18 francs in the 1820s and a mere 24 francs in the late 1850s. Apparently the quality was not as fine as it could have been had the makers used a shorter and more careful primary fermentation. Certainly the reds of the Loire Valley did not win the same esteem as the whites.

As we move into the lower valley, we enter the old province of Anjou, now the department of Maine-et-Loire. At Saumur and Angers whites predominated again. The grapes were white Pinot, Muscat, Chasselas, Gamay, and Groslot. In the vineyard of the Château de Varrains, there were Carbonets as well. Such a variety offered local wine merchants the possibilities of blending on a large scale, and an abundance of diverse beverages entered the market. Some were excellent, others less so, hence the average price was only 26 francs in the 1820s. In the Layon Valley a moderately sweet wine, quite distinct from that of Saumur, sold for 27 francs.

Anjou, capital of the medieval Angevin Empire of the Plantagenet kings of England, was a wine center since the fifth century A.D. The English connection greatly stimulated vine cultivation and both nobles and churchmen were active planters, looking upon the possession of vines as a mark of distinction and proudly sending their wine as gifts to kings and high-placed persons from whom they sought favors and esteem. England, therefore, was an important market, but by no means the only one. During the seventeenth and eighteenth centuries the wines of Angers and especially of Layon were sold to the Dutch and other north Europeans who liked a full-bodied strong drink. Unfortunately French revolutionaries declared war on England, so the British blockaded the coast from 1792 to 1815, cutting off that traditional seaborne trade. The conquest of all the lowlands by the French did not recover these markets because overland travel did not improve. In addition the Vendée counterrevolution beginning in 1793 disturbed the economy, especially of the Layon Valley. If these misfortunes were not enough, Angevin wines that had once enjoyed large sales in the North were hurt by a shift in taste, as in Belgium, from white to red wine, a shift, ironically, introduced by the French occupation army. These whites, therefore, sought to win a place in the local and national markets, but their success was uneven. The destruction of the Layon vineyard during the Vendée uprising and the high costs of replanting gave Saumur wines the advantage in England, even after 1815, as well as in the North. The Layon vineyard recovered only slowly, as did the local population, from the effects of an exceedingly bloody internal war.

Recovery also involved a greater concern for public taste. Saumur wines became associated with their white variety, and there was no longer much effort to turn out reds. However these latter continued to be grown on the north bank of the Loire, but vines there were part of a mixed agriculture, low in quality although high in pretense, and shipped to Paris, that garbage pail of all the inferior products of the provinces.

On the south or left bank, where the best grapes were grown, there appeared a sparkling saumur by the 1840s, with production limited at first to only a few thousand bottles, but leaping by the 1890s to six million. The way was shown by the owners of Château Varrains, Louis Duvau, who planted the vineyard, and E. Chapin, who created the sparkling wine industry. From a mere 600 bottles at midcentury, their production rose to a half million yearly by the 1890s, rivaling the middling champagne houses because the reputation of the château's whites was solidly based. There were two harvests: the first gathered the ripest grapes destined for first-quality wine; then came "le tri" or the second gathering, for lesser wine. The grapes were collected in wooden buckets carried by hand and poured into wicker baskets attached to men's backs for transport to wagons and thence to the cellars. There they were pressed immediately, usually twice, in order to get a clear wine free of color. For *ordinaires* the first racking usually came in December or January and bottling in March, when warm weather awakened the yeast and renewed fermentation gave a natural sparkle that attracted buyers more concerned with bubbles than quality. This was before the use of the champagne method to get sparkle. The finer wines were bought by northern merchants, but usually early, in fact, on the lees, long before bottling.

In the Layon district, after recovery, the best wine came from the central valley, where the slopes were steep and the soil ideal, since it was too meagre and stony for any other crop. The lesser wines to the north and south of these slopes sold for about 15 to 20 francs and were shipped to Paris, where merchants used them to give body and strength to Midi wines, hence their designation as *"vins pour Paris."*

Moving westward we come to the Nantes vineyard, but it will not detain us, for it produced wines that are better lost in the historical past, and we should be grateful for not having to drink them.[16]

The Atlantic Vineyard

Charentes and the Southwest

Turning southward from the Loire, we come to the Charentes region. We may refer to it as the northern gateway into southwestern France, and note that it was the most extensive regional vineyard in the world prior to the phylloxera invasion of the 1870s. Only along the coasts of large bodies of water can such widespread grape-growing areas come into existence. Those of river valleys can be long, but they are also confined in space and tend to be narrow. The West and the Southwest, in their vast space, produced every type of wine ever conceived by man with one exception, sparkling. On the other hand this region enjoyed a unique characteristic in that a sizable proportion of its wine served as the basic raw material in the distillation of the most renowned of brandies, cognac and armagnac.

The two departments of Charentes and Charentes-Inférieur (today Charentes Maritime) contained in the 1820s about 221,000 hectares of vineyards, roughly 10 percent of the total. Over their great expanse stretching westward to the coast lay an oceanlike, undulating surface of vines and among them the most prominent was the Folle Blanche. This variety had only recently become important in the area, its introduction on a massive scale having begun only in the eighteenth century, when viticulture there underwent a marked change. Until then quality grapes were grown for the manufacture of good whites capable of traveling to England and the North of Europe. La Rochelle and Rochefort were chief ports and the most famous wines came from the nearby area around Aunis. The extensive planting of Folle Blanche occurred when local growers sought to expand the quantity of juice in order to produce brandy (*eau de vie*). In the seventeenth century an oversupply of table wine had induced them to distill it and they found that there was more profit to be made from brandy, soon known as cognac. In the eighteenth century they resorted to the Folle Blanche because it satisfied their demands, producing "like crazy." And after the Eden treaty with England in 1786 they exported their brandy in considerable amounts until 1793, when the war seriously curtailed their trade.[1]

With the rise of a brandy trade there occurred a shift in the locus of commercial viticulture, from Aunis on the coast to an area around Cognac farther inland. Lands once extensively planted in grains now received the vine, because the profits to be made from it far exceeded those to be made from cereals and other food crops, especially since the Folle Blanche offered high yields, required relatively little outlay, and was also resistant to several diseases. Other grapes grown in small quantities were Colombard, productive in poor soils, the Saint-Emilion, the Jurançon, the Balzac *blanc*, Chalosse (often blended with Folle Blanche and Jurançon), and Saint-Pierre. None of these grapes were considered to be producers of good table wines, but various blends of them in the distilled product made the world-famous cognacs. In many vineyards the actual process of wine-making was carried out in a careless way because the quality of wine, while not unimportant, was of less concern, since the wine was to be distilled. Of chief importance was alcohol content.

In time winemen came to recognize differences in the quality of the brandies grown in different sectors of the entire region. The one just south of the town of Cognac was known as the Grande Champagne and immediately around it was the Petite Champagne. Here the great brandies were made, the true cognacs with their special appellations. Vines grew in an earth that was whitish grey in color, containing either lime or silica mixed with clay and resting on beds of chalk or marl. As in the real Champagne district, this chalky, calcareous soil was excellent for viticulture. Vines were pruned short in the best vineyards in order to curb production and make a better wine for distillation. In the outlying districts encircling the Champagne, the trim was longer in order to raise yield. This broader circle comprised the *bois*, themselves divided, according to decreasing quality, into the *borderies, fins bois, bons bois, bois ordinaires* and, along the coast, the *bois à terroir*. Divisions such as these had come into existence rather recently at the behest of cognac merchants, who determined both quality and prices. Local growers, of course, had their own views, but they could not ignore these divisions. Consequently each sought to be associated with the Champagne without the adjectival distinction. Until the twentieth century there was no official distinction; and all these boundaries, loosely drawn at best, differed on maps prepared by local growers and merchants.

To continue our voyage we move southeast into the Dordogne region, a romantically beautiful, wild, arid place of deep valleys and steep hills honey-combed with caves where Stone Age people dwelled thousands of years ago. It was an area of considerable viticultural activity and expansion. In 1804, when the first Napoleonic empire was created, there were over 64,000 hectares of vines. In 1834 the vineyard had grown to nearly 90,000, and in 1870, when the second Empire of the third Napoleon collapsed, it comprised 107,000. Most of the vines were in the districts of Bergerac, Périgueux (famous for its cuisine), and Serlat. It rivaled Hérault in size, and most of its wine, like that of Languedoc, was *ordinaire*. Nonetheless profits from wine sales were absolutely necessary in this economically backward region. In the 1860s the average yield was distressingly low, 16 hectoliters, with an average price of merely 20 francs. Gross revenue came to 200 francs per hectare but costs, 80 to 100 francs, left a ridiculously low net revenue. According to Dr. Guyot, the viticulture was inept; growers insisted on the short trim, which curtailed the quantity of juice, without, unfortunately, improving its quality.[2] In addition, local growers practiced mixed planting with other crops, a common usage where land was flat or moderately sloping. Under these conditions they turned out an opaque liquid that they either consumed locally or shipped to central France or in some years sent to Bordeaux to give color to weaker wines there.

Within this vast wasteland of *ordinaire*, there was, however, an oasis— which is almost always the case. It was situated in the Bergerac district, astride the Dordogne River. On the north bank, just above the town of Bergerac, vignerons made a pleasant red table wine that Guyot classed with the better beaujolais and even with common saint-estèphe. They added a small quantity of white must to give it mellowness, deeper color, and more "generosity" or alcohol. White juice, when added to red must on the skins, had the effect of extracting more coloring matter from them. When mature, it was dry, light, with a good bouquet, and rarely went to market under its own name because it was snatched up by Bordeaux merchants for blending. On the south bank lay the far more well-known district of Monbazillac. Vineyards here had been created in the sixteenth century by rich bourgeois of Bergerac who set up large domains on lands they found inexpensive to buy. The resulting wine, sweet and alcoholic, enjoyed markets in northern France and Holland until the 1790s, when radicals of the French Revolution broke up the large estates. Auctioned in rather large blocks, most of the vineyards fell into the hands of merchants, only a few into those of peasants, an injustice from the social point of view, but the only means at this time of preserving the quality of the wine and its reputation. By the 1830s it recovered its former markets, and although it gradually lost Holland, it found new markets in nearby Libourne and Bordeaux to the west.

Monbazillac was made with considerable care. Even after the break-up of the large estates the old custom remained of picking the Muscat and Sémillon grapes after 15 October, when they were "*sorbés*" or dried up, even becoming rotten. The practice of gathering grapes after they acquired the "noble rot" began here as it did in Sauternes. What apparently had been discovered was that repeated racking would halt fermentation and so prevent all the sugar from becoming alcohol. In this way a naturally sweet wine resulted, a practice taken up in Sauternes in 1850.[3] There was some resemblance between the two wines because the same grape, Sémillon, predominated in both, with the Muscat composing about one-sixth of the must for Monbazillac. Although expensive to produce, Monbazillac during the 1850s sold for just under 100 francs per hectoliter when four to five years old. So it was better to keep it, because when new it brought only 18–19 francs.[4] This price could hardly cover expenses.

Continuing southward we encounter the extensive vines of the old province of Quercy. This is the country washed by the upper Garonne and Lot rivers. The wines of Cahors and of the departments of Lot, Lot-et-Garonne and Tarn-et-Garonne were almost in a class of their own. The grape was the Auxerrois (of the Cot family), often planted in thin soil and pruned too short for abundant production, yields being only 30 to 40 hectoliters per hectare. This grape naturally produced a deeply colored wine, but the peasants had acquired a predilection for a truly black wine and sought to "improve" on nature in several ways. First they boiled a portion or all of the must with its skins to extract extra coloring matter, then fermented it for a period of from ten to thirty days to get an even darker tint. To add strength they prepared a "vin rogomés," that is, they added a liqueur called *rogome* to make up a third of the total. This wine they sold for 40 francs per hectoliter in the 1820s. The *rogome* was made of Auxerrois must boiled five minutes, to which a 33 degree wine alcohol was added in proportion of one to four. These highly alcoholic wines, especially those from Cahors, were shipped to Bordeaux for blending and could live for thirty to fifty years.[5] The simple nonalcoholized *vin noir* was usually consumed locally or shipped to the mountain folk of the rugged lands in south central France. The peasants of Auvergne prized this black liquid; in fact the local merchants, to judge its salability, used to throw a glassful against a white wall, and if the stain was ineffaceably dark they prized it as suitable.[6] There were also stories of peasants, when no white wall was available, using their white shirts to make the test!

As we now swing westward, we encounter the extensive vineyards of the lower Southwest, in particular the Armagnac district. However, we need not pause here because most of the information given about cognac applies to armagnac, even prices were similar. Beyond this huge district of about 100,000 hectares lay the small vineyard of Béarn, just south of the lovely town of Pau, in the foothills of the lower Pyrenees. With only 25,000 hectares in 1852, it was notable for the quality of its product. The Jurançon slope, extending only about three miles in length, profited from a southern exposure and could produce whites of good quality using the Camarao, Courbut, and Mansenc grapes. Victor Rendu, in the 1850s, referred to them as "full-bodied, generous and with a good nose,"[7] a judgement in which Dr. Guyot concurred, comparing it to Rhine wines, but more alcoholic and less sweet. They enjoyed a good market in the Low Countries. The red wine, on the other hand, had almost no market save the local population, and yet Guyot wrote of it as having a magnificent color, generous, clean of nose and taste.[8] The grapes were the Bouchy, Arroyat, Camarao, Mansenc, and Mourast, hardly known outside of the locale, yet their must sold at harvest time for the good price of 40 francs. Far less interesting were the wines of the Landes district, along the Atlantic. These were nothing more than *ordinaires* and need not delay our entry into the Bordeaux area, where wine was a whole way of life.

Bordeaux

As we ascend into the Bordelais we enter another great wine area, the peer of Burgundy and Champagne for quality, and almost an equal of lower Languedoc for vineyard area. No one is certain, however, of the physical extent of vineyards in the early nineteenth century. According to Cavoleau, Gironde department possessed 137,000 hectares of vines in the 1820s, nearly all of which were classed as Bordeaux. Official figures for 1842 gave 133,000 hectares, 32 percent of them in the Bordeaux *arrondissement* (Médoc and Graves), 26 percent in Libourne (Saint-Emilion and the eastern cantons), and the remainder spread out along the Gironde and Garonne rivers.[9] Local growers, using these data, argued that the decline in planting had resulted from the depressed condition of viniculture, a condition that should have encouraged the central government to reduce taxes on wine. Fiscal agents, using their own data, insisted that planted area had increased; indeed they held that the quantity of wine had also risen by 20 percent from 1808 to 1826, not only because more land was planted in vines but also because of improved methods of trimming, and the greater use of fertilizer spread among more productive vines planted in richer soil. These early evaluations were crude in the extreme. More to the point is a report, dated 1851, pointing out that net profits by the 1820s had fallen along with prices. Thirty thousand *tonneaux* (900 hectoliters each) of wine at 300–500 francs each earned a large income in 1789, whereas in 1850, due to rising costs, 100,000 *tonneaux* at 100–180 francs brought losses. The fiscal agent who prepared this document did not explain his reasoning, but we know that increasing costs and declining prices were behind the fall of net income, as will be shown later.

Another cause of financial stagnation was the difficulty of foreign trade after 1800 and the imposition of protective tariffs. The better Bordeaux wines had always enjoyed foreign markets, and their improvement was further stimulated by their overseas trade, which itself was encouraged by the fact that the vineyards were located so near the Atlantic Ocean and on the large transport network created by the Dordogne, Garonne, and Gironde rivers. Since the Middle Ages a large part of Bordeaux wine was destined for Anglo-Saxon and north European markets; it therefore had to be a first-rate, sturdy wine, capable of living through the shock of distant travel; in fact, it became desirable to produce a wine that would improve with travel, and better-than-average wines did just that—at least by the nineteenth century. But, of course, not all Bordeaux wine could meet this standard.

The very extent of the entire district, comprising a sizable part of the department of Gironde and some communes of her eastern neighbors, made for diverse qualities. Most of the wine in this large region was common, like most of the wine of Burgundy, also a sizable area. The higher-quality wines were the result of fortuitous factors in a rather limited zone: upper Médoc, the Bordeaux Graves, and Saint-Emilion for the great reds and the lower Graves and Sauternais for the equally famous whites. Here the soil was ideal for vines: gravelly, sandy, with sufficient lime and iron. For centuries merchants considered the upper Médoc to have a nearly ideal combination of favorable ingredients: dry, porous soil and relatively good weather. However conditions in Médoc seemed to offer a serious challenge to vintners and this too was a factor stimulating improved viniculture. First the Atlantic did not provide ideal climate; on the contrary it often brought cold winds and fog and heavy rain. Moreover there were no slopes as such and no ideal exposure; the topography was flat and had only good soil to recommend it. Slopes do not appear until the lower Graves and Sauternes districts and even there they are very gentle, sometimes hardly noticeable. So the fine wine districts of the Bordelais seem to belie all the assurances of the experts that "vines prefer hills," a proverb repeated even by the ancient Romans. Soil, extreme care, heavy expense, and fine grapes explain the excellence of the wines. Both the médocs and the red graves were chiefly made of Cabernet grapes, with smaller amounts of Merlot and Malbec. The sauternes and barsacs used the Sémillon, the Sauvignon, the Muscadelle, and a few other species to give a special, complex bittersweet flavor.

Far more hilly were the regions of Saint-Emilion and Pomerol, where the almighty Cabernet was seriously challenged for supremacy by the Merlot and Malbec. In the richer soil of this inland district and on its steep slopes with their favorable exposures, these grapes, blended with some Cabernet, made it possible to turn out wines more soft and full than the austere médocs. They were quicker to mature, but also quicker to fade. This was presumably the reason for refusing to classify them in the highest ratings for Bordeaux wine. They were well known in the earlier years of the century, but their quality was considered lower in scale. A first growth of theirs was at best held equal to only a fourth or fifth growth of upper Médoc and usually it was lower than that. A look at prices is a fairly sure indicator of the merits merchants attributed to a wine. In 1815 the three highest-rated wines of Médoc (margaux, latour, and lafite) sold for 2,600 to 3,000 francs per *tonneau*, while the finest saint-emilion received only 550 to 650 francs, the price paid for the best peasant wine of Médoc ("paysans des bonnes paroisses"). The leading vineyards were Ausone, Beauséjour, Belair, Canon, and thirty-odd others; the seconds were Cheval-Blanc, Figeac, and fourteen others. The price differential between first and second growths was only about 50 francs, an indication that Bordeaux merchants did not see much distinction between them, whereas that between first and second growths of Médoc was about 500 francs, the same as between seconds and thirds.

At this time the finest Saint-Emilion vines grew on the north slopes of the Dordogne Valley. Although their quality undoubtedly improved over the years, their price standing remained about the same, and few were the years when their highest prices rose to equal the next higher standing of the médocs, the bourgeois growths. The big merchants and Médoc growers were undoubtedly determined to keep the saint-émilions in a lower place, and the classification that they drew up in 1855, in connection with the International Exhibition of that year, did not include any wines from there. Among the reds, only one listed in the top rating was not a médoc; it was haut-brion, a product of the Graves. The médocs were clearly the choice wines in their ideal vineyard. Unfortunately for Saint-Emilion, the 1855 classification excluding them became official and therefore more rigid. Most importantly, its rankings rather than the intrinsic quality of a wine strongly influenced prices. Once the commission agents settled upon a price for the first growths of Médoc, they fixed the prices for all the lesser wines proportionately, and although there were years when this plan was upset by weather conditions, the official classification gave more rigidity to the price structure than did the older unofficial hierarchy. This should have encouraged owners of lower-grade vineyards to improve quality, because there now existed a pecuniary advantage to entering a higher status. But this was as true before 1855 and there is no certainty that upward and downward mobility became easier, rather the reverse was more likely to occur.

There was certainly no hope of ascension for the ordinary wines produced between the Bordeaux and Saint-Emilion districts. The *palus*, relatively low lands of alluvial soil and dried marshes along the three rivers, produced an ordinary wine (precisely called palus), that was highly regarded. The best of them came from the Queyries, opposite the city of Bordeaux, and in price they rivaled the better saint-émilions and middling médocs. They were rich, generous, and deeply colored, slow to mature and improved with the years. They were exported to tropical markets, because they endured the heat capable of destroying lesser beverages stored in the holds of slow sailing ships. Some were sent as ballast and returned to Bordeaux much improved by the trip. Queyries were also blended with weak médocs to give body and color, and, according to Franck, mixed better with them than did hermitage or the alcoholic wines of Roussillon. The chief grape was the Verdot, but its vines were difficult to grow because of the humidity and spring frosts coming from the rivers. In 1815 they fetched 500 to 550 francs per *tonneau*. The middling palus sold for 420 to 430 francs and the lowest rated for 350 to 380. These latter were harsh, strong, and colored, and went to colonies or to northern Europe for blending with whites.[10] Bourg, Fronsac, and Blaye were located on the right banks of the Gironde and Dordogne rivers. Growers there produced good and less good *ordinaires*, both red and white, from vines on slopes well above the rivers and the palus. Their wines were generous and, when young, of a fruity taste. But they were generally sold and consumed when still immature and therefore were never able to show their true character. Blaye sold for about the same price as middling palus, while bourg went for 500 or 430 francs in 1815.

The Entre-Deux-Mers and Premières Côtes de Bordeaux were areas of white wines, with a minimal amount of red. These beverages were ordinary, dry in the northern part of the Premières Côtes and sweet in the southern part and in much of the Entre-Deux-Mers. The better of them were used for blending and sold without label. Exceptional were those of Sainte Croix-du-Mont and Loupiac, with prices between 480 and 500 francs for the whites. For the remainder, chiefly Entre-Deux-Mers, their value put them at the bottom of the hierarchy, 260 to 275 francs.

They were in the unofficial rankings as early as 1815 and probably earlier than that, since the classing of wine by quality and therefore by price seems to have started between 1725 and 1735 as a convenience for wholesale merchants who had to determine prices for the finest growths of Médoc.[11] Save for the best of them, wines were graded by their commune of origin and a price was affixed to the commune, allowing, of course, for some variation within each commune. A price list prepared by the Chamber of Commerce of Bordeaux for the period 1808–1850 listed wines by region and subregion rather than by commune.[12] The classification for Médoc indicates not merely a price structure, but also a kind of social structure. The first three growths formed a blue-blood aristocracy from which parvenus were vigorously excluded. The fourth and fifth were the *bourgeois superieurs*, then came the *bons bourgeois*, then the *bourgeois ordinaires* of the best parishes. Here we have an upper, middle, and petty bourgeoisie, and a kind of artisan class, *Médocs ordinaire bourgeois*. This last stood between the *paysans* of good parishes and the *petit médocs* or simple *paysans*. There was some overlap in prices between the fourth and fifth *crus*, the lowest of the nobles, and the *bourgeois supérieur*, the highest of the middle class. In contrast, social and price rankings in Burgundy were far more simple than in Bordeaux, but then the former had a republican tradition, the latter did not.

The finer vineyards in Bordeaux were in the possession of the parlementary and landed nobility before the Revolution and there was little change of ownership by class after the Revolution, save that some rich wholesalers, bourgeois par excellence, began to buy estates of the higher growths, and peasants bought some small vineyards producing common wine. The great châteaux, entirely in the hands of the rich, were well established by reputation in the eighteenth century, and compared to Côte d'Or and Champagne, the church's role in their creation was minimal. They had been set up and developed by aristocratic families, most of whom probably were nobles of the robe, that is, were high court judges and lawyers and obtained much of their wealth through the parlement, the high court in Bordeaux. They invested heavily in their vines and cellars, not merely for *gloire* (although that was not absent) but also for profits, which were significant.[13]

During the early decades of the nineteenth century high returns continued. With costs estimated at 320 francs per *tonneau*, according to Charles, the high prices of 1846 and even the much lower ones of 1847 provided a good profit margin for many châteaux.[14] On the other hand, rates of profit continued to fall after 1830, because costs went up while prices either fell or leveled off. The little vigneron who tended his own plants probably enjoyed a higher rate of return than the larger owner. The latter, to cultivate his vines, usually resorted to the system of *prix-fait;* that is, he or his overseer engaged a skilled vigneron to cultivate about 2.5 hectares of his estate. The vigneron received 120 to 150 francs per year, a house, a garden, some land to grow cereals, and other advantages in return for performing specific tasks. For other tasks he received a daily wage and could double his cash income, indeed he had to in order to live. Small wonder that vines were carefully cultivated and trimmed. As in the rest of France many vines continued to be grown in bunches, and some other crops were also planted between the rows. By 1815, however, this gross usage had disappeared in the better vineyards; specialization had really set in with the eighteenth century and the continued rise of prices. As in lower Languedoc, income from wine became too important to plant crops other than vines in suitable land. In the lesser regions peasants and rural artisans purchased or rented or sharecropped small holdings and relied on polyculture for survival. But gradually in the nineteenth century they too began to separate vines from other crops and to imitate the technology of the great and near great châteaux. When Jules Guyot and other traveling enologists visited the area, they were full of admiration for the skill, care, and innovations there. For indeed the many steps required to produce a master wine were fully developed. The vineyard had, after all, been created by urbanites, men with a more forward look on life, more original than the purely rural notables, not to mention the tradition-bound peasants. For this reason Bordeaux resembled the Marne area more than the Côte d'Or, where property was small and vintners, however talented, were less innovative.

CHAPTER FOUR

Northern Italy

A tour of Italian vineyards is a unique experience, if only because we do not encounter a wine referred to by the local growers as an Italian burgundy or an Italian bordeaux. As early as the nineteenth century these two denominations acquired such monumental prestige that even in Spain, with an old viticultural tradition of its own, and naturally in areas of recent vine planting, such as the United States, there were persistent—and absurd—efforts to identify with the French. California "burgundy" can and does arouse indulgent smiles, but Spanish "burgundy" can provoke little else then the most profound irritation. Italian winemen, for all of their faults, which they freely admitted, were less inclined to exploit for commercial purposes the enological reputation of France. Of course they borrowed considerably from the vinicultural know-how of their Gallic neighbors (as the Gauls had borrowed from the Romans), but they did not slavishly imitate them. Rather they sought to learn and to advance the reputation of their own regional wines in the Piedmont and Tuscany; they sought to implant in the public mind the idea that a barolo equaled a bordeaux and that a chianti was the peer of a burgundy. That they did not fully succeed in this endeavor is less important than the fact that they managed to improve enormously the produce of their better vineyards. That they did not progress as far as the more visionary among them hoped, and that progress was slow, was perhaps the result of forces beyond their limited abilities to change within a mere three or four generations. The entire peninsula was backward in economic activities; it lacked investment capital, rapid cheap transport, and active national and international markets. These weaknesses were exacerbated by political disunity, a condition that had not hindered Italian states rising to eminence during the Renaissance, but that was a serious detriment in the nineteenth century. National unity had become indispensable for the creation of a large market without internal tariff barriers, tolls, confusing weights and measures, and local political rivalries. In France the centralization of power begun by the Valois kings in the sixteenth century was nearly completed by Napoleon Bonaparte, and in consequence the wines capable of traveling enjoyed the benefit of a large domestic market, as well as the power and prestige of a powerful state in the foreign market. The French, when they were not making revolutions, put their energy into building up their economy, and the wine industry certainly benefited from the general increase of wealth. French economic energy was equal to her political vigor.

The Italians, on the other hand, expended their political energies either in fighting one another or in struggling to achieve national unity. Until 1861–70 all of the Northeast (Lombardy-Venetia) belonged to the Hapsburg Empire; the Austrians ruled there directly and indirectly in small satellite states throughout the Po Valley. Hapsburg rulership by the 1790s was unenlightened, untidy, and unpopular. As a sense of Italian identity grew among the younger generations after 1800, energy and wealth went into the *Risorgimento*, the unification movement, with the result that economic life, while not stagnant, failed to bring throughout the peninsula a revival of the wealth and well-being so necessary for encouraging the wine, or any other industry. In fact the wine industry grew to significant proportions and excellence only in two limited areas, Piedmont and Tuscany, where economic growth stood well above the national average. To be sure, we must not ignore the fact that both these areas contained a growing viticultural tradition needing only the stimuli of leadership and general economic progress to make them the leading vineyards of Italy. As these northerly areas rapidly distinguished themselves in the making of fine wines, they reversed the ancient wine map of the peninsula, for when Rome ruled the world, her great vineyards were all in the South. Since then nearly all of Italy enjoyed a tradition of wine-growing, and yet Bacchus could hardly have been happy with the general quality of his favorite drink; neither were many Italians whose tastebuds did not pretend to divine inspiration. Barolo and chianti were truly nectars of the gods, everyone agreed, but was the rest of Italian wine fit for consumption even by mere mortals? Let us tour the vineyards to find out.

The North

Piedmont, with its capital in Turin, aspired to achieve glory on several levels. In politics it assumed leadership in the struggle for national unification, and its reigning dynasty finally succeeded in becoming the hered-

MAP 2: *Wine Areas of Italy*

itary kings of unified Italy in 1860–61. The middle class sought to transform Turin into a center of industrial and commercial capitalism. With
aspirations no less grandoise, the best enologists there sought to produce
Italy's most glorious wines, and their devotees are convinced that they
succeeded.

The viti-vinicultural tradition of Piedmont goes back several centuries;
indeed there are numerous indications that some native growers made a
superior wine in the early modern period, especially during the high and
late Renaissance. As in the rest of Italy the immense wealth earned by
enterprising bankers and merchants, which they spent so lavishly to encourage artists and humanists, was also expended for high living. And
who wants to live high without wine? But the subsequent decline of this
economic prowess led to a slackening of both cultural and living standards, along with a marked narrowing of the wine market. In Piedmont,
as everywhere in Italy, the urbanized nobility became effete, while the
middle classes lost much of their ambition, and, unable to rise socially as
in former times, accepted a minor place in society. The peninsula re-
laxed into a predominantly agrarian condition with a depressed
peasantry.

In the eighteenth century Piedmont-Sardinia was merely one of many
states in the peninsula, and her upper classes, apparently unconcerned
about local viticulture, preferred wines imported from France. According to Don Paolo Staglieno, a knowledgeable producer and connoisseur
French wines were more durable and healthier than Italian ones.[1] What
then was wrong with the latter?

One of the chief forces encouraging the production of fine wine is
active trade, especially foreign trade. Wine, like culture, must have a
universal appeal to achieve excellence. The major defect of nearly all
Italian wines was their inability to travel and seek out external markets.
Rebaudengo has found at least one example of a Piedmontese wine
trying to enter the much prized and inspirational English market. England, above all London, was truly the holy land of wine. Success there
put one on the road to heaven. In the mideighteenth century two British
merchants bought some of this Piedmontese wine, but it seems to have
turned sour on the bumpy road to Nice, still a long way from London.
Apparently the beverage, although produced with the best intentions,
was not adequately clarified or protected from the air. The London merchants, drawing on their experience with French produce, urged that all
wine be prepared for travel, first by clarifying it, then by adding some
good alcohol, distilled from wine, to give it force, and finally by pouring
a thin layer of olive oil over the wine's surface to protect it from air and

oxidation. They also insisted on receiving only the best wine and mentioned "Barol," undoubtedly for barolo.

We do not know whether the experiment was repeated. Some wine, advertised as Italian, found its way into London shops, but given the absence of authentic labels, it could have been a blend of French or Spanish-Italian. In 1800 there were quite good wines at bargain prices available to Londoners, but they seem not to have been tempted by them. By this same time Napoleon's armies had invaded Italy, seized Piedmont, and cut off foreign shipping. The loss of a few foreign markets was probably less damaging, however, than the opening of Italy to French wines. Napoleon also carried out some land reform initiated by the revolutionaries, but local peasants were in no better position to purchase the highly rated vineyards of Piedmont than their newly emancipated counterparts were in France.

In the hill country southeast of Turin, owned chiefly by well-to-do Turinese, local growers had for centuries cultivated one of Italy's finest grapes, the Nebbiolo. In the small district of Alba this grape, when properly tended, was the main ingredient in two quality wines: barolo and barbaresco. Since barolo enjoyed a decidedly higher reputation, the locale of production, the soil, exposure, methods of vinification, and, in certain years, the blends used made a great difference. The qualities of barbaresco were hardly recognized until the 1880s, when Domizio Cavazza arrived in Alba as director of a new school of viticulture and enology. He quickly recognized its distinctive qualities and began producing it under its own label. It has a notable advantage for small and peasant growers in that it matured in three or four years, whereas a true barolo was still a harsh stripling at this young age.[2] The distinction was similar to that between upper médoc and saint-émilion in Bordeaux. The true barolo family of wines was located in the villages and towns of Barolo, Castiglione, Falletto, LaMorra, Monforte, and Perno, all in the province of Cuneo.[3]

The most extensive wine area of Piedmont lay farther northward, in the lands around Alba, Asti, Alessandria, and Casale Monferrato. Here growers turned out above average and average wines, some of them blends of nebbiolo and local varieties. Indeed these vineyards contained a constellation of lesser but worthwhile grapes, such as the Barbera, Dolcetto, and Freisa, whose wines ranked with the various bourgeois growths of France for vinosity, color, and body, and became so popular that they are still produced today. Also widely planted was the Bonarda, but it did not survive the late-nineteenth-century vine blight. The Brachetto, equally widespread, was equally unfortunate: some growers used it to make a red sparkling wine, but when public taste swung decidedly to white *spumante*, they limited its planting to Acqui and parts of Alessandria. Pelaverga also enjoyed a wide domain, but has disappeared today. More enduring was the Lambrusco, grown in an almost wild state, with its long vigorous canes climbing up trees for support. Its wine, like those of the Balestré, Balsamina, Crove (or Crova), and Malvasia, was useful for blending. These were all quality juices added to the musts of noble and bourgeois growths to give color or strength, and because of their quality they often constituted up to one-third of the finished wine. The Grignolino, of low consideration and found chiefly on peasant holdings in the early decades, has come to enjoy much higher esteem today. Grape varieties, like human families, have their ups and downs over time.[4]

Among the white varieties, the Cortese enjoyed the highest esteem throughout the nineteenth as well as the twentieth centuries. The Erbalus, also widely planted, produced a bitter wine unless mixed with the sweet Cascarolo, but it faded quickly. The Muscat came into favor, often replacing the Malvasia, especially when it became the basic ingredient of the sparkling wine industry that grew rapidly after midcentury in the Asti region. Asti spumante resembled sparkling vouvray because both were made from grapes of the large Muscat family, but while it was possible later in the century to find dry vouvray, all Asti spumante was sweet, indeed too sweet for many palates. There were in addition numerous red and white grape varieties, indeed far too many occupying valuable soil, that disappeared in the later nineteenth century.

Apart from the large vineyards, most of them covering the low hills of the Po Valley and benefitting from a relatively moderate climate, there were also vineyards in the Alps to the north. Given the topographical layout of Italy, with the Alps to the north and the Apennines running nearly all the way down like a backbone, inevitably there would be some vineyards high above sea level. A comparable situation was rare in France, where vines nestled close to the sea, the ocean, and long river valleys, avoiding the highlands of the interior and the east. Vines liked hills, but apparently not mountains. Exceptions were the quality vines of Savoy, rather high in the Alps.

Not so notable was the small amount of second-rate wines that came from vineyards located high in Aosta, where a somewhat acid white beverage enjoyed regional popularity. More interesting were the reds grown in larger amounts in the northern area of the province of Novara. In and around Gattinara and Ghemme local *vignaioli* cultivated the Nebbiolo—calling it the Spanna—which over time they had adapted to the climate, soil, and exposure, enabling them to produce wines of superior quality rivaling those of the hills in the Po Valley. The work of these local growers proved once more that a quality grape, if protected against excessive cold and frost by southern and eastern exposures, was capable of giving a first-rate nectar. We have noted that the northernmost quality wines of France were whites; the opposite was true of Italy where the finest Alpine wine was a clear, rich red, and easily the equal in quality of the finest Alsatian whites.

Vines and wines in Piedmont evolved throughout the century, acquiring better quality as enological knowledge spread. For centuries landowners outside of the finest vineyards had cultivated an excessive number of vines of different varieties. Their planting was haphazard, with several varieties thrown together in the same row, or hung onto the same tree; no adequate experimenting was done to adapt vines to soil or to achieve an improved beverage by blending their juices in various proportions. They picked grapes of different varieties at the same time and used them all simply because the fruit was there. Their tradition was to adapt man's taste to these concoctions rather than vice versa, being ruled more by the availability of grapes than by rigorous norms. Low prices and limited markets seemed the will of the gods and nothing encouraged change for hundreds of years. The only important improvements had occurred in the late seventeenth and eighteenth centuries when informed growers replaced the live trees, on which vines were customarily hung, with poles or stakes and trimmed their vines low. This change was not a sudden step, but a rather long evolutionary process; it was neither universal, being limited chiefly to the Barolo area, nor accompanied by the elimination of other crops from the wide space between vine rows. Not until the coming of better transport, new market opportunities, and technical education in the mid and later 1800s did cultivation become more quality-oriented and the lesser grape varieties disappear.[5]

The wines of Lombardy and Venetia never acquired a comparable reputation, save for several regional varieties. Lombardy until 1861 and Venetia until 1866 were ruled from Vienna by Hapsburg officials, and their economies were tied to the needs of that sprawling empire. They naturally traded with their southern neighbors in the Romagna and with Piedmont. In fact Lombardy, with its large capital city, Milan, never devoted a significant proportion of its land to viticulture, so it relied heavily on its neighbors to quench its thirst. Therefore when the Austrians imposed a tariff on imports, many north Italians were furious, since it diminished Piedmontese exports and raised prices for Lombards.[6]

Wines sold in foreign markets came almost exclusively from two small districts: the Oltrepò, south of Pavia, with superior reds and whites resembling those of Asti, and the Valtellina, the Alpine heights well north of Milan. In altitude the Valtellina was Italy's highest district for wines of good quality. The main slope was long and narrow, about the size of the Golden Slope in France, and somewhat resembling it when seen from afar. However the differences were fundamental, unfortunately for the Valtellinese and their bank accounts. The local red grapes, Chiavennasco and Rosolo, could not produce a wine truly comparable to the Pinot; and even when the Nebbiolo was later planted, it did not give a great wine resembling barolo, not to mention the finest of Burgundy. Nonetheless Valtellina wine, spurred on by the Swiss and Austrian markets, became one of Italy's better products. For the natives, isolated until the coming of railroads, wine was the basis of life. It was their only money crop and all cash transactions were carried on after the harvests, when Swiss merchants made limited advances either for grapes or must. All other crops were for home consumption so that the Valtellinese really lived for and off of wine. In this respect they were closer to French specialist growers than to their Italian compatriots.

They worked hard for cash incomes. Whether as cropper or owner, they and their ancestors, since Roman times, had cut into the steep mountain sides north of the Adda River, had built terraces about three to six feet wide, supported them with stone walls, and carefully planted their vines, doing all the labor by hand. Only good wine, selling at high prices, could justify such egregious expenditures of human effort. Even today the slopes, 40 to 60 degrees steep, must be worked by hand, and for centuries the soil washed down by rain had to be returned on the peasants' backs, an annual task. As in the Rhône Valley, vines had to be trained for protection from the strong west wind called *breva* that began in the spring. The branches of two or more vines planted in rows were interlaced along a series of supports, leaving the appearance of an open fence. The vines were pruned low to protect them from the winds of winter and to obtain some warmth from the soil in summer. Although far north, the upper Adda Valley enjoyed moderate temperatures; the mountains shielded it from the bitter north winds and Lake Como to the west reflected some warmth. The best wine, grown in the small districts of Grigioni, Sassella, Grumella and Inferno, was capable of fetching high prices in the Swiss market, at least until the railroads brought in cheaper wine from Piedmont and the South. After the 1870s Valtellinese wines, priced high because costs were high, had to face stiff competition and suffered when Austria imposed a tariff against the rebellious and now independent states.

Venetia, the last major territory to win independence from the Hapsburgs, was somewhat more viticultural than Lombardy and also produced large amounts of common wine. However, as in Lombardy, viticulture there left something to be desired. Hanging vines on trees exposed them to the long Alpine winters, causing many to perish from the cold. The growing season was generally too short for grapes to mature fully, so their wines were harsh and bitter, and old vinicultural habits, more suitable to warm southern vineyards, added to the acidic taste.

The limited areas of quality wine were located around Verona, in the zones of Valpolicella and Valpantena. There, on hills facing the blue, warming waters of Lake Garda, were the vineyards of Lasize, Bardolino, Garda, and Cazzano de Tramigna. The Corvino grape served as the basis for excellent reds, and local growers blended in about 20 percent of the Terodola, or 12 percent of the Negrara. Although red wines made the reputation of Verona, there were excellent whites from the communes of Soave and Monteforte, whose qualities were enhanced by blending in the juices of the Garganega and Trebbiano. The vineyard of Verona consisted of gentle slopes compared to those of Valtellina, with vines trimmed rather high off the ground, a system permitted by the moderate climate. The finished beverages went to Lombard and Venetian cities and to Vienna, where the upper classes willingly paid high prices for them.

The limited production in these Alpine regions was amply compensated by the quantity from the vineyard of Emilia Romagna. It lay between the Po River on the north, the Apennines on the south and west, and stretched from Piacenza eastward to the Adriatic Sea. The Lambrusco grapes for reds dominated in the west, various whites in the east between Bologna and the coast. Unitl the 1860s the northern sector remained under Austrian rule, while the southern sector was part of the Papal States, and scattered along the Po Valley were small principalities dominated by one or the other of these larger states.

The wine industry here differed from that of Piedmont and much of France in that nearly all the care of vines and making of wine had fallen into the hands of simple peasants unsupervised by proprietors. Supervision would have been slight anyway because not more than a handful of landowners sought to acquire the requisite knowledge to direct their wage workers and sharecroppers. Moreover many peasants had acquired their own land during the French occupation—often church land—and were not dispossessed of it afterward; they were simply taxed on it, and quite heavily. Whether crop sharers, wage workers, or owners, they formed part of the north and upper central Italian agricultural population and shared a generalized outlook on farming. Practically none of them were truly *vignaioli*, that is, persons prepared to spend most of their energy tending vines, who planted other crops only as necessary supplements. They were, rather, general farmers, carrying on a highly diversified type of cultivation in which vines were only a part, and by no means the most important part. Grape production was useful as a cash crop, which enabled a peasant to obtain the specie he needed to pay taxes. This necessity, incidentally, was by no means limited to Emilia; it was a condition existing everywhere in both Italy and France and undoubtedly a force encouraging peasants to abandon subsistence for commercial agriculture. Even where peasants did not possess the means of making wine, they began selling grapes for money to larger growers or merchants, a practice that became increasingly widespread in both countries during the century as wine-making became more complex and required capital outlays far beyond the simple peasants' means.

Given the need for cash in Emilia Romagna, vine culture looked toward quantity rather than quality. The Lambrusco, planted everywhere between Piacenza and Bologna, gave an abundance of low-grade wine, inferior to that of Piedmont where it was more carefully tended. As was the custom in the North, vines were hung on live trees planted in rows separated by intervals of fifteen to thirty feet in the low rolling hills and up to ninety feet in the valley plains. The trees provided farmers with either wood, fruit, olives, or leaves for silk worms, and the tilled soil between rows offered them food crops such as cereals, corn, vegetables, beans, and oftentimes industrial crops like hemp. Under these conditions the three or four vines planted around each tree had to compete for sustenance not only with the trees but also with the other crops, not to mention grass and weeds. Manure and other fertilizers were, when used, good for these crops, but bad for the quality if not the quantity of the grape's juice. Even so, yield under these conditions was extremely low, from one to six hectoliters per hectare in flat land as well as hills. Moreover the grapes, hanging from six to ten feet off the ground and partly concealed by trees, did not enjoy sufficient direct sun in the summer and nearly no reflected heat from the ground, covered as it was with other crops. Also an absurd number of different grape varieties were grown, reds, whites, some maturing early, some late—and all in the same row, all harvested at the same time, so that good, rotten, and green fruit were crushed and fermented together.

This condition was an enological nightmare and it would have been difficult—if possible at all—to produce quality wine from such raw material. But the peasant growers knew nothing of viniculture save what they learned at their fathers' and their grandfathers' side. Tradition ruled and it was bad. But since we shall go into winemaking elsewhere, suffice it to say that most of this wine had to be consumed locally and before the next summer's heat, when the remainder of it was distilled before it turned sour.

There were, of course, landowners who sought to innovate and a few succeeded. Their number increased after the oïdium crisis of the 1850s and their wines began to appear in national as well as international exhibitions. There were numerous viticulturists and enologists who wrote books and pamphlets condemning bad practice, each trying to be the Doctor Guyot of Italy. But peasant growers were stubborn. To the urging that they plant vines low on dead wood stakes, they replied that the stakes would be stolen for firewood before the vines could bloom. In addition they feared heavy reliance on one crop, and with good reason. Venetia and much of eastern Emilia were subject to unstable weather, heavy rain and winds, hail, fog and unseasonably cold spells coming off the Adriatic. Peasants therefore rejected the idea of a true vineyard, with all vines planted in one place. Fearful of hail, they put vines in widely separated locations, if they possessed enough land, and harvested everywhere at once. Some forward-looking owners urged the Hapsburg and papal rulers to impose restrictions on grape harvesting, the *bando di vendemmia*, forbidding peasants to pick immature grapes, but the emperors and the popes, deeply devoted to tradition, would not interfere with what they erroneously believed to be age-old practices of harvesting. In reality, the prohibition was traditional; freedom a revolutionary innovation in both Italy and France.

Far more traditional were highly protective tariffs, imposed by both states to maintain prices. In Lombardy, Venetia, and Hapsburg Emilia there was a loud outcry from growers in 1833 when the Austrian government lowered tariffs on Piedmontese wines entering the empire. Continued pressure, probably from Hungarian wine producers, and growing distrust between the royal houses of Savoy and Hapsburg led in 1846 to a new tariff higher by 100 percent. As noted above, the Piedmontese were outraged. They faced a serious crisis for prices were already low, and they began demanding freedom from the Austrian yoke for all Italy. Certainly a compelling force in the *Risorgimento* was the desire for political unity, for unity meant both national freedom and an enlarged domestic market free of internal tariffs. Equally interested were growers in

Austrian-dominated areas and the Papal States, who hoped to win freedom from the heavy fiscal impositions of Vienna and also to sell their wine as before to merchants from north of the Alps.

They were mistaken, especially the growers in Emilia, who belonged to the Papal States with its protective tariffs. They had usually sold grapes or must to Lombard, Swiss, and German merchants, and in years of scarcity they could obtain 30 to 35 lire for a quintal of Lambrusco grapes. But after unification and the improved transport that followed it, all the growers found their once privileged markets flooded with cheap grapes and wine from the South, the Mezzogiorno. In this respect they found themselves in the same sad state as the makers of ordinary wine in the upper Rhône and Saône valleys and throughout Burgundy in France who angrily saw their markets invaded by Languedocian beverages.

For all these regional producers who had traditionally sold their ordinaries in local and northern markets, this problem became acute in the second half of the century. To stay in business they would have to modernize their vinification methods drastically to keep costs and prices down, because their average lower-class consumer was not able or willing to spend ostentatiously for drink and therefore found it convenient to acquire a taste for cheap southern wine. On the other hand the growers and merchants, precisely to discourage a change of taste for the worse, would have to improve quality and standardize it year in, year out. In short their problem was tantamount to squaring the proverbial circle. As we shall see, they nearly managed to do this by blending some of their musts with those of the South: in this way they would create a truly national product, transcending regional divisions.[7]

CHAPTER FIVE

Central and Southern Italy

The Center

For most of north central Italy the generalizations we made about the low quality of most Lombardy and Venetian wines hold good. However there was a time when the lower Romagna produced a superior wine, capable of traveling and therefore of commercial value. The finest came from Cesena, until the general decline of commerce discouraged the making of a quality product. Foreign markets were lost and the growers abandoned high-cost methods and settled down to turning out mediocre beverages for the economically backward local markets.

This decline was a cultural phenomenon, not the result of ruined soil or atmospheric changes or a shift in the sun's exposure of the best hillsides. Past and present conditions indicate that it was not an enormous problem to make wines in central Italy. In midcentury several enologists studied conditions in the Marche and Abruzzi areas and concluded that soils, combining clay, lime, and marl, were very suitable for quality vines. Not only did vines flourish, grapes matured without great difficulty; therefore man, not nature, was at fault. Viti-viniculture was ill adapted, above all in Ancona, and this situation was all the more deplorable because there were fine grapes suited to the area: the Verdicchio *bianco* was capable of becoming an excellent dry white and the Verdicchio *nero* a good red. The Balsamina and Dalmazia also made quality reds and the Lacrima, a salable rosé.

Apart from throwing rotten, green, and mature grapes into the same vat, central growers widely practiced cooking a part of the must so as to evaporate excess water. In the Abruzzi fields were regularly irrigated, often making the grape juice thin and low in sugar, so that cooked, concentrated must was added as a fortifying substance. Without it the resulting wine might turn sour with the warmth of spring. This addition could preserve but could not improve the wine because it added a disagreeable cooked taste to the finished concoction. Some of the wine, boldly but unwisely entered in an Italian wine fair in 1872, where it was practically thrown out because it had not fully clarified, was discolored from cooking, lacked bouquet, and had an odd taste. The taste resulted from mixing too many varieties of grapes in the fermenting vat.[1]

After midcentury an increasing number of growers, educated in the new principles of enology, began to make wines of high quality which were quite capable of traveling. Their reds, solid and wholesome *ordinaires*, could compete with beverages of the same quality from Piedmont and Tuscany and sold for .90 to 1.40 lire a bottle, a most remunerative price. In contrast the whites, especially in the Abruzzi, left something to be desired, not as regards taste but as regards color, for growers persisted in keeping the skins in the must during the primary fermenting period, which gave the wine an unwanted yellow tint and lowered its value. Perhaps for this reason the whites, once dominant, gave way to reds. The major exception occurred in the district of Jesi, west of Ancona, where local growers made a verdicchio, golden yellow in color, and highly praised for its quality. Here, and in a few other areas, small-scale growers began to specialize in grape production and found it quite lucrative. In fact in this poor farmland grape and wine sales were the sole means out of extreme poverty. Farther inland the population of the Abruzzi remained poor, for the region was not suited to becoming an important vineyard. The Marche was more fortunate, with soils and exposures that offered fairly good opportunities to modern enology. And yet production and sales during much of the century continued to be chiefly local affairs. The regions of the Marches did not enjoy large urban centers nearby, their population was economically poor, and they looked out upon a viniculturally dead sea, the Adriatic. Beyond it were the Balkans with their own vines, and the Near East where the Moslem majority was forbidden to consume alcohol. In consequence conditions became more promising only after unification and the building of railroads.

In the central Apennines the only vineyard worth noting was that of Orvieto, where vine culture as an art had its beginnings in antiquity. Yet the wine's more modern renown resulted at least in part from an accident. When Perugia fell under papal rule, Orvieto became a secondary residence of the pontiffs, who served the local wine during their gastronomic celebrations and encouraged its purchase by the ecclesiastic and lay notables of Rome. Hence this growing religious capital became the wine's largest market, and a most profitable market after 1870 when the capital of the Papal States became the exalted capital of Italy. The fine savor of orvieto comes from the Trebbiano grape, blended with the Verdello and Malvasia, varieties that were not truly native but brought in from Tuscany.

From the lightful and delightful whites of Orvieto, one has only to travel a short road westward to enter that more serious paradise of red wine known as chianti. If Rome was the gateway to heaven, chianti must be the ruby river to the gods. But this was true only of the wines from a rather small district within Tuscany, a green undulating surface reaching north and south between the great dome of Bruneleschi's cathedral in Florence and the high serene towers of Siena. Here in 1812 vines occupied some 18 percent of the total arable.[2] The Chianti district was of course not the only one in which vines were cultivated, for they stretched westward along the gentle Arno's valley to the Ligurian coast. In consequence, growers turned out a considerable amount of common wine, nearly all of it for local consumption. Quite distinct, however, was the Chianti district with its constant succession of perfectly exposed slopes, its fine soils, and moderate climate. Equally important was the rather healthy economy of the Grand Duchy, admittedly fallen from its Renaissance splendor, but still active enough to provide both capital and consumer purchasing power. And of equal importance was the rational tradition of the eighteenth-century Enlightenment with its emphasis on reason, utility, and science. Here Piedmont and Tuscany were of a piece, and both were major centers of the enological advance during the eighteenth and nineteenth centuries. It is not surprising that each state, prior to and after unification, came under the influence of an empirical, innovating farmer-statesmen, active in the improvement of vines and wines: Camillo Cavour in Piedmont and Bettino Ricasoli in Tuscany.

Both men found Italian agriculture in a sorry state, and both set out to improve it. In Florence, Ricasoli became a member of the Accademia dei Georgofili in 1831 and began to collaborate with an elite of learned gentlemen bent upon improving the antiquated methods of farming. The peasants, though liberated from the legal bondage of serfdam, continued to bind themselves to traditional practices of tillage. Ricasoli, who would make a major contribution to classical chianti, was able to learn about general agriculture and viticulture from his more experienced colleagues, Gino Capponi, Raffaele Lambruschini, and Casimo Ridolfi, all empiricists in the mode of English gentleman farmers.

Since the Georgofili represented the noble and gentry class, they advocated neither small peasant property nor large feudal or capitalist latifundia. Rather they favored medium and moderately large estates, populated by peasant families working the land on a corp-sharing basis and supervised by benevolent, progressive landowners. They believed that Italy, in order to expand its rural wealth, must educate and raise the moral level of her peasants. Rural notables, therefore, must not only apply science to farming, they must seek moral leadership over those families tilling the soil. They saw in crop-sharing *(mezzadria)* the means to avoid rural democracy with its demand for peasant ownership and its abiding distrust of the gentry, and also the means by which a technically educated peasantry would become more profitable to itself, to their lords, and, just as important, more docile.[3]

Undoubtedly the Georgofili influenced an elite of the gentry, who improved their own estates, but many owners and probably most peasants remained untouched by their pamphlets and lectures. There is little indication that grape-growing and wine-making turned out a better product. In fact there is the possibility that viniculture suffered a setback; at any rate its exports to England declined from their level in the previous century, although this decline may have resulted from adulteration of the wine by merchants. Whatever the cause, the value of wine exported in the 1820s was less than 3 percent of the value of olive oil and about 10 percent of that of grains. Prices were too low to encourage heavy capital outlays for fine vines, new equipment, and greater effort, with the result that most wine did not go beyond the local market, a situation that nearly always discourages innovation and betterment.

This lethargy and indifference struck Ricasoli when he moved to his family estate at Brolio in the 1830s. City bred and academically learned he knew little of agriculture; nor is it clear whether his motives for the move came from his need for a regular income, a love of country life, or the decision to isolate his beautiful young wife from the temptations of Florentine high life. But while he became a most able farmer, he is mostly remembered as a great innovator in the making of chianti.

When he settled on his land, he found that cultivation was badly organized; there was, however, an old tradition of grape-growing and vines were well tended. As everywhere else, vines were hung on trees, but happily the peasants had not been tempted to use manure and irrigation as a means of increasing yield, even though they practiced mixed farming. Baron Ricasoli hoped to plant vines separately, but his crop-sharers, each of whom individually farmed a plot of 5–6 hectares, stubbornly refused to abandon mixed farming. However docile they were as regards social status and politics, they were veritable rocks of resistance concerning age-old farm practices, which once provoked Ricasoli to exclaim, after he had entered politics, that it was easier to rule the Italian state than his own estate. His impatience was all the greater because he was an ardent experimenter, seeking to improve old ways by trying new ways. To complement the knowledge of vines he acquired from books, he traveled extensively in France, visiting Bordeaux and Burgundy, in Piedmont, and even in the Rhineland of Germany. Like Cavour, he brought back vines of different varieties and planted them in an experimental vineyard directly under his control.

What he had in mind was to produce a wine that could travel over the bumpy roads leading from Brolio to the port of Leghorn and then over water to foreign markets, especially to England. He was no enologist, but he followed the best advice, which was perhaps better than being an enologist. He patiently taught the fifty-five families settled on his estate to cultivate vines more efficiently and to harvest grapes more carefully, picking only the mature ones. As a good manager, he gave each person a simple task to perform at a given moment. Above all, he insisted upon the cleanliness of the vat room and of the vats. Customarily in Tuscany numerous red grapes, not all of them fully mature, were poured into large vats made of chestnut or mulberry wood and crushed by men entering the vats barefoot over a three- or four-day period, after which the resulting must fermented for twenty to thirty days before it was transferred to casks. During this longer period it was not uncommon for naked men to enter the vats, in order to push the floating grape skins (the cap) down into the liquid, a custom widely practiced in Burgundy and sometimes fatal.

Chianti was famous for its red wines and the predominant grape was the black Canaiolo, to which were blended varying amounts of Sangioveto (or Sangeovese), Mammolo, and Marzamino. For the lesser renown whites the grapes were the San Colombano and Trebbiano. Ricasoli, chiefly interested in red wine, not only introduced a more rational vinicultural process by making use of crushing machines and larger vats, he also overturned tradition by reversing the proportions of grape blends. After considerable experimentation he arrived at this mixture: 80 percent Sangioveto, the grape that added the deep, intriguing aroma and although requiring many years aging—like the Cabernet and Pinot *noir*— gave body and durability to the finished product; 15 percent Canaiolo, for it, much like the Malbec and Merlot of Bordeaux, hastened the aging process by moderating the harsh early taste of Sangioveto; and 5 percent Trebbiano, the white grape that softened the taste by aging quickly. But since Trebbiano did not live long, he replaced it with the Malvagia in wines intended for storage. Following in his tracks, some producers abandoned these stellar Italian grapes and substituted Bordeaux vintages, presumably either Merlot or Malbec or both, to hasten maturing.[4]

Tuscan producers, however, had long ago invented a method of production intended to make wine more readily available for drinking. It is known as the *governo*, and as a process it is quite simple. Either just before or during the grape harvest workers pick the best grapes and lay them aside to ripen further in the sun, in order to encourage the evaporation of water and the concentration of sugar. Meanwhile the must of the other grapes is made to ferment and allowed to settle. About a month later the overripe grapes are examined, the best are stemmed, crushed, and made to ferment, and this rich, full-bodied, deep-red liquid is poured into the regular must in a proportion ranging from 2 to 10 percent of the whole. If the cellar is adequately heated, a second slow fermentation begins, hastening the maturing process, so that the wine will not only be ready for drinking when spring arrives, it will become slightly sparkling (*frizzante*). Customarily the *governo* was widely practiced in the province of Florence, the Val di Nievole, Valdarno, here and there in the province of Siena, and in the Montepulciano, southward of Siena. This last area grew a *vino nobile*, using the same grapes as those of chianti, which was quite capable of rivaling it. As early as 1830 a local connoisseur and enologist, Ulisse Novellucci, proposed a method of heating wine in bottles in order to hasten its aging.[5] It does not seem that his proposal was widely practiced, albeit the Marquis of Ridolfi recognized that it prevented renewed fermentation, a grave problem for wines bottled too early, since the wine then became cloudly and unsalable. This technique, however, was rediscovered independently by Louis Pasteur thirty years later, not to age wines, although that was a desirable side effect, but to preserve them from harmful bacteria. The *governo* had tradition behind it and remains in use to this day. It not only adds maturity and roundness, it aids in the creation of a "typical" wine, an objective that Tuscans sought before most other Italians. However many producers of fine wines, as prices rose, decided to abandon the *governo* in favor of normal aging, for while it added roundness to a light or medium beverage, it might render a naturally full-bodied wine too heavy. The new enology with its practice of short fermentation, or of using hermetically sealed vats for longer fermentation, made such old practices useless.

Such fine wine made up only a fraction of the large production of Tuscany. The greater part of it, often called chianti despite its birth in other parts or even entirely outside of the Grand Duchy, was shipped out to Italian and foreign markets. We can assume that much of it was of poor quality, for enologists later in the century were still lamenting its lowly condition. They held that too many grape varieties went into the wine and that immature grapes were used as well as defective equipment, especially old, musty wooden barrels. Unfortunately this lesser product tended to give a bad reputation to the finer wines of Chianti and made its sale on the international market more difficult.

Moving down into the lower central provinces, the growing of vines diminished considerably, save along the Mediterranean coast. In the Lazio region, stretching southward from Perugia to Latina, with Rome as its focal point, the predominance of the Trebbiano and of white wine continued. In antiquity Lazio boasted of two famous vineyards, Albano and Velletrano; but in modern times it was no longer a highly rated viticultural center: neither the soil nor the climate, having become too warm, was favorable to high quality or great abundance.[6] Perhaps more effective leadership might have preserved ancient bacchic glories. Elsewhere in Europe the church, or at least several religious orders, had played a major role in perfecting the art of viti-viniculture, and the popes at Avignon had encouraged the creation of châteauneuf-du-pape. But the clerical heads in Rome, who ruled over most of central Italy and were highly appreciative of good wine, did not actively participate or encourage wine production except by purchasing it. But then the Roman pontiffs did relatively little to encourage any sector of the economy in their state, with the result that poverty was widespread, and the long coast, lacking a prosperous hinterland, witnessed neither a dramatic rise of cities nor of population. Absent, in consequence, was the domestic economic and social basis of a flourishing viticulture, and since the wine that locals produced did not travel, exporting it was out of the question. The denizens of Rome, each capable of consuming 135 liters per year in 1850–62, were the chief market for the worst and the best. Nearly everywhere farmers produced the worst; the good was rare and limited to several districts. In Viterbo, in the vineyards of Montefiasconi overlooking Lake Bolseno and where Tuscan viniculture had many imitators, a quite pleasant white was made from the Trebbiano grape. It achieved some renown, if only because of its name, est est est (sometimes written est! est!! est!!!). The origin of this name has been lost, but one story has it that a bibulous ecclesiastic traveling from Germany to Rome instructed his servant to proceed him, to taste the wines along the road, and to write the word "est" (it is) on the walls of inns serving notable beverages. Apparently the wine of Montefiasconi so aroused the servant's spirit, he gave it the triple "est." The exclamation points were surely added later by the Chamber of Commerce. The Romanesco grape, more widely grown for the abundance of its juice, gave an inferior wine for the locals.

The Trebbiano appears once more just to the south of Rome in the marvelous district of Castelli Romani, where the hills rise like green velvet from the sea. In a typical commune, such as Frascati, at least two-thirds of the population lived principally from the sale of grapes and wines, a rare occurrence in rural nineteenth-century Italy. Here one found authentic vignaioli and even vineyards from which other crops had been banished. Land given over to the grape reached about 24,000 hectares after midcentury. The growth of Rome in population and wealth, especially after 1870 when the government of Italy moved there, encouraged viticulture, for the city could easily absorb all the local wine and still call for more.

The Castelli Romani, like the district of Barolo and some parts of Brolio, resembled the quality vineyards of France. There were also examples of specialization pushed to the extreme. Normally, in a mixed culture, there were 2,000 to 3,000 vines per square hectare. In France the average was 6,000 to 8,000 with row planting and 10,000 or more with bunched planting. In the Castelli Romani, it was not uncommon to plant 15,000 vines, using a system called "vigna stretta all'velletrana" or 13,000 under one called "vigna a filone a coppia." A third method, designated "Vigna alla genzanese" called for 6,000 vines. Yield varied according to method, being only 25 hectoliters per hectare with 15,000 vines, and 50 with 6,000. In a normal year low yield denotes high quality, but in most years in the Castelli the third method, using fewer vines, gave both higher yields and superior quality. The grapes profited from more free-flowing air, sun, and warmth. In earlier times there had also been extensive specialized planting in the Viterbo district. However growers there received for their grapes only 6 lire per quintal, compared to 10 in the Castelli, and they returned to mixed farming. Larger owners in Viterbo and the Castelli had the advantage in that they could procure sufficient equipment and store their wine in cool cellars. In the Castelli, these cellars had for ages been cut out of tufa or sedimentary rock; each was small, with space for a single vat of 8 to 12 hectoliters at most. Small owners, without sufficient cellars and cooperage, had to sell either grapes or musts to local or Roman merchants.

The wine that reached the Roman market was often the produce of merchants, and, given the limited quantity of wine and the city's rapidly growing population, they sought to meet demand in dubious ways. They added water to expand volume, aniline to disguise the water and deepen color, and alum to give a dry taste or lead salts to sweeten it. The pontifical government before 1870 did not enact or enforce legislation to prevent fraud, and the royal government after 1870 did not reveal much more enthusiasm for pure food laws. On the whole the largest cities of

Europe—London, Paris, Lyon, Milan, and Rome—were surfeited with beverages called wine but that were more like products of chemical manipulation than of sun-kissed grapes. Only with the coming of mass-produced natural wines and cheap transport did it become possible both to quench the thirst of teeming urbanites and provide them with pure beverages. This was the destiny of the great vineyards of the South.[7]

Southern Italy

By the 1860s southern vineyards in France and Italy could probably have produced enough common wine to satisfy the world market. The enthusiasm of Dr. Jules Guyot for French Mediterranean viticulture led him to believe that production for a mass market would bring undreamed wealth to growers. For a brief moment in history it did, both in France and Italy, but age-old economic conditions, while modified somewhat in France, were hardly changed in Italy.

Southern Italy, the wild dry austere Mezzogiorno, seems always to have been Italy's principal economic problem. Before and after unification it did not follow the path of modernization opened by the northern and some central provinces, but stubbornly remained the perennial Kingdom of the Two Silicies, misgoverned, compulsively bound to its feudal past, and beset by chronic poverty. There was a steady flow of peasants to other parts of Italy and to other lands, chiefly France, where they found subsistence as laborers in vineyards, and the Americas where they went into industry or the services.

South Italian wine, it would seem, was like the regional economy, a product of a retarded technology and medieval social system that did not encourage innovation. Like that of the lower Midi of France, the wine was a low-grade ordinary, an authentic proletarian beverage. However, here and there, a few sectors were capable of turning out sweet and alcoholic dessert wines of higher quality, similar to those of Languedoc. It rightfully boasted the oldest wine tradition, tracing the earliest plantings back to Greek settlers at least, and probably earlier, even to prehistoric man. The famous Campania vineyards, Falerno, Formiano, and Cecubo, had produced wines highly prized by ancient Romans, wines that could live for a hundred years. As with other celebrated vineyards of antiquity, the decline of the empire had led to neglect, and malarial swamps inundated the vines. In contrast the region of Apulia, the heel of the boot, became the center of a brand new wine industry that had much in common with lower Languedoc.

The depressing poverty of most of the Mezzogiorno was undoubtedly a factor working against quality viticulture there. Elsewhere, in the finer vineyard areas of Italy and France, grape and wine production contributed to a relatively high standard of living, and enological progress reaching toward excellence profited in turn from rising standards. An awakened, enterprising, and technically educated population of growers, at least after midcentury, encouraged a flourishing wine industry catering to the local, national and international market. In the Mezzogiorno, however, excessive poverty bred illiteracy and indolence, interspersed with exhausting labor on sun-bleached, ungrateful soil, and the kind of submissiveness that sanctified gross hostility toward innovation and higher taste. Naturally if the vinicultural traditions of the South had enthroned over centuries both finesse and solid quality as goals, then man, as a grower, might have overcome the deficiencies of nature: the torrid climate, the arid soil baked by the unrelenting sun. The unfortunate presence of poor people is not the point we wish to emphasize here; the poor were, like vice and virtue, omnipresent inside and outside all viticultural regions. It was rather the crushing weight of generalized poverty that impeded nearly all industry, including the wine industry. Lacking were aggressive bourgeois, the only class—given the incompetence of nobles and clergy—that might have organized a wine industry comparable to that of southern France. But the bourgeois were weak and subservient, despised by nobles and distrusted by peasants. Not even national unification changed this state of affairs. Consequently, where a significant improvement or innovation in viniculture did occur, foreigners were largely responsible for it. Englishmen built up a Marsala wine trade, while French and Austrian merchants were among the leading promoters of expansion in the Apulian vineyard.

Given the semitropical climate of the Mezzogiorno, growers there, however skillful, could not have created a truly fine wine, but there is ample reason to believe that a more skillful viti-viniculture could have markedly improved the product. And indeed, where there existed a more discriminating local market, such as the middle class of Naples, some quite pleasant dry and sweet wines appeared.

The vineyards of Campania produced most of this superior wine. It was a region of transition; in the upper provinces of Caserta, Benevento, and Avellino, at least two-thirds of the vines were cultivated with other crops and hung on live trees as in central Italy, but in the lower provinces of Salerno and Naples more than half of the vines were cultivated in specialized vineyards.[8] In the lower Mezzogiorno many growers before and during the nineteenth century decided to plant vines *a la francese,* closer to the ground and apart from other crops. By midcentury some of them, following the teachings of Jules Guyot, began to line up their vines in rows, a practice, as we have noted, not yet widely followed in France. During most of the century, however, progress toward a truly specialized culture was slow. There is reason to believe that most vines, while not interspersed among other plants, were still attached to olive and fruit trees and that land classified after 1860 as *specializzata* often combined vines and olive trees. Growers in the Neopolitan district trimmed their vines up to twenty-four feet, but those on the slopes of Vesuvius favored six feet, and those in the islands of Capri and Ischia also preferred a low trim.

The grapes most widely used were the Aglianico, especially for calcareous clay soils, in which it produced a salable red. The Falanghina grape, widely used in Caserta, made a wine called falerno, but it could hardly have been comparable to the falerno of the Romans. The only beverage of more than a local reputation was called lacrima christi; served chiefly with dessert, it was the sort of strong, sweet beverage for which the southern climate was ideally suited.

Equally characteristic of lower Campania, Calabria, Basilicata, and Apulia were the heavy alcoholic liquids called *vini da taglia,* useful only to blend into weaker northern wines in need of color and body. The objective among growers was to produce an industrial raw material rather than one to be consumed directly. As the need for such wine grew, a new wine industry developed in Apulia almost exclusively geared to the blending needs of north Italian and foreign wine merchants. *Vino da taglia* made up over half all wine produced.[9] There followed a marked transformation of agriculture. In midcentury the area of Bari produced 8,000 casks of wine valued at 240,000 ducats. The value of olive oil, however, came to over two million ducats and that of grain to 384,000.[10] It was the olive and grain harvest that truly decided the fate of the local population. Then in the 1870s and 1880s the phylloxera extinguished over half of France's vines with the result that merchants there desperately needed south Italian wine to blend into and give a vinous taste to the various concoctions they were putting on the market. As long as these merchants frantically bought wine, and at high prices, vineyards sprang up from Foggia to Lecce at the very heel of the peninsula, amidst all the bustle and growth that normally accompanies gold rushes. New populations moved in, villages and towns grew, wages rose, and peasant growers found it possible to purchase land. Apulia in the 1880s came to resemble lower Languedoc in the 1860s, when a similar boom took place. Certain regions in both France and Italy, favored by their natural resources and man's ingenuity, became the centers of dynamic growth that markedly changed ways of life.[11]

Calabria was suited for low-quality viticulture, and vineyards there were fairly widespread, along with olives and citrus fruit. The vine was a specialized crop, well suited to the soil and the dry, hot climate. In the North chilling frost and heavy rain were deadly enemies of vines; in the South summer drought and myriads of insects were the eternal menace, but the South suffered fewer bad years because late spring frosts or hail or heavy rains at harvest time were not frequent occurrences. Nature was kind; unfortunately, man did not take full advantage of it.[12]

Viti-viniculture in Calabria throughout the nineteenth century remained what it had been in preceeding centuries. Innovation was as absent from the wine industry as it was from all other human activities. This static quality was common in peasant culture, even one, as that of Calabria, where wine production was carried out by peasants for a commercial market. The local merchants, buyers of peasant musts and wines, were as indifferent to new techniques as the peasants. In Reggio di Calabria, the growers crushed their grapes with their feet, often unwashed, and brought the juice to the merchant in town, a distance of five to eight miles, a voyage requiring the better part of a day. In the heat of an intense sun, musts began to ferment in the small barrels and animal skin bags containing them. They were considerably jolted and shaken, carried as they were on the backs of mules and asses. Transport costs were moderate, but the means of locomotion were inefficient and therefore too slow. Due to a redundancy of manpower that was terribly underpaid, there was a peasant to accompany each mule, despite the ease with which one man could lead five or six of them. A wagon would have saved on animal power, but the roads were often mere pathways, not wide or smooth enough for wheeled vehicles.

The enologists of the *Annali di Viticultura* were shocked in the later decades of the century to discover both the backward methods of transporting must and the merchants' method of making wine. The local producers first bought the juice made in the lowland plains, where grapes matured earliest. They fermented it in large open vats, and then, as the grapes of the lower hills matured, they acquired juice from there and poured it into the same vats, greatly disturbing the fermentation process of the earlier juice. Finally they bought the juice of high hill grapes, last to mature, and nonchalantly poured it into the same vat, further disturbing the fermentation and, of course, prolonging that of the first grapes far beyond the recommended time. The result was a beverage imperfectly fermented and ready to turn acidic, a malady common to

Calabrian wine. The incidence of spoilage remained high because producers did not close their casks soon enough or adequately.

Of course there were a few learned gentry and nobles who, like their counterparts in Languedoc, made quite good wines, even some that won medals in enological fairs at Bordeaux and Philadelphia, and their wines found buyers as far away as Holland and Scandinavia. But, alas, they were the exceptions, for in Reggio, where viticulture showed some improvement, the making of wine remained as unprogressive as ever.[13]

The situation was not greatly different in Sicily, just west of Calabria. The large island was part of the Kingdom of the Two Sicilies until 1860, when Garibaldi and his Red Shirts landed there, liberated it, then crossed the narrow Straits of Messina to overthrow the Bourbon king. Sicily immediately became part of the brand new Italian kingdom. These changes did not modify the economic poverty or the social inequality of Sicily, nor did the fine viniculture of the North exercise an influence over that of the South. North and South remained two separate worlds. And yet political unity did end internal toll barriers, so that wine could flow freely from one end of the island to the other. This turned to the advantage of Sicilian winesmen who, like other southerners, could now ship their beverages northward for the happy marriage between the bitter, thin wine of the cold regions and the sweet, full beverages of the semitropics. After 1860 the acreage devoted to vine planting expanded egregiously, above all in the coastal plains where there was easy access to the sea. Large estates producing wine on a sizable scale were at an advantage, because laborers were quite cheap and the plow, extensively used where vines had been planted in rows, further reduced the cost of production. This situation was similar to that of Roussillon, and at about the same time as Roussillon, from the sixties to the eighties, Sicily enjoyed a wine boom accompanied by rising incomes. The riches derived from viniculture did not spread evenly across the island, for although peasants everywhere grew grapes and made wine, production for the quality wine trade was limited to the western and northern coastal areas, that for blending wine to the eastern coast. However some good ordinaries could be found in the provinces from Messina to Siracuso where blending wines were not as predominant as in Apulia.

In the southeastern province of Siracuso, viticulture was characteristic of the island. Vines were trimmed low "ad alberello," more or less in the French fashion. They were supported by wood posts, with lengths of cane in between, or grew wild, without supports of any sort. Close to the ground, the grapes received the sun's rays directly as well as the heat reflected from the torrid earth and stones, with the unhappy result that in hot summers the temperature rose excessively and heat scorched the grapes. Peasants, refusing to believe that the fault was theirs and determined not to waste their crop, pressed these grapes and the resulting wine had a cooked, bitter taste. Normally sugar content was high and acidity dangerously low but ideal for blending with the highly acid wines of the North. In earlier times peasants grew a large variety of vines. A mark of progress, therefore, was the spread of the Muscat grape, which has become the basic ingredient of the sweet, alcoholic dessert wine exported to outside markets. It was the only white wine of any consequence in the area; the reds, made from the Nero d'Avola and the Frappato, interested local consumers, chiefly, but some was shipped for blending.

In Catania, just to the north, about 10 percent of the arable was cultivated in vines, roughly the same as in Siracuso, and slightly above the 7 percent in Messina farther north. Mount Etna provided an ideal terrain and vineyards ran up its slopes for several thousand feet, with the Nerello Mascalese grown for reds and the Carricante and Catarratto for whites. The cool air of high altitudes has always helped to moderate the excessive heat of summer and make it possible to turn out a juice more evenly balanced between sugar and acid content. Wines from the south slope have traditionally enjoyed the highest reputation.

In Palermo province the vineyard area declined to a mere 5 percent and most of it occupied land to the west of the city of Palermo. Here more knowledgeable growers in and around the commune of Casteldaccia learned how to make red and white table wines that became popular in trade under the labels either of corvo or salaparuta. The local population seems to have preferred a concoction made of the red Perricone and the white Cateratto grapes, quite alcoholic, and of a yellowish orange color. The Cataratto and Inzolia grapes were cleverly blended to make a wine falsely labeled as marsala because that name had become so popular.

The original home of marsala was, of course, the district of that name in the western province of Trapani. During the nineteenth century vine planting expanded considerably, arriving at more than 13 percent of the arable, undoubtedly the highest in Sicily. The calcareous soil in which the Catarratto grape was cultivated gave the finished wine a distinct flavor. Marsala remains the best-known Sicilian wine on the international market, and it owes it reputation to an Englishman, John Woodhouse.

About 1770 he came to Sicily in search of soda ash. He noted, when traveling in Trapani, that the local wine had a pleasant, bittersweet taste, and considerable alcohol, and attribute highly regarded by the English, and that it resembled madeira, a wine also appreciated by his country-men. In a stroke of genius he dropped his original project and shipped some of the beverages he had tasted to London, where it soon attracted a devoted clientele sizable enough to encourage Woodhouse to expand production.

The local growers, however, were too impecunious to undertake the planting program he had in mind, so he invested heavily in vineyards and supplemented his own harvests with grapes and juices purchased from peasants, nearly always on his own terms. In 1773 he constructed an elaborate plant for wine-making and also for heating some of the wine in order to give additional body and alcohol to the finished product. In this same year he was able to ship 2,800 hectoliters from the port of Trapani—he and his local growers were in business.

From all accounts marsala's reputation was considerably enhanced during the Napoleonic wars. There is no indication that the emperor tried it, but the British Admiral Nelson did, and he bought a large stock for his officers, who acquired a taste for it and spread its fame. Wood-house himself was a staunch conservative; he was particularly friendly toward the Bourbon ruler restored to power in Naples during 1815, even lending him funds. In fact their relations were such that when the local Trapanese government levied a tax on his wine exports, the king at Naples vetoed it. Before his death in 1826 Woodhouse had become a kind of benefactor to the city and province of Trapani. He had created a profitable wine industry, built a port and a good road leading to it, and provided grain in times of food shortages.

Somewhat more expansionist was another Englishman, Benjamin Ingham. In 1812 he began sending marsala to his homeland, then he enlarged his markets to include the United States, Brazil, and other parts of the world. Aware of the fortunes won in its sale, native Sicilians began to produce it and soon "marsala" came out of Siracusa, Catania, Messina, and Salerno. Since Italy had no laws respecting labeling rights, the name marsala became simply a trade name applicable to a particular type of wine grown widely in Sicily and perhaps also on the mainland. The product of Trapani, however, retained its true character and enologists defended it as the best among all the varieties, the most worthy of remembrance. Indeed it won a place for itself in the Risorgimento, for natives used this local beverage to greet Garibaldi and his Red Shirts when they landed in Trapani in 1860. Marsala now ceased to be simply Sicilian, it became an Italian wine made in Sicily.[14]

Needless to say, the national revolution did not change the technique of producing it. Like vermouth, it was a manufactured concoction, and the addition of various raw materials, such as alcohol, acids, and herbs, rendered it less likely to deteriorate. The production of sweet wine presented no problem in the hot climate of Sicily, but to make a moderately dry wine required know-how and skill. In a hot climate the temperature of fermenting must often rises to the point where yeasts are discouraged from further fermentation, which leaves sugar in the must. These sweet beverages are lacking in acids and likely to become defective unless "doctored." One safeguard against deterioration was chalk, and Sicilian growers added it in powdered form to many of their wines, for it not only preserved the wine, it hastened its clarification and improved its color. "Vino gessato," or chalked wine, became so common that foreign buyers grew distrustful, and merchants offered higher prices for unadulterated produce. Yet the practice persisted until the phylloxera blight invaded the massive vineyard, after which calamity came the modernization of winemaking. But first let us look at the traditional methods of vitiviniculture.

PART TWO

Technical, Economic, and Social Aspects

CHAPTER SIX

Wine-Making:
Tradition & Innovation

Viticulture in France

Grapes, like all other plant life, are products of nature, and their use to man has been influenced on the one hand by nature's benevolent forces: the sun, the warm air, the spring rain, the fecundity of earth, and the gentle winds that aerate the leaves; on the other hand there are her malevolent forces: frost, hail, violent winds, rain in excess, cloudy skies, and a frightful array of insects. Since grape vines have existed for millenia, the benevolent forces must have been stronger, and the wild, natural vines survived. Their grapes could hardly have produced other than a harsh acid juice. However our concern is not with wild fruit but with certain of its numerous derivatives, those which man adapted to his needs and to his taste over centuries of selection, manipulation, and hybridization. By the nineteenth century the important wine vines of Europe were as much, if not more, the products of man as of nature. And yet malevolent natural forces were still awesome and hardly understood. For man had never truly conquered his environment; rather he had selected certain vines in order to improve them and their produce, and his taste had been his guide. By the early nineteenth century this adaptation was still incomplete, and nature retained her sway, for the good as well as for the bad. Nature's attack came in three forms: climatic, cryptogamous, and entomological.

Climate was undoubtedly the most important, for it influenced the vine day after day, year in, year out. It was the eternal, unremitting factor, the hope and despair of the vignerons. It came often in the guise of natural disasters that were catastrophic in about two or three years out of ten, and unfavorable in two or three more years out of the same decade (see chapter seven). In the northern vineyards of both Italy and France, there was the menace of winter kill, cold of such intensity and duration that dormant vines perished. Everywhere save in the deep

South vines were threatened with spring frost capable of killing buds or the fresh flowers from which grapes would emerge. An equally terrible enemy was hail; it could and did on many occasions destroy a vineyard's crop in less than an hour. A man had to be dogged, of stout heart, to witness such a catastrophe and return to prune his vines for the following year. Excess rain in spring or early summer also caused flowers to fall, or it encouraged the growth of other maladies. In southern lands the chief menace was summer drought. Good vines never want much humidity, lest their grapes and wine become watery, but prolonged drought as could occur in Languedoc and the Mezzogiorno caused grapes to dry up and produce little or no juice.

Vine-dressers, like other farmers early in the nineteenth century, were not equipped to defend their vines against these climatic hazards. Some growers devised schemes involving straw mats to be used as covers, but these were prohibitively expensive and wine prices from the 1830s to the 1850s were too low to cover their costs. Against cold, vignerons built straw fires among the vines and the heavy clouds of smoke helped retain soil warmth and heated the air slightly. Against excess rain and humidity they sought to provide good aeration by cutting away unnecessary foliage, both from the vines and from the lands surrounding the vineyards, hedges and forests for example. They also avoided bottom lands where damp mists settled. All of this practical knowledge had grown over the centuries; some of it was even present in ancient times. In fact, learned landowners acquired much of their vine lore by reading the manuals of ancient Roman and Greek agriculturists. Numerous were the aphorisms handed on from father to son:

> "To cut back a vine is to renew it."
> "The success of the vine trimmer is in his pruning knife."
> "To use fertilizer is to fill one's vats."
> "Spading before the buds come earns two cultures for one."
> "A vine in flower wishes not the sight of vigneron or lord."

Yet even with centuries of practical knowledge, vine men could rarely ward off the ravages of nature, and even in villages organized for defense, where men, women, and children would rush into action at the clang of an alarm bell, damage to vines was inescapable.

Weather influenced vines both directly, as described above, and indirectly, by fostering cryptogamous maladies. The chief ones were anthracnose, various kinds of rot, especially black-rot, and mildews, above all powdery mildew. These were all fungi of some sort that thrived in hot, humid conditions and fatally attacked either the bark or the leaves.[1] Not all of these maladies were indigenous to the European vine, the *vitis vinifera;* some were unknown until vine specimens were brought to Europe from the United States. Such was the powdery mildew (*oïdium*), which appeared in France in the late 1840s. It spread widely, reaching Italy and Spain in the 1850s, when it became a national calamity in each country. Vine experts already knew that sulphur under various forms was a preventative, but it was not widely used in Europe until midcentury. Henri Marès, working in collaboration with the Ecole d'Agronomie of Montpellier, proved that it was indeed a preventative, and in 1853 Frederic Laforgue used it on his vines near the town of Béziers, where they flourished in the midst of ruined vineyards.[2] Almost immediately M. Duchâtre developed a practical process of dusting on a field scale, and growers soon discovered that sulphur dusting increased the set of fruit and led to earlier harvests.[3]

On the other hand sulphur used for dusting presented several drawbacks. Their application increased the costs of production, since it was discovered that at least three applications were required to prevent the return of mildew. Moreover if the last application occurred after July, there was an increased likelihood that the chemical would remain on the grape skins and finally settle in the wine, becoming hydrogen sulphide, and infect it with the odor and taste of rotten eggs. The problem of chemical residues was already apparent. Partly for this reason, partly because of reluctance to adopt unproven techniques, the great châteaux of the Bordelais were hesitant to apply sulphur on a large scale until 1857–58. Indeed for large employers of workers there arose another difficulty. In warm weather laborers became quite ill after the third day of sulphuring; they suffered particularly from eye sting. Therefore a shorter workday became obligatory, limited to the early mornings when dew on the vines absorbed the fine powder.[4]

The struggle against the third enemy, insects, also turned out to be quite costly. All of the insects were bugs, grasshoppers, or caterpillars that laid their eggs in the bark or on leaves or on berries and shoots. The larva that emerged fed on various parts of the vine, including the grapes, and ended by destroying the vine itself. There were numerous instances of insect invasions and the near destruction of whole vineyards. From 1825 to 1837 the pyrale ravished vines, especially in the Rhône, Saône, and Loire valleys. The next year the Charentes were its victims. The loss ran into millions of francs.[5] Since time immemorial men have defended their produce by gathering entire village populations to crush caterpillars and bugs, especially may-bugs. Beetles were also destructive and it was only in 1844 that M. Raclet in Beaujolais discovered he could destroy them by pouring boiling water over the stock. Advocated by the agricultural journals, his idea was rapidly adopted.[6] Propagation became increasingly important, because the use of boiling water went back to 1828, at least in the Mâconnais, but it was hardly known elsewhere.

Butterflies, however, were more difficult. There are stories of numerous tricks to destroy them. One involved spreading muslin sheets, smeared with honey, and lighting devices at night to attract the butterflies toward the sheets where they would become stuck against the honey and perish. The insects, disturbed by the lights, soared up, but not toward the honey, and escaped. By the 1860s most enlightened vine growers agreed that sulphur and copper chemicals were more effective, because they killed the larvae on the vine before they could evolve into caterpillars and butterflies. But since four applications were necessary, once more the costs of production were increased. Science was coming to the aid of vines, but the expense involved was to influence the entire industry.

Practical science had long been in the service of vine culture, and from 1800 to about 1850 books on the subject had a remarkably modern ring. Chaptal, Cavoleau, and Thiébaud de Berneaux in France, Fabbroni, Rovasenda, and Dandolo in Italy displayed a remarkable and essentially accurate knowledge of soil conditions and of techniques of trimming. Their knowledge was based chiefly on practical experience and intelligent observation. But they were not lacking in some laboratory knowledge about the physiology of vines, such as the influence of pruning on the flow of sap and the function of leaf structure in the process of nourishment. Gradually from the 1820s on, a considerable body of literature—books, pamphlets, some articles in the agricultural press—helped spread their teachings. Growing knowledge and interests encouraged leading amateurs and experts to go beyond the limits of their local agricultural societies and to organize in 1842 a "Congress of Vignerons" in France. It was a happy success and the papers read during its sessions were published for wide distribution. Of course it did not resolve all the problems of vine growing; on the contrary, its sessions were marked by extensive debate on the merits or lack of them of fertilizer, the use of wooden supports, and other issues. These congresses were held annually, and the volumes of their proceedings grew thicker in the next years, from 196 pages in 1842 to 640 pages in 1846. As yet there was practically no special, formal education in viticulture, nor were there laboratories or official experimental vineyards in either France or Italy.

Viticulture was merely a part of agriculture in the eyes of government agencies and institutes, and not the most important.

What then, was the state of viticulture in France and Italy in the early nineteenth century? The fact is, it was not greatly different from that two thousand years earlier among the Greeks and Romans. Indeed, "advanced" vineyard owners still read the tracts of ancient agronomists, a habit resulting from their classical education. The owners of large estates called themselves vine dressers at this early time; their national conventions in the 1840s used the title "Congress of Vignerons." Of course they did not tend vines, but hired the workers who did, and they could impart their knowledge to them. After 1848, when class feelings were intensified by the revolution of that year, the big owners assumed the title "viticulteur" (viticulturist), abandoning that of vigneron to the peasant workers.

Improvements in vine culture, once carried out extensively in monasteries by monks or on noble estates by either learned resident aristocrats or other hired technicians, now were carried on by a combination of noble and bourgeois owners. Those who resided on their domains were the innovating landlords, comparable to the "improving lords" of the agricultural revolution in England. They were in a position to control the activities of their vignerons; they had the capital to carry out the costly processes of vine culture and to experiment with new tools and equipment; and they had the education to acquire technical information and to disseminate it in periodicals and in congresses.

The conditions for a viticultural revolution were nearly all present, but none took place before late in the century. Several major factors were still missing. There was not as yet adequate land transport; both in France and Italy railroad building was just beginning in the 1840s, and therefore markets were as yet inadequate to encourage more extensive vine planting. Each region tended to be self-sufficient in grape production and planted varieties that had long been domesticated to local weather conditions and soil; taste had accustomed itself to local varieties of wine. Only the great vineyards grew grapes capable of making those few wines with the body and strength to travel overland and overseas. Equally important, the culture of enlightened growers urged them to emphasize quality over quantity, high-grade production at high prices for a select, élite market. Gentlemen growers drank their own wines and sold to other gentlemen consumers; not only the techniques of mass production, even the idea of it, were repugnant. This mentality was already growing weak before midcentury, but a new generation was required, plus other factors as we shall discover, before the old ways were swept away by a floodtide of wine in the 1860s. What might be called a viticultural revolution came with the industrial revolution—vineyards changed, but only when a whole way of life changed.

The early nineteenth-century vineyard seemed almost at one with the Romantic ideal, closer to the unkempt wildness of English gardens than to the neat geometric patterns of the grounds at Versailles. There were, in the South, some vines neatly laid out in rows, as they are now, but most of them were planted in bunches (*en foules*). The bunching resulted not from a preference, but from the method of replacing old stock—layering (*provignage*). To obtain a new vine, the grower chose a healthy, long stem or branch, laid it in a trench so that only two or three of its buds emerged at the far end, and buried its middle part with a soil and manure mixture. For a year or two the stem would receive nourishment from the mother stock and, meanwhile, it would put out its own roots. At the right time, the dresser would sever it from the stock, and it would become another vine. Over the years a cluster of vines would grow up, quite close to one another, resembling a small crowd or *foule*. All the major vineyards of France were planted like this and had adapted cultivation to it.

It had advantages and disadvantages. In its favor was the fact that several vines could be trimmed "in pyramid," that is, attached to one large stake, thereby realizing an economy in the number of stakes required. There was possibly an economy of labor too. However it was more difficult to work the soil around the vines, and the soil could only be turned by hand, since there was no path between rows for a plow to follow.

The vignerons' tools were still remarkably primitive, essentially those used by ancient Romans.[7] There was the widely used double-pronged hoe; the single-blade hoe called the *fessu* in Beaujolais and by different names elsewhere was used extensively in stony soils, along with various rakes and shovels (see Figure 1).

Hand labor with these simple tools meant that the soil was never turned deeply. It was well known that the plow, drawn by oxen or mules, was far more efficient and cheaper for labor costs. And the plow had its champions among vine growers meeting with local agricultural societies. But most owners and probably every vigneron looked upon it with suspicion, arguing that an animal in a vineyard was like the proverbial bull in a china shop: they wreaked havoc by trampling the vines and nibbling new shoots. Because of these views plows were not widely adopted until a labor shortage made them indispensable.[8] A similar attitude prevailed concerning pruning tools. The pruning knife (*serpe* and *serpette*) was widely used both for pruning and harvesting. But if not razor-sharp, it often ripped the bark, and it also shook the branches, causing grapes to fall prematurely. On this, however, knowledgeable winemen did not stand by tradition; rather they urged using the more efficient shears and indeed after 1850 there was hardly any doubt about their advantages.[9]

Perhaps the most controversial issue was fertilizer. Here growers and vignerons debated at length, but most were agreed—and experience was on their side—that certain types and heavy use of fertilizer had an undesirable effect on the wine grape, as on any fruit. When vigorous growth occurred, the sappy fluids reached the cellular tissues of the fruit in such abundance that they could not be properly prepared, resulting in the diminution of sugar and aromatic elements. The whole art of vine-dressing was intended to slow the movement of sap from the roots to the grape clusters, for only then could the berries, aided by the sun, assimilate the sap in suitable amounts and acquire the sugar content needed to make quality wine. High-minded growers sought to control juice yield in the interest of quality. Other growers—and their number rose after mid-century—sought to increase yields. Their bloated grapes made the thin wine they sold to merchants, who, in turn, blended it with alcohol to

Hoe for rocky soil (Drôme)

Hoe to break soil (Burgundy)

Hoe for rocky soil (Vouvray

Hoe for heavy soil (Médoc)

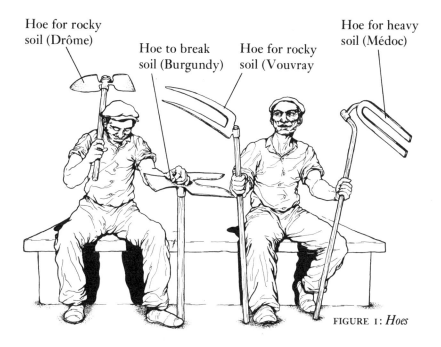

FIGURE 1: *Hoes*

raise its strength, added plaster to deepen its color, and sold it to the burgeoning lower classes of the cities. In contrast quality growers held their noses at the very idea of manure in the vineyards, apart from a limited amount for layering. They approved of carrying new earth to the vines, especially the soil washed down slopes by rain, and many of them took the pommace (grape skins left after the final pressing) to work into the soil around the vines; others made composts of dung, leaves, twigs, and earth, but they spread it only every third year and sparingly.[10] They also recognized that the quality of grapes depended, not only on the soil and its constituents, but also on the year-round care of vines.

In both France and Italy there were two distinct vine civilizations. Predominant in most of France and in the southeast of Piedmont in Italy were vines growing either without support or tied to stakes from three to five feet high. Predominant in most of Italy and in some areas of southern France, were vines attached to trees for support and interplanted with other crops. Since France was undeniably the leading country in viticulture and progressive Italians looked to her better vineyards as models, we shall begin our description of vine care there.

A new cycle of vine culture began after the grape harvest. The winds would rise, the rains come, and the autumn chill would turn vineyards into stretches of red, yellow, green, and brown as the leaves changed color before falling. A first pruning often took place at this time, if only because workers were entitled to keep most of the pruned branches for cooking during winter. For this reason they had to be supervised carefully, as at other prunings, lest they cut away too much wood, including the canes required for the following year's growth. They also, in the northern climates, piled earth around the vines to prevent the upper tender roots from freezing. These tasks seem more arduous than skilled, but in reality, pruning required a true knowledge of viticulture, and even turning the soil with the heavy two-pronged hoe demanded enough skill to avoid harming the roots that were so precious. Additional prunings took place in February and March, when the cold numbed the fingers of vine dressers in most of France. In late March came a turning of the soil to remove it from the vines, moderately aerate the roots, and expose any threatening insects. In April came layering and the placing of stakes to which the vine canes were attached as they began to grow. This was also the time to put sulphur on the vines to kill off the larvae of insects and harmful fungi in their early state. Very few vignerons employed sulphuring as yet; their ancestors had lived with insects and so would they. Not until the 1850s, when mildew appeared, did they resort to it seriously. They turned the soil again in July, chiefly to root up weeds, and for a last time in August.

Meanwhile the skilled vine dresser was tending to the vine in order to improve the quality of the grapes. In April and May, when he was not weeding, he or his womenfolk began nipping the buds of old canes in order to discourage precious sap from rising in this wood. Shortly after he carried out an operation called topping: young shoots bearing fruit were snipped about an inch above the spot where they were attached to the support, the purpose here being to prevent undue growth of wood that would steal sap from the fruit. And in some high, cold regions, they nipped off the lower end of each cluster to improve the quality of the remaining grapes. Finally, a couple of weeks before harvest, excess leaves were cut away so that the bunches of grapes could receive more sun. This was a most delicate operation because an excess removal would harm the vine; it was already known among savants of the vine that two or three leaves must be retained above each cluster, for they were necessary to draw sap up to the cluster.

By now, September, the time was approaching for the harvest, the *vendange*. Before the Revolution of 1789, in communes where grape-growing was an important part of the local economy, there existed the *ban de vendange;* that is, a custom which prohibited picking until communal authorities had tested the grapes and determined their ripeness. This custom had tended to disappear during the Revolution; it seemed to violate the principle of individual freedom. But growers did not everywhere abandon it completely, and the larger ones, recovering communal control after the Terror of 1793–94, reimposed it, relying on provisions in the Rural Code of 1796. The ban prohibited peasants from going into the vineyards before the time set for picking, and, consequently, protected their grapes from peasant fingers all too ready to snip as many as possible for themselves before the owner's arrival. Theft had been a nuisance before the Revolution; it became a greater one after the 1790s, because some peasants had managed to acquire a few yards or an acre of vines contiguous to those of local notables and they claimed the privilege of going among their own vines at any time. The ban could at least exclude them on the crucial days when grapes were nearly but not yet fully mature. Gradually, however, and more rapidly after 1830, the ban fell out of usage, and it was rarely applied a decade later. The Revolution of 1848 and the coming of universal male suffrage dealt it a death blow, because now all peasants elected their mayors, who refused to enforce any restrictions even where the custom still existed.

The *vendange*, then, could bring some disquietude to larger owners, but, except for bad years, when grapes were few or of very poor quality, harvesting brought gaity and great expectations to growers big and small (see Figures 2 – 3).

For a full year the folk of wine villages had been awaiting the day when they would see in their fields the results of all their labors. Excitement seemed to give energy to their muscles as the entire village went among the vines to begin in festive joy a labor that became increasingly arduous as the day wore on. Among the natives were many peasants from nonwine villages and from nearby mountainous or isolated areas. They came—men, women, and children—to earn a few francs to add to their meager incomes. Most were hired by the larger owners, who housed and fed them. Among the vines women and mature girls did the picking, while sturdy men carried the grapes in baskets to a nearby wagon. They all had to work hurriedly and as a team in order to gather enough grapes each day to fill one or more vats. In Burgundy, at Nuits Saint Georges, the carriers' baskets were long, with a narrow portion that fit over the shoulders and rounded bowl-like ends for the grapes (see Figure 4). Carrying this, each man looked like some winged creature scurrying along the ground. Elsewhere the basket was long and resembled a truncated cone, with straps to attach it to the carrier's shoulders.

On some domains the porters carried their loads to women seated around tables, whose job was to remove green, rotten, or dirty grapes from each cluster. This step certainly slowed production and was costly, therefore only growers of premium wines selling at high prices resorted to it. In medium-quality vineyards the women pickers attempted to cut out bad grapes from each cluster before placing it in her basket, and experienced pickers could do this quite rapidly. In common vineyards selection was done summarily, if at all, and most grapes went into the hampers.

At customary times, the pickers and porters stopped to rest. In Champagne they had early in the morning received soup and brandy, the former to give them strength, the latter gaiety. They had started work while dew was still on the grapes, because vintners insisted that dew-covered grapes made a more limpid, lighter wine. It also added to the quantity of juice and helped defray part of the high cost of grape selection that was extensively carried out in the region. Elsewhere, picking did not begin until the dew had evaporated, after nine o'clock, so the work continued on into the evening. The task was hard; the women had constantly to stoop to reach low-hanging clusters, and the porters handled baskets with up to 150 pounds of grapes. At the midday meal there

FIGURE 2 & 3: *Transporting Grapes from the Vineyard*

FIGURE 4: *Baskets for Transporting Grapes. A. Nuits Saint Georges, B. Burgundy, C. Clos de Tart*

was considerable wine-drinking, flirting, joking, and, after the evening meal, even more. Then when the heat of the day gave way to the cool of the evening, they slept on straw until aroused the next morning.

Viticulture in Italy

Italy in the nineteenth century stood for an old viticultural tradition, essentially adopted from that of the ancient Romans, while France had been more directly influenced by the Greeks who had settled in her Mediterranean littoral. The Greeks had trimmed their vines close to the ground, while the Romans, even in their great vineyards, had hung their vines high on trees, a practice found everywhere in the peninsula and which continues even today from the central provinces to those of the upper South. Now, if it is true that men are more burdened by their past than liberated by it, then vintners were indeed the prisoners of their history. But this may be a sweet burden to bear if one feels at home with traditions. Innovation may be an improvement, or it may be a degradation. In Italian viticulture there is little doubt that the nineteenth-century call for change was a call for improvement, a cry for better grapes to make wines that would be superior to the beverages poured out upon a nondiscriminating market. Reforms in grape culture had made their appearance in several areas: the quality vineyards of Alessandria, Alba, and Asti in Piedmont, in the Tuscan hills of Chianti, in those of Campania, in the Castelli Romani, and in some on the high slopes of the Apennines and the Alps. Everywhere else viticulture was, and had been for centuries, an integral part of agriculture. In the North and Center, vines were "promiscuous;" that is, they consorted not only with trees but with cereals, fodder, vegetables, and other fruit. Only in the deep South, the true Mezzogiorno, were vines dominant in the fields where they were grown because nothing else would grow there in the arid climate. But in the upper South they were not truly masters of the terrain, for the growers continued to attach them to olive and fruit trees and to let grass and weeds grow all around them.

During the first half of the century, there was practically no improvement in the dressing of vines. In Venetia farmers considered it a forward step when they changed to the maple tree as a vine support, because its slower root development robbed vines of less food, and its acceptance of closer pruning removed some of the leaves shading grape clusters from the sun.[11] Because maples did not grow on hills, the mulberry was also widely used, particularly since its leaves were fed to silkworms in the hill regions, where silk production loomed large in the peasant economy. Other trees used as living supports were the elm in the North, because it also provided good wood, the olive in the South, because olives were more profitable than wine, the oak, and other trees common or useful in a particular region. These trees were planted in rows as much as twenty-five to fifty feet apart, and from fifteen to twenty feet from each other. Usually four vines were planted at the foot of each tree, trained up along its trunk, and suspended in various ways over its branches (see Figure 5). Often two vines were extended from one tree to meet two vines extended from the neighboring tree, and they were all bound together in midair. One can readily understand the impossibility of measuring the number of hectares of vines in such an area, as well as the low yield of their grapes and the poor quality of their juice. It was impossible to treat vines high in the air against the various maladies and insects that afflicted them, an additional cause of low quality, given the indifference of peasants who picked diseased and sound grapes together. A common complaint that knowledgeable observers raised against peasant growers was the variety of vines grown in the same field, ten or a dozen kinds in many cases; sometimes different types even hung on the same tree. At

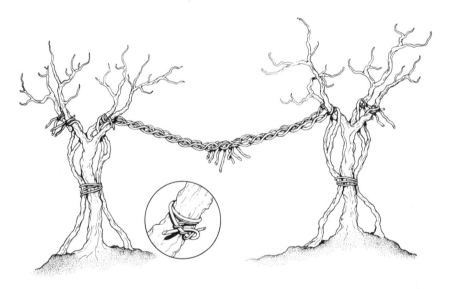

FIGURE 5: *Vines Hung on Trees*

harvest time pickers gathered them all, though some had not yet matured while others might be past maturation, and threw them into the same vat.

Evidently not even Tuscany differed from other regions as regards viticulture. The educated members of the Academia dei Georgofili were certainly improving landlords. The celebrated Bettino Ricasoli, a name that has become synonymous with excellence in Italian wine circles, did not bring the vines down from the trees; nor did he induce all his peasants to give up mixed planting or change the dependent status of the peasants. What these amateur agronomists did was to improve viticulture within the context of improved agricultural production and to demonstrate that even a relatively backward vine culture need not seriously hinder the making of high-class wines. Of greater importance was the selection of quality grapes, such as the Sangioveto and Canaiolo *nero*, and their proper blending both in the vineyards and in the fermentation vats. Nonetheless grapes remained, up to midcentury at least, merely one of many crops, and their production was limited, given the low yield, from 2 to 6 hectoliters per hectare. Tuscany, it is clear, was not the equivalent of Bordeaux or Burgundy; it barely produced a sufficient vintage for local needs and had to import wine.[12]

During the nineteenth century southern Italy, including Sicily, remained the major vineyard of the peninsula. Only in the South did mixed culture give way to real viticulture. This was not true as regards the quality of vines, for the best were not grown there; but it was as regards the quantity and solidity of wine. Out of the Mezzogiorno came enormous grape harvests, rich in sugar and capable of producing the full-bodied, alcoholic beverages that northern merchants required to reinforce the sometimes thin, faded liquids they called wine. But no one could accuse the South of innovations in grape-growing; it was too impoverished, too backward, to leap or even to crawl ahead. The one wine for which it became famous in midcentury, Marsala, was not even a fully Sicilian creation.

Why then this difference? Geographically Italy had a more ideal location than France for growing grapes. Vines existed nearly everywhere in the peninsula, whereas most of northern France was ill-suited to them. Let us begin by affirming that the difference can be overstressed, that most France vineyards were hardly superior to the Italian, that the Gallic peasant grower was as recalcitrant to change as his Latin brother south of the Alps, that while French vines had descended from trees, as had man's simian ancestor, long ago, the extremely short trim widely practiced could be as detrimental to sound grapes as the long tree-hung vines of Italians. And yet there were two distinct viticultures, and consequently, two distinct vinicultures.

Perhaps the distinction resulted not so much from the peasant growers as from the class that ruled over them during most of the century. There existed, it seems clear, a difference of mentality between the French and Italian landowner. While by no means given to tradition-shaking innovation in agriculture or well supplied with rural credit, the Frenchman invested more time, skill, and money in his vineyards, probably because there was an incentive to do so. He had enjoyed since 1789 a national market of millions of drinkers and he had fairly good access to it even before the railroads came during midcentury. On the other hand there was not, in a true sense, an Italian market until the unification of the peninsula between 1860 and 1870. Until then the grower of Piedmont could sell neither his grapes nor his wine to the sizable market in Lombardy or Venetia, because the ruling state, Austria, imposed a high tariff on imported wine—at the request of Lombard and Venetian growers! The five major states of the peninsula were more hostile toward one another than toward non-Italian states. Even if frontiers were opened, transport of grapes and wines was difficult. Canals and roads were few and in need of repair. The great vineyard of Brolio, in Chianti, was nearly isolated. On the other hand France had access to the rich markets of Britain and northern Europe, where heavy alcoholic wine was in wide demand. Her growers and her merchants profited from the stimulus of international trade and commercial expertise, plus the capital accumulation resulting from it. Finally, the higher standard of living in France, as well as the exquisite taste and refined culture there, were especially encouraging to fine vineyards and the wines coming out of them. The Italy of the nineteenth or even of the eighteenth century had declined both materially and intellectually from the Renaissance. Her churchmen and her nobility were as powerful as ever, but neither was as rich or progressive as in the past. More important was the relatively weak position of the middle classes, that is, businessmen, professionals, and bureaucrats, for it was these men who had to take the initiative and, as landowners, teach the peasants. In Italy, however, this group preferred to live in cities and have their land tended by crop-sharers whom they left to their own devices with the indifference of city dwellers. It is almost symbolic that the Italian language made such a distinction between the man of the city (*cittadino*) and the man of the countryside (*contadino*). The former lived off the fruit of the land for his own profit; the latter worked the land, produced the fruit and, alas, the wine thereof.

Viniculture

The motives that led men to grow fine grapes were precisely those that led them to make fine wines. And of these motives, the lure of distant and foreign markets should be underlined. Wines produced primarily for local consumption rarely attained greatness; rather, according to the enologist Renato Ratti, those that were consumed "by palates ever accustomed to a fixed taste . . . fatally tended to decline." [13] This observation sounds extreme, but it accords with that of Henri Enjalbert, a learned geographer of the University of Bordeaux.

The nineteenth century forms a rather long watershed between the making of wine as it was practiced for millenia and the quite new enology or science of wine that emerged from about midcentury and continues today. The word "viniculture" refers to the practical knowledge acquired by wine-makers since the Greeks and brought to the point of perfection in the late eighteenth and early nineteenth centuries in the writings of Chaptal and Fabbroni. This last phase of a long tradition was also the jump-off point of the new science of enology. We shall give more attention to enology in a later section of this book; however, in order to understand it we should first investigate the viniculture of the earlier decades of the century. We shall not here give much attention to the peasants who made wine on their own. Every writer on the subject condemned their beverages as a crime against Bacchus. Of course all of these commentators were bourgeois or nobles, prejudiced against peasants anyway, if only because they were landlords. But their judgments were undoubtedly veracious. Most peasants harvested too early; they crushed grapes with dirty feet in unclean vats; and they fermented their grapes too long, for their aim was to obtain alcohol and color in preference to savor and finesse. They poured their wine from container to container when removing it from its lees, splashing it and provoking oxidation. Finally they stored it in ill-treated wood with the result that it acquired a moldy taste and could neither travel nor live until the next harvest. Few peasants were equipped to make healthy wines; they possessed neither adequate utensils nor cellar space; probably most of them stored their wine in a crude shed containing animals, their droppings, hay, rotting fruit, potatoes, vegetables, all of which gave off odors noxious to fermenting must. Most small makers who produced for the market sold their wine early, often while it was fermenting violently, because they lacked the casks and space to store it. This practice, it should be noted, was not limited to the lower classes but was normal procedure in reputable vineyards, even in the great Château Latour.[14] Wine, when it was destined for commerce, was not always made by the landowner or peasant but was "reared" by a merchant who usually purchased it shortly after the primary fermentation and stored it in his own cellar. There, hidden from the public gaze, he blended it with other wines, added alcohol and, often times, various chemicals. After suitable maturation he distributed it either to distant markets, if it was a superior drink, or, if it was an ordinary, to local cafés, bars, restaurants, and neighborhood grocers who, watering it, dispensed it out of the barrel to customers furnished with their own bottles. The large cities of western Europe were well supplied with this wine, for surrounding them were peasant vineyards doing a fairly good business until midcentury, when transport by railroads flooded their markets with cheap wine from warmer areas far better suited to mass production. A certain number of large owners, using hired labor, also brought forth a peasant-type wine for the burgeoning urban markets. Not until later in the century, however, did there appear wine "factories," churning out by new mass-production techniques wine for the masses. The future of cheap wine lay not in the hands of peasants, who had made it since time immemorial, but in those of vinicultural and enological entrepreneurs, whose presence was hardly felt until the transformation of transport by steam power.

Less dramatic but just as significant was the development of good or superior ordinary and fine wine, two types that achieved marked improvement in the early nineteenth century. These wines were less affected by later mass-production techniques because their character and appeal were the results of essentially artisan methods of production. Mechanization of the steps followed in their fabrication, therefore, remained limited, which meant that their costs remained relatively high, as did their prices. The cost factor included both grape-growing and winemaking, and the extent of mechanization was limited in both activities. What, then, were the steps required to turn out a good wine?

To answer this question we can take up our narrative from the section on viticulture. Practical experience had taught growers that bad grapes must be separated from each cluster before crushing. This process was rather summarily carried out in ordinary vineyards, if at all, but was accomplished with great care in the finer ones by women specially trained for this task, working around tables in the open. The sound clusters were then carried to the fermenting sheds as rapidly as possible so as to avoid their premature fermentation. When enough to fill a vat were ready, work began. But what kind of work? Here educated growers were not all of one mind. They recognized that the skins must be broken in order for the juice to flow freely and for fermentation to begin rapidly. They did not agree, however, as to whether the grapes should first be stemmed. On the whole the most experienced recognized that there was no absolute rule on this matter. In good years when grapes reached maturation, they either did not remove the stems or removed them in part. They knew that mature grapes contained a high sugar content and that the acids in the stems were necessary to balance the sugar, encourage fermentation, and make a healthy dry beverage. In bad years, when grapes contained insufficient sugar, they stemmed completely to avoid making a wine too high in acid. They also knew that it would be desirable to add sugar in years of rain and cold, when the natural glucose of fruit was at its lowest. Without sugar the finished wine would be too high in acid and too low in the alcohol it derived from sugar during the primary fermentation. The classical scholars among the landowners—and most had a smattering at least of Latin—knew that the Romans had added honey to weak musts as a corrective. And if they had a guilty conscience about adulterating the must, Jean-Antoine Chaptal relieved them of their sense of sin with the assurance that sugaring was the natural thing to do. Of course he was a wise and honest man and warned against an excess of it. He also urged the use of a sugary syrup made previously from grapes. On the other hand he recognized that cane and beet sugar, in a pure state, were compatible with grape sugar and would achieve the desired results: more alcohol and a healthy wine. There were also growers who heated a part of a thin must in order to evaporate some of the water in it and poured this syrupy liquid into the vat to enhance the sugar content. That this practice gave a cooked taste to the finished product was ample reason for makers of better wines to avoid it, and Chaptal warned against it.

This was quite easy to grasp. After all, he was only telling learned growers what they already knew, and Italians, if they were patriotic and detested Bonaparte for conquering them—Chaptal was a peer of France—could turn to Adamo Fabbroni, their own patron saint of wine. My impression is that few did this, that nationalism was almost wholly absent in viti-vinicultural circles until some nationalists appeared in the 1880s. Winemen who thought about the issue at all were rather committed to a kind of international fraternity and held that vinicultural knowledge was part of a humanistic world view, quite above the narrow interests of this or that nation. Wine was a drink for all men, and the knowledge of its manufacture was, like the humanism of the ancient classics, a bond among men, not a divisive force. Debates over technology never assumed a national character; when the first congresses of grape-growers began meeting in the 1840s in France, their German and Italian colleagues immediately despatched messages of congratulations, encouragement, and friendship. Save in periods of crisis, as we shall see, winemen were remarkably universalist in their outlook. One sees this in their literature, particularly in their constant interchange of ideas and their readiness to acknowledge foreign influence. For Pasteur, Fabbroni was a précurseur; for Italian enologists, Jules Guyot was another patron saint. And below these giants were the simple artisans, who picked up ideas regardless of national origins and who spread their technological know-how with the same indifference to frontiers. Most of these artisan inventors have been forgotten, yet their work laid the basis of the vinicultural revolution.

By the early 1800s there was a market for the earliest crushers. Most skilled winemen recognized the importance of a thorough crushing of all the grapes. Traditionally vignerons placed the clusters on a large grill made of dried wood, with boarded sides. To stem they plunged and turned a wooden pitchfork or rake among the fruit and freed most of the berries from the cluster to which the stems remained attached (see figures 6 &7). Then a number of men trampled the free grapes, breaking their skins and forcing them between the small openings of the grill and

FIGURE 6: *Workers Stemming Grapes with Rakes*

into the vat below. They not only trampled the grapes; with their bare feet—hopefully cleansed—they danced over the grapes to the sound of a violin (see figures 8 &9).

In fact two or three francs per day were usually budgeted for a violinist. In certain areas this whole process became an elaborate ritual. In the rich châteaux of the Bordelais the lady of the house—as all the men held their breath—removed her boots and with exquisite coyness, deftly trod upon a few grapes, and this in the presence of a handsome male costumed as Bacchus. Then the workers began their dance in earnest, continuing it late into the night in order to fill the vat. This was common practice and was stoutly defended by most makers against the use of mechanical crushers recently introduced.

These crushers, made for the most part by local artisans at the suggestion of innovative vintners, usually consisted of a wooden box containing two parallel rollers turning in opposite directions toward each other when activated by a hand crank. From a bin at the top grapes passed between the rollers and were crushed. Widespread opposition to it resulted because some early models had rollers too closely spaced, which crushed the grapes seeds releasing an oil that spoiled the wine. Improvements included channeling or grooves in the rollers and spacing them

FIGURE 7: *Carrying Grapes to the Tops of Open Vats for Stemming or Crushing*

farther apart so that the seeds passed through untouched. Resistance remained firm, however, and many—perhaps most—makers preferred crushing by feet, arguing that the human foot, soft and arched, was naturally designed for crushing grapes without the danger of breaking the seeds. They meant, of course, the naked human foot, yet wooden clogs were apparently used in Clos Vougeot early in the century without ill effect.[15] Whatever method was used, the crushed grapes were poured into the vat, if the wine was to be red, or pressed at once, if it was to be white.

Red wine derived its color during the primary fermentation from substances in the skins. This led many wine-makers to reason that primary fermentatoin should last a long time in order to intensify color. Throughout France and Italy skins were left in the must for two weeks at least, sometimes four. But quality-minded growers recognized that a long fermentation, while it might add coloring elements, also exposed the must to air and the risk of oxidation, of turning sour. They therefore shortened it to six or eight days.

As might be expected, not all winemen agreed. They all knew that fermentation was a process transforming grape sugar chiefly into alcohol

FIGURE 8: *Crushing Grapes by Feet: Large Scale*

and carbonic acid and gas. Now the gas gradually forced the skins toward the surface of the must, where they formed a large mass called the hat or cap (*chapeau*). Traditionalists argued that the cap protected the must from the air, that there was nothing to fear. Yet they also recognized that the mass of skins should be forced into the bubbling liquid to enhance color and to reinvigorate the yeast. In some cellars workers did this with large wooden rakes. In Burgundy an old custom called for naked men to enter the vats and force the skins down, but as mentioned before, there were reports of workers inside deep vats suffocating from the carbonic acid gas. To avoid this they carried candles; if the flame went out, they were to retreat at once. This practice, incidentally, continues to the present day in a few cellars of Côte d'Or.

A far more ingenious device became fairly widespread by the 1830s. It consisted of a heavy wooden cover, slightly smaller in circumference than the vat, which was placed over the cap to force it down into the juice. The gas could escape from the small open space between the edge of the cover and the interior walls of the vat. More sophisticated makers argued that this cover did not diffuse the skins throughout large vats, so they introduced a series of wooden grills, fitted at different levels inside a

FIGURE 9: *Crushing Grapes by Feet: Small Scale*

high-walled container, with a portion of the crushed grapes between each one. This, of course, involved more expense and only big makers resorted to it (see figure 10).

Far more innovative was the invention of closed vats. In fact, it would not be farfetched to equate this invention with some of those appearing in the eighteenth century in textiles and metallurgy, the mechanical crusher being perhaps the equivalent of the spinning jenny and the closed vat that of the puddling process for smelting. But while mechanical crushing gradually became a universal procedure in large and medium wineries, the closed vat has not, and debate still goes on. The idea of a closed vat is very old; the Romans discussed it, and they may have made a few. Fabbroni and Chaptal believed that a more agreeable wine resulted from closed-vat fermentation, but to my knowledge no one put closed vats on the market or insisted on their superiority until the 1820s. At this time Mlle Elizabeth Gervais of Montpellier invented not a closed vat as such, but a special cover for any vat of suitable dimension. In a small brochure her brother, J. A. Gervais, claimed it protected the must from cold, preserved warmth necessary for complete fermentation, prevented the evaporation of bouquet, alcohol, and must, and consequently could make more and better wine than an open vat. Numerous letters,

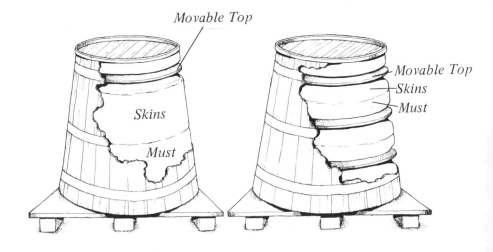

FIGURE 10: *Fermenting Vats*

including one from Chaptal, attested to the benefits of the Gervais system. In an experimental operation, the Royal Academy of Gard obtained 12 percent more wine with it for the same weight of grapes than in an open vat. The special feature of the cover was a condenser in which "alcoholic vapors" that normally evaporated in the air were trapped, condensed, and returned to the must (see figure 11). Carbonic acid gas escaped through an airtight water seal and therefore the juice inside could ferment for four weeks or more in perfect safety from oxidation.[16] All the other devices in these illustrations use various forms of water seals, i.e., tubes connecting vats to barrels or receptacles containing water, thereby allowing gas to escape and preventing oxygen from entering (see figure 12).

In short order a Monsieur Delavan published a report of his own experiments in 1822. He argued that closed vats produced better wine than open ones, but the Gervais cover possessed no special merits; any sealed cover with a small hole for gas to escape was suitable, and a lot cheaper. Reports to the Congress of Vignerons in 1843 took the same view as Delavan and recommended closed vats with S-shaped water locks made of galvanized iron or tin. They also took note of water locks used in Bordeaux for sealing the bungholes of casks containing wine going through its slow malo-lactic fermentation in winter.[17] Open-vat fermentation continued to dominate, particularly in small and medium wineries unable to increase their costs of operation. Larger growers, with those in the Midi of France leading the way, increasingly adapted covers to their large vats. Some of the great growths of Bordeaux adopted closed vats and extended fermentation from two to four weeks.[18] But even today many fine vintners are convinced that the best wine is made in open wooden vats, with a short rapid fermentation.

Other steps in the wine-making process changed little, if at all, until the turn of the century, and even in wineries seeking a superior product it remained customary to transfer must by hand from the vat to barrels after its primary fermentation. The liquid, bright red at this stage, poured from a spigot in the vat or press into a wooden tub and a worker poured it with a bucket into a barrel (see figure 13). A good cellarer splashed the wine as little as possible and used a funnel long enough to extend to the bottom of the barrel to minimize splash and contact with air. But the very process made exposure unavoidable. A more advanced technique called for siphoning wine through leather hoses from vats at the ground level into casks below ground in the cellar, practically eliminating splashing. For two barrels side by side, several writers suggested running a leather hose from the full to the empty one and, with a bellows inserted into a small hole in the upper head of the full barrel, forcing air in and the wine out and into the empty barrel. Only a small amount of air was needed and the wine flowed freely in relative safety.

The wine that had emerged from the crushed grapes was always considered the best. Fine vintners kept it separate and in new casks. It was called free-run wine or *vin de goutte*. After the vat was emptied of it, the skins were also removed and put in the basket of the press. The wine extracted from the first and second pressings, the *vin de presse*, was also highly considered and was either mixed with the free-run wine or put into separate containers for topping. Sturdy workers, after each pressing, used wooden shovels or pitch forks to break up the nearly solid mass of grape skins, the cake. Then flowed the wine of the third and fourth pressings, which being of inferior quality was separated for sale as cheap table wine, for distilling, or for home consumption. Finally the cake was broken up once more and covered with sugared water and allowed to ferment again to produce a second wine, the *piquette*, which was distributed to the workers as part of their wage. With this in mind, we can more readily understand why the vignerons manipulating the press were reluctant to exert themselves to the utmost, lest they leave little substance in the cake for their own wine. These peasants were stubborn and

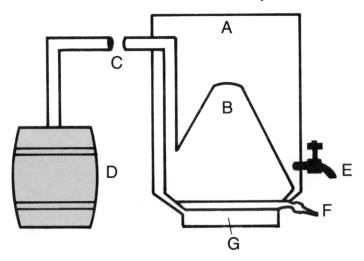

FIGURE 11: *Vat Cover of Elizabeth Gervais*
A. *Cooling unit,* B. *Condenser head,* C. *Gas escape tube,* D. *Gas escape barrel containing water,* E. *Water outlet valve of cooling unit,* F. *Condenser liquid outlet from head,* G. *Attach collar to vat cover*

clever; in some Italian wineries they physically resisted any pressing at all, arguing that the cake belonged to them by custom. Few were the owners who accepted this argument and most insisted on adequate pressure.

Presses were still large, requiring two or more sturdy men to work them, and quite expensive, and small wine-makers either had to rent them or sell their unpressed must to local merchants. The little independent man was thus at a serious disadvantage, because he had to bring his must to the press, few presses being movable, and this step exposed his must to the air. The press of the Clos Vougeot was either the largest, or one of the largest, ever built (see figure 14). It was the lever-and-capstan type, with a wooden screw, a design that goes back to Roman antiquity, perhaps earlier.

But even a relatively smaller press, such as served at the Clos de Tart, or at Hermitage was an extremely costly item, (see figure 15). These illustrations make clear that technological innovation came slowly to the winery, for the very mechanism of the press, the wooden screw, the rope and capstan, and the large flywheel, were already centuries old. Mechanically they were not highly efficient, which pleased the peasants no end since a fair amount of juice remained in the crushed grapes. After

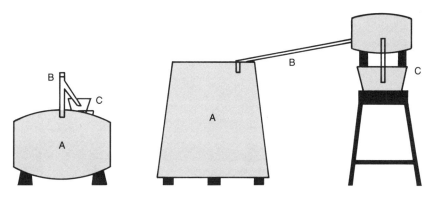

FIGURE 12: *Water Locks*
A. *Fermenting vat*, B. *Gas escape tube*, C. *Water-filled vessel*

the cake was squeezed out, the skins were either fed to the farm animals or spread among the vines as a desirable soil nutrient.

Other steps in the wine-making process were far less controversial: topping (keeping casks filled), airtight enclosures, racking (removal of wine from lees by transfer to another vessel), aging in wood, cleanliness, and fining to remove solids suspended in the liquid. The extent to which wineries adopted all these steps depended on the quality and price of its finished product. Since each step added to the costs of production, most growers preferred, after pressing their grapes, to sell the new wine at once and leave all the added expense to the merchants. The costs of cultivation, fermenting, and pressing alone could become prohibitive, indeed could lead to bankruptcy, if the year was too cold or too hot, too wet or too dry, if insects devoured the wine leaves or the fruit, or if an error in vinification harmed the wine. We have already noted some of the steps a vigneron could take against the enemies of his vines; what could he do against the enemies of his wines?

When his ignorance was his worst enemy, he could only instruct himself, a defense that grew in proportion to the quantity of articles, brochures, and books on the methods of growing vines and making wine. Unfortunately neither the government of France or Italy felt obliged to

FIGURE 13: *Racking Wine*

educate its lower-class subjects, and illiteracy was high until the last decades of the century, with the result that few peasants profited from this literature and peasant wines did not improve. For the educated, however, there was a considerable amount of information on the treatment of wines, even sick wines.

For a must low in sweetening agents they learned how to add sugar, and with the aid of new precision instruments such as the hydrometer they could measure the amount of sugar in a must and know how much to add to get the desired amount of alcohol. They also learned to expose some grapes to the sun for several days so as to concentrate their natural sugar prior to crushing them and pouring their juice into the vat. Another practice that became widespread and highly recommended was to heat about 5 to 10 percent of the must in order to concentrate the sugar by evaporation. To get color they could add various berries or a small amount of black wine. To protect their product against harmful microbes they resorted to sulphur, the miracle drug for vines and wines. They heated it to a liquid, dipped cotton in it, and attached the saturated cotton to a metal rod that they lowered into a barrel half filled with wine. Igniting the cotton, they let sulphur fumes penetrate the interior of the container as well as the wine, sterilizing both. Blending also might conteract a weakness: a sour wine with a sweet one or vice versa, a heavy one with a light, and so on.

Blending however was not undertaken solely to disguise wine; the grower frequently carried it out to improve quality. Not much of the wine entering commerce was the juice of one type of grape, although there were notable exceptions to this generalization. The great burgundies were all made from the Pinot *noir*, exclusively in the *têtes de cuvées*, the best, and the *premières cuvées*, but even in the *bonnes cuvées* and the *cuvées rondes*. The differences among this vinicultural hierarchy proceeded not from the grape type but the soil, exposure, location on the slopes, and the expertise and effort put into growing the grapes and making the wine. Beaujolais was made solely from the Gamay, just as authentic Chablis and the Pouilly wines were products of the Chardonnay or the Morillon *blanc*. In Piedmont the excellent reds of Barolo and Gattinara were made either exclusively or chiefly from the Nebbiolo grape. All other wines were blends of two or more grapes. The Burgundian *passe tout grain*, a common wine, was made of the Pinot and the Gamay, the great hermitage of Petite Syrah and Roussane, the côtes-roties of Sérine and Viognier, champagne of Pinot, Plant Doré, Plant Vert, and Épinette *blanche*, and the médocs of Cabernet, Malbec, Merlot, and Verdot. We also know that wholesale merchants brought full-bodied, richly colored wines from Banyuls and Hermitage for blending with the weaker wines of Bordeaux in bad years. Such practices as blending juices or mixing grapes was not merely a way of doctoring weak wines, but was part of a wine policy that made it possible to create a "typical" wine, of a constant taste, year in, year out. This was what Italian wine publicists constantly clamored for; they looked to the French producer as a model, while deploring the peninsular vintners either for not blending or for combining too many grape varieties. A typical wine, however, was more the merchants' concern than the growers'. The merchant blended wines, the grower grapes, and each sought to keep his blend a secret. Our knowledge therefore is scanty. In Médoc the estate owners planted about 80 percent of their land in Cabernet-Sauvignon, a hybrid introduced in the eighteenth century, 10 percent in Merlot, 6 percent in Malbec, and small amounts of Verdot or other grapes.[19] The aim was to produce a wine that would be long-lived because of the Cabernet, but mellowed or softened fairly early by the Merlot and Malbec. Before ten years of age, the cabernet was astringent and harsh, but after that it matured slowly, smoothly into a magnificent beverage. Its astringency was enhanced by the use of new casks with a high content of tannic acid in the wood. Tannin gave staying power to wine, but seriously prolonged the period

FIGURE 14: *Press at Clos Vougeot*

before it became drinkable. The costs of this type of wine were enormous, for they included not only the heavy expense that was normally part of vinification but also the long years of storage. The temptation, therefore, has been to add larger amounts of Malbec and Merlot to hasten maturing, a temptation to which lesser growers had already succumbed in the earlier years of the century. G. Bord gave the following proportions as those commonly used in the cantons of large-scale production; it is apparent that only in the cantons of quality wine did the Cabernet hold its own (See Table 1).

In the Libournais superior growths blended ⅓ Cabernet, ⅓ Merlot, and ⅓ Malbec. Elsewhere the Malbec, Merlot, and other grapes, such as the Verdot and Mancin, made up the blends.[20] Partly for this reason the leading growths of Saint-Emilion and Pomerol, as regards prices, were classed below fourth and fifth growths of Médoc.[21] East of the Gironde River the Merlot ruled, and while it was blended with the Cabernet, it did not live as long or reach the high state of development of a great *cru* of Médoc. The Merlot was also a relatively new grape, introduced in the later eighteenth century.

Chianti in Tuscany in the early century was also a blend, "a large part of Mammolo and of Marzamino." [22] As time passed they were aban-

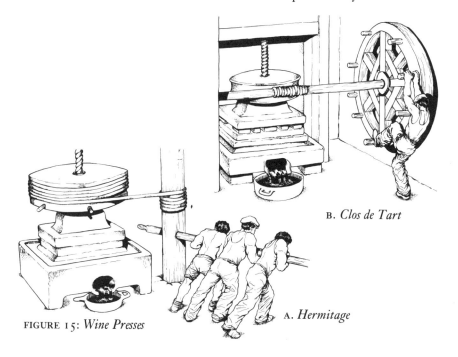

B. *Clos de Tart*

A. *Hermitage*

FIGURE 15: *Wine Presses*

TABLE 1: *Blending Formulas in Upper Médoc*

Canton	Cabernet	Merlot	Malbec	Merlot and Malbec
Pauillac	3/4			1/4
Saint-Laurent	3/5	1/5	1/5	
Castelnau	2/5			3/5
Blanquefort	2/3			1/3
Pessac	1/2	1/4	1/4	
Brède	2/3			1/3
Brède (peasant growths)		4/5		1/5 (Merlot, Verdot, Cabernet . . .)

doned and the Sangiovese took precedence (50–80 percent) over the Can-aiolo *nero* (10–30 percent), and to it was added a white grape, either the Trebbiano Toscano or the Malvasia of Chianti (10–30 percent). The white gave softness and finesse and like the Merlot in Médoc hastened maturation. In Tuscany, however, the *governo performed that function.*

The Viniculture of Sparkling Wine—Champagne

The viniculture of sparkling wine is not fundamentally different from that of still wine; rather it is an addition to the normal process of produc-tion, because the gaseous bubbles that give the sparkle are induced to appear in a wine as still as any other. The territory of Champagne, where the process was perfected in the last century, grew into one of the three great vineyards of France, the most recent to enter the limelight. Perhaps for this reason the vinicultural traditions there were less rigid than in Bordeaux and Burgundy. In fact Champagne's rise to success occurred because local wine makers and merchants were willing to revo-lutionize their industry, first by shifting from a still to a sparkling bever-age, and then to changing its color. Until the late seventeenth and early eighteenth centuries the best wines were red, or reddish (the whites were held almost in contempt by connoisseurs), they were still or non-sparkling, and they were consumed early, after the first racking in Janu-ary. Young wine was considered the best, and any that was more than a year old was condemned as faded, insipid, and bitter.[23] Merchants pre-ferred red still wine at least until the 1690s. Bubbles in wine, they be-lieved, were a trick used by producers to disguise a harsh taste. By the eighteenth century, however, their views began to change. Effervescent wine was attracting favorable comment, even though only a small quantity was purposely made to bubble, and white wine had revealed its superior quality for this purpose.

Undoubtedly the work of Dom Pérignon either started or hastened this change. Although he lived in the seventeenth century, his work was fundamental and markedly influenced our period. In a sense he made champagne what it has been ever since: a blended sparkling wine. We have already noted that for various motives, both high and low, nearly all wine was blended. Pérignon greatly improved the quality of his monastery's wine by acquiring grapes from various vineyards in the area between Reims and Epernay and then blending them to make his final beverage. His sense of taste was marvelously acute, perhaps all the more so because he became blind, and he made his mixture by tasting grapes, not wines.[24] This method, since few had his sensibility, was not followed by later procedure; however they did learn to blend wines made from different grapes of various areas in the Champagne region in the hope of rediscovering the wise monk's happy proportions. His blend encouraged the formation of carbonic acid gas to create bubbles, a whiter color, and long conservation. He also used strong bottles, tied string over the stoppers to keep them from blowing out, and availed himself of Spanish corks as stoppers.[25] His wine, when it rightfully acquired a wide reputation in the nobility, enhanced the fame of champagne wines.

Until the mid-nineteenth century, however, red still wine remained predominant in the region. Yet it was amazing that good red wine could be made so far north. In the seventeenth century it had even rivaled red burgundy for the favor of Louis XIV and his court. However growers discovered after the Napoleonic epoch that sparkling whites were easier to sell at high prices, even though they were more complicated to make. Their red wine was often sour, because grapes grown in the cold northern climate lacked sugar, and had to compete against Burgundy and Bordeaux, both more favored by nature; on the other hand sparkling wines, sweetened by the addition of sugar, were almost a novelty.

The leading position of red wine becomes clear from these figures of 1832 for Marne Department:

	Hectoliters
Total wine production	480,000
Ordinary red for local use	310,000
Quality red for export	120,000
White for sparkling	50,000

Not until the 1840s did reds decline in quantity and, soon, in quality. In the 1860s Henry Vizetelly complained that the red still wine of St. Thierry, recalling a Médoc for its tannin and a Côte d'Or for its vinosity, was "almost a thing of the past." [26]

The whites might continue to be snubbed by conservative connoisseurs, but many nobles and upper bourgeois were eager to try them, if only to enliven a party by letting the froth spew out over giggling ladies. In such company sugar and bubbles could not only lend gaiety, they could also disguise the wine's mediocre quality, a marked commercial advantage. Mediocre champagne doubtless entered the market, but the world reputation champagne acquired could hardly have been based on such trickery; rather it was the consequence of the rapid development of techniques far more innovative than those in other regions, aggressive entrepreneurship, and the making of a high-quality product.

Making wine in Champagne was not more difficult or expensive than in other parts of France. As in Côte d'Or the Pinot *noir* offered the highest quality juice which, fortunately, was pure white until colored by the skins. Makers pressed it, then immediately separated its juice from the skins so as to prevent their giving color to the rich, bright liquid. According to Rendu, the juice of the first three pressings made the best wine.[27] Evidently practices differed among large companies selling their own blends as they did among small wine-making vignerons, but everywhere the fourth or fifth pressing, called *rebêche*, was used to make the *piquette*. On their way to the vats or casks the juices were usually filtered through wicker baskets as a guarantee that no grape skins would enter to darken the must. As an additional precaution some houses poured the must into large vats where, during twelve to twenty-four hours, it deposited its heaviest lees; then it was transferred to casks for fermentation. Racking came in late December and then blending. The true art, then, was not in making wine, it was in blending various wines to make "champagne," a special kind of product. This complex process, requiring more manpower and equipment, explains why champagne was, and still is, so expensive.

As the wines aged in wood each blender followed their development to discover the unique qualities of each before deciding on the proportions he would need. Like growers in most areas where a mixture was deemed necessary to achieve a typical wine, the Champenois developed an elaborate system. In fact from the first step of blending to the final step of bottling, champagne was the most "manipulated" wine on the market. Blending had two goals in Champagne: first to correct deficiencies in the year's vintage and second to achieve a quality and well-established type of wine regardless of the vintage. To accomplish the first objective the blender used strong wines to correct the weak, sweet wines to balance the sour, old wine to age the young, and heavy wine to give body to the light. As we have noted, all makers married wines to save their year's production from the adversity of nature. Champagne houses gathered rather distant wines when the local harvest left something to be desired, for only by following this practice could they liberate themselves from the climatic vagaries of nature and turn out a good wine year in year out. Ordinarily most of the firms obtained the various juices they required from local or regional growers. Wines of different areas were brought together, usually before Christmas, and each blend was called a *cuvée.* The vintners more or less agreed that wines from the Mountain of Reims added body, vinosity, and solidity to the final product; those from the slopes in the Marne Valley brought softness; and those from the Côtes des Blancs (white-grape slopes) added a whiter color, finesse, lightness of body, and encouraged the fermentation needed to make bubbles. Rendu believed that the best champagne consisted of a one-third portion from each area.[28] But the proportions remained house secrets, for the distinctions among the several quality champagnes, each under a distinct label, derived in large measure from the blend. To keep faithful to the quality of his label, the type of wine expected of it, each blender had to follow his formula faithfully. In bad years, however, he might have to modify it, even to the point of bringing in musts or grapes from far outside the district.

The desire to keep the blending formula secret entailed all sorts of problems similar to those of early industry. It was a common practice for entrepreneurs in metallurgy to hire away skilled workers from their rivals in order to obtain trade secrets. The British government even forbade its workers going to France lest they carry blueprints of new inventions with them. Now there can be little doubt that champagne companies hired some German winemakers to profit from their skills and that they sought by every device to keep their knowledgeable blenders from being lured away by rivals. Great blenders were rare, as were fully professional enologists. The easiest solution, of course, was for the company manager or owner—when firms were nearly all owned by a family—to be his own blender. Combining management and wine-making was fairly common in the early history of the companies, and managers were often sons of wine merchants who had learned their trade during an extended apprenticeship. At this time there were no agricultural schools as such, certainly none organized to teach enology. Wine-makers learned their trade, as nearly everyone else did, by apprenticeship, by doing, and by perfecting an inherited sense of taste. Even in the late nineteenth century many sensitive blenders were still largely self-taught in the old way. André Simon told of meeting an aging blender risen from the peasant class. Into a dozen glasses, each filled with new wine from a different vineyard, the old man put a spoon of sugar. When Simon said that he could not tell the difference among them but only smell the sugar, he replied, "Of course you can smell the sugar, *mon p'tit,* . . . but try again and you will find that all those wines are slightly different: the sugar is there as a uniform background against which slight differences will stand out." [29]

Making the blend in large companies involved elaborate systems of pulleys, cranes, and lifting devices. With these workers sorted out the casks of wine, lifted them over a huge vat, and emptied the contents into it.

The marriage of the various wines was consummated by a large mechanical paddle or stirring device, activated by a hand crank, which mixed them into a harmonious whole. When satisfied the blender then had workmen return the new wine to casks where it matured until the moment of bottling.

The date of bottling was extremely important. Wines normally sleep in the cold winter months, especially after the malo-lactic fermentation in December; they then awake, or ferment, again in spring, at about the time that vines show new signs of life. From March to May, new wine was bottled and stacked on its side deep in the large cavernous cellars of each company. Here the wine stayed in a cool temperature so that its maturation would continue slowly and carbonic acid gas build up pressure. During the eighteenth and first half of the nineteenth centuries this was a critical period for the financial future of a champagne-maker; atmospheric conditions during the summer following the bottling could either make or break him. During July and August the pressure of carbonic acid gas grew, sometimes causing bottles to explode; in very torrid years champagne cellars were said to sound like a battlefield under an artillery barrage. This is why companies enlarged the deep chalk quarries they originally used as storage cellars or dug deeper ones. The deeper the cellar, the cooler its air, and even one or two degrees of cold could save thousands of bottles from destruction. The wine that survived remained in glass for a year or more, depending on its quality. Meanwhile the reactivated fermentation continued building up pressure and depositing lees of dead yeast and other chemical products. Finally the time arrived for the next major step leading to the finished product, riddling.

In this step the sediment lying on the lower side of the bottle was directed into the neck, where it settled on the interior side of the cork. It marked an important technological advance. Until the later eighteenth century most champagne was not shipped as sparkling wine because the weak bottles of the time broke under the pressure built up during transit. Since only rich men could afford the wine, each customer bought an entire cask of it; the maker sent him the wine, bottles, corks, string, and instructions for bottling so as to get a *mousse* or bubbling foam. A small amount was shipped out in bottles, however, and with proper handling stood a fair chance to reach the customer. Before these bottles were shipped, the lees were sent against the cork by holding the bottle upside down and striking its sides with the hand in order to detach them and let gravity draw them downward. This was a long, costly process, and not always successful. Subsequently, tables with holes in the surface were used. Workers inserted bottle necks into the holes and counted on gravity for the rest. Around 1818 a cellarist of the famous Widow Clicquot suggested that the bottles be agitated with their necks remaining in the holes so that sediment would be detached from each bottle's sides and descend more rapidly and completely.[30] Because these tables occupied too much room, other cellarists hit upon the idea of *pupîtres*. These were tables turned on their ends, so to speak, nearly vertical to the floor, like an inverted V, with rows of holes into which the necks of filled bottles were inserted, parallel to the floor (see figure 16). A group of workers call *remueurs* were then assigned the task of *remuage*, that is, of giving each bottle about one-eighth of a turn every day after the worker first marked the top side with white chalk so that he would complete a full rotation with eight turns. As time passed he would not only turn each bottle but also oscillate it and lift its bottom slightly so that, in a specified time, it was, like the *pupître*, nearly vertical to the floor, with its neck pointing downward. At the end of the cycle, all the solid matter was supposed to be lying against the cork. If it were not, the worker, as he turned and raised the bottle, let it fall into its hole with a slight bump so as to force the sediment downward. Particularly important was the deftness of hand that displaced lees without clouding the wine. This process required two or three months and began with the wines that were ready to be shipped out. There are numerous stories told about the workers who carried out this job. They spent most of their lives in the dark, damp cellars, with only a candle or other preelectric light, moving among the *pupîtres*, using each hand to twist two bottles at a time; a good man could turn about 30,000–40,000 bottles in his ten- to eleven-hour shift. These men were like miners, their world was the underground. After a few years of this life they grew morose, became heavy drinkers, and imagined they saw apparitions in dark caverns, sometimes devils who shook the bottles to stir the lees and cloud the wine. Pale from lack of sunlight, they were easy victims of illness and, it was believed, died early.[31] (In 1971 I saw an old-timer doing this job on the eve of his retirement. I could not help wondering, how long will he live in the sun?)

When the lees were all against the cork the time had arrived for *dégorgement* (see figure 17). Bottles upon bottles, all turned with necks downward, were carried to the *dégorgeur*, who, keeping the neck at about a 45° angle, cut the strings or pulled off the wire holding back the cork, which immediately blew out along with the sediment in a frothy explosion. At once the deft artisan, righting his bottle, wiped away the sediment remaining in its neck. stuck his thumb over its opening and passed it on to the *doseur*, the worker who replaced the bottle's lost wine. He refilled it with the *liquer d'expédition*, a wine sweetened with either cane or beet or grape sugar (this last blending most harmoniously with wine) and some brandy.

Even in the early nineteenth century the degree of sweetness varied with the demands of the market. Of course all champagnes were sweet, but those destined for Russia and east Europe were considerably sweeter

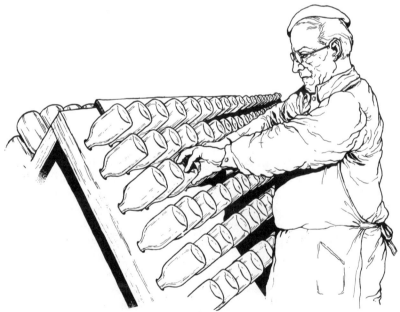

FIGURE 16: *Using Pupîtres for Riddling*

than those being sent to western Europe. At first there was no market for an unsweetened beverage. However the desire to expand sales by encouraging people to drink sparkling wine with their meals as well as after proved an irresistible force, and champagne labeled "dry" came on the market in the 1860s. But even the "very dry" still received a *dosage*, however slight.

Since it had to age longer, the new dry champagne was more expensive and the *doseur* had to have even greater skill to refill the bottle. This was a quite difficult task in the earlier nineteenth century because the worker had to get wine into a bottle from which froth wanted to rush out the moment he poured in a small amount of liquid. Happily his errors could be corrected by the next worker in line, the corker who regulated the level by pouring out or adding wine. Until Dom Pérignon champagne bottles were stoppered with wooden dowels wrapped in a cloth dipped in tallow. Pérignon, however, began the use of authentic corks, which presented the problem of insertion. At first a mallet was used to pound the corks in as well as to round off the upper portion. Then the next worker tied them in place with string and wire. Here, indeed, was an almost modern assembly line. The final tasks took place after the wine had recovered from such active manipulation and pressure had reap-

FIGURE 17: *Disgorging, Refilling, Corking, Tieing Champagne*

peared, an interval of several months; then it was labeled, packaged, and shipped off to the pleasure capitals of the world.

Shipping presented difficulties because motion further increased pressure inside the bottle and breaking remained a serious problem. Indeed it was a serious problem long before the bottles were put on wagons and ships for export. Both the use of sugared musts and of white grapes to encourage the second fermentation increased the pressure inside bottles during maturation and could provoke considerable breakage (*casse*). Normally each company expected a 10 percent loss, but in certain years it was catastrophic. If the summer turned hot, *casse* took horrible tolls: 85 percent at Avize in 1801, 35 percent in the Moët cellars in 1833 and 25 percent there in 1834. 1842 was the *année terrible;* cellars were flooded with running wine and broken bottles throughout Champagne, for even a mere 10 percent breakage in 1842 amounted to two million bottles.[32] In 1850 a Reims cellar suffered 98 percent loss; bankruptcy surely followed such a misfortune. Profits declined when the reverse happened; that is, when no sparkle appeared, because the merchant then had to start all over or sell his wine as still at a ridiculous price.

Little wonder that the champagne trade was considered highly speculative. Until the 1830s makers were viniculturists rather than scientific enologists. They knew little about fermentation and even less about the chemical changes taking place as wine matured. Some of them knew that adding sugar assured a sparkle, but not all of them resorted to it because it also could bring on too much gas and cause breakage. But failure to add sugar sometimes meant that no gas remained by springtime and no sparkle appeared in the summer. They also knew that heat was a causal factor.

Breakage, even of average dimensions, added considerably to the retail price, and had it continued at its early rates it might have priced champagne out of the market. In order to save their produce, lower costs, and expand sales, company managers had to find a way to lessen it. Relief came from several different sources. Bottle manufacturers gradually improved their technology and by the 1830s and 1840s put on the market bottles able to withstand thirty atmospheres of pressure, far above the six required for a *grand mousseux*.

At the same time wine technology moved ahead with the aid of science. The first significant work was carried out between 1829 and 1836 by a Châlons pharmacist named François. He began by showing how to measure the quantity of sugar in wine by a process that came to be called the "reduction method." He reduced a bottle of wine to four ounces, then measured its sugar content by means of the glucometer that Cadet de Vaux had recently invented. Once the sugar content was known, François then drew up a table indicating the amount of sugar to add in order to obtain a desired pressure. His book, *Traité sur le travail des vins blanc mousseux* (1837) was a technological breakthrough of such importance that his method was still used in the early twentieth century, for although his method was and remained an approximation, it was sufficiently accurate for practical wine-makers. The later researches of J. Maumené were, theoretically, an improvement over François's work, but they were not effective in practice.[33] His chief contribution was an *aphromètre*, or manometer, to measure gas pressure in the bottle. It consisted of a long, hollow needle, shoved through the cork and attached to a measuring device. He also experimented considerably with the wine of Champagne and became the leading enologist there.[34] As a result of these technological discoveries breakage was cut at least in half, costs reduced, and production increased to meet a rising demand. And yet one must not imagine that growers were eagerly awaiting a new technology and readily accepted it. Moët of Epernay was the first to adopt the recommendations of François, but producers in Reims were resistant to such innovations and continued to rely on personal testing to determine the amount of sugar to add.[35] A new generation, younger and part of the new scientific age, would have to appear before a new technology and science could take over champagne-making.

The generation following Napoleon's empire did not overly welcome innovations that smacked more of theory and speculation than of practicality. To men who believed that their sense of taste was superior to scientific measurement the findings of François seemed over-expensive trifles. They were much more attracted to practical inventions that improved the productivity of the assembly line beginning with the disgorger and ending with the labeler. And their generation saw the invention of several new machines: in 1827 a corker that resembled the guillotine, in 1844 a machine facilitating the dosage of liqueur, a machine to wash bottles, and one to attach the *agrafes* or metal hooks holding on the first cork; in 1846 appeared a machine to tie on the second and permanent cork after the first had been pulled out by the *dégorgeur*. It also became a practice to brand the second cork with the maker's name so as to insure the buyer of the authenticity of the bottle's contents.

The job of the *dégorgeur* was greatly facilitated in the 1880s by the use of ice and chemicals to freeze the wine in each bottle's neck. Henceforth when he pulled off the *agrafe*, and the first cork popped out, so did the sediment contained in the frozen plug of wine. Less wine and less gas were lost as a result. Mechanization, of course, had not yet appeared. All the new inventions were activated by hand and required highly skilled workers combining dexterity and rapidity. By the 1840s a good crew could handle at least a thousand bottles a day, and as the demand for champagne increased these technical innovations helped meet that demand. They were labor-saving devices to a certain extent, but they did not eliminate the workers, nor avoid an increase of the labor force. Greater demand required a larger number of crews until electrical power was applied to more efficient machines. But that came only in the twentieth century, when mechanization began to influence the economics of the wine industry.

CHAPTER SEVEN

Economics of Wine

Vintages and Income

The geographic spread of vineyards was not the result of hazard but of man's response to the exigencies of climate, soil, and economics. Among these three major determinants of vine location, soil has always been a constant factor, unvarying from year to year. Climate, on the other hand, while it reveals a certain constancy over long periods of time, displays marked seasonal instability, ranging from cold to warm, or dry to wet. Weather, therefore, has to be taken into account by the commercial grape-grower, because his annual income is always highly dependent on it. Climate in the long run and weather in the short run are major factors in any wine economy and to ignore them when planting a vineyard is the height of folly.

The men who survived as grape-growers and wine-makers were fully aware that climate and soil determined the more enduring quality and reputation of a particular grape and its wine, year in, year out. A vougeot, or a château latour were great wines, and although their vintage of say, 1821 was decidedly inferior to that of 1822, they retained their reputations all the same.

The difference between 1821 and 1822 was due to weather, and it was the annual combination of sun, rain, and temperature that decided the economic value of vine-growing. In a good year, when grapes contained sufficient sugar and acid, the wine made from them sold well and procured a profit for everyone in the business. In a rainy cold year, when grapes lacked the desirable balance among their chemical ingredients, prices might tumble. Fine wines were often not sold under their usual labels; sometimes they could not be sold at all, or only after several years, when another poor or insufficient vintage might induce a merchant to take them at practically give-away prices.

These wet, cold years have always been the great bane of wine-growers, and no healthy, profitable wine industry could appear in regions where bad years were more numerous than good, or even balanced the good. This situation explains in large measure why, in the course of the century, commercial grape- and wine-growing became concentrated in the most favored locations. To be sure, a favorable climatic balance was not the only factor—improved transport was another—but modern transport merely gave an added value to climate precisely because it made geographic concentration possible. Vineyards in less suitable situations were economically feasible where a local market closed to outside wines offered a near monopoly for regional beverages. When easy transport ended these privileges by introducing wines from other regions, local growers abandoned vines for crops more suited to the climate. Cold and wet years have several effects on vinemen. Psychologically they are demoralizing. For many growers viticulture was an act of faith, a sacrosanct profession, almost a priestly act in honor of the gods. Ever since the Greeks, and undoubtedly before them, vine planting and cultivation, the harvest and the making of wine were carried on with appropriate incantations and exhortations to one or more deities. The coming of Christianity did not in any way change these rituals; there merely evolved a series of saints—such as Saint Martin in Burgundy or Saint Verney in Central France—to replace the anthropomorphic gods of old. If the immortals of heaven were on one's side, one could hope for abundant sun, dry weather with sufficient moisture, and rich, full grapes. Prolonged cold and rain, or drought, or vine maladies, or an excess of insects brought long days of prayer and nights of holy vigil, and all too often the fading of hope as grape flowers withered in a poor season.

Mediocre years, of course, have usually been economic as well as psychological catastrophies. But this was not always the case, especially if the weather reduced yield along with quality; a decline of grapes following on several abundant harvests could and did have the meritorious effect of cleansing the market and holding prices steady. An ideal location encouraged both an adequate yield or quantity of grapes and high quality during as many years as possible.

The vineyards enjoying the highest prestige had to meet certain minimal criteria as regards quality and our task involves the discovery of those criteria. At this point we must confess that the data for such a study create problems; they are chiefly verbal and rather subjective, while our method of measurement is numerical. Our conclusions, in consequence, remain somewhat tenuous and subject to revision. On the other hand the French relied on several key words when reporting on the quality of vintages and this makes it possible to assign a numerical value to each of them as follows: 7 exceptional or superior, 6 very good, 5 good, 4 average or ordinary, 3 mediocre, 2 bad, 1 very bad or disastrous. The first four categories identify a wine that was readily salable and therefore profitable, if not excessively abundant; the last two or three identify wine whose sale usually resulted in a loss unless it was in extremely short supply. The first four categories we shall classify as A, the last three as B, which enables us to see how they line up in table 2.

These data include most of the important quality-wine districts of France, the Côtes du Rhône being the main one missing. Since these were the regions in which quality wine-growing became concentrated, they were presumably the ones selected by commercial producers in search of profits, and profitability apparently required that two out of three vintages produced an average or better crop of grapes. The Mâconnais seems not to have met this requirement; however the data available is limited to the 1870–1914 period, when fully half of these years were adversely affected by phylloxera, the vine blight. Touraine was far luckier, apparently suffering less from the blight and recovering early. Most likely the grower in the Mâconnais, over a century of time, was not more adversely affected by the weather than those of Côte d'Or just to the north and those of Beaujolais just to the south. In fact the data for Saône-et-Loire can be combined with that of its largest vineyard, precisely the Mâconnais, for a total score of 60 and 40 for nearly a century. This was almost identical to Côte d'Or, 62 and 38.

These data clearly indicate that the growing of grapes and wine was a particularly hazardous enterprise. It was the least stable in growth of all agricultural produce, with a coefficient of variation more than four times higher than other crops.[1] The enterprise was especially hazardous in the Mâconnais, Côte d'Or, and Touraine. Serious vine maladies, powdery mildew in the 1850s, phylloxera in the 1880s and 1890s, and rot in the 1890s drag down the percentages. But the use of sulphur, a regular part of vine culture after the 1850s, had a marked influence on the years following the phylloxera and pull them up. Extensive replanting using sturdier, improved varieties, more sophisticated viticulture, and sulphur chemicals caused the flowers to set earlier and hastened the maturing of grapes. Harvesting began a week or so earlier and "good" years increased in number, as table 3 indicates. (It includes regions for which data is available. A = average or above, B = below average).

Quite clearly the most notable gains in the post-phylloxera period were made in the Bordeaux and Champagne districts where replanting brought about a notable improvement in the quality of vintages, which undoubtedly helped vintners to recover some of their losses. Equally

TABLE 2: *Quality of Harvests, France*

Area	Number of Years, N	A as percent of N	B as percent of N
Rhône Dept. (Beaujolais)	109 (1805–1914)	66	31
Côte d'Or	114 (1799–1913)	62	38
Gironde	120 (1795–1914)	65	35
Saône-et-Loire	52 (1812–72)	69	31
Champagne	115 (1800–1914)	63	37
Bouzy and Ambonnay (Champagne)	59 (1815–74)	69	31
Maine-et-Loire	60 (1812–72)	68	32
Mâconnais	43 (1870–1914)	51	49
Touraine	33 (1881–1914)	60	39
Mean		64	36

Sources: Garrier, II, 164; Goujon, 169: Laurent, II, 175, 248; Bernard, 1–10; Simon, 142; Lafforgue, passim; Petit-Lafitte, table C.

important were the number of post-phylloxera years with above-average production, that is, good and excellent harvests as regards quality. Under this heading came, in most favored position, the vineyards of Champagne (51 percent), Rhône department, (50 percent), Gironde (48 percent), Touraine (45 percent), Côte d'Or (43 percent), and Maine-et-Loire (42 percent).

One would imagine that the most northerly region, Champagne, would suffer most from winter cold and spring frost. It, however, was protected from frigid winds by the high ground of the Montagne de Reims, while the equally famous Côte d'Or was less favorably situated; other factors, such as soil and transport rather than the uncertainties of seasonal climate, encouraged the continuance of viticulture there, at least in quality vineyards. The high prices of its wines undoubtedly helped to allay the disadvantages of bad years, a situation similar to that of Bordeaux but by no means identical. Compared to these northerly vineyards, the Gironde had a highly favorable climate. The winters were less rigorous, the summers warmer. In fact the climate of the Bordelais approached that in which truly fine vines could not grow because of temperatures too high and summers too long. To produce grapes that will make the finest beverages, the noble vine must be stimulated, or, so to speak, challenged by certain aspects of its environment.[2] In Champagne

TABLE 3: *Quality of Pre- and Post-Phylloxera Harvests*

Area	Before phylloxera			After phylloxera		
	A	%	B	A	%	B
Rhône dept. (Beaujolais)	63		37	68		32
Côte d'Or	61		39	63		37
Gironde	60		40	79		21
Champagne	59		41	79		21

and Côte d'Or, as in Alsace, the cold winters proved suitable to challenge the Pinots and Rieslings to produce their best fruit; in Bordeaux the decisive factor—if there is really one that stands above the others—was the soil; thin, gravelly, hardly nourishing, and arrogantly demanding of the Cabernets and Merlots to push down their roots. But, to repeat, these were permanent factors, forming part of the microecology of vineyards. One cannot, as noted already, ignore the annual weather as both an ecological and an economic factor.

The tables in Appendix 1 provide additional information about the weather; they attempt to indicate the quality of vintages by decades and set up a raw score at the end of each row, enabling us to evaluate the influence of weather during shorter time spans than was the case in table 2.

Most notable was the relative equality of the average score for the four major regions, with a range between 42 and 45, and Champagne's rating of 45 may be due to semantics rather than reality. There the high number of years rated excellent, 21 percent, seems unduly optimistic; indeed, it seems to be either a sales device intended to influence buyers or simply high-flown rhetoric. The large champagne houses were more actively engaged in publicizing their product than most merchants of still wines, and they were keenly sensitive to public opinion, especially outside of France. It was good business to have either superior or very good years—Champagne accumulated thirty-four, or 38 percent of our eighty-nine-year sample. In the chilly north this was a remarkable achievement when compared to Bordeaux (20 percent), Beaujolais (23 percent), and Côte d'Or (25 percent). More convincing was the low score everywhere for the 1820s, a decade of weak income due, apart from poor quality, to low prices and limited yields. The 1850s, when vines were plagued by mildew, also recorded low scores for quality, and Champagne suffered her worst decade of the century. Conversely the 1840s and 1860s were the best decades for quality before the phylloxera blight. Apart from

TABLE 4: *Quality of Vintages Related to Net Income, Côte d'Or*

Period: 1820–54 (N=34) Quality Rating	No. of Years	Percent of N	Index of Yield, Mean	Net income/*ouvrée* self-employed vigneron producing Fine wine Ordinary mean of sample	
7–6	6	17	72.5	42.0F	25.4F
5–4	12	35	91.8	21.3	13.4
3–1	16	47	102.3	16.7	16.4
Mean net income of all years 1820–54				26.6	18.4
Period: 1855–79 (N=25)					
7–6	10	40	124.1	113.9F	47.9F
5–4	8	32	113.2	101.1	59.9
3–1	7	28	80.0	22.8	29.6
Mean net income of all years 1855–79				79.2	45.8

Source: Laurent, II, 171, 198–99

these years of similar performance, the major vineyards went their separate ways; there were few years of either very good or very bad weather everywhere. Among the best were 1802, 1811 (the year of the comet), 1822, 1825, 1834, 1846, 1858, perhaps 1865 and 1893. Among the worst were 1809, 1816, 1824, 1845, 1853, 1860, 1866, and 1910 (worst vintage since 1800). The best and the worst balanced each other.

The years of high quality were, if the Côte d'Or was typical, years of highest net income for growers. Thanks to data furnished by Professor Laurent it was possible to prepare table 4, which relates quality to net income.

For the period 1820–54 the six harvests rated very good and excellent amounted to 17 percent of all the harvests and returned net incomes well above the average for the entire period. Undoubtedly the relatively low yield also accounts for the high prices of these years, but it was the outstanding quality that sent prices high enough to compensate for limited supply and therefore to return a quite profitable net income. As it turned out, net revenue during these six harvests was high enough to raise the mean net income above those of average and mediocre years for the entire period 1820–54. Years of low quality, on the contrary, were usually economic disasters for fine wines, in part because the new wine was hard to sell and had trouble surviving the summer heat; in part because yields were high in these years, a condition that by itself pulled prices downward. On the other hand ordinaries returned a higher revenue because quantity was sufficient to compensate for lower prices. Good and average years, of which there were twelve, maintained prices at profitable levels, but they did not bring in substantial returns. Two hectares of fine vines averaged 1,065 francs, while ordinary vines on the slopes averaged 670 francs. But quantity was insufficient to compensate for low prices.

It is apparent that yields also influenced wine economics in the first half of the century. There was a remarkably high correlation between the amount of wine and prices (r = −.7 − .8) in all the vineyards, and this was true especially for ordinary wine. When harvests were large, prices fell, and vice versa. However high prices, resulting from a scarcity of wine, did not always engender equally high net income unless quality was superb. As table 5 indicates, average yield (about 20 to 30 hl/ha) was the most remunerative level in terms of net income, and that was true of both fine and ordinary produce in the Côte d'Or and Mâconnais.

So far we have touched on only two variables as regards the Côte d'Or vineyard. The above tables leave no doubt that quality and quantity influenced net income, but the correlation between them is less significant than for prices alone. Using multiple regression we derive the following results for wines grown by independent vignerons (See Table 6).

The coefficients indicate significance and reveal that quality was a more important determinant than yield for fine wines, while the reverse was true for ordinaries. As regards high-quality beverages, the elasticities indicate that a 10 percent increase in yield produces about a 7 percent increase of revenue, whereas a 10 percent increase in quality will produce nearly a 12 percent rise of revenue. This is to be expected. What is equally significant is the limited explanatory power of the variables, for both yield and quality explain just less than half of the variance. Clearly there were other variables that acted on revenue. Demand as well as wine in stock must have played a large part in the workings of the market. Unfortunately we do not have the data needed to measure them and can do no more than make assumptions. Apparently the three prosperous decades after 1850 augmented demand, hence the leap of prices and net income. That prices fluctuated considerably is beyond doubt. This was as true for an ordinary as it was for Château Yquem

TABLE 5: *Optimum Net Income Based on Yield*

Years	Index of Yield	Fine Wine	Mean net income/hectare Côte d'Or Ordinary of Slopes	Mâconnais Ordinary
1815–51	Below 50	618F	544F	137F
1855–79	(Under 10hl/ha)	519	735	312
1815–54	50–99	1488	885	242
1855–79	(10–19 hl/ha)	3413	1901	590
1815–54	100–149	1758	1315	333
1855–79	(20–29 hl/ha)	4719	2384	650
1815–54	Over 150	1424	859	258
1855–70	(Over 30 hl/ha)	6185	3274	711

TABLE 6: *Determinants of Net Income, Côte d'Or, 1820–79*

Type Wine	Variable	Coefficient	T Value	Elasticities	R^2
Fine (of Slopes)	Yield	44.844	3.82	.6975	
	Quality	1386.5	5.51	1.1625	.46
Ordinary (of Slopes)	Yield	11.802	5.57	.8602	
	Quality	3606.4	2.94	.5001	.43

whose new wine sold for 6,000 francs in 1859, less than 1,000 in 1860, shot up to 6,000 in 1861 and plunged to 2,500 in 1862, and then to 1,700 the year after.[3] Since prices and quantity were closely correlated, it would seem logical that net income would reveal greater stability, with larger quantity compensating for meager prices. Graph 1 should dispel such a belief. Profits from year to year revealed the same wide swings as prices, a clear indication that no compensating mechanism existed and that the independent wine-grower was almost totally at the mercy of weather and of a wider market he could neither understand nor control. His only means of salvation was to put aside some of his income in prosperous years so as to have ready funds during those that were lean.

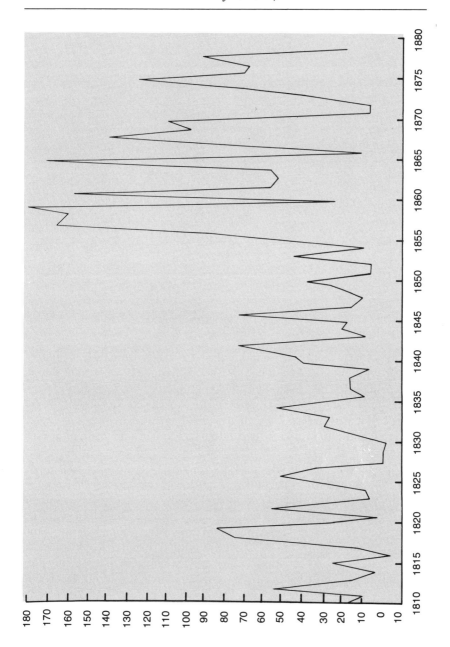

GRAPH I: *Net Income per* ouvrée, *Independent Grower of the Golden Slopes*

If the lean years were too numerous, like the 1820s, then his chances of survival were dangerously diminished.

Up to this point our analysis has focused on aggregated data for the purpose of generalization, and the Côte d'Or has been the center of attention because Robert Laurent's careful research has provided ample data for that district. So far we have concluded that the first half of the century was a period combining depression in the 1820s and slow growth with modest income afterward. In other words the French wine economy was not significantly different from the general European economy, caught in a long phase of stability if not stagnation, after the Revolution and Empire. The quality and quantity of vintages influenced economic conditions, but until midcentury weather was not favorable enough to overcome the limited demand of the market, another powerful determinant of income. The peak years for profits—1818–19, 1822, 1826, 1835, 1843 and 1846—were not sufficient to compensate for the troughs in between.

Vintages and Prices

Particular years, then, were important and we must now look at them to discover what influence they had on the vigneron. His bills were due in weeks or months, not years, and the appearance of sun or rain was not a number on a scale but a moving personal experience. In this discussion we shall deal with prices more than with net income, which will enable us to include the Bordeaux district and its abundant information on each vintage.

As we attempt to find relationships among prices, quality, and quantity in the Bordelais, we encounter one problem peculiar to that region. Before 1789 all the other major quality vineyards of France had large interior markets, whether in France or in Europe, and therefore were not immediately threatened by coastal blockades. Rivers, canals, roads, and limited coastal shipping in the Baltic Sea offered them sales opportunities quite similar to those existing before war began with Britain in 1792. Both Burgundy and Champagne were geographically close to the sizable wine-bibbing populations of Paris and northern Europe, and Napoleon's territorial conquests after 1800 actually offered them expanded markets free of previous restrictions and tariffs. In the gay frenetic world of imperial war wealthy persons increased in number and were more spendthrift and thirsty than ever for the wines once made chiefly for the pleasure of nobles.

Bordeaux's problems, on the contrary, were magnified by the Revolution's bellicosity. Since the Middle Ages wholesale merchants had shipped wine, more often illegally than legally, to the British. Not even Anglo-Portuguese treaty arrangements in the early eighteenth century designed to aid the sale of wines from Portugal, their ally, had turned the English entirely away from their claret. And the Eden Treaty of 1786, allowing French wines to enter Britain nearly duty free, had encouraged the Bordeaux growers, since they were closest to England, had long-established connections with it, and turned out the type of wine that the English monied classes preferred. Considerable profits resulted for the brief period until 1789, but after the revolution broke out, a mutual British-French hostility grew. Then the totally unexpected occurred: the Girondins, a liberal political group centered in the Gironde, where claret was made, came out in favor of war against "perfidious Albion." They could not have concocted a better way to destroy the Channel wine trade. This, of course, was not their intention, since they imagined that war would provoke an English revolution and this happy event would be celebrated with a great quantity of wine-drinking. As it turned out, the war that began in 1792 lasted until 1814, with only one short period of peace in 1802–03.

Although we are not here concerned directly with the war or the wine trade, but rather with harvests and prices, the war naturally influenced prices. Exactly how it did so is not always clear because precise information on prices is hard to find. On the whole they seem not to have fallen unduly before 1799; some rich vineyard owners' heads fell, but the new owners maintained production and good-quality wine held up. In 1799 prices dropped because of bad weather and low quality. Then they rose very sharply because quality improved, also because the harvests remained small. Then when yield rose and prices would have normally declined, political forces intervened. In 1802–03 the Peace of Amiens was signed and demand rose in Britain. This, combined with the low-yield vintage of 1801, pushed prices upward drastically in April-May 1802. Red *ordinaires* of Saint-Emilion rose to 460 francs per *tonneau* (900 liters) compared with an opening price of 260 francs in October 1801.[4] The peace, unfortunately, was short-lived, hostilities began again in 1803, and the British reimposed their blockade on all French goods. However the price structure held up, regardless of yield and quality, because of the licensing of trade between France and the British Isles, where demand remained high; that is, illicit trade was given a badge of innocence in the form of export licenses issued by Napoleon. The British blockaded the coast of France, but merchantmen plowed their way back and forth without undue interference. By 1806–07, however, the English blockade tightened, Napoleon's troops in Spain began retreating, and in 1811–12 he moved across Europe and invaded Russia. Prices fell in Bordeaux and did not improve much until his overthrow in 1814, when a general rapid rise occurred until 1819–20. It would seem, then, that the state of belligerency rather than the harvest, influenced prices. In the spring of 1802 and in 1807–14 it apparently did.

However one must look at other, more permanent forces that acted on the price structure. For the first and second growths of Médoc between 1811 and 1847 we have a sample of fourteen years for which there are reasonably accurate data on opening prices, quality of vintages, and quantity. We have divided the sample into two groups, one of above-average prices, the other of below-average prices. In the first group were nine years when prices were above average, and since they were all years of peace, it is possible to discover some normal price determinants.[5] The most decisive of them, even for high-quality vineyards, was the quantity of the harvest; second was its quality. The years of highest prices, 1818, 1825, 1834, combined low quantity with high or fairly high quality. The year 1837 produced a reverse combination, high quantity and mediocre quality with slightly above-average prices. Normally they should have fallen. At this point it is important to note that the preceding year, 1836, was a vintage low in quantity and quality, indicating that a gap existed in the market and that the 1837s could hold their prices up by filling it. But the market did not always function so mechanically. The year 1831 produced a very small quantity of high quality wine, while 1830 was deficient in both quality and quantity. Why, then, were prices for 1831 bordeaux just average for the first growths and only slightly above average for the seconds, as was the case with all other Médoc wines? The wines of Côte d'Or and Beaujolais revealed the same tendency toward the average, low yield notwithstanding. Apparently the revolution of July 1830, albeit a mild affair resembling a coup d'état more than a true revolution, was sufficient to disturb demand, not only inside but also outside France. England was deeply disappointed that the new government of Louis Philippe was as protectionist as the Bourbon regime that it replaced. Probably the reduction of taxes on wine by one million francs influenced prices, perhaps holding them down. If so, it did not help growers, because their incomes remained depressed for several more years.

The year 1841 is also exceptional in that both quantity and quality were high—as was the average price of first growths, making for handsome net returns. But since other Bordeaux wine prices were well below average, quality had saved only the wine of kings; the beverage of mere mortals followed the law of the market. For the nine vintages of above-average prices, only 1837 turned out a large quantity, and since quality was low that year, the general price was just barely above the average of an eighteen-year period.

We can now look briefly at the group of six years when prices were below average. As regards the first two growths, the rule of the market respecting quantity is unclear, for quality plays a role. (More on the part of quality later.) In 1816 and 1823, when quantity was very low, prices for all wines were, contrary to market rules, also low. The explanation is that quality was inferior and checked the price rise that would normally have occurred, at least for ordinaries. There was an equal disaster in Beaujolais and Côte d'Or in 1816, when prices tumbled for both fine and common beverages. The years 1823–30 were also catastrophic in Côte d'Or, but slightly more promising in Beaujolais. Everywhere rains were heavy and wines were excessively acid.

As for Bordeaux the other four years of this group with below-average prices reveal that high yield was a significant factor in lowering price, quality notwithstanding. Our somewhat larger sample of the fourth and fifth growths (ten years) does not reverse these findings, but rather reinforces them for the years when prices dropped below average. The influence of Napoleon's wars also shows up clearly. The years 1808–1813 were catastrophic for growers; vintages were generally average, but prices were below average by 40 to 50 percent. Although 1808–10 in particular were years of normal vintages, when prices should have been about average, they were not.

The year 1811 is a curious one in Bordeaux. Its vintage was said to be the "best of the century," the "wine of the comet." Its quality ranked seven on a scale of seven, and connoisseurs still tasted and praised it in the twentieth century. Yet opening prices of the first *crus* were only 800 francs per *tonneau*, a mere 88 francs per hectoliter. As regards the fine wine of Château Latour the price was a mere 50 percent of the average price from 1775 to 1825.[6] By August 1812 the first growths had risen to 1,350 francs, still below the forty-six year average of Château Latour by 300 francs. Second growths began at 525 francs per *tonneau* or 58 francs per hectoliter and later rose only to 900 francs. Fourth and fifth growths opened at 410 francs and rose to 450. Did quantity affect these prices? The harvest was "abundant," a four rating on a scale of five, and therefore it probably did. The remarkable quality could not seriously affect the price, although it might have partially salvaged the better *crus* if war-time conditions and uncertainties had not pressed on the market. Again in 1812, when quantity was below average and quality normal, opening prices should have risen, but they remained low. This was the year of Napoleon's defeat in Russia, an untoward event that dealt a terrible blow to the wine market.

Unfortunately the evidence for Saint-Emilion is sometimes insufficient or lacking in clarity. According to Moquet, opening prices for first-quality wines of Saint-Emilion and Cannon averaged 140 francs a *tonneau* in 1811. But Butel and Roudié put it at 300 francs.[7] Moquet indicates that the price doubled by August 1812, rising to 275 francs. The prices of Butel and Roudié seem to agree with this. These differences for opening prices are vexing, but even if we accept Butel and Roudié, the better saint-émilions were still below average for the periods we are studying. And this proves our point, the same as that of Butel and Roudié, that quantity is the dominant factor in the price of lesser wines. They add "demand," but neither they nor I have found a way to measure demand save indirectly: peace apparently intensified it, as exemplified by the vintage of 1802 and the unbelievely lucrative ones of 1815–18. But in all these years quantity was also down.

As regards Bordeaux, Monsieur Lafforgue claimed that vintages of high quality usually came in years of abundant harvests, with the result that great quantities of wine, even of high quality, restrained the rise of prices.[8] This observation remains more or less valid for the period 1853–81, years familiar to the famed enologist. During this time span there were ten years combining above-average quality and quantity, and only five with superior quality and low quantity. But it is hardly valid for the vintages from 1801 to 1852, when there were seven harvests combining above-average quality and quantity and eight combining above-average quality with below-average quantity, a situation that excludes generalization other than that there was a balance between the two variables; that is, high-quality vintages were as numerous in lean as in abundant years. Nonetheless quality was rarely a negligible factor in determining price. When wine was in short supply and its quality above average, prices rose more dramatically than would have been the case if the quality had been inferior. This point is borne out in Côte d'Or and Beaujolais, where, unlike Bordeaux, quantity in 1811 was seriously reduced by spring frost and summer drought, but quality was above average. These areas saw prices move to their highest peak between 1805 and 1851.

Undoubtedly the safest observation is that quality in wine-making was of primary importance in establishing the reputation of a region or an area. It therefore influenced the permanent price structure more powerfully than the price of a particular vintage or year. There was a significant, but not a truly high, correlation between the quality of an annual vintage and its price. Quality was a regional factor: a morgan beaujolais enjoyed a higher price structure than a beaujolais de villages, a château margaux or a château lafite cost ten times more than a bourgeois *cru* of Bordeaux, a bottle of clos vougeot equaled about ten days wages of a vigneron whereas an upland *ordinaire* from Côte d'Or equalled about thirty minutes at most.

The Growers' Budgets

The broad generalizations in the preceding sections are useful for understanding the particular or exceptional forces that influenced the quantity and quality of vintages and the prices that growers were able to command. In order to obtain a more intimate and personal understanding of the growers' economic condition, however, it will be necessary to study several typical budgets. This will make it possible to discover how costs affected income, regardless of the weather. Happily several Bordelais archives and libraries contain quite detailed budgets. The information in each is probably accurate; whether it is typical and can be used for generalization about financial conditions is another matter. Hopefully it will serve as a corrective of local views about conditions. But one note of caution in advance. In calculating the incomes of small owners I have not included the cost of their own labor. This is because I am not certain how to do so. Their hours of work were quite irregular on a daily and seasonal basis and the entire family worked without pay; also I am not primarily interested in the rates of return on their investments, but rather in the income available to them after deducting all costs for which they paid cash. This was their "net income" as far as they were concerned, and as far as I am concerned. This sum, rather than their rate of return on investment, was uppermost in their minds and motivated their actions. Fully accurate accounting was not their objective; making a living was. They seem never to have calculated the cost of their own labor, at least not in figures. Work on the land was a form of self-identity, a human dimension rather than an economic calculation. Life was hard enough without having to place a monetary value on it.

Although trade was brisk and prices high immediately following Napoleon's overthrow, almost all growers became pessimistic when prices fell precipitously in 1819. The bleak twenties seem to have fixed their outlook for the following decades. Data gathered by the Bordeaux Chamber of Commerce justified their mood: while prices rose for quality wines, they declined or were stationary for ordinaries from 1786 to 1828. And all growers, although prices had improved for some, were going through difficult times, because rising costs had either eroded their profits or reduced their incomes to unacceptable levels. Costs of materials had more than doubled, while wine prices had risen by only 10 to 20 percent. The Chamber, like most winemen, blamed their setbacks on protective tariffs and exorbitant taxes. Tariffs would not be reduced until 1860, but the 1830 revolution put a new king on the throne and he, to win the favor of a wine-drinking people, reduced the tax on alcohol. There followed a modest rise of prices, but it did not last. In fact the years from 1835 to 1846 were, according to the Chamber, disastrous.[9] And all recent studies on economic growth agree that the period 1815–48 was depressed everywhere in Europe. Demand, therefore, must have fallen from its previous high level. Nonetheless government fiscal agents, ever alert for tax evaders, were not much impressed, positing that the wine industry must be economically sound because the acreage of vineyards had gone up since the Revolution. This assertion the local growers denied and they also challenged the accuracy of the agents' data.

A more balanced presentation of budget data gathered for no apparent partisan cause can be found in two fairly detailed and useful books, one by Franck and one by Jouannet.[10] Most of the calculations in them are based on a division of soil called a *journal*. It was 32 ares in size, nearly one-third of a hectare (100 ares). In the Graves of Bordeaux, according to Franck, the cultivation of vines and the making of red wine on a particular but typical estate involved a cost of 200 francs per *journal* during the early 1820s.[11] The *journal* produced about 684 liters of wine, which fetched an average of 225 francs gross income. So the net return was 25 francs per *journal* or 78 francs per hectare. This not particularly handsome return resulted from low yield (only 20.5 hectoliters per hectare) and poor quality. This red wine sold for only 300 francs a *tonneau* (900 liters) or 33 francs per hectoliter (100 liters). It was a common wine, but the owner of the land in question hired vignerons to dress his vines, till the soil, and pick the grapes, so his costs were quite high, far too heavy for the value of the finished product.

Labor costs came to 27 percent of the total, a rather modest component of the overall expenses, only slightly above the expense of three barrels. These barrels were presumably new, and given the quality of the wine, it is highly doubtful that they were renewed each year, so the

TABLE 7: *Costs of Vineyard in Graves, Bordeaux, per* Journal

Labor	55F.	00C.
Vine supports	25	
Manure (6 wagons at 12F for 4 years)	18	
Harvest	6	
Three barrels at 180F per dozen	45	
Upkeep of wine-making equipment	2	50
Upkeep of walls and other tasks	3	
Taxes	7	
Transport to Bordeaux	2	
Brokerage at 2 percent	4	50
Interest on annual advance payments (5 percent)	8	40
Cellar roof and vat cover	2	
Renewal of vines	2	
Expense to turn soil, every 5 years	4	
Privation of revenue during these same years	4	35
Indemnity for losses, at 1/20th of total produce	11	25
	200F.	00C.

figure of forty-five francs is certainly too high. This list of costs, incidentally, is quite detailed and reveals that the landowner kept his books carefully and that he was his own manager. He was not a vine trimmer, but probably a middle-class professional living in Bordeaux.

If the owner had been a vigneron who did his own work (with his wife and children), he would not normally include his own labor but only the costs of materials, wear and tear, and taxes. Without the heavy costs of labor his net revenue would have been 249 francs per hectare. The owner who did not cultivate his own vineyard, therefore, had to possess a considerable amount of land in order to receive a revenue worthy of consideration. If the vigneron-owner possessed two hectares, an average size in the Bordelais, his net return came to nearly 500 francs. This was not a princely sum, but since he grew part of his food and always sold chickens and eggs, he could make ends meet. On the other hand he had little to fall back on in bad years when there was no wine or bad wine that sold at a much lower price, as in 1821, 1823, 1824, 1826, 1827, 1829. We can well appreciate the vigneron's lament during the 1820s, a decade with six bad years, but only two very good and two good years. Not until the 1840s, with seven good to exceptional years, did the wine-growers feel prosperity. But then, as though fate was against them, came the 1847 depression, when no one could afford high wine prices. The 1848 revolution aroused men's thirst for justice rather than for wine, which led to further economic dislocation.

Noncultivating owners faced similar problems, especially if they did not have income from sources other than their lands. In the Médoc district, the well-to-do owners of fine vineyards enjoyed a modest net return, about 500 francs per hectare, according to Jouannet, for classed growths, and about 414 francs for *crus bourgeois* in the early 1820s.[12] After this decade, however, their vineyards became less lucrative investments than before, particularly for the first growths. As regards Château Latour, for example, from 1784 to 1807 and 1812 to 1823, the rate of return on investment came to just over 14 percent. These fine estates were considered a *mine d'or*, and indeed they were. From 1808 to 1835 net income remained high, about 1,500 francs per hectare, roughly 1,000 francs above Jouannet's average for all classed growths. But Château Latour did not escape the general malaise when prices fell precipitously in the 1820s, and for the period 1836–53 its rate of return came to a mere 1.66 percent.[13] Dividends slipped seriously; however the accompanying graph makes clear that even with rising costs, income remained rather high, save in 1838 and 1842. In 1844 the owners of Latour contracted with several Bordeaux merchants for the purchase of the next ten vintages at a fixed price. This arrangement spared them the fall of prices in 1847–49 but seems not to have been in their longer term interest, since they were not able to profit from the rise of prices after 1849.[14]

During the first half of the century net income on the lesser estates in the Gironde region varied from area to area. In the Bourgeais (the area surrounding the town of Bourg) it came to 107 francs per hectare, in the *palus* to 120 francs, in the Libournais to 204 francs. In the last named, costs were slightly lower and net revenue considerably high for a *journal* of vines, as table 8 indicates.

Wine here sold for only 175 francs a *tonneau*, and since the average production was 1,140 liters, total revenue came to 218 francs 75 centimes, leaving a net income of 67 francs 70 centimes per *journal*, or 204 francs per hectare. The cheaper and abundant wine of the Libournais was more profitable than the slightly better wine of the Graves, but only on condition that the landowner resided on his property, supervised the cultivation of his vines himself, and was his own wine-maker. The absentee owner, hiring a chief vine-trimmer and a wine-maker, could not possibly have made money on his vineyard. Residence and technical qualification were, if our data is accurate, prime requisites for a profitable operation.

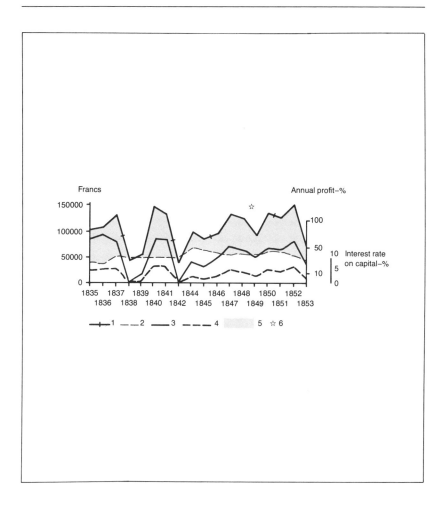

GRAPH 2: *Economic Situation of Château Latour, 1835–53*

1. Gross profit
2. Costs
3. Net profit as percent of gross profit
4. Interest on capital investment
5. Net income
6. Period of contract (1844–53)
Source: Higounet, I, 346.

138 Technical, Economic, and Social Aspects

TABLE 8: *Growers' Budget in Libournais for a* Journal

	Francs	Centimes
Labor	31	
Vine supports	15	
Layering	1	
Harvest	8	
Five barrels at 144F a dozen	60	
Taxes	4	
Manure	0	
Upkeep of wine-making equipment	1	
Upkeep of walls and other tasks	1	
Transport to Bordeaux	3	
Courtage	3	75
Interest on annual advances (5 percent)	6	38
Renewal of vines, expense to turn soil every 5 years, privation of revenue	6	
Indemnity for losses, at 1/20th of total produce	10	92
	151	05

Source: Franck, *Statistique du Gironde* (1824 edition) p. 113

The prices, yields, and profits changed from year to year. But there was also a permanent or nearly permanent variance based upon more durable factors such as climate, soil, grape species, and technology, with the result that there were hierarchies of grapes and of the wines made from them in all the major vineyards. The Gironde district is a good example of this, for the wholesale merchants there early developed an evaluation of growths (*crus*) and determined prices accordingly. Therefore when their professional organization proclaimed in 1855 a kind of official classification of growths, it based its rankings on at least two centuries of experience. As early as 1822 the as yet unofficial classification is laid out in table 9.

It is obvious that the price spread from top to bottom was considerable, 2,300 francs, a ratio of 1 to 12.5. There was a similar, but less structured, hierarchy for white wines. At the top was that of Château Yquem, "the king of wines and the wine of kings" as its motto goes. Then came the wines of the upper districts of Sauterne, Barsac, Preignac, and Bommes, then the prime-quality Graves and so on. There was probably more justice in this vinicultural hierarchy than there was in the social strata existing in French society. A good wine was usually good

TABLE 9: *1822 Classification of Bordeaux Red Wines*

Growth	Prices per tonneau (900 liters) in francs
1st growth	2500
2nd growth	2000 to 2100
3rd growth	1300 to 1500
4th and 5th growths	800 to 1200
Médoc bon bourgeois	500 to 600
Médoc ordinaire	380 to 450
Petit Médoc, paysan	300 to 350
St.-Emilion	400 to 500
Queyries	420 to 500
Montferrant	300 to 400
Cotes and Bourg	220 to 320
Palus	200 to 300
St. Macaire and Blaye	160 to 200

Source: Moquet

year after year, or, so to speak, generation after generation, whereas among men, an heir, even a degenerate one, inherited titles, status, and wealth. Such degeneracy in a wine would soon cause it to lose its standing, would bring about its "downward mobility," as sociologists say. There did occur some upward mobility after the official classification of 1855, chiefly among the quality growths, but it should be noted that the tendency to rigidity in French social structure of the nineteenth century became a salient character of the vinicultural structure. Vineyards in the highest categories have not fallen since then, and many of the lower have not risen. No one has put forward a case for dethroning the highest growths, but improved methods and management have led many tasters to believe that several lesser growths should climb upward. This has rarely happened. In society such a phenomenon often caused a revolution; in the world of wines revolts have rarely occurred; perhaps incipient revolutionaries found other outlets for their frustrations, such as prices comparable to those of higher-classed growths. They were like enriched bourgeois, mildly frustrated but too content to make barricades of empty wine casks.

Profitability in Burgundy does not seem to have differed much from that of Bordeaux. In fine vineyards the costs of labor, where labor was paid in money, came to about 50 percent of gross revenue in the first half of the century, only about 25 percent where the owner participated directly in cultivation, and 20 percent under the half-shares system. In ordinary vineyards these percentages were 65, 27, and 16. As in Bordeaux the years between the fall of Napoleon and midcentury were stagnant and the 1820s and 1830s brought sharp falls in revenue. From 1818 to 1846 the average gross profit in fine vineyards was 1,014 francs per hectare, in ordinary ones it was 699 francs. For owners of fine vines, net income came to 735 francs when they cultivated directly, but merely to 469 francs when they hired wage labor, and 398 francs if they used half shares. Ordinary vineyards produced 495 francs, 223 francs and 292 francs respectively for their owners.[15] These are not high returns and they are about the same or slightly higher than those in comparable vineyards of Bordeaux. From about 1808 on income fell; it did not seriously improve before the 1840s, when it rose until 1847, only to plunge again during the midcentury revolutionary crisis and oïdium plague of the early 1850s.

The Golden Years

The years from about 1854–55 to 1876–80 were memorable for winemen; old-timers of the later nineteenth century looked back upon them as the golden years. Undoubtedly they were, for gold lined the growers' pockets after the lean—even starvation—years of 1846–53, when prices fell so low and remained there for so long that the growers began to ask whether the wine economy had not come to the end of the road. At that time their problem was high production and low prices, a problem normally solved by weather bringing seasons of low yield and consequent price rise. But at midcentury the natural resolution of their difficulties did not take place because a political revolution broke out during February 1848. Starting in Paris, it spread rapidly to the provinces, aggravating a general economic crisis that had begun in 1846–47. Indeed near panic resulted in the economy, with bankruptcies and massive unemployment. In all the vineyards wine prices fell to their lowest point since the terrible year of 1805. Despite this great reduction in prices, and the availability of good to excellent wine, there were few buyers. Money became scarce and former consumers hoarded their wealth, fearing current disorders and an uncertain future.

Growers were particularly hard hit, because they had practically no reserves to fall back on. The thirties and forties, while not as depressed as the twenties, had not been happy decades. Both vine-owners and their vignerons had suffered, for actually they had operated without profit or at a loss from 1838 to 1842, and from 1845 to 1847.[16] Things would have been even worse if food and other prices had not followed the downward trend of wine. During the years of upheaval, 1848–49, those vineyard owners able to sell their wine, albeit at low prices, profited from the drastic and general fall of prices to levels below those of wine. Vignerons working for a wage in Côte d'Or also profited early, while those in the Mâconnais did not until late 1849. Statistically at least, wine-sellers seem to have improved their real incomes in 1848–1850, but we know that wine was hard to sell because large numbers of consumers were out of work or struggling with low incomes and unwilling to buy items not listed among their prime necessities (see graph 3).

The so-called "golden age" therefore did not begin until the Second Republic (1848–51) finally succumbed to the coup d'état of Louis Napoleon in December 1851. By the next year, when he restored the imperial regime of his uncle and styled himself Napoleon III, the revolutionary upsurge that had swept across Europe four years earlier had been completely suppressed. The restoration of order probably contributed to the economic revival that accompanied it. As early as 1850 prices of most goods, including wine, began to climb, and a sense of optimism spread, helping men to forget that many of them had either lost or abandoned the political freedom they had clamored for only two years earlier.

Unfortunately the wine industry did not enjoy the full benefits of the revived European economy, for both in France and Italy a new malady settled upon the vineyards. European scientists called it oïdium, a name menacing enough in its sound. In English it is called "powdery mildew," almost poetic. An English savant named M. J. Berkeley first described it; he believed that it had originated in the United States and been brought to England where it spread to France and the major European vineyards. It was a fungus that settled on vines, destroying the leaves, flowers, and finally the clusters. It covered everything it attacked with a whitish powder, and grapes burst open, dried up, or fell victim to a grey-colored rot. It had first made its appearance in 1846 but did not cause widespread damage until about 1850. In France average yield per hectare was 20.75 hectoliters in 1850; in 1852 it dropped to 13.26; in 1853 to 10.45; in 1854 to 4.97. Total production in 1850 stood at over 55 million hectoliters, in 1854 at 10.8 million. Recovery came in 1857 when yield rose to the 1851 level of 18.24.[17] Gross income, having fallen to about 100 francs per hectare in 1849 because of the revolution, then had moved upward to over 250 francs the next year, tumbled now to under 200.

Regional vineyards, whose conditions determined national levels of

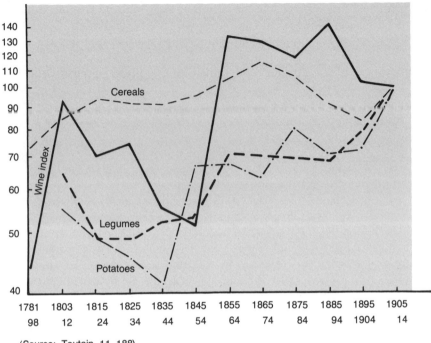

(Source: Toutain, 11, 188)

GRAPH 3: *Index of prices, 1781–1914. 1905–14=100*

Source: Toutain, II, 188

prices and production, showed little variation from the norm. In the Bordelais, production fell from 2,297,000 hectoliters in 1850 to 319,900 in 1854; in Marne from 450,000 hectoliters in 1851 to 50,000 three years later. The broad totals fell so precipitously, not because vines had been uprooted as a result of the economic crisis of 1848–49; rather yields per hectare of full vineyards clearly indicate the extent of the catastrophe; in the Beaujolais region, yield fell from 33 hectoliters in 1850 to 6.5 in 1853, "the worst year of the century," [18] in Côte d'Or from 39 to 19 in the same years.

This marked fall in production did not take place in a vacuum. Growers were quite lucky that the oïdium struck at a time when general economic conditions had taken a turn for the best. Had it appeared in the 1830s and 1840s a large number of them would have been ruined beyond repair, for the market at the time was sluggish and demand, even when prices were low, was limited. But the discovery of gold in California and Australia gave a fillip to the world economy. Employment rose, incomes improved, and an almost frenetic desire to spend money settled over the European populace. In France the founding of the Second Empire in 1852 enhanced that feeling. The population abandoned the Republic with little reluctance and looked to the revival of Bonapartism for the salvation of private property (which had never been threatened) and economic prosperity (which had). Their hopes were justified. Neither of the two previous regimes, the July Monarchy (1830–48) and the Second Republic (1848–51) had used political power to stimulate the economy significantly. They had been run by men who believed in the "hands-off" policy of orthodox liberalism. Napoleon III, on the other hand, was not part of the liberal tradition. Action by the state loomed large in the Bonapartist ideal, and the emperor regarded it as part of his prerogative to use state power for any end he deemed necessary to preserve that power, whether silencing free speech or fostering the economy. As might be expected, Napoleon did both. He suppressed democratic movements on the one hand; he established land banks, built railroads, and negotiated trade treaties on the other. France's economy therefore was stimulated both by a more roseate world situation and an interventionist state.

The wine industry responded to this condition at once: extremely short supply and extremely high demand (absent from the wine market since 1816–19) caused prices to shoot up at a rate unknown to this generation of growers and merchants. Only the generation that had suffered the defeat of the first Napoleonic Empire had experienced a similar rise of prices from 1815 to 1819, and they, at least, had wine to sell. In the early 1850s, however, most growers had practically no wine, with the result that they suffered serious declines of gross and net income, regardless of whether they made fine or ordinary beverages. Worse, the price of food, especially cereals, and of vineyard and cellar materials kept up with the inflationary trend, so winemen suffered a decline of real income as well.[19] It is evident, therefore, that most wine-producers were caught in a scissors-grip between low income and high costs, a situation becoming increasingly common in agriculture as inflationary trends continued.

In this respect the powdery-mildew crisis marked a new era in the wine industry, both for ordinary and fine wines. Until its arrival, costs of production had remained rather moderate, amounting to under 25 percent of gross revenue for ordinaries and from 40 to 50 percent for fine wines in the case of owners cultivating their own vines. Included in these expenses were the amounts spent to ward off harmful insects and maladies that were a normal part of viticulture and that had existed since time immemorial. In the past when these blights had been particularly disastrous, vinemen were impotent before them because their knowledge of science and chemistry was too limited to be used as a defense against nature. By the nineteenth century, however, science had made enormous progress and agricultural chemistry, thanks partly to Liebig, came to the farmers' rescue. In France from the 1850s on growers and agronomists came to rely more heavily on the use of chemicals to protect vines. The application of sulphur in various forms brought salvation to both the vine-trimmer and the wine-maker. The mildew was all but conquered by the late 1850s. This was a signal success, but just as notable—and ominous—was the rise in production costs; henceforth growers had to sulphur their vines regularly in order to prevent a return of the malady, because once acclimated to Europe the fungus from America was ever ready to reappear and did so periodically.

The Golden Age began only when rising costs were easily absorbed by rising prices. In fact the true characteristic of the period from the mid fifties to about the mid or late seventies was the dramatic reversal of the relation between price and yield. Formerly yield had been the primary determinant of price for ordinaries; a high yield meant a low price and vice versa. But from the mid fifties demand first of all, and then quality, became the chief determinants. If the vintage was good, an increase of production brought not a decline of prices but their greater rise and hence a leap upward of both gross and net income (see tables 4 and 5). Not even the increase of taxes and new costs rising to nearly twenty francs per hectoliter seriously hurt net reveues.[20] This economic "miracle" was brought about not only by the general prosperity of the times;

the weather also helped. For no reason we can discover, there occurred over two decades of remarkably fine climatic conditions for grape-growing. From 1855 to 1880, a quarter of a century, there were only four really bad years as regards quality of harvests (1860, 1866, 1872, 1879) and only three years that could be called slightly below the century's average. The vast majority of vintages were above average, with six rated at very good to excellent. Favorable weather and strong demand, therefore, account for much of the prosperity of the wine trade (see Appendix 1).

In addition, there were at least three other factors that not only enhanced prosperity, they transformed the wine industry itself. First and most epoch-making among these was the introduction of steam power in transport. Wine had always reached its overseas markets stored in the holds of slow-moving sailing vessels and its inland markets either in wagons or in barges, both drawn by oxen or mules. Transport was slow, which raised its costs, and hard on wine because of the tossing and jolting that small ships and poor roads imposed upon cargoes. Only well-made beverages fortified with alcohol could withstand such trials, and they were expensive. For this reason people availed themselves of local wine, even when it was acid and harsh to the taste, or else they consumed beer. With the appearance of steamboats and the locomotive, however, transport became rapid and far less expensive. In consequence lesser wines began to enter the national market and competed successfully with local drinks. This change encouraged specialization of commercial wine production in the regions most favored by nature for the growing of grapes, which led to a shift of the geography of viticulture toward the South and the Mediterranean.

Second, the trade treaty signed between France and Britain in 1860, and soon extended to other European states, nearly abolished tariffs on wines sold in international trade. The finer beverages benefitted chiefly from this provision, but an increasing quantity of high-grade ordinary wine now also entered foreign markets. It commanded a highly remunerative price when it came dressed up in a flashy label to conceal its origins.

Finally, the expansion of credit encouraged business growth and purchasing power at all levels of the social hierarchy; easier credit in the countryside enabled vignerons to purchase new land and increased France's vine area. From 2,193,000 hectares in 1849 it rose to 2,429,000 hectares in 1873. It is evident that the golden age increase of acreage was not dramatic, merely about 236,000 hectares or 10 percent. What was dramatic was the sustained high level of yield on the national level. As

best I can determine, yields in the 1830s and 1840s were under 15 hectoliters per hectare; in the 1860s and early 1870s they ranged between 20
and 30 with an average of 23 hectoliters per hectare. The fact that prices
rose along with yields meant that profits expanded as they had not since
1815–1819. For example, in the Beaujolais, prices between 1852 and
1882 went up 176 percent and net income followed in their wake.[21] This
situation further stimulated vineyard extension, as little and big growers
both borrowed and used their own profits to buy land and to plant it in
vines; like industrialists they preferred self-financing to heavy reliance on
banks.

These general conditions of prosperity seem to have hastened the rise
of the common man, and among them was the common vigneron. This
rise was not sudden; it had begun on a small scale in the eighteenth
century and was abetted by the Revolution of 1789 when some large
estates were divided up and auctioned off. Quality land planted in vines,
like quality land planted in other crops, fell into the hands of the well-to-
do, whether noble or roturian (everyone was a citizen now); some was
even bought by previous owners through dummy bidders. The rise of
the common man in the countryside took place on the fringes of the best
soil and usually in areas were there was neither a nobility nor a middle
class rich and powerful enough to thrust the peasants aside in auction
sales. Within these circumstances many vignerons became property owners, even if they did not acquire sufficient acreage to get a full livelihood.
Vignerons continued to buy parcels of vines during the early nineteenth
century, and the high incomes they obtained during the Second Empire,
as well as easier and cheaper credit, truly stimulated their ascension. At
this time they did not always purchase vineyards; rather they bought
land—much of it rich farmland—and covered it with vines. And the
vines they cultivated on both their new and their old land were the most
productive. Because there was a rising demand for wine, peasant growers turned ever more willingly to varieties offering high yield but producing mediocre wines. Quantity rather than quality was their goal, and
from their point of view they were quite correct. Since they dressed
their own vines, usually without hired labor, their costs remained low
and their net profits were quite high in these good times. With their solid
incomes they did relatively little to improve cultivation and viniculture;
instead, the more enterprising bought additional land and vines and became independent.

Now peasant growers were not the only group to produce low-grade
wine for the rising urban markets. Many business and professional men

and bureaucrats bought vineyeards and hired overseers to manage them; by no means were they all preoccupied with quality young shoots. Naturally planting in bunches gave way to planting in rows; layering went out and nurseries appeared offering for sale vine cuttings grown in hothouses. The vines in neat rows were now more likely to be supported by two or three wires attached to tall posts than by individual pickets. The old practice of letting vines grow without support of any sort seems to have nearly disappeared, save in Roussillon and some backward areas, as peasant growers increasingly imitated the improvements of others. Many of them were part-time workers on large estates and learned from the knowledgeable managers who hired them. During the sixties many large estates became veritable wine factories, managed professionally, with dozens of vine-trimmers hired by the year, by the job, or by the day. Since many well-established estates showed the same trend, the managers of large holdings, with the backing of local credit and the owner's capital, embarked on a new phase of modernization.

Old vines were rooted out and replaced by new ones promising higher yields. In Burgundy the Gamay gained ground over the Pinot in a viticultural revolution comparable to that of 1789: the bourgeoisie lorded it over the nobility. But the revolt of the grape masses did not stop there, for an even lower group, the Persagne or Mondeuse of Savoy, won out over the Gamay in the calcareous clay soils of the new vineyards in Beaujolais; its yield could rise to 80 hectoliters in a good year. New techniques of long trimming raised the normal yields, as did the addition to the soil of recently discovered chemical fertilizers. Since many of these new vineyards were established on relatively flat lands, cultivation with the hoe gave way to innovative plows drawn by oxen or horses with baskets over their mouths to prevent them from nibbling.

This transformation of the social hierarchy in viticultural areas did not always bring about a permanent improvement in status. The bourgeois growers who happily climbed upward on the Gamay and the peasants who followed them on the Persagne or Mondeuse soon discovered at their heels the real lumpen proletariat of growers, those from the Mediterranean coast. With the cheapest of cheap wines made from the Aramon and various Alicantes they set out to conquer the Center and the North, and thanks to the railroad they invaded the markets formerly reserved for more northerly growers. The great rising urban centers such as Paris and Lyon opened their gates to this vinicultural rabble and at last the Albigensians were avenged. A similar phenomenon took place in Italy, but not until much later.

Italy: Costs and Profits

For Italy it is difficult to obtain information about the economy of wine production. Data on this subject has not come to light for the earlier decades, and that for the postunification era is extremely sparse, hardly lending itself to generalization. The information most conveniently available and perhaps the most accurate was published by the Jacini parliamentary committee after its extensive investigation of all aspects of Italy's agriculture during the 1870s and 1880s. Particularly useful are the account sheets showing the costs and profits of some general farmers and grape-growers. In this respect it is more informative than the shorter survey of French vineyards carried out by Jules Guyot, whose data was too general, often so abstract as to be worthless for analysis.

The Jacini study offers considerable detail about local conditions; it even goes down at times to the family level in its search for information. For example, we learn about a very small vineyard (38 are) in the territory of Bra, near Alba, where fine Dolcetto grapes were grown. The owner did not make his own wine but sold his harvest to local wine producers, and his gross profits came to 196 lire. This would amount to 514 lire per hectare, a fairly good income considering that the grower produced only a raw material to make wine, not the finished product. However his costs were remarkably high, amounting to 64 percent of his gross income, and leaving him 185 lire net per hectare. More typical of the North was a farm near Acqui, in the province of Alessandria, which engaged in the widespread system of mixed agriculture. Vines occupied 20 percent of the 10 hectares that made up the total surface. With grapes selling at 2 lire per miriagram, they brought in 47 percent of gross income and 70 percent of the net.[22] This percentage indicates how important viticulture had become in mixed agriculture. We cannot be certain, however, that this balance of crops and income was typical, because during the late 1870s and 1880s the entire Italian wine industry was enjoying extraordinarily good times, thanks to the near distruction of the more southerly French vineyards by the phylloxera. Before this event, income from grapes may not have occupied so high a percentage of total income in the general farmer's budget.

In Tuscany, where mixed farming was also prevalent, vines seem also to have been more profitable than other crops. Given the greater spread of crop-sharing, the peasant growers and land owners combined their grapes to make wine which they sold in the local market. A farm of 22 hectares, located in the hills near Siena, is a good example of a larger holding. Grains occupied 10 hectares, while vines, typically hung among olive, mulberry, and other trees, occupied 7 hectares, and forest and pasture accounted for 5. In this layout, with vines occupying the same space as living trees, it is impossible to know precisely the hectares devoted to them, but it was probably about three or four at most, or roughly 18 percent. Since the wine sold for only 20 lire it was certainly not of high quality but was rather the cheap red known as chianti and shipped in straw-covered *fiaschi*. Net revenue derived from it represented nearly 25 percent of the cropper's total returns and 28 percent of the owner's, therefore it did not hold such a high economic position, compared to its acreage, in the hierarchy of crops producing incomes. Wheat held the apex, producing nearly half the incomes of both men, a percentage equal to its share of the acreage.[23] Despite wine's financially inferior ranking, it nonetheless was more profitable in terms of the space it occupied. This farm, incidentally, was hardly an advantageous enterprise, for it returned to owner and cropper only 65 lire net per hectare.

Another equally diversified hill farm of 5 hectares obtained from wine only 18 percent of its net income for each party, the owner and the cropper, and the vines produced a mere 9 hectoliters per hectare. This was above average for mixed farms and, as in France, the smaller holding produced a higher return than the larger, 225 lire per hectare, thanks to more intense exploitation. Olive oil was the major source of income on this farm near Pescia in Lucca province.[24] Another hill farm of similar size in Arezzo which was more heavily planted in vines derived 40 percent of its income from wine, with a yield of 10 hectoliters and net income of 260 lire to the hectare.[25] A farm of 7 hectares near Florence derived 32 percent of net income from wine and enjoyed the highest price, 25 lire compared to 22 lire in the above examples, and attained a yield of 24 hectoliters per hectare. Table 10 is a summary of an average year's accounts.

It is important to bear in mind that there is no entry in this account for the land tax or for the costs of transporting goods to market. Undoubtedly the peasant family transported most of the produce itself, since it owned a horse and a wagon; and most likely the owner made all the wine and either transported it himself or had the peasant family do it.

Also notable in this account is the low cost of tillage, less than 3 percent of gross income for materials. Labor of course was provided by the peasant family, consisting of four men, three women, and two children. For the owner, who had to share the gross revenue with his cropper, costs amounted to over 50 percent, since he received only half and

TABLE 10: *Costs and Incomes of a Tuscan Farm*

Production

Source of Income	Area in hectares	Quantity	Value in lire
Wheat	4.50	35 hl.	805
Legumes	2.50	—	155
Fruit	—	—	20
Wine	—	42	1040
Olive oil	—	6	720
Raw silk	—	15 cg.	60
Stable manure			360
Income divided between owner and cropper			3160

Costs of Tillage

Materials	Total in lire
Sulphur for vines	16
Silkworm food	12
Manure	50
New vine stakes	10
Total	88

the cropper's share was the equivalent of a wage. More precisely the total costs for him came to nearly 65 percent (50 + 15), and this high figure does not include taxes. In France, specifically in the Côte d'Or, when costs rose to this height owners abandoned sharecropping in favor of hiring workers by the day or the job. In Italy, however, the sharing, or *mezzeria*, system prevailed well into the twentieth century. Peasants were not as given to buying land as their French counterparts, and owners looked upon sharecropping as a form of social control, since it tied the lower classes both to the land and to themselves. This was the case regardless of the crops cultivated, it was by no means limited to wine-producing areas. In the plains along the Arno River and the coast wine did not enjoy as important a place in mixed agriculture, its revenue rarely rising to more than 20 percent of the total, yet crop-sharing was equally prevalent.

The 1870s and 1880s in Italy were about equivalent to the 1860s and 1870s in France, a golden age of high profits, and in consequence there

TABLE 10 (*continued*)

Income of owner		Costs of Owner	
½ of produce	1580L	½ cost of tillage	44L
Sum owed by cropper	35	Upkeep of tools, etc.	85
		5% interest on stock	102.50
		5% interest of anticipated costs	4.40
	1615		235.90
Net income	1379.10L		
Income per hectare (7 ha.)=197L			

Income of Cropper		Cost of Cropper	
½ of produce	1580L	½ cost of tillage	44
Produce of truck garden	50	Payment to owner	35
Wages for extra work	20		
Sale of chickens	50		
Sale of pig	40		
	1740		79
Net income	1661L		
Income per hectare (7 ha)=237L			

Source: Giunta parl., III, 292

was a tendency to plant vineyards *alla francese*, that is, separate from other crops. This tendency was fairly well developed in Piedmont and Tuscany, but was much less so in the Northeast and the Center. Fortunately there are some data on the average income per hectare in Tuscany under the changed method of planting.

Average yield in the best areas, Chianti, Empolese, and Florence came to 35 hectoliters; in Elba and the Transappennine it was 30, and in Mugello and elsewhere to 25. As regards the *colono* or cropper, table 11 gives his average gross and net income per hectare (A) and the net of a small owner farming on his own (B).

A hectare on shares normally produced twice the above sums, but the other half went to the owner. The net income in column A is perhaps too high, since various supplementary costs, especailly those involved in making wine, have not been included. However the peasant under the *mezzeria* benefited from the fact that the owner paid most of these expenses.

TABLE 11: *Income of Cropper and Small Owner, Tuscany*

District	Gross Income (A)	Net Income Cropper (A)	Small Owner (B)
Chianti	640L	543L	810L
Empolese	603	505	735
Mugello	405	308	340
Transappennine	380	297	290
Elba	305	208	140

Source: Giunta parl., III, 305–8

Where the land belonged to the *vignaiolo* and the Guyot trim was used, net return came to the sums indicated in colomn B. Combined ownership and labor, it is clear, proved worthwhile only in the Chianti, Empolese, and Mugello districts.

Net income from specialized vineyards therefore was about equal hectare for hectare in Tuscany and Piedmont, and in both areas vineyards were considerably more profitable than mixed farms, more than double in the fine wine areas during periods of prosperity. Naturally the arrival of the phylloxera curbed this advantage, but the aphid proved to be less catastrophic in Italy. It spread both later and more slowly than in France, so Italians learned how to combat it from the French. Also they suffered less because they had other crops to fall back on. As in France vineyards in good locations usually offered a higher rate of return than most other cultures. Only olives, livestock, and truck-gardening rivaled vines for high income.[26]

For the vineyards of the deep South, there is only scanty published information of an economic nature until the twentieth century, when the Ministry of Agriculture undertook a major study of agriculture there. By 1905 the southern wine-growers, particularly those in Apulia, had only the memories of the golden age of the 1880s. They had lost most of their markets in France and Austria, as we shall see later, and they were now in a state of retrenchment and, worse, experiencing the destructive effects of the phylloxera.

Despite these drawbacks local officials pointed out that emigration overseas was not serious and that profits were still satisfactory. In the vine region around Barletta, not far from Bari, these were the average accounts for a hectare of vines of the medium and little *vignaioli* renting vines. Gross profits came to 512 lire and costs to 302, leaving a net of 210. The heaviest item in the cost column was the labor hired to fight against the phylloxera, 176 lire. Also the 30 lire for renting barrels and storage space pulled down income. The vineyards in question were not sufficiently productive, given the mediocre quality of the wine, to make up for low prices. Vines planted in richer soils had higher yields without loss of price, with the result that net income rose to 318 lire.[27]

Small farmers, despite the drawbacks of vines cultivated in unproductive land, avidly sought to rent plots there because the rent remained low and the revenue superior to that of grains, which rarely ascended above 127 lire net. These low incomes were favorable compared to those of peasants in other areas of agriculture. The major problem of the southern Italians was their indifference or inability to transform the technology of wine-making; it remained, like their entire culture and outlook, rooted in the tradition of the past. Indeed these roots into the past were so deep that many of them remained stubbornly impervious to the attacks of the phylloxera.

CHAPTER EIGHT

The Phylloxera or the Terrible Vine Blight

France: The Beginning

The vine blight that struck France in the 1870s was unprecedented in its impact. It was, in a sense, a revolution, but not the kind that men made or understood, for it was egalitarian in natural rather than human terms. Ignoring all hierarchy, it destroyed the finest and the meanest of vines, the noble and the proletarian. There were no truly safe areas in France or Italy where vines could take refuge, save in a few sandy places; moreover the invasion hit both countries at almost the same time and with nearly equal destructiveness. The blight did spread more slowly in the peninsula, not because the Italians put up better defenses, but because, as we shall see, they were briefly safeguarded by their past, by the viticulture their Roman ancestors had left them centuries ago.

Now vignerons were quite familiar with blight; indeed, less than a generation earlier they had been victims of the powdery mildew or oïdium, but they had overcome it in a few years. Then winemen north and south of the Alps rejoiced, for they believed they had ended all such blights and that henceforth the future would be festooned with grapes of gold. And yet only twenty years later came another invader bringing death to the illusions of growers as it did to their vines.

The phylloxera was another native of America. It was a yellow aphid or plant louse which lived by sinking its pointed snout into the vine roots and sucking out their sap. This act was deadly enough, but the insect also secreted a saliva that infected the root at the point of attack, preventing the wound from healing. This caused the vine to wither and in short time to die. The mildew was a fungus that killed crops rather than vines, even though in time it might kill plants by exhausting them, but the phylloxera was a killer of the *vitis vinifera* of Europe, destroying the source of wine for good. In addition, the powdery mildew was easily conquered by sulphur; the deadly aphis has defied all efforts to destroy it and lives on today. The salvation of the European vineyard, therefore, required a method entirely different from the one used against oïdium.[1]

History is often the confirmation of irony: idealists with moral goals commit crimes to attain them, and the villains of their own times become the heroes of later generations. The history of wine also has its ironic episodes. The phylloxera "emigrated" from America to Europe in the 1850s on native root stock, but the only salvation from its devastation turned out to be—American root stock! Ironic also was the fact that the steam power which had brought prosperity to wine producers in the 1850s and 1860s had provided precisely the greater speed necessary to transfer live phylloxera from the United States to Europe. In the days of sailing ships the voyage took so long that at its end either the vine cuttings or the aphid on them had died. The substitution of steam for sail so speeded up the crossing that a live cutting with equally live aphids could survive it, as well as the overland journey by railroad. And once planted in a garden, the pest could begin its work of destruction.[2] The oïdium also played a part in this tragedy of errors, because it is most likely that certain American vines, in particular the Isabella, noted for their resistance to the powdery mildew, were imported into France to replace the vines affected by it. Of course these were the vines carrying the aphids on their roots and once planted in France, they made their presence known without ado.[3]

Ironically—the word keeps coming up—their deadly work first attracted attention in France during a very good vintage year, 1865. Vines in several communes of Gard and Vaucluse died without apparent cause. On 8 November 1867 a veterinarian from Arles described in a letter the sudden demise of vines planted east of his native town. Other notices appeared in the agricultural press around this time and vine owners became increasingly alarmed. As was their custom they called upon a local agricultural society to send a team of experts to find the cause of the trouble. When a request arrived the society of Hérault sent Gaston Bazille, J. E. Planchon, and F. Sahut to a vineyard near St. Rémy.

They painstakingly studied the phenomenon, even while the aphid made its way down the Rhône Valley, spreading eastward and westward. Planchon, the first to note the tiny insect, called it the *phylloxera*, Greek for "dry leaves," and *vastatrix*, Latin for "devastator." He was immediately convinced that this minute creature caused the vines' death. Other savants stubbornly took the opposite view, arguing that the phylloxera attacked vines already sick and on the point of death; its presence was not a cause but a result.[4] Planchon finally won out, but the opposite view served as an excuse among many middle-class and peasant growers for doing nothing to destroy the destroyer until it was too late.

The actual work of saving Europe's vineyard was, like the work of enhancing its quality in centuries past, undertaken by well-to-do, educated owners and agrarians who not only had an economic stake in its salvation but who also lived by their belief in the intrinsic goodness of a rural way of life of which the vine was an essential ingredient. After discovering the tiny culprit, their problem was to destroy it, but unfortunately they were confronted by events far beyond their control. In 1870 the phylloxera was relentlessly expanding in the departments of Gard, Bouches-du-Rhône, and Vaucluse, the great Rhône estuary. Vines, once green, fruit-burdened, and productive of considerable wealth, withered and died, leaving their owners penniless and burdened with debts. In that same summer France and Prussia went to war; Frenchman focussed all human effort and finance on destroying the human enemy seeking to cross the frontier rather than the insect one already within it, yet the latter, measured in terms of money and ruined lives, proved to be the most costly. France recovered from the war in six years; she required over a generation to restore her vineyard.

The phylloxera had as profound an effect on the course of history as did the Franco-Prussian War. Military defeat, of course, changed governments: a Republic (the Third) replaced an Empire (the Second). There was a change of names, of symbols (Marianne pulled down the imperial eagle), and of men (republicans replaced Bonapartists). In the long run, however, the Second Empire in its last days had begun to look like the Third Republic in its first days. There is good reason to doubt that republicanism in France seriously changed the conditions of the people, their style of thought, or their modes of life. Administrative centralization continued intact, the bourgeoisie remained the ruling class, and the fact that its lower elements could rise to positions of local, regional, and national power resulted not from forms of government but from universal male suffrage and education, both of which Bonapartism had encompassed in its programs.

And yet in the minds of men and in their grandiloquent gestures, the struggle against the Germans, the tragedy of defeat, the bloody civil strife of 1871 in Paris, the heroic efforts to found a republic and to make men free (even when they did not want to be) and to curb the power of the church (when the devil still seemed real)—these were the great events of the last third of the century. Beside them the lowly phylloxera plunging its snout into vine roots seems as infinitesimal as it physically was, as historically dimensionless as men's rising in the morning, working for a living, dining and wining, and going back to bed.

And yet, there was no measure of the despair the southern vintner felt as he watched helplessly, obstinately unbelieving, while his vines faded and died. A quarter century earlier he had seen whole clusters of grapes wither and, if they survived, give only an acid, thin wine. Now he watched not merely the withering of his grapes but the dying of his livelihood. The sun, the rain, the warm air of spring and summer, his skill and constant efforts were of no avail against the myriad lice sucking the sap of life. These tiny creatures, beyond the capacity of the human eye, marched across the vines of France as defiantly as the Prussians had marched down the main streets of Paris in their hour of triumph. The Prussians were bought off with the province of Alsace and its fine vineyards and the payment of five billion francs; the phylloxera was more demanding: not until nearly twelve billion francs were spent and as many tears shed, did it bow to superior forces. Even then it did not consent to die, but rather to cohabit as a neighborly enemy in the new vineyard of France.

What then was taking place in the obscure shadows that few historians bother to penetrate? First there was a great deal of human wreckage. By 1876, when the first general elections of the new republic returned a republican majority in the Chamber of Deputies, the vines of the Côtes-du-Rhône and most of southern France were dead or dying. By the early eighties nearly all of the major vineyards south of the Loire River and in the Rhône and Saône valleys were either destroyed or succumbing. By the early nineties vineyards in the north were the scenes of battle. Man felt himself powerless.

Science and the Vine

The scientific knowledge that gave men steam locomotion also gave him the means to combat the phylloxera, if not to conquer it. But knowledge cannot be used without organization. Once the louse was discovered, numerous problems dealing with how to attack it arose. First there was the question of leadership: who was to conduct the campaign against it? There was not a strong tradition of governmental intervention in France. Bonapartists, of course, claimed that the central power enjoyed the right to initiate, to innovate, and Napoleon III had used his power to influence the economy. Republicans, however, especially the middle-of-the-road men who ran the government after 1877, expressed a repulsion for strong government, associating it with the absolute monarchy that their forefathers had overturned in 1789 and that they had finally put to an end in 1870. Highly individualistic, they wanted a laissez faire economy, a hands-off state. Most vignerons were at one with them, for perhaps no other segment of the rural population was more individualistic. It was, rather, the well-to-do landowners organized in agricultural societies, and large wholesale merchants organized in chambers of commerce and buyers of many vineyards during the 1850s, who first realized that the magnitude of the crisis would require governmental aid in the form of subsidies far beyond the capacities of local growers. Few of the emerging leaders recognized what gigantic proportions the struggle would take, but their experience quickly made them aware that, to repulse the invader, both money and nearly military discipline would be required from each rank-and-file vigneron. They, as leaders, would certainly have to display more skill and daring than did the Franch commanders sent against the Prussians in 1870. Bravado was useless; scientific modernization became the prime need.

It must be remembered that both the man in the street and the man in the field were highly skeptical of science and especially of entomology. Few of them believed the theories of Charles Darwin, and even fewer believed that science had anything to offer agriculture. The vast hoard of vine-trimmers were simple peasants who had survived the oïdium, had made good during the Second Empire, and proved incapable of accepting the wild notion that a tiny yellow bug could take it all away. They were particularly aroused because the first step their leaders took was to set up agricultural commissions consisting of large owners and middle-class experts who demanded the destruction of infected vines, truly a "scorched-earth" policy. This practice, urged in the midseventies, soon won legal sanction and the support of local authorities. By this time, however, local authorities were not as universally respected as before the war. Until 1875 France had been torn between monarchists and republicans, and many peasants distrusted the gentlemen savants who came around in city attire to inspect their vines. On many occasions they turned out with shovels, hoes, picks, and rakes to put the inspectors to flight, and comic were the scenes of top hats and coat tails flying a few steps ahead of angry vignerons. When signs of a phylloxera attack appeared, local cultivators rarely reported them to the departmental commissions for fear of having their vines uprooted. As the plants died, however, peasants became increasingly resigned to intervention.

But by no means did resistance disappear. When the aphid finally made its appearance in Champagne, the struggle took on political over-tones. In 1891 the departmental professor of agriculture detected its presence in a vineyard and the departmental surveillance and defense committee decided to uproot the vines. A strong protest went up, and René Lamarre, claiming to speak for the independent vignerons, con-demned the decision as a trick by the big champagne companies, the buyers of grapes, to subject the vignerons to their power. When agents of the committee arrived, they too, were chased away by peasants carry-ing pitchforks. In part this problem resulted from the obstinacy of the peasants, who refused to uproot their vines merely because a professor declared them infected; in part, however, it was caused by the system of basing representation on the committee on the amount of money sub-scribed for its work. Since the big champagne companies paid substantial dues, they obtained a majority vote. Their decision to uproot had some wisdom behind it, but Lamarre and his peasant followers demanded more democratic representation. When they received it, they were not satisfied, and many refused to pay their dues, claiming that the commit-tee was not legally organized. The committee finally expired in 1896 and the work of defense fell to local communal councils, whose tasks were subsidized partly by the central government, partly by the champagne companies.[5]

The Champenois's refusal to uproot their vines did not result wholly from ignorance and blind hostility to the companies, for by the early 1890s the rest of viticultural France had gone through twenty-odd years of experimentation with palliatives, and nowhere had uprooting stopped the aphid's spread. Given the cold climate and the relative isolation of the Marne vineyard, uprooting seemed a drastic but necessary measure to an enlightened man such as Gaston Chandon and he paid for the vines he destroyed. But similar programs had failed in Bordeaux and Bur-gundy and both regions had already undertaken other measures that were far more effective.

Efforts to find a cure for phylloxera-infested vines go back to the last years of the Empire and the founding of the Republic. At this time Frenchmen were uncertain about how to cure both their vines and their politics. While still debating the ideal form of government, the provi-sional regime decided to offer a prize of 300,000 francs to any man who could rid the country of the terrible scourge. The prize commission examined over 700 proposals and tried out 317. Every imaginable scheme was suggested, including toad venom, tobacco juice, arsenic, urine, magic and exorcism, and even a beating mechanism intended to drive the insects either into the sea or over the frontier, hopefully to

Germany. Others suggested electricity, magnetism, ants, and moles. There really was an insect that devoured the aphids in the United States, but transferred to Europe it mysteriously lost its appetite for them. Commission members despaired of the state of man's knowledge and roundly condemned the educational system of their time. Needless to say, the government kept its prize money.

The only realistic proposals were palliatives, not cures. The earliest was the suggestion of Baron Paul Thénard, who in 1869 had deep furrows plowed in two vineyards near Bordeaux, in which he spread carbon bisulphide (800 kilos per hectare). Of the eleven vines involved in this experiment a few died and the remainder recovered the next year. But while all the aphids were destroyed, their eggs survived and grew to become adults.[6] To many the experiment was a failure; however in 1873 near Montpellier in the South a M. Monestier, using much smaller doses of the chemical, killed many aphids without harming the vines. Additional trials were carried on by L. Vialla, who discovered not only that the chemical was effective but also that it was dangerously flammable, even explosive, and its fumes could be poisonous without proper ventilation.[7] Numerous experiments were required before growers learned the dosage most suitable for varying soil conditions, and in due course the plowing of furrows gave way to the use of an injector, called a *pal*, that was quite efficient. It consisted of a pole holding a tank for the chemical and a hollow pointed metal end. This was forced into the ground and the desired quantity of the chemical allowed to flow out. The problem that remained now was for owners to induce their vignerons to fill the tanks of the injectors, a nasty task due to the viscous, smelly nature of the chemical. There are stories of workers and crop-sharers, disbelievers in chemicals anyway, who injected empty tools into the earth all day long, as though the gesture alone was as effective as the chemical! On large estates more complicated—and expensive—machinery appeared. Another chemical, sulphocarbonate, (discovered by S. B. Dumas of the Academy of Science) came on the market, but it never received the wide application of carbon bisulphide.

These chemicals presented many problems and dangers—when improperly used, they were more destructive of vines than of insects—yet their appearance made it unnecessary to root up infected vines all at once. Since the life of a vineyard could be extended from five to ten years and even longer, there emerged a school of men who ardently favored defending the *vitis vinifera* of France and Europe and keenly opposed uprooting and other methods of defense. They formed the school of sulphurists.

Up to a certain point logic was on their side. True, the use of chemicals was expensive. Defenders of chemicals estimated that the cost of carbon bisulphide came to 150 francs per hectare. In addition vines subjected to this treatment needed 300 francs worth of fertilizer each year for the first two years, bringing the total to 450 francs, a sum eventually reduced to about 300 francs. Since sulphocarbonate came to 700 francs the first two years and 500 francs thereafter, it was at a distinct disadvantage, despite its superior capacity both as a killer of aphids and as a restorer of vines. The question was, could earnings cover the expense of these chemicals? Given the high prices of wines when they were in short supply during the phylloxera period, most growers could afford them and used them. This was especially true in the areas not attacked before the late seventies, when the methods of using chemicals had improved considerably.[8]

Opposed to the sulphurists, or chemists at they were sometimes called, were the Americanists. These had come to the conclusion that the use of sulphur chemicals could at best prolong the life of a sick vine, which despite all efforts must soon die. They therefore turned to a solution that appeared to them more durable. Some remarkably ingenious experimenters had discovered that cetain native American vine species, the *vitis labrusca* for example, were not harmed by the aphid, so the early Americanists advocated replanting the vineyards of Europe with resistant American root stock. But trails with wine made from American grapes soon revealed the persistance of an off taste, referred to as "foxy" and not at all acceptable to the European palate. Then came the idea of grafting native French vines onto American roots, an idea put forward by Gaston Bazille in 1869 and perhaps earlier by Leo Laliman of Bordeaux. This notion was taken up with some enthusiasm in the lower South of France because vines there had been the first victims of phylloxera and by the early seventies were far beyond salvation through chemicals. Growers had to replant; the question was, with which vines? Those in Hérault were especially hard hit and they hoped for an answer from Planchon, who set off on a voyage to the United States in 1873. There he met C. V. Riley, a noted entomologist, who had devoted great energy to studying vines and insects. Planchon was too old to travel extensively and Riley showed him several vines quite resistant to the aphids, whereupon Planchon returned home a hero of sorts. Growers induced the local administration to lift the ban on imported vines, and they grafted local varieties onto Clintons, Taylors, and Concords. To their horror they discovered that these roots, resistant though they were, did not thrive in the chalky soil of their vineyards. Next they resorted to the Riparia and Rupestris, both of which died of chlorosis, then they sadly discovered that the Jacquez, while resistant to lime, was far less so to the phylloxera. These experiments were costly and time-consuming, and their failures furnished the sulphurists with ample ammunition against the use of foreign vines and for the continuance of import bans.

Meanwhile scientists began to cross French and American vines, creating hybrids, in their search for a root capable of resisting phylloxera and thriving in calcareous soils. Crossing a Riparia with a Rupestris produced a suitable root; so did Aramon and Riparia, and Cabernet and Rupestris.[9] Henry Marès of Hérault, in conjunction with the famous agricultural school there, carried out numerous experiments. With the use of American stock, grafting came into its own. Few vignerons knew anything about it or had been trained to make a graft. As demand for grafted vines rose, so did the price of master graftsmen. Consequently local authorities soon established schools to train vignerons who, in turn, trained others on a cooperative basis. This particular aspect of reconstitution proved to be the easiest, the most friendly, and indeed the most fraternal and successful. And when growers learned to graft their own stocks and scions, they reduced their costs.

Costs of reconstituting a vineyard were also a factor to consider. According to Marès soil preparation came to about 2,150 francs per hectare in the Midi, and new vine stock to 2,000 francs, plus 600 francs interest on the total (borrowed from local banks) for three years. These were heavy sums for small vignerons, most of whom had abandoned their vineyards or converted them to other crops. Leadership in the movement and its financing therefore fell to middle and large owners, many of whom had other sources of income because they were also medical doctors, lawyers, merchants, or professors. As we shall see, reconstituting the southern vineyard drastically changed its character. Since the demand for wine had grown so intense after 1875, the last big harvest of France, and since prices rose accordingly, investors willingly supplied the capital required for such a vast operation. The attraction was all the greater when experiments indicated that grafted vines were more fertile than others, flowered earlier, and matured about eight days before native root vines.[10]

Growers also tried submerging their vines under a foot of water for a specified time, usually several weeks, and it proved to be effective for drowning the phylloxera. Louis Faucon of Graveson, near Arles, concluded that he could flood a hectare of vines for 60 francs, a cost much below that of chemical treatment or replanting. For this reason there are still vineyards flooded once a year in the lower South. But this method has been feasible only in several low-lying coastal areas of France, and acceptable only for the most common vines.[11]

When the International Phylloxera Congress met in Bordeaux in 1881, the Americanists were in a strong position to sway opinion. They had the backing of the venerable Planchon himself, of Pierre Viala, who would travel in the United States in 1888 to complete the work of Planchon, of two lady viticulturists, the Duchess of Fitz-James of Gard and Mme Ponsot of Pomerol, and finally the striking success of recent experiments. Table 12 indicates the new direction.

The most persistent opponents of grafting were growers long renowned for their quality wines. In Côte d'Or and Médoc the voracious aphid did not appear until the mid eighties, and when it did arrive, the owners of fine vines employed chemical treatment at once, for its effectiveness had been proven whereas grafting had not. Moreover the growers had no compelling reason to uproot all their vines and plant anew, nor could they have afforded to. The superiority and high price of their wines depended upon the age of their vines, and by no means other than a miracle could a newly planted stock of Cabernet or of Pinot produce the kind of wine demanding high prices in the market. Therefore there was little replanting among them until after 1890, and for the next decade they experimented with various grafts in limited areas. In this way they could continue to employ chemicals on their old stock and make good wine during the eight to ten years required by a noble vine to produce its best grapes.[12] Just as important as the phylloxera to these makers of fine wines was the reappearance of mildew and various rots during the two decades after 1880. If Château Latour is typical, the problem confronting them was the decline of quality resulting less from the aphid than from the deadly fungi or mildews. From 1880 to 1891, the wine of eight vintages turned sour when put in bottles, the result of mildew rather than of phylloxera. So when the botanist Alexis Millardet discovered "bouillie bordelaise," a preventative mixture of water, copper sulphate, and plaster, he became as much a savior as Planchon and other Americanists. To maintain quality, therefore, not more than a small part of the total vineyard was turned over to grafts at one time.

In opposition to the sulphurists were hordes of small growers who could not profitably convert their lands to other crops or continue to bear the heavy costs of sulphuring. Their number was legion everywhere and their will to act could not be denied. In Burgundy, however, an even sharper division arose when the growers of Gamay grapes, most of whom were small, independent vignerons, but far fewer in number than their Bordeaux or Midi counterparts, came to favor the use of American

TABLE 12: *Various Vine Treatments*

Year	Submersion	Carbon bisulphide	Sulpho-carbonate	Grafted American Roots
1878	2,800 ha.	2,500 ha.	800 ha.	1,300 ha.
1880	8,000	5,500	1,500	6,400
1885	24,300	40,500	3,200	75,000
1890	32,700	62,200	9,300	436,000

roots over the continuous effort to save their native vines. Like many little growers they had at first refused to believe that the phylloxera would dare enter their well-kept vineyards and refused to inform the authorities of dying vines. Pinot owners, however, were determined to save their fine vines and feared that American roots would produce inferior juice. They condemned the Gamay growers for wanting to bring foreign roots into the area, for this would replenish the aphid population and make treatment more difficult. This vinicultural elite, in contrast to the departmental government and the defense committee, sought to force their opponents to use carbon bisulphide and to maintain the 1874 prohibition against American stock.[13]

They were successful until 1887, when American vines won the right to be planted in Côte d'Or, but 1891 was the turning point, when the peak of 4,250 hectares received chemical treatment. Then the number declined. By 1900 only 340 hectares still received treatment, whereas 18,900 had been reconstructed on American roots. We should note, however, that the owners of renowned vines were remarkably successful in using chemicals to safeguard them. Their losses, therefore, were less disastrous and, once convinced of the necessity to replant, they had sufficient capital and experience to carry out the operation effectively and without great loss. The peasant growers of Gamay, on the other hand, were at a disadvantage; during the early years they could neither legally replant nor always pay the heavy expense of chemical application, even when partially subsidized. In consequence many of their vines died and they had no options apart from moving away or taking jobs working for rich owners. Many believed that the fine vine owners had acted arbitrarily to keep a labor force at their disposition.

Eventually both North and South suffered, but at different times and in different ways. The South bore the brunt earliest and was the area of extensive experimentation. Only vines in the coastal zone escaped attack, because phylloxera could not survive in loose sandy soil. Stretches of land that had been worthless before the invasion appreciated many times in value afterward. But, like submersion, the recourse to highly sandy soil was available only to ordinary vines.

Both in the short and long run the phylloxera invasion was a severe trial; only the areas truly committed to viticulture survived and recovered. The marginal ones, where general farmers had painfully grown vines since time immemorial for the local market or where men had turned to vines during the Second Empire, were now abandoned quite simply because reconstitution did not pay. This abandonment encouraged a trend toward regional specialization, which cheap transport had initiated, so in this way, too, the blight had a marked effect on the rural economy.

Most striking was the drastic decline in hectares devoted to vines. According to government data, the peak of planting occurred between 1866 and 1869, with 2,643,174 hectares, an increase of 24.8 percent since 1835, the first year for which national data was published. By 1885 the total had fallen to 1,971,000 hectares, and in 1900 it stood at 1,609,000 a drop of 64 percent. The continued decline after 1900 resulted from a serious fall of prices and was only indirectly related to the phylloxera. The national loss between 1873 when the aphid was rampant in the Midi, and 1900 was about 1,220,000 hectares, or 51 percent. Most probably the figures for 1873 and 1900 refer to areas of producing vines and are therefore comparable. The total for 1885 undoubtedly does not. In that year 24,000 hectares were flooded, 41,000 were treated with carbon bisulphide, 5,000 with sulphocarbonate, and 75,000 were on American roots. This gives us a total of 145,000 hectares and leaves 1,826,000 untreated. It would be absurd to believe that all these vineyards contained producing vines; probably more than half were dead and uprooted, but the land remained classed as vineyards. To get a clearer idea of the impact of the phylloxera, it is more meaningful to calculate average yield between 1870–75, 24.54 hectoliters per hectare, and that between 1885–90, 15.2 hectoliters per hectare. The second group made up the worst six-year period of the crisis and revealed a decline of just over 61 percent. Normally such a small crop would encourage a sharp rise of prices, and in fact there was a marked rise, especially in the earlier eighties, but a downward trend after 1885, combined with continued low yields, resulted in a shocking fall of gross income. The cause of this downward trend was the massive importation of foreign wine from Spain, Italy, and Portugal, as we shall see later.

Another result of the blight was a notable increase of dishonesty in the wine trade. The mideighties witnessed the appearance of various fraudulent wines on the market. Because of the shortage vignerons now began making second wines, the *piquettes*, to put in trade as first wines. This was a simple process. After pressing the grapes for the first wine, the maker had traditionally added water and some sugar and allowed this liquid to ferment on the pressed skins. We have already noted that many wine workers had no desire to press the grapes too heartily because this second wine, which was given to them, acquired a better quality if some of the original juice and coloring matter remained in the "cake." This wine, by custom, had not gone into commerce. The owner kept some, he gave most of it to his workers as part of their wages, and he gave some to friends and relatives. But during the eighties they sold even third and fourth wines, made by adding, in addition to sugar, coloring agents such as fuchsin (which since it contained arsenic could be dangerous if applied too liberally). The government encouraged the use of beet sugar by lowering the taxes on it, with the result that large quantities of sugar wine appeared on the market. In addition a so-called wine made of raisins also emerged and competed with natural wine because it could be made anywhere. Huge quantities of raisins were imported from Greece through Marseille, and this port city as well as Paris became important centers for the manufacture of this beverage. Since its production costs remained low, enterprising "vignerons," who had never seen a vine, discovered it was a quite profitable enterprise. Of course it was not labeled as raisin wine, nor were second, third, and fourth grape wines as such.

It is impossible to discover the precise quantity of false wine turned out annually, but government figures offer some data on general trends. In 1885 just under 8,000 tons of sugar were sold to make the equivalent of nearly 800,000 hectoliters of wine; in 1888, the peak year, 38,763 tons of sugar were used to produce an equivalent of 3,633,000 hectoliters. These data include sugar used to increase the alcohol of the first wine and the *piquettes*, which means that not all the wine made with it was false, but as we shall see, probably far more wine was clandestinely produced and marketed than official data indicate. According to this data, 2,272,000 hectoliters of raisin wine appeared on the market in 1885, 3,178,000 in 1890, the peak year, and only 108,000 in 1899, after which the quantity dropped sharply because of high taxes.[14] However most legitimate growers of grapes vociferously denounced official statistics for not including much fraudulent wine. By the 1890s these legitimate growers, who had survived the phylloxera, were replanting on American roots and rapidly expanding their production by improving their technology. Now, with their vats full, they cried out against the competition from false beverages.

Clearly not all survivors had clean hands—or should we say casks. Many lived through the crisis by turning out sugar and raisin wine as a supplement to their natural product. Taken as whole, their average production of legitimate wine from 1867 to 1871 came to just over 54 million hectoliters, from 1872 to 1881 to just over 49 million, and from 1886 to 1895 to 30.5 million, a drop of 77 percent. This was a far greater decline than was the case with vineyard acreages. As for prices, the average price in the 1850s was 21 francs, in the 1860s 28 francs, in the 1870s 29 francs, in the 1880s 38 francs; it then declined as yield increased. In fact there was even a glutted market in 1893–94, forcing the price down to 23 francs.

Under these conditions only growers fully committed to wine-making or whose land was unsuitable for other crops decided that it was worthwhile to hold on. Their number in 1869 came to 1,342,000, in 1875 to 1,865,000, but by 1896 there were 1,492,000. So there was actually an increase over 1869, but a marked 25 percent decline after 1875, when the dread aphid began its conquest of southern vineyards. Now most of these growers were not monoculturists concerned exclusively with vines; the full-time grower lived chiefly in the lower South and Southwest, but even in Gironde the majority of vignerons cultivated a few other crops, though grapes remained their most lucrative one. Maps 3 and 4 show where vines were rooted up by discouraged farmers who returned their fields to other uses. The 1866 map reveals how the prosperous era of high yields and prices had attracted peasants to the vine. The viticultural square is clearly still there but somewhat deformed by the expanded planting in interior departments such as Allier, Indre, Dordogne, Lot, Tarn-et-Garonne, and Lot-et-Garonne. By 1900 production in these areas had dropped sharply, and this was to be expected. Also to be expected was the decline of vines in northern climates, where wine was profitable only as long as transport was too expensive to allow competition from regions admirably suited to grapes, such as the South. Both phylloxera and railroad reduced the profit of northern vineyards and discouraged farmers there. Somewhat more rare was the reduction of vines in sectors with a long history of their cultivation. The most dramatic cutbacks occurred in Vienne and the Charentes, where the blight was devastating, forcing the peasants to turn their holdings over to grazing. From an area of vast wine production for distillation, the Charentes became a major dairy center, because the price of the common wine distilled to make cheap cognac did not cover the costs of treatment and reconstitution. A more limited number of quality vines was replanted on resistant roots. Undoubtedly the lower Midi vineyard would have suf-

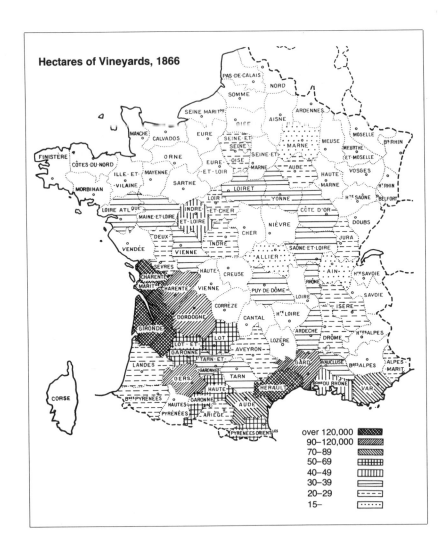

MAP 3: *Hectares of Vineyards, France 1866*

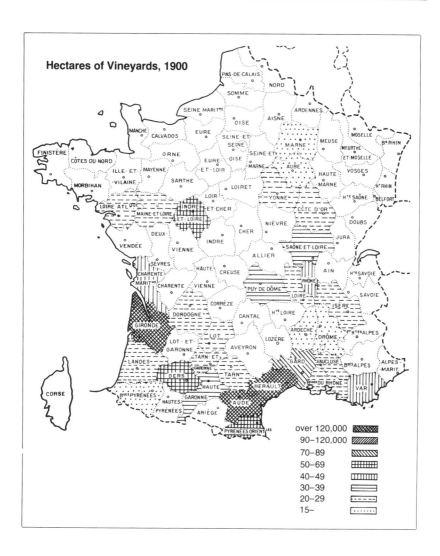

MAP 4: *Hectares of Vineyards, France 1900*

fered the same fate had small growers there continued to produce low-grade wine for three-sixth brandy, but the Languedocian vignerons had shifted after 1850 to the making of table wine, and this act saved them from extinction, if not from near poverty for a while. In the department of Charente, however, vines that had occupied 110,000 hectares in 1877 were left only 15,000 in 1900 and juice from grapes gave way to milk from teats. The department of Charente-Maritime was somewhat less affected, thanks to sandy soil along the coast, but its vineyard declined from 130,000 hectares to 46,000. The vineyard of the Southwest also suffered, destroying the hope of vast wealth for this isolated, economically backward region. The department of Gers was an exception, because its vine-covered hills were the source of Armagnac brandy. Where vines perished or did not produce quality juice, low income plus poor transport and isolation left the population with no choice but to go elsewhere. Perhaps state intervention might have helped, but politicians did not take action.

Several historians today criticize the French government for acting too late and doing too little against the phylloxera. This statement is correct by today's standards, but it is unhistorical. The phylloxera reached its peak of destruction during the 1880s and early 1890s, when the republican form of government was still too concerned about sinking its own roots in society to give prime attention to a bug sucking at vine roots. The crisis in wine occurred during the period when Jules Ferry sought not only to provide free education for all children, but also to weaken the control of royalist clergymen over them, and his actions diverted public attention by creating extreme bitterness in a still strongly Catholic country. In addition there was war in Indo-China and imperialist expansion in Africa. Worse yet, a general economic depression that began about 1882 deflated most prices at the same time that those of wine inflated, which adversely affected the wine market. Possibly this general decline of prices saved many vignerons by lowering their costs of living precisely when the source of their livelihood was vanishing. For Burgundian vignerons their real income during most of the three decades from 1852 to 1881 had actually fallen slightly, due to rising food and supply costs. But when the aphid appeared, general prices fell so low that the real income of surviving growers took a turn for the better.[15] Burgundians of course profited from the disappearance of the Languedocian vineyard in the 1870s, and by the time the aphid appeared north of the Loire a means of defense existed. This partly explains why the vignerons of Beaujolais and Côte d'Or resisted the rooting up of their infested vines when local authorities demanded it.

The point to note here, however, is that most politicians did not want to compel people to act. They believed in the natural laws of economics—save for tariffs—and preferred that winemen find their own solution to their problems with minimum governmental intervention. One can hardly blame politicians for taking this view when most vignerons agreed with it. To them the government was the levyer of taxes, and therefore an impediment to economic growth and well-being. It was natural for them to resist—even violently—the efforts of local authorities to fight against the phylloxera by rooting up vines, by treating with chemicals, and by assessing them for part of the costs. In all these respects vignerons were hardly different from the bulk of the peasant class and of much of the middle class. Public opinion was divided on the role of government in economic and social arrangements. Many large landowners who accepted and demanded official aid in their economic activities denounced it when it interfered concerning their workers' living conditions and wages. They were, nonetheless, the chief promoters of official intervention in the phylloxera crisis.

Governmental action was carried out at three levels: in international congresses that were quite ineffective; in national law that first sought rather unsuccessfully to curb the importation of American vines and then to encourage their entry for grafting purposes; and finally at the departmental and local level, where agricultural committees and defense or vigilance syndicates, backed by higher authority, sought both to prevent the spread of the aphid and to obtain funds to combat it. These funds derived in equal parts from monies voted by the central government, on the one hand, and the departmental council (*conseil général*), on the other. That is, Paris matched the sums raised locally either by taxation or, more often, through dues paid by all the growers of a locality to the syndicate. Given the total number of grape-growers in 1879, nearly two million, table 13, prepared by Barral [16] makes clear that most growers did not want to assess themselves by organizing a syndicate, nor did they reach out desperately for matching funds, since the existence of a syndicate was required to receive them.

Barral noted that small owners were predominant among the membership in order to get public subsidies. If this is true, in 1882 the average owner would seem to have possessed under three hectares. Some large growers, on the other hand, provided much of their own financing perhaps out of distrust of the government.

The role of government, local and national, was not negative. Despite the often obvious incompetence of the ministers of agriculture, all of them political appointees, and the frequent preoccupation of the regime

TABLE 13: *Growth of Wine Syndicates*

Year	Number of Syndicates	Number of Members	Hectares Owned by Members	Hectares of Vines in France
1879	8	153	390	2,299,000
1880	74	1,507	6,672	2,258,000
1881	223	6,414	17,126	2,245,000
1882	369	12,338	32,685	2,180,265

in Paris with other matters, it is clear that politicians from viticultural districts were able to press for measures favorable to growers. The law of 2 August 1879 forbade the planting of foreign vines and that of 15 June 1878 compelled the treatment of vines, partly at government expense, and granted to local syndicates the power to distribute monies for buying chemicals and injectors. The subsidy arrangement worked on a decreasing scale: 100 francs per hectare for the first year, 60 francs for the second year, 40 francs for the third, and then nothing. Thereafter the local syndicate had to provide all of its own funds from dues and private gifts, such as those of the PLM railroad and the big champagne companies. To supervise the entire program these laws brought into existence a Superior Phylloxera Commission, composed of viticultural experts and scientists.

Without doubt the phylloxera crisis created a precedent in the field of state action at least comparable to that of laying railroad track during midcentury and after or of modernizing the major cities during the Second Empire. The disbursement of public money was massive, though I am not certain it is now possible to discover exactly how much was spent. On the basis of the Agriculture Ministry's budget, over 36 million went into the struggle between 1881 and 1909, averaging over a million per year. This money was spent for research, subsidies for chemicals, root stock, and grafting schools, and miscellaneous activities among governmental agencies.[17] To this must be added the loss to the treasury of about 17,617,000 francs as a result of exemptions from the land tax between 1887 and 1894.[18] Phylloxera-related exemptions rapidly dropped thereafter and subsidies, which had been greatly reduced, ended in 1904. It has been estimated that the phylloxera caused a money loss of about 12 billion francs, a figure that includes some 4 billion spent for imported wine. This outlay was certainly unprecedented in peacetime.

Equally important, it was the first major effort by a public power to force producers to assemble, organize, and act in their own defense, which, ironically, was done not always in the public or consumers' interest, as we shall see. This period provoked the creation of the earliest large-scale growers associations and the law of 1 April 1898 encouraged the formation of mutual credit societies. In the long run the blight was largely responsible for modifying the ferocious individualism of most vignerons and at least indirectly stimulated their willingness to modernize.

Italy

The story of vine maladies began in Italy, as in France, with the powdery mildew which spread in the peninsula during the 1850s. As was the case north of the Alps, it came shortly after the unsuccessful revolutions and wars of liberation of 1848–49. In those years large numbers of Italians gathered to fight against the Austrians in order to end Hapsburg rule in Lombardy and Venetia. The *Risorgimento*, the movement for national unity, had briskly descended from the lofty sphere of ideals to that of practical politics and war, but there it suffered a crushing defeat at the hands of the Austrian armies. The task of reviving it fell to many men, but two in particular stand out—Cavour, the scientific farmer, and Ricasoli, the champion of the *governo* method for making chianti classico. As they continued the effort to rally opinion behind their political goals, leading viticulturists undertook the effort to combat the mildew. Cavour was not so single-minded a nationalist that he ignored Italy's economic needs; on the contrary, as prime minister of Piedmont he commanded the Royal Academy of Agriculture in Turin to study the malady and to seek a remedy.[19]

Despite all these efforts, Italian politicians as well as viticulturists discovered that the aid of France was, if not desirable, then necessary. Cavour appealed to Napoleon III, whose intervention on the Italians' side in 1859 made it possible for them to win national independence from the Hapsburgs. Winemen also looked to France for methods to overcome the mildew, and, following the example of their Gallic brothers, resorted to the use of sulphur. Unfortunately Italy, like France, was peopled by large numbers of uneducated peasant growers who refused to apply chemicals to their vines simply on the advice of "experts" or of Cavour, who was too far removed from the land to induce them to take action. More influential was Garibaldi, already assuming the proportions of a folk hero, who when he became convinced of sulphur's efficacy urged the peasants to use it.

There is a story about the little growers in Bielle, who refused to use sulphur until their bishop saved his own vines with it, supposedly on the advice of the famous red shirt.[20] This story has the ring of fictitious folklore, but in Latin countries in midcentury the authority of churchmen was still considerable. And the superstitions of peasant farmers were enormous. The story continues that the peasants imitated the bishop, not because they believed the sulphur would work, but because they suspected that Garibaldi had told the bishop the magic word for destroying mildew! Certainly the mass of peasant growers were not won over until enologists, special commissions, and local leaders gradually drove into their heads the effectiveness of scientific methods. The fact that in 1856 only the growers using sulphur had a crop to gather, also won them over.[21] Given the failure of rulers to provide the nineteenth-century peasant with schools, seeing did not always lead him to believing; a constant pressure had to be exerted to induce him to act. This was true both in France and Italy, not only as regards the oïdium, but also as regards the phylloxera.

The story of the phylloxera in Italy is less dramatic than in France. In both countries, political upheavals deprived the aphid's attack of the public attention it deserved. Indeed the overthrow of the Second Empire in 1870 as a result of military defeat was a minute event compared to the near destruction of a millenium of vine culture. In Italy unification was at last achieved in 1870 with the capture of Rome and the immediate transfer there of the Italian capital. This final gesture was a moral victory, but it did not change the economic policy of the national government. A change of men did not bring about a serious change of viticultural policy because there was none—at least not in the 1870s.

It is possible that the phylloxera had come to Italy early; its penetration was not an invasion, having quick, devastating effects, as in France, but rather an infiltration that went unnoticed until 1879. To be sure, the Italian growers did not assume at once a posture of stately calm. In fact the same amazement, frenzy, and recrimination that had stirred up French growers spread among their counterparts south of the Alps. Large landowners, dominating the National Phylloxera Commission that the national state quickly set up and modeled on the one in France, insisted that the government take action to check the spread of the louse, either by treating all vines with carbon bisulphide or by uprooting them. The peasants responded in the same way as their brothers north of the

Alps: they denied that the phylloxera existed, they refused to believe that their vines could be attacked by it.

Agricultural experts were hard put to convince the mass of small growers of the need for quick, decisive action, because while they had reason and the French experience on their side, the peasants had logic on theirs. Throughout northern and central Italy there were hardly any large consolidated vineyards to tempt the invader, so the experts could not frighten the peasants with the reality of a mass, destructive invasion; moreover the Alps were undoubtedly an effective barrier. Although one strain of the aphid had wings, it could fly only a few yards, therefore the Phylloxera Commission was fairly certain that the louse arrived on vine stock imported from France.[22] The earliest official notice of its presence came in 1879 in the communes of Valmadrera and Civate in the province of Como in the North and from there it spread into the provinces of Novara and Varese. Since these areas, although productive of some high-quality wines, were not widely planted in vines, the small growers in Piedmont and elsewhere did not feel threatened, and indeed they were not until the 1890s or later.[23] Mixed planting with vines hung on trees and in widely spaced rows, did not encourage the aphid. Not only the distance but the style of cultivation saved northern Italian vines. Hung on trees, they were rarely plowed, so they had long deep roots in firmly pressed soil. The aphids had no chance to enter the surface soil through cracks in order to attack the roots.[24] For these reasons independent peasant growers were as rebellious toward inspectors as their Gallic counterparts. To make matters worse, Italian officials, like those in France, could not decide quickly on whether to uproot all infected vines or to treat them at any cost. Most peasants, of course, wanted to do neither; their solution in the North was to plant more vines, especially in the plains, after the aphid struck those on the hillsides. The result was an excess of wine of poor quality.[25]

Far more serious—far more similar to that of France—was the true invasion of Sicily and Reggio Calabria, the toe of the Italian boot. The vineyards in the lower Mezzogiorno were quite similar to those of the lower Midi—vines were planted in closely spaced rows, trimmed close to the ground, supported by stakes rather than by trees, plentiful enough to attract aphids, and situated in a looser, more frequently plowed soil which encouraged their propagation. By 1891 Sicily made up about half of the infected area of Italy while the lower mainland accounted for another large portion of the national total of 136,000 infected hectares. Not until 1893–94 was there widespread destruction in Piedmont and other provinces in the North, especially in Cuneo, Alexandria, and Pavia. By 1889 the government estimated that about 300,000 hectares were infected; since it also estimated the total vineyard area to be over three million hectares, infected vineyards even then made up only 10 percent of the total.[26] The government's figure is patently absurd, but even if we reduce it by 30 percent, the evidence proves that Italy suffered far less than France. As late as 1912 only about 7 to 10 percent of her vineyard was dead or dying.

In a sense Italy even profited from France's catastrophe. Her growers were able to borrow the techniques the French had developed at great expense to kill the root louse. They resorted to carbon bisulphide, with disastrous results for those practicing mixed agriculture. Unskilled applications of it killed most of the vines—which was perhaps a blessing in disguise—but also it was fatal to support trees and other crops in the nearby area—which was not a blessing in any guise. With time and experience, of course, the same chemicals used in France were skillfully applied in Italy. But as in France, chemicals did not eliminate the insects, consequently replanting on American root stock proved to be the only permanent solution. Like the French government, that in Italy aided the growers by lifting the tax on their dying vineyards and, in conjunction with provincial authorities, it contributed about 850,000 lire each year to help root up dead vines and treat living ones. Submersion, effective in parts of Siracusa and Catenia, also enjoyed subsidies. Unlike the French, however, the state did not encourage replanting. Rather it sought to limit the vine area, reasoning that if there were fewer vineyards, there would be no wine crisis comparable to that of 1888–92.

The new government in Rome found itself in difficulty precisely because the phylloxera in France had so curtailed the quantity of wine there that Italians, especially in the Mezzogiorno, greatly expanded their production to fill the vacuum. Trouble occurred when the French, having recovered from the phylloxera, began producing their own wine again and no longer needed large quantities from foreign growers. To worsen matters for the Mezzogiorno, the governments in Rome and Paris nearly broke off commercial relations in 1888, with the result that southern wine producers found themselves with a huge surplus of low-quality wine in their cellars. Given this situation the coming of the phylloxera to Bari and Brindizi seemed merely a minor catastrophe; in fact, its destruction of much of the southern vineyard came to be looked upon in governmental circles as a blessing of sorts, a view which undoubtedly helps explain why official policy refused to subsidize replanting. Rome clearly wanted to deplete the vine population throughout the peninsula; the Agricultural Ministry therefore subsidized defensive measures designed, in reality, to preserve the smaller quality vineyards of the North whose markets were not as adversely affected by governmental tariff policies. Moreover private capital more readily came to the aid of northern growers, in part because the major money centers were north of Rome, in part because northern agriculture had already come to rely on heavy amounts of investment capital to improve both the land and the methods of farming it. In addition as the phylloxera killed newly planted vines in the northern plains, peasants planted cereals and rice there, crops far more profitable when their prices rose in the 1890s.

The Mezzogiorno, on the other hand, was and would remain Italy's number one economic problem. Adverse events seemed to arrive there in a never-ending file. At about the time that the root aphid began its deadly invasion of France's Mediterranean vineyards, southern Italy suffered a severe decline of wheat prices, a decline made doubly severe by the fact that farmers had greatly expanded cereals earlier in order to profit from high prices following national unification. Now, despairing of cereals, peasants and landowners searched about for another, equally profitable crop. They found it in the vine.

The rapid, disorderly growth of the south Italian wine industry would have undoubtedly come about even without the thirsty French market. On both the Mediterranean and Adriatic coasts, as well as in Sicily and Sardinia, vines had always been cultivated, but market conditions and political disunity had not encouraged their spread. After 1860, however, conditions in Italy promoted economic expansion as internal tariffs, that had hampered progress for centuries, were ended. At last Italians achieved a free internal market, roughly eighty years later than Frenchmen. Other conditions paralleled those of France: increase of urban population, expansion of rail communication, growth of industry in the north, and a rising standard of living. In exactly what way or how rapidly the southern wine industry would have developed without the French market remains impossible to determine. Assuredly its flowering would have been slower than that of France, if only because general economic and social wealth were slow to expand south of the Alps, and a higher percentage of the population remained on the land, largely self-sufficient in both food and drink. Moreover the French southern vineyard broadened production energetically from the late 1850s to the 1870s, a period of great prosperity and rising demand; the era of the southern Italian vineyard came just before a general depression set in. The opening of the French market in the 1870s and 80s, as well as the rising price of wine, undoubtedly saved Italian farmers from both falling cereal prices and the closed economy of depression. The French market

TABLE 14: *Blending Wine as Percent of Total Wine Production*

Province	Percent
Lecce	62.6
Bari	59.8
Foggia	49.2
Potenza	23.4
Cosenza	21.9
Catanzari	31.1
Reggio Calabria	37.3
Palermo	27.4
Messina	37.4
Catania	35.6
Siracuso	37.8
Trapani	21.9
Cagliare	16.1
Sassari	26.3

Source: Focardi, *Produzione*, 5

effectively determined both the rate of growth and the character of the south Italian vineyard. We can see this particularly in Apulia, the heel or lower southeastern part of the boot.

Before the 1850s the peasants of Apulia (Bari, Brindizi, and Lecce provinces) relied chiefly on oil and grains for their livelihood. When the olive and wheat failed, widespread poverty resulted.[27] The local farmers made wine, badly as we noted earlier, but during the 1850s, because of increased demand for wine and rising prices, producers began to improve their methods and the quality of their beverage. The Pugliese were truly blessed by the fact that the oïdium barely touched their area. Their wine readily found a place in the peninsula, even though it was not yet united, as well as in the international market—England, Austria, Russia, and Greece. Planted under the scorching sun in calcareous, dry soil the vines produced a heavy, alcoholic drink that wholesale merchants found useful for blending with weak wines in both northern Italy and France (see table 14). Although poverty remained extensive, even degrading, the peasants began to acquire enough cash from their three crops to purchase some of the land they farmed; in fact small landowners grew in number, without acquiring, however, a notable measure of independence, because the return on their land was too small. The crop-sharing system remained basic; so did extensive poverty and malaria, even after unification. Prices of wine rose as they had in France before the phylloxera and poor families became comfortable while those who enjoyed some wealth earlier now grew rich, at least by southern standards. As in France earlier, the sons of peasants could now go to school and daughters receive a dowry and silk clothing, for *"pezzi d'oro"* were piling up in the family treasury.[28]

Apulia, of course, was not the only section of Italy to expand production rapidly to supply France. Table 15 makes this clear:

TABLE 15: *Italy, Expanding Production (millions of hectoliters)*

Region	1870–74	Average Yield 1879–83	1892–95
Adriatic South	3.5	4.9	4.1
Mediterranean South	3.7	5.2	3.2
Sicily	4.2	7.8	4.4
Sardinia	.5	1.2	.8
Center	7.4	10.0	2.2
North	7.8	7.6	1.8

Sources: 1. *Rivista di viticoltura*, I (1877) 47
2. *Giornale vinicolo italiano*, XVI (1890) 613
3. *Revue de viticulture* II (1895) 602

All the above data should be viewed with caution. Until about 1901 the figures given by the Ministry of Agriculture were not considered accurate by winemen, who insisted that they were too low. We can only hope that these data were at least uniform in their inacurracy, so that our table really shows the evolution of wine production. It probably does, since the averages coincide with verbal testimony from knowledgeable men. Both the data and the assertions of commentators indicate a great increase in production during the 1880s and a sharp decline beginning in the early 1890s, a decline undoubtedly resulting from the spread of the phylloxera, barely noticeable in the Adriatic South but terrible in the Mediterranean South, in the Center and the North. It also reveals the effects of the closing of the French market as growers there, having recovered from the phylloxera, demanded and got tariff protection from Italian wines. The French tariff of 1888 practically excluded all but high-grade wine, and a separate law prohibited the blending of French and all foreign beverages, which destroyed the reason for importing both Italian and Spanish wines. As we shall see, the Mezzogiorno suffered severely as a result. If table 15 is fairly accurate, it would seem that the North and Center were more adversely affected than the South. However the data is certainly less accurate for the North and Center, because planting was mixed almost everywhere except in a few areas of Piedmont. In addition the North and much of the Center (Emelia, Tuscany, and Latium) had a rising industry and commerce to fall back on, as well as a greater facility for conversion to other crops. The new vineyards there had been planted in soils unsuitable for vines and produced an execrable product whose low price no longer covered costs. In these cases the aphid had come as a justiciar to condemn these vines guilty of violating good taste.

On the eve of World War I the phylloxera had not yet completed its deadly work. In the North and Center replanting was well underway; in the South it was just beginning. The war, of course, seriously interrupted this task and therefore long after France had learned how to live with the aphid, Italy continued the heroic struggle. And in the heat of battle a new wine industry emerged to aid the cause.

CHAPTER NINE

The New Wine Industry

At certain turning points in its history the wine industry appears to have followed a course similar to that of textiles and metals, for it too went through a technological or industrial revolution beginning in the 1850s and 1860s. The Golden Age seems to have been the "take-off" stage and the phylloxera period nothing more than a long slump or depression, rather like those endemic to the clothing industry. And like depressions in general, the phylloxera had the effect of eliminating the weak, the inept growers so that the strong and aggressive ones were eventually in a better position to further the industry, really to modernize it. Michel Augé-Laribé has suggested that there occurred in Languedoc in the later nineteenth century a phenomenon of this sort to which he applied the term "viticulture industrielle." [1] He was quite right. However, excluding the Mediterranean South and perhaps Champagne, the transformation of the wine industry tended to be slow rather than rapid, and it did not lead to a great degree of concentration and rationalization or even to rising levels of production. It must also be noted that viticulture underwent far less modification than viniculture, for the former often remained in the hands of peasants whereas the latter increasingly came under the control of trained technicians, enologists, and professional men bent upon increasing efficiency and profits.

But what precisely were these changes, and what were the main events that signal their occurrence during and after the last third of the century?

We must first emphasize the constant interchange between the vineyard and the vat, between the grape and its fermented juice. This interchange began long ago when men first learned to select the grapes most suited to a particular region and to cultivate, among the suitable vines, those most capable of producing a superior wine. What was new in this process was, first, the fact that the vineyards of France and then of Italy were almost completely renewed. Never before did man start from scratch.

Second, never before had growers experimented so extensively and carefully with so many types of vines and dressings and worked so hard to adapt vines to soils, always with the ultimate goal in mind: a good wine and plenty of it. In former times changes of this magnitude required generations, even centuries. But the young vigneron who saw his vines die in the 1880s was hardly middle aged when he could cultivate newly planted species, and his Italian brother was not much slower in making the transition. Such a quickening is perhaps revolutionary, but we must note that the old viticultural order was not dethroned, the status hierarchy was not upset. The "noble" vines retained their lofty status, and those beneath them remained there. The only novelty was that they all stood on American feet, but this one concession to equalitariansim changed nothing as regards the end product, the grape and its wine, for in these, inequality was as marked as before.

Third, there was distinct from the act of replanting a considerable increase of practical knowledge about vines, their cultivation, and their classification. Most of this information had to do with grafting and adaption; it emerged from the careful, extensive research carried out in major agricultural schools, such as the one at Montpellier. The work had a sound empirical, or experimental, approach, more concerned with practical application than with theory, even though theoretical efforts were by no means absent, because taxpaying growers and budget-minded politicians emphasized quick solutions to immediate problems; there was little time or money to support purely theoretical research. Even where the national government was prepared to support it, local pressure discouraged it, in Italy particularly, which explains why the experimental vine station at Gattinara closed several years after its opening; local subsidies ceased when its researchers showed a growing interest in theoretical problems.

The fourth new factor to emerge, despite the narrow vision of practicing growers, was the wider dissemination of the new pragmatic knowledge. Expanding literacy among peasants, the availability of books and periodicals authored by both teacher-researchers and trained growers, an increase in the use and number of peripatetic lecturers, of experimental stations, of agricultural schools, and of local agricultural societies—all of these contributed to the improvement of viticulture. Only where illiteracy remained high—in parts of southwest and central France, in much of southern Italy—did the new knowledge fail to penetrate.

A fifth factor was the considerable input of capital investment, both to renew the vineyards and to make them increasingly profitable. This factor appeared in nearly every locale where vines had occupied an important place in the rural economy, but it predominated in areas that lent themselves to grape-growing on a mass scale: Bordeaux, Languedoc, Roussillon, Piedmont, Tuscany, Sicily, and Apulia. Considerable amounts of capital were needed, not merely to renew the vines, but also to meet the higher costs of their cultivation.

A sixth factor, and perhaps the one most responsible for raising costs, was the growing use of chemicals. In viticulture, as in general agriculture, the massive application of chemical products to plants was undoubtedly one of the major innovations of the nineteenth and twentieth centuries.

Innovations in Viticulture

Considerable changes had begun in the cultivation of vines before the arrival of the fatal phylloxera. Not all of these had been desirable, for among them was the massive extension of vine-planting in flatlands and rich soils not at all suitable to the production of quality wine grapes. In addition various long trims were devised to augment the quantity of juice, to the detriment of quality. On the other hand, greater attention to beneficial innovations in pruning began to appear, along with a new willingness to experiment, perhaps best typified by Jules Guyot, the energetic propagandist of the new viticulture during the 1860s. He reminds us, and indeed was the rural equivalent, of the innovating champions of laissez faire and mechanized industry. Certainly he was dogmatic and naively visionary, a utopian of vignerons, with his belief that the produce of the vine could bring endless well-being to millions of Frenchmen working the soil and dressing the vine. But whatever his faults, he was a true apostle of Bacchus and his influence (as well as the new trim that he developed) spread throughout Europe and the New World. His students were legion and rose to important posts in newly established viticultural schools. In Italy his mission was carried out by Ottavio Ottavi.

After Guyot came the phylloxera and an end to his complacent assertions about vines as an inexhaustible source of riches. Its devastating impact was evident: it cleared away the old vineyards, the best, alas, with the worst. A whole army of new heroes now appeared; we need not repeat their names or their heroic combat against the dread disease. What emerged under their guidance were new vineyards with vines lined up in military ranks and files, neatly spaced, so that each could be easily treated with the chemicals necessary for its preservation. Gone were the best of the old vineyards, the product of centuries of layering, where the great haphazard profusion of vines resembled a disheveled mass covering the hillsides. When these withered and died, it left the land free for major modifications in vine culture. Under the former system, all cultivation was necessarily carried out by hand, but with vines neatly lined up, and with spaces between rows ranging from three to five feet, numerous growers abandoned the double-pronged hoe and shovel and resorted to various forms of plows.

Now the use of plows was not a complete novelty; owners of some large estates had introduced them and row-planting as early as the 1820s in order to reduce labor costs and turn the soil to a greater depth. In Burgundy the Viscount de la Loyère used horse-drawn plows so efficiently that his crop-sharers could cultivate a hectare in half a day. Consequently a small family was able to tend vineyards of five to six hectares, where by hand a single family could rarely handle more than two or three hectares.[2] Plows would probably have become more extensive during the 1850s and 1860s, as in the Mâconnais, Beaujolais, Languedoc and a few other areas where ordinaries were grown, but vignerons lacked skill in their use. Their blades frequently ripped through the tender roots lying close to the surface—a characterstic of hand-cultivated vines—and destroyed a year's crop. Besides, oxen, mules, horses, the only tractive power then known, nibbled the shoots on which the flowers had to grow to produce grapes. And finally labor was abundant and cheap and most vignerons distrusted innovations of this sort anyway.

But once the phylloxera destroyed a vineyard or demanded major changes in the struggle against it, once workers became scarce as a result of outward migration, and with capital for replanting less difficult to find, then new techniques formed part of the struggle for survival.

The first tasks in the revival of a vineyard were the uprooting of dead vines and deep-plowing to renovate the soil. The plowing had always been a tremendous labor, and had often been imperfectly carried out with the simple tools formerly available. During the phylloxera, however, there appeared various deep-plowing instruments activated by steam engines, or by animal power in smaller holding where steam proved too expensive. The steam tractor, recently introduced in France, was not feasible in most places, either because the area to be turned was too small or the hillside too steep. So a deep plow (*charrue défonceuse*) of large dimensions was hitched to a stationary engine and drawn forward by the use of steel cables. Since steam power was very expensive, animal traction often took its place, as indicated in figure 18. Even with animal power, the equipment needed for deep-plowing was far too expensive for most growers. They therefore either rented the equipment, needed rarely anyway, or contracted to have the work performed by a specialist.

Quite different were the much lighter, less expensive, plows for turning surface soil, that is, for light dressings. These were used frequently. One pioneer in the use of this sort of plow, as already stated, was the Viscount de la Loyère of Savigny near Chalons-sur-Saône. In the early nineteenth century he invented several horse-drawn cultivators, which could both turn the soil and uproot weeds. With his multishared cultivator a worker, using one horse, could dress nearly two hectares in a day, provided the rows of vines were forty inches apart (see figure 19). With his single-share plow he could bare vine roots without ripping them in the spring, and then, by attaching a "hiller" he could later pile or "hill" dirt to cover and protect them against winter cold.

In the second half of the century, as the planting of vines in rows won new converts, more efficient plows came onto the market. They were not radically different from earlier instruments, but their makers introduced devices which enhanced their efficiency, making it possible to plow closer into the row. These maneuvers were controlled by the contours of the plowshares, as illustrated in figure 20. Figure 21 illustrates an even more advanced instrument, the shares coming together (left) to pile earth on the vines, or (right) removing it to form a mound in the space between vine rows. Although vine plows did not come into general use before World War I, they were particularly prevalent in the Médoc, the Southwest, and the lower South, where many vineyards were newly planted on a large scale, making the plow almost mandatory. Muzzles were put over the mouths of draft animals to prevent them from feeding on vine shoots.

Two other factors encouraged larger owners to use plows: first, skilled vignerons became scarce, then wages doubled after midcentury, and, as we shall see, climbed even higher after 1900. Vineyards on moderately sloping hills in the Gironde, Burgundy, and Champagne could also accept plows without great difficulty. However on steep slopes no animal could drag a plow and maintain its equilibrium, nor could farmers turn their plows at the end of each furrow. They resorted therefore to plows attached to cables and drawn uphill by stationary winches worked by men or animals, a device similar, but on a miniature scale, to the deep plows described above. Even a small grower could manage with such a device, and yet few did so. Most peasant growers continued to till their lands with their hoes and picks; indeed, many workers employed to till

FIGURE 18: *Deep Plow with Stationary Engine*

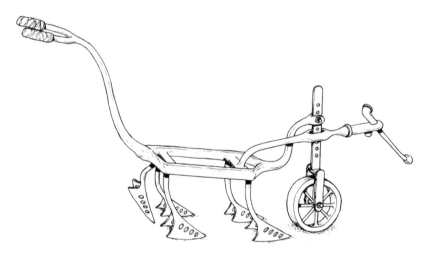

FIGURE 19: *Multishared cultivator*

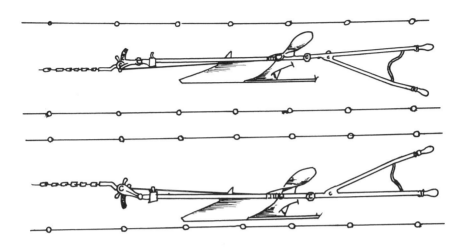

FIGURE 20: *Vine plow. Above, to pile soil on vine row; below, to pile soil between rows.*

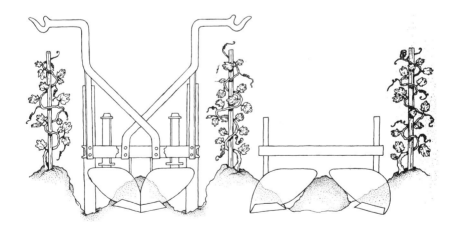

FIGURE 21: *Vine plow*

fine vines distrusted plows and held to the methods of their forebears. Such distrust was really a part of the same superstitious mentality which led vignerons to disbelieve in the existence of the phylloxera, or that it would invade their vines, and to refuse to take energetic measures against it when its destructiveness cancelled any doubts about its presence. On the other hand, the appearance of rows did encourage the long-recognized need of attaching vines to two or three levels of metal wires hung on posts planted along the rows. The use of wires, and the Guyot trim which necessitated them, spread rather rapidly, bringing additional order and discipline into the vineyards.

The new vines, the grafted Franco-Americans, imposed major changes on nearly every grower. Far more than before he had to become a skilled cultivator. Dressing ordinary vines had never been a complicated task, since several practices—weeding, pinching, nipping, etc.—had never formed part of peasant viticulture. But grafted vines were more demanding. American roots, constantly attacked by phylloxera, required far more nourishment than the old native roots. When vines had formed part of a polyculture including the extensive pasturing of animals, manure had been fairly abundant and was spread among vines. Growers of fine vines, of course, were horrified at the idea of frequent manuring. Branches that they layered received it, and mixed with vegetation as compost it was spread sparingly among bunched vines every three or four years, but they preferred to bring washed-down or new soil to their vines in place of manure. Growers of common vines, seeking quantity over quality, had not been reluctant to use it, but during and after the phylloxera many in southern France and Italy turned to viticulture exclusively. They pastured few animals, so gone was that reassuring pile of manure located near their cottages to protect it from theft.

Their problem was mitigated by the dread aphid itself, for the efforts to kill it ushered in the new age of chemicals. Of course chemical products had been applied earlier on a limited scale and a far more extensive use of sulphur beginning in the 1850s conquered the oïdium. The phylloxera was, none the less, the fillip to the new viticulture relying heavily on chemicals. Growers used them extensively against the aphid itself. Then when they turned to American roots, they discovered that these required chemical fertilizers both to survive the aphid and to produce a marketable crop. After growers overcame this problem, they discovered with consternation that grafted vines were especially subject to "mildieu," that is, mildew, a parasite which could and did (with insect assistance) ruin a year's crop in the late 1880s and 1890s. Vignerons soon recognized that they must chemically treat their new vines as a preventive, for once an attack of parasites began, the cure was inevitably too late to save the crop. The application of chemicals therefore became a regular practice and an additional cost in truly commercial undertakings.

Because growers had to apply the chemicals, there appeared not only a new industry to produce chemicals, but also a second to manufacture the instruments for their use. Since most chemicals were sold in solid form, then mixed with water, a large number of sprays entered the market. There were small ones that fit on the backs of men and worked by a hand lever and large ones with several nozzles and tanks that fit on wheeled carriages drawn by animals.

In addition to purchasing chemicals, the prices of which reflected their heavy demand, and the need of equally expensive applicators, there were labor costs for growers who hired others to cultivate their vines. The little grower, as part-owner, part-worker, could, by hiring himself out, profit from these added tasks, so long as the price of wine remained high enough. But the cost of dressing a small vineyard such as he owned or sharecropped rose proportionately: the cost of using the new machines went up in inverse proportion to the size of a vineyard, the cost per unit of chemicals also remained high for the limited quantities he required. This new method of cultivation, then, remained profitable during the 1880s and 1890s, because wine prices remained high.

No chemical, however, could protect the vigneron against the ravages of storms. Unlike parasites that required a certain time to attack a vine, a sudden hail storm could batter a vineyard in a few minutes, destroy much or all of a year's crop, and prove fatal to plants themselves if it wounded their wood. The new viticulture, although it conquered or at least learned to cohabit with phylloxera aphids, never achieved an adequate and generally applicable defense against excess rain, heavy winds, or hail. The best the small grower with limited capital could do was to plant his vines in widely spaced areas, so that hail could not affect them all, and to trim them adequately, so there was sufficient vegetation to allow for leaf loss and to protect grape clusters and wood. This was good advice but in severe storms no more effective than a wooden wall against a tidal wave.

A wooden wall could offer security against high winds and hail. Its costs, however, limited its use to the finest of vineyards—and these were chiefly in France. Hail, of course, plagued northern Italy and in the vineyards of Venetia it was a fairly frequent occurrence. However, as far as I can discover, Italians did not adopt walls or attempt to cover their vines, largely because so many of them were hung high on trees and simply uncoverable. Possibly some growers of the Barolo district in

Alba, who trimmed their vines *alla francese,* resorted to them, but I found no indication that they did. But some of the finer domaines in Bordeaux, Burgundy, and Champagne did use various materials against hail storms.[3]

There were two types of *abris,* or shelters, vertical and horizontal. Vertical defenses consisted simply of portable walls or screens, about two to three feet high and of varying lengths, usually two to six feet. Those made of wood used in Champagne were six feet long and cost 2,500 francs to defend one hectare. They lasted about twenty years, so the annual expense, including labor to install and remove them each year, plus amortization, came to 230 francs per hectare. These were the cheapest. Screens made of thin lathes came to 360 francs per year, those of *planchots* (small planks) to 340 francs. Horizontal screens made of heavy cloth laid on poles cost 390 francs, while those used in the vineyards of Moët and Chandon, made of straw mats laid on upright poles, cost about 445 francs. The severe winter of May 1897 revealed that vertical screens, while sometimes useful against winds and hail, offered no protection against frost.

Small vignerons, of course, could not bear these heavy expenses, even if they performed their own labor. Against hail, they continued to resort to thick smoke screens caused by burning damp straw, but this was hardly successful. In fact the syndicates or corporate groups organized to give the alarm and build these fires even dissolved themselves after a few years in Champagne. Nonetheless smoke remained a low-cost defense in the vine-grower's struggle against nature and proved effective on occasion against frost.

Against hail every tested method proved to be expensive and inconvenient. The screens were too costly for most growers, especially when grape prices began to fall after 1900. Around this time another device came on the market: cannons. These were not ordinary cannons; they shot no balls and were not designed to kill. Rather they looked like the smoke stacks of old-time locomotives, narrow at the breech, wide at the muzzle, and pointing straight up toward the sky. By setting off an explosive charge in a special chamber in the breech, the makers argued, a wave of turbulent air rose high up, disturbed atmospheric conditions, and disbursed any storm clouds threatening to form hail stones. One cannon alone could not do this; victory required, as in war, a whole battery spread over a geographic district, and some mountain growers of Stiria claimed to have achieved signal success with them. In high hope several Italian and French scientists attended demonstrations both in Switzerland and northern Italy.[4] Apparently there was some reason to believe that these barrages were effective if carried out repeatedly on a large scale, for some north Italian communes set up consortiums to purchase cannons (*antigrandini*), along with explosive charges. In consequence another industry quickly came into being as several industrialists began manufacturing them, and, of course, making pretty wild claims about their efficacy. On the basis of evidence available to us, none of these cannons set up over several hectares exercised a noticeable influence on the weather, but in northern Italy, where numerous consortiums were set up, experiments were not adequately carried out. The many small owners were too individualistic to join, and they also refused to help defray the costs of experiments, believing that someone else would bear the expense and they would profit anyway.[5] This was a repetition of their attitudes toward fighting the phylloxera.

More encouraging were the improvements in methods of trim and the use of chemicals to bring about earlier maturing of grapes in the fall. In the Bordelais the former wide dispersal of picking dates began to narrow around 1900, which meant that growers could prepare their equipment for making wine with greater confidence.

Science, Machines, and Viniculture

The manufacture of wine followed an evolution identical to that of grape-growing, for it too came under the influence of science. In fact a rather new and complicated branch of chemistry named "enology" now appeared and became a distinct field of study in several university curricula. It denoted the science of wine-making and maturing, and its practitioner became a highly trained scientist. The term viniculture did not disappear; on the contrary, it applied to the large majority of lesser-trained persons who made wine, almost always from their own grapes, using traditional or newly learned skills. Viniculture meant the general knowledge of wine manufacture, the know-how required, without necessarily including an understanding of the chemistry of wine. Many peasants and cellar masters were quite efficient viniculturists, but they could not qualify as technically trained enologists. The *tastevin* (wine taster) was their artifact; the test tube, microscope, and chemical formula were hardly familiar save to those few among them who had attended the special courses set up in several technical high schools.

It was undoubtedly inevitable that a special science of wine would emerge. Before the midnineteenth century there were no enologists in the strict sense, nor were there any schools specifically devoted to training them. Rather there were scientists, Gay-Lussac and Buchner, for example, who studied problems of great importance for growers, such as sugar content, the nature of fermentation, and so on, but who did not devote their full time to wine. Not even Pasteur, a major contributor to the industry, was an enologist in the true sense; he was a bacteriologist who devoted some time and effort to specific problems of wine and beer.

Now it will not do to be too stingy with awarding the title of enologist, because there existed in the eighteenth and nineteenth centuries—and today—a large number of men who combined an extensive knowledge of practical wine-making with some knowledge of chemistry. Men like Chaptal, Fabbroni, and François of Reims have been called enologists, with just cause. That they were amateurs does not weaken their claim; after all Darwin was an amateur in that he was largely self-taught. These early wine-makers were the major writers on the problems of the industry; they were the true popularizers of the knowledge available in the eighteenth and early nineteenth centuries. Chaptal was undoubtedly the most influential viniculturist at the turn of the century, rivaling Jules Guyot in popularity. Although he made no new discoveries, he knew the fundamentals of the trade and all the tricks of it, above all those developed over the centuries to safeguard new wine and improve its quality. He was translated into many languages, including Italian, and was probably more widely read than his contemporary Fabbroni. Chaptal was more the practical man, Fabbroni more the theorist; indeed the Italian came remarkably close to explaining the nature of fermentation. Had he not so firmly believed in the Phlogiston theory, he might have made a great advance in explaining the mysterious transformation of grape juice into wine. Most scientists and educated viniculturists understood superficially the process of fermentation, the chemical changing of sugar into alcohol and carbonic acid; but they did not know why this change took place nor the full extent of it, since many other changes occurred also.

As early as 1810 Joseph Gay-Lussac had worked out a chemical equation to explain the fermentation process, but not until Louis Pasteur, influenced by the suggestive mind of Fabbroni, did the learned world know why fermentation took place. Until the 1860s and 1870s many scientists believed in spontaneous generation and that fermentable liquids contained their own ferments.[6] Pasteur rejected this notion and proved that fermentation was caused by germs that settled on grapes during certain times of the year. He was able to demonstrate that yeasts were living organisms and responsible for causing fermentation. His work was expanded shortly before 1900, when Buchner discovered that the yeast cells themselves did not cause fermentation, but rather that they secreted the enzymes that were most directly the cause of it. Buchner's experiments, like those of Pasteur, proved that fermentation is an extremely complicated chemical reaction, in truth a long series of reactions, and that Gay-Lussac's equation was only a summary statement of it.

Pasteur also provided additional information about the importance of temperature as a factor in fermentation. By long experience viniculturists knew that excesses of cold and heat either prevented fermentation from beginning or brought it to a halt after it was underway. Once they understood the origins of fermentation, they set about to search for an ideal temperature for the best rate of fermentation. However neither they nor the generation of trained enologists who followed Pasteur discovered an ideal temperature because they could never agree among themselves about an ideal type of first fermentation, some favoring a long, slow action inside a closed vat, others a quick violent action in an open vat. This controversy shows the limits of scientific knowledge in the realm of taste.

Nonetheless Pasteur's studies did enable vintners to grow the kinds of yeast that encouraged the fermentation process and enhanced the finished product by protecting it from harmful yeasts; they also pointed the way to eliminating harmful bacteria that had, in the past, threatened maturing wine with terrible maladies. In short Pasteur did for large producers of still wines what François of Châlon had accomplished for those of sparkling wines: both greatly lowered the risk in production. François as regards bottle breakage, Pasteur as regards spoilage. Much spoilage had resulted from mannitic fermentation, a process that gave wine a bitter, unsavory taste. This was a problem serious enough when vinification occurred on a small scale; it was a major concern by the fifties and sixties, when the wine industry became truly big business. In the South, especially the still wine industry had followed sparkling wine into large-scale capitalist techniques; now Pasteurization offered such producers a form of quality control hitherto unknown, which certainly made for a much more secure investment.

Pasteurization was not merely a theory, it was a practical process invented by Pasteur himself. Since time immemorial wine had periodically turned bad, the result of numerous maladies: *piqure, graisse, pousse, tourne, amertune,* and so on. The great savant demonstrated in 1864 that microbes developing under favorable circumstances caused all these problems in the beverage. Winemen, though ignorant of the microbes' existence, used to burn a sulphured wick inside a half-filled barrel as a precaution against souring. This simple technology was often effective, but if sulphur ash got into the wine, it gave the final product a bitter taste as well as a putrid odor. Besides, sulphuring was not always effective. Pasteur found a more successful method for sterilizing wine—heating it. Since the Greeks at least, heating wine was considered a means—a trick even—for giving body to a thin must by causing some of the water in it to evaporate. The resulting product, however, generally acquired a "cooked" taste, which reduced its commercial quality. Naturally makers of fine wines looked askance at Pasteur's proposals and no rush to pasteurization occurred in 1868 when he first made it known.[7] Skillful viniculturists had always safeguarded their wines by maintaining cleanliness in their cellars and by carefully following strict methods of manufacture. Above all they meticulously cleaned their casks and racked with sufficient frequency. The microbes that attacked wine often settled and developed in the sediment, so the early and regular removal of the liquid from its sediment usually safeguarded it from contamination. Also good wine usually had sufficient alcohol and acidity to safeguard it from *mycoderma aceti* and *mycoderma vini*, two bugbears of the wine world.

Yet Pasteur proved that microbes could ruin fine as well as common wines. Through pictoral reproductions of his microscope slides he revealed to winemen the minute life that abounded in their beverages; he pointed out the presence of germs and the differences between alcohol yeasts (that turned sugar into alcohol) and harmful yeasts (such as those causing *tourne*). Then he displayed the corpses of this microscopic life in wines that he had subjected to heat, that is, had pasteurized. Certainly the merits of this process were quickly recognized by a new generation of enologists, many of whom were his students. Many became university professors in science faculties, where they spread his ideas. Among the most renowned was Ulysse Gayon, a leading member of the school of science in the University of Bordeaux, whose work with his colleague Dubourg during the 1880s and 1890s complemented that of their master. Remembering that Pasteur had experimented with some of Burgundy's fine wines—Nuits, Volnay, Chambertin, Romanée, and Vougeot—they used various wines of Bordeaux with equally successful results. Of course during the phylloxera attention turned toward vines, and the heroes of the world of wine were viticulturists. But by the late 1880s, as wine became a rapidly rising economic force and science a dominant factor in public opinion, the lessons of Pasteur came to the fore. Not only growers, but wholesalers and shippers came to recognize the usefulness of pasteurization as a means of safeguarding their investments. Soon a new technology emerged for the quick sterilization of wine as well as other liquids.

The process was rather simple; it required merely the heating of wine to 55 or 60 degrees centigrade or in some cases to 65, depending on the amount of time that particular liquid remained at the required temperature. The experiments of Pasteur as well as those of Ulysse Gayon revealed that all wines with at least 8 percent alcohol became sterilized if heated to 60 degrees for fifteen seconds; if of 12 percent alcohol, they became germ free at only 57 degrees centigrade in the same amount of time. Pasteur was forced to manufacture his own instruments or at least design them, but Gayon was able to experiment with several heating devices recently put on the market. There were small ones, designed for wine; later larger industrial types originally produced for pasteurizing beer were adapted to wine.

Gayon experimented for several large Bordeaux merchants, using wine in bottles. Naturally the liquid could not simply be poured into a caldron and cooked directly over a fire, a *bain-marie* or double boiler was necessary. Because wine expanded under high temperatures, bottles had to be solidly made to withstand the heat and all corks had to be tied on, or special corking devices inserted. A nimble worker could prepare the corks of about a thousand bottles a day. There were boilers of various sizes in which bottles stood in water up to their necks, as shown in figure 22. For the simplest, a worker inserted a thermometer in a water-filled bottle that served as temperature indicator, filled the boiler with water, and prepared a fire under it. A large commercial model made by the German firm of Boldt and Vogel, had a capacity of 5,000 bottles a day and cost 1,750 francs, plus the expense of installation. There were also large heaters made of masonry, able to contain up to 10,000 bottles at one time. These, like the Boldt and Vogel type, used steam rather than hot water, but Gayon complained that it was not possible to obtain a uniform temperature throughout the boiler, and filling and emptying it of bottles required too much time.

Without doubt these were serious problems for large wine-growers and merchants, particularly for those handling common wines. After each heating in a small boiler, all the water had to be emptied and replaced, requiring money and time for reheating; in a large boiler only half the water was replaced but it still had to be heated. Steam obviated this cumbersome process, but generating steam required costly equipment and fuel. With the decline of wine prices in the 1890s and the startling rise of other costs, pasteurization in bottles represented a serious obstacle in a competitive market. Growers or merchants handling 30,000 hectoliters or more required a less cumbersome method, which they found in devices that heated the wine while it was still in wood. Under this system wine flowed or was pumped from a filled cask into a long metal coil immersed in suitably hot water; it then flowed into another coil to be cooled before returning to a clean, disinfected cask. Rapid and easy, this process had only one serious disadvantage: the wine might come into contact with air and if the air were cool and the wine still hot, the latter would acquire a harsh "cooked" taste. Despite this danger the big southern winemen, with their mass production, sophisticated techniques, and rising total costs, were able to fit in this process in the many already required. By more efficient use of machinery they were able to absorb the extra costs—if only to insure the good condition of their products.

Pasteurization offered certain advantages beyond the killing of germs. Even properly balanced wine not likely to be harmed by microbes could at times be improved by heating. Hot wines which returned before cooling to wooden casks underwent chemical transformations that gave them the reddish-brown color and rich taste of old vintages. In this way young wines too acid and harsh could be "mellowed" by artificial aging, a result of interest to sellers of ordinaries. Skeptics insisted that heating gave wine a burnt taste. Gayon replied that wine suffered a cooked taste only when pasteurization was improperly carried out, and even then the taste

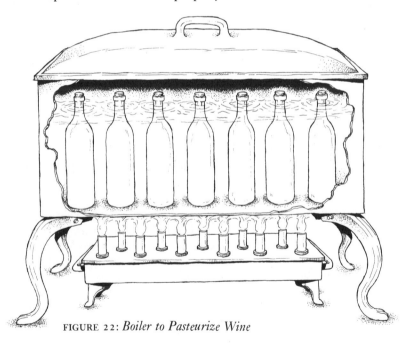

FIGURE 22: *Boiler to Pasteurize Wine*

disappeared with time. He organized several blind tastings, as had Pasteur, and experts could not distinguish between treated and untreated beverages; in fact, some experts believed that the bottles subjected to heat were superior to the others.[8]

Pasteurization was probably the most important innovation in the wine industry after the 1860s. It undoubtedly saved many wines from going sour and it secured a considerable degree of quality control over the final product. It made the chemical laboratory an indispensable part of the cellar, for wine, both during and long after its primary fermentation, had to be analyzed periodically for its alcoholic and acid content, its double pulse, so to speak. A loss of alcohol, a rise of acidity forewarned of deterioration and the need for immediate action, first with the microscope to discover the microbe, then with the sterilizing apparatus. Instruments to measure alcohol and acidity, some dating back decades, were improved in order to increase their accuracy. For the small grower, unlearned in chemistry and lacking precision instruments, there soon appeared several publicly supported enological laboratories, as well as many private enologists, who examined and reported on samples sent in. Unfortunately no process could save a wine already badly stricken by germs and harmful yeasts. Pasteurization was chiefly preventative, not curative, and frequent chemical analysis was necessary to catch a malady in time.

Happily not all wines became sick. Good vinification practice was the best prevention and remained so. What occurred was an expanding knowledge of how to make good wine, and, after commerce grew, how to make it in massive quantities. In terms of quantity there occurred a little vinicultural revolution. The wine industry tended to follow in the track of all industries; that is, it became increasingly mechanized. Had it been centered in England where the Industrial Revolution began, perhaps steam power would have been used earlier. But the major wine areas of Europe—the Rhine Valley excepted—were located precisely in those areas where mechanized industry made only slow progress. In fact the new viniculture had its widest application in the lower South of France and Italy, two economically backward regions. These were not even centers of an agricultural revolution; economically and technologically they were stubbornly backward, save for wine. But then even economically advanced areas such as Bordeaux and Turin offered little incentive for either the Gironde or Piedmont, where according to contemporary reports there was little machinery. The major innovation there was to use more productive vines in order to get more juice, but winemen fermented and processed very much as their forbears had done.

Unfortunately we do not know how many mechanical devices driven by nonhuman power were introduced into the cellars of France and Italy. (Animals could be used in the open, but inside the cellars the odor of their excrement would harm the delicate aromas that winemen sought to preserve.) Governments published data on the number of machines in use, but did not distinguish between viniculture and other forms of production. Undoubtedly mechanization went ahead more slowly in wine-making than in other industries; the mass of growers displayed an entrenched technological conservatism and capital was not available for investing in machines. Italy was seriously deficient in liquid wealth, while France, where rural credit was somewhat more available, staggered under the blows of the phylloxera. The aphid not only wiped out many vignerons, it diverted most of the money reserves they had built up during the golden age away from viniculture and into viticulture. The wineman who grew his own grapes and produced his own wine could hardly both replant his vineyard and modernize his cellar. Here is to be found part of the explanation of the extensive transfer of wine-making from landowners to merchants who enjoyed easier access to investment capital.

There were, of course, wine producers who had other sources of income, because they were large industrialists, financiers, and rentiers holding stocks and state bonds, and who could divert some of their nonagricultural wealth into new equipment. However even these persons tied up much of their surplus capital in replanting. Far more independent of viticulture were the large wholesalers who bought newly fermented wine, aged it in their own cellars, and sold it on national and international markets. They were, to be sure, adversely affected by the phylloxera in France, but they readily discovered that they could import wine from Italy and Spain, doctor it if need be, blend it with their native beverages, and sell it as an authentic French creation. Their revenues did not suffer long; in fact, some of them purchased vineyards at drastically low prices and used their capital both to replant and to modernize their vinicultural equipment. Such concentration of production and merchandising became particularly noticeable in the Bordelais and the lower South of France. It did not, however, seriously reduce the number of small vignerons, whose comeback became apparent by the 1890s, and whose presence remained a necessary complement to large landowners who hired them as part-time laborers. Big merchants also required large numbers of vignerons and continued as in the past to buy either their must or their newly fermented wine. On an increasing scale, moreover, they purchased grapes from small growers and made the wine them-

selves, or rather, they hired professional enologists and cellarers to make
and age it. This policy became the ideal of a new generation of winemen,
the creators of the new agricultural schools, the men who wrote most of
the articles in the newly established wine journals. But more on this
later.

Mechanization also depended on the foundation in greater numbers of
truly large-scale viti-vinicultural establishments, literally wine factories,
hiring many workers and using power-driven machinery as normal procedure. This phenomenon was not a novelty; there had been big producers before midcentury using hand-driven devices, and their number went
up after 1850. What was new was the increasing application of steam to
drive machinery and, after 1900, of internal combustion engines. Naturally only large plants found it profitable to use steam power; but small
gasoline-driven engines and then electric motors made it possible for
smaller growers to function more efficiently and to compete with their
larger homologs.

Wine factories were most prominent in Champagne, the lower South,
and the Bordelais. A good example was the Domaine of Jouarres, located
in the Minervois, in the department of Aude, purchased by Leopold
Roudier, a banker from Béziers, after the phylloxera ruined it. With 215
hectares of vines, he and his manager could produce 30,000 hectoliters of
wine in a good year, though not high-quality wine, since the grapes were
chiefly Aramon, Carignane, Alicante, and Terret Bouschet, typical
grapes of mass-producing vineyards. The labor force varied between 120
and 140 men and women, nearly 30 of whom were lodged and fed on the
premises as part of their wage. During the harvest this number rose
considerably, for a day's picking could produce 1,400 hectoliters of
grapes. This amount required the use of twenty fermenting vats, each
with a capacity of 350 to 360 hectoliters.

The use of steam power to activate nearly all the wine-making equipment permitted a considerable reduction in the labor force, a mere four
men could handle most of the miscellaneous tasks, while four others
carried out the pressing. A separate room housed a steam engine, an
internal combustion engine, and a distillery. Here were generated the
twenty-two horsepower needed.

When fresh grapes arrived, workers loaded them into small wagons on
rails which carried them to mechanical elevators with hoppers that
hauled the grapes up to a rapiely turning crusher. From there they fell
into a stemmer and then, on steeply inclined metal slides, moved downward into fermenting vats made of special masonry. The crusher could
handle up to 400 kilos (800 pounds) of grapes per minute, a remarkable

capacity, but necessary, to insure that all the grapes picked in one day would be crushed and loaded into vats within several hours. The stemmer had to function at an equally high capacity, especially for grapes destined to make white wine. Two large and four small pumps facilitated the movement of wine through large tubes from vat to cask or from cask to cask. The total capacity of this wine factory could be racked in a week. Four large presses stood near the vats and after four days of fermentation for red wines the skins were transported to the presses on a conveyor belt. The presses were the only machines not mechanized. The explanation given was that these presses required much less manpower than other types—two men sufficed for the functioning of each. In addition steam power and hydraulic equipment would be too expensive for machines used only during a few weeks of the year.[9]

The construction of the wine factory of Jouarres was planned with the latest enological discoveries in mind. On the whole there was little information about crushing and stemming, save that both were recommended in the North. But some Frenchmen and most Italians recommended against stemming the highly sugared grapes grown in hot southern climates, since these grapes often combined excessive quantities of sugar with insufficient acidity and the stems provided the must with additional tannin. Now, however, laboratory technicians could, for a fee, offer all growers more exact measurements of the sweet and bitter elements in a given must. Knowing this in advance the grower could either add sugar or acid before fermentation began and profit from a better balanced product.

When the insufficient natural acidity and excess sugar of southern European and North African grapes combined with overly high temperature, the yeasts sometimes simply stoped functioning, and the fermentation become "stuck." Or they might fall victim to mannitic fermentation, when harmful microbes grew, causing a sour taste and spoilage. Pasteurization was the most effective way to preserve such a wine.

Various solutions were offered for overheating. This problem only occurred when large quantities of must had to be handled, about 300 or more hectoliters, in one vat. Since wood did not absorb and radiate much heat, it was preferred in the North, the East, and central areas of France and Italy, where the chill nights of October could discourage fermentation. In the South, however, growers turned to reinforced concrete for vats with large capacities. The necessariely thick walls of a concrete vat, by absorbing a part of the heat, stabilized the must's temperature, encouraging a more even and fine development. When vats contained over 400 hectoliters, however, not even concrete sufficed.

Technicians than began adding pipes through which the must could circulate outside of the vats, exiting from the bottom, passing through cool water reservoirs, or cool air, and returning in a showery spray at the top (see figure 23). This system not only maintained the must at a desired and uniform temperature, it also provided for its more even distribution in the vat. Because it was difficult to control temperatures in the South, enologists concerned with quality recommended relatively small vats, like those of Jouarres (of course the large number of small vats brought their accumulated capacity to 7,200 hectoliters). But despite the advice of enologists winemen tended to use masonry and to prefer truly large fermenting vessels. Just after midcentury the Estate Puech-Ferrier erected eight vats, each with a capacity of 650 hectoliters. And in the late phylloxera period the big Salt Company of the Midi, as it began to diversify its activities, used vats with over 700-hectoliter capacity, massive containers about four meters high and four meters square. These vats of chemically treated cement, apart from the decided advantages they offered for the special heat problems of southern vintners, were also less expensive to buy, costing only three or four francs per hectoliter of capacity, compared to four or five for wood. On the other hand, according to Jules Guyot, the wine made in them was less colored and substan-

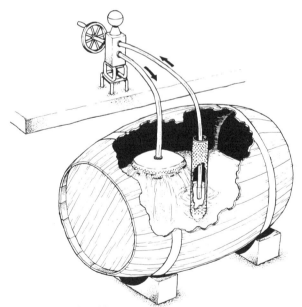

FIGURE 23: *Spray to Cool Fermenting Must*

tial than wine made in wooden vats. And of course the makers of fine wines would have nothing to do with cement. With suitable disdain, they remained faithful to oak, at least most of them did, up to World War I.

This conservatism revealed not a distrust of innovation as such, but a refusal to accept new techniques that seemed to sacrifice quality for quantity. Winemen were far more willing to utilize new equipment if it conformed to their goals, and this was particularly the case as regards crushing and pressing operations. Since time immemorial grapes had been crushed by feet, either by a man stomping up and down upon them in a barrel with one end removed, or by several men dancing upon them and forcing them through a large grill positioned atop a sizable vat (see figure 6). Then after the primary fermentation reached its end, sturdy men placed the skins in huge presses, activated by enormous flywheels or capstans (see figure 15). Probably the press in Clos Vougeot was the largest in existence, requiring eight to ten men to bring its mighty weight down on the mass of grapes placed in its square basket. Even smaller presses demanded the energies of three or four stout peasants to get all the liquid from the skins, and they were quite expensive, far beyond the means of simple vignerons.

In their favor, then, was the combination crusher and press, which the Morineau company put on the market in the 1880s (see figures 24 to 25). Similar devices bore the brand names of Poinsteaud and Mabille. In each case two men could rather easily set the mechanism in motion, and in a brief time grapes were both crushed and pressed. This apparatus was especially useful for making white wine from red grapes, since the juice could be separated from the pulp before the coloring agents in the skins had time to affect its color. In the models displayed, the crank handles clearly are designed for hand use; but mechanical power could be easily applied. Even where it was not, this press lent itself to small production and a father and son, or two sons, could readily set it in motion. The endless-screw press offered other advantages to the small producer: it was mobile, that is, animal-drawn, and therefore could be rented by little vignerons (see figure 26). It produced not only economic, but social consequences, since one man could activate it.

Other advances came about in the enological laboratories, in the study of wine chemistry. Through the use of microscopes and various chemical analyses a new generation of scientists came to learn more about the physical structure of wine. In the cellars of agricultural schools and experiment stations true enologists studied such various phenomena as fermentation and the chemical composition of wine, the influence of soil on

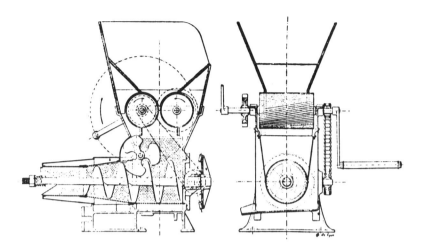

FIGURE 24: *Combination Crusher and Press*

FIGURE 25: *Crusher-Press in Action*

that composition, the role of various sweetening properties in grapes, that of acids, and how to apply sweetening or aciduous additives in order to achieve a balanced must and from it a marketable wine. Enology did more than satisfy man's ever-present curiosity about his world; it certainly encouraged the making of better wine and it helped safeguard the sole or chief source of income of well over a million growers, to say nothing of wholesale and retail sellers. In addition, much of the government's income derived from its taxes on alcoholic drinks. The new enology could not guarantee to save producers from all the catastrophes of nature. Nor did it encourage the doctoring of any beverage to the point of fraud or to the detriment of public health. Rather, with its safeguards against maladies and its remedies for wines lacking balance it offered a more solid basis for determining wine policies.

There were at least two fairly well-defined schools of thought about wine policy, that is, about the goals and values of production. For one school, whom we can call the gastronomers, the making of wine was an art requiring love, care, even self-sacrifice, in order to achieve the ultimate in quality. Monetary considerations did not have to be ignored, but they should not lead to an abandonment of excellence, because quality wine would always sell, even in less than good years. The fact that wine

FIGURE 26: *Portable Grape Press*

of a given year would differ from that of other years was not a misfortune. Rather this variety enhanced the interest and excitement of tasting by allowing for surprises, the *inattendu,* and increased all the more the value of great vintages. Refinement and elegant taste must prevail in wine for the same reason it prevailed in all the arts, to give a sense of quality to life. Needless to say, this was an aristocratic and esthetic attitude, which found its echo in the upper levels of society, if only because fine wine was expensive. However modified versions of it appeared frequently in wine reviews and in the local press. An educated person did not have to buy the most costly beverages to enjoy both good savor and exciting variety. What was important was to avoid the boredom of standardization.

At the opposite extreme was a school of enologists calling precisely for a standard wine. In France Jules Guyot and many agricultural professors urged both a viticulture and a viniculture capable of producing the same type and quality of wine, year in and year out. In this way a buyer would know precisely the taste of the wine he preferred and become habituated to it. He must never be disappointed by it, lest he turn away from the market. Such a policy was less the goal of vignerons, often ignorant of the market, but was decidedly that of large merchants, who looked upon a standardized product as a safer investment. The mass production of wine that began after midcentury encouraged standardization, and the new enology enabled the seller to achieve it. There would no longer be bad years; but there would no longer be good ones either.

Because this policy was considered indispensable for the conquest and retention of foreign markets, some of Italy's most prominent enologists began to preach it. Discerning in the phylloxera invasion of France an unprecedented opportunity for their compatriots, they encouraged the imitation of French methods in order to invade markets the French could no longer satisfy.

Their goals reflected vinicultural conditions in the peninsula. Italian wine publicists went further than the French in condemning peasants as producers. Parliamentary committees, vinicultural journalists, professors in agriculture schools, and practically everybody else who could write and taste deplored the low quality of peasant wine. And they were undoubtedly correct in their disapproval and in their call for improvements. This new direction became discernible even before the phylloxera struck France. At the first enological congress, meeting in Turin in 1875, the roster of professors who took the lectern unanimously denounced the uncertain quality of peasant wines and the lack of uniformity and of a standard wine. They were made aware that compatriots living in foreign countries complained of the low quality and excessive variability of wine Italy exported. The first shipment was often acceptable; subsequent ones fell below its quality. This was not necessarily an act of fraud, but often the result of a deficient harvest and the mediocre wine resulting from it. Led by the Ottavis, the professors called for a new policy. They wanted vines to descend from trees into regular vineyards; they wanted growers in a given area to concentrate on the fewest of vine varieties and to concern themselves chiefly with growing grapes. They pushed the division of labor to its extreme: educated peasants were to grow vines and sell grapes to professional winemakers organized in large companies directed by competent enologists and market analysts. These companies would then sell their produce to large commercial firms that possessed the ability to open and hold new markets. The tastes of foreign peoples must be studied and, as in France, wine produced to satisfy those tastes. Italian enology had become almost totally dominated by the commercial spirit. Against it arose the aging count Ernesto di Sambuy of Piedmont, who denounced the addition of sugar, acid, or other ingredients as a fraudulent practice. Enologist, he insisted, should not encourage producers to fabricate "little Bordeaux" wines but to produce natural, authentic local beverages.[10] The Sambuy brothers, along with the great ampologist Odart, had long emphasized quality for the produce of Piedmont. By no means did that policy die with them, but as world demand grew, the siren song of quantity pealed louder, even in the Astigiani and Barolo districts, where the great Nebbiolo yielded some ground before that bumptious commoner, the Barbera. In Tuscany the Ricasoli firm continued to produce fine chianti, but on the world market its plebeian imitations, dressed in the already famous straw-covered *fiasco*, became better known, even though large quantities of it had no more relation to the Chianti district than the name.[11] While these dicta came to be held by a majority of market-minded growers and enologists, they did not penetrate the vineyard population, did not bring the vines down from the trees, and did not, in consequence, make it possible for Italian winemen greatly to change their social conditions.

CHAPTER TEN

The Human Element

The human element in the wine industry was like the weather, uncertain and unpredictable. And yet without the intervention of man there would be no wine worth drinking, because it was he who transformed the small, hard, bitter grapes of ancient wild vines into the lush, sugary fruit of today, and it was he who created from them a beverage capable of becoming the nectar of the gods.

By no means were all vignerons so lofty in their aspirations that they had the gods in mind when they fermented their juice. The vast majority were simple peasant farmers of varying skills growing vines and making wine for home consumption and, until the 1850s, for a local market. Undoubtedly most of them cultivated vines as a secondary or lesser occupation. According to French government data their number stood at over two million in 1828, a total undoubtedly including nearly every farmer who harvested grapes, whether or not for wine-making. The huge numbers for several northern departments make it obvious that table-grape-growers and numerous farmers with a few vine rows planted among other crops were listed. For example, the cold northern department of Seine-et-Oise alone boasted nearly 95,000 viticulturists, while the great vineyards of Gironde counted merely 60,000, and Hérault only 76,000!

More realistic for the production of wine grapes were the figures for 1869: 1,342,000 growers, and at the peak of 1875–1876: 1,865,000. Because of the phylloxera the total for 1896 fell to 1,492,000 and then, with that menace overcome, the total rose to 1,700,000 in 1905. The crisis years of 1906–10 drove desperate vignerons once again to abandon vines, and their ranks diminished to about 1,498,000 in 1913.[1]

A comparison of 1828 and 1913, although the data are of uncertain value, indicates approximately some of the changes induced in the viticultural population. Notable was their retreat from the North as table 16 makes clear:

TABLE 16: *Geographic Location of Vignerons*

Department	1828	1913
Seine-et-Oise	94,838	4,690
Seine	5,580	391
Seine-et-Marne	27,100	5,413
Aisne	16,579	2,628
Meuse	30,190	5,696

Source: Vidalenc, 142; *Ann. statis*, vol. 33 (1913) 124–26

TABLE 17: *Geographic Location of Viticulturists, 1908*

Region	Total numbers
Mediterranean South	199,827
South West	382,373
East	306,087
Loire Valley	195,422
Other	481,202
Total	1,564,911 (excluding Corsica)

Source: *Ann. statis*, vol. 29 (1909) 155.

Where did all of these northern growers go? A large number went to Paris or northern industrial cities where they became drinkers rather than makers of wine. There is no reason to believe that they emigrated in large numbers to more favorable locations after 1850, because the rising price of grains provided them a good income and the urban market for table grapes encouraged many to abandon commercial growing of wine grapes when cheap wine carried in railway cars invaded northern markets. The same tendency appeared in the mountainous regions of central France. In consequence vignerons finally clustered in the regions most favorable to the vine.

Since the figures in table 17 do not include the families of growers, they must be increased about four times. And to define quantitatively the true wine population of France, we must add nongrowers whose livelihoods depended entirely or substantially on the wine industry; their numbers, with their families, attained perhaps a million. Included among them were persons in the wine trade. Wholesalers alone rose from 24,693 in 1969 to 33,960 in 1908, and retailers in spirits were legion.[2]

There were also the personnel of large wholesale houses as well as those of the champagne companies, not a negligible figure. Moët and Chandon employed about 1,150 workers full time in 1880 and 400 part time. Two important groups heavily dependent on wine were the coopers and bottle makers; however their number seems to have declined in the later nineteenth century as these industries became mechanized. In compensation there was an increase in the population of workers engaged in the manufacture of vinicultural equipment and of the chemicals widely used in postphylloxera viticulture and wine-making. Added all together these wine people accounted for between 7 and 10 percent of France's total population from about the 1840s on.

Probably the *vignaioli* constituted roughly the same percentage of Italy's people, but documents to identify them as a definite group are incomplete and far more untrustworthy than those of France. Given the highly mixed planting system south of the Alps, even in the areas of fine wine, local administrators could not pick out and count the true vine-trimmer with even a pretense of accuracy; they could not even survey precisely the number of hectares devoted to viticulture when vines not only stood interspersed with other food crops but hung from live trees that were also part of general farming.

Social Structure

For reasons hardly requiring explanation man has played the primary role in the history of wine. Nature in her whimsical ways gave forth the soil, the grape, the sun, and rain, but there was no wine until man deliberately set about making it, and the wine of his making became an equally deliberate reflection of his taste. Wine has been for many centuries a social product; that is, an industrial and commercial object of varying value, both made and consumed on the basis of a division of labor and on unequal distribution of wealth. Grape varieties varied in quality and man conceived of them as a pyramidal hierarchy. His conception grew partly from his recognition of their natural qualities and was partly a projection of the historical stratification of his own society. The class structure of society at large reproduced itself in that of viticulture.

Landlords

Prior to the Revolution of 1789 in France and the Napoleonic invasion in Italy, the production of most fine and much good ordinary wine was in the hands of clerical, noble, and bourgeois landowners. It is clear that the long evolution of techniques for growing fine grapes and making superior wines was carried out by a handful of knowledgeable and patient churchmen and nobles whose search for quality was part of their elevated outlook on life, part of their savoir vivre. By the seventeenth and eighteenth centuries more well-to-do commoners—bourgeois—had purchased large domains partly planted in quality vines and, like the nobles, participated actively or through their hired managers and cellarers, in the creation of estimable beverages. The production of fine wine had finally become a badge of distinction, a confirmation of lofty status, and in some lucky instances, a source of income. The eighteenth century, when rising prices and growing markets encouraged vine-planting, was one of expansion, both of production and knowledge. Landowners of the higher social levels, noble and nonnoble, consolidated their positions, while some owners of lesser stature began their social rise. At the bottom of this social pyramid were numerous peasant vignerons and rural artisans with small holdings and laborers in the vineyards of the well-to-do. There was a blurring, but by no means a serious weakening, of social lines in the world of viticulture.

The Revolution of 1789–94 modified this socioviticultural structure, and we underscore the word *modified* because it did not completely upset or eliminate acquired positions. By no means was the pyramid turned upside down in France, and the spread of revolutionary ideas to Italy had even less practical effect, because the Italian middle and peasant classes were less active than their French counterparts in accepting the ideal and practice of social mobility.

The most significant change was the near elimination of churchmen from the highest rank. In France even moderate revolutionary governments confiscated church lands and put them up for sale. The best clerical vineyards now fell into the hands of a rich middle class enjoying wealth chiefly of financial and mercantile origins. Some noble land was also confiscated and bought at auction by well-to-do bidders, but it is now clear that the nobility was not eliminated from the highest echelons, for it recovered about half of its land through official restoration or repurchase.

Modification was far more extensive in France than in Italy. French Jacobins urged their Italian allies to take over church lands in the north, but completion of this process had to await the unification of the peninsula after 1860. The nobility was hardly disturbed in the possession of its lands and vineyards in the vast Po Valley of the North, and not all in the Center and South.

What then, was the social structure of winemen in the first half of the nineteenth century, and what were the general tendencies? The peak of the pyramid was probably as narrow as before 1789, but the church had been replaced by a plutocracy in which the remnants of the old aristocracy rubbed vine stems with newly made nobles deriving their titles from the Napoleonic and Orleanist regimes and with a relatively new category of rich commoners. The term "commoner" here must not be interpreted too literally. Among its members were wealthy bankers, realtors, some industrialists, and, of increasing importance, big wholesalers (*négociants*), all men who, if they were not noble, were surely notables. There was a certain amount of intermarriage between the nobles and the notables, especially in the Champagne region.

From a purely viticultural point of view, the disappearance of the Church was unfortunate. It had provided considerable capital and remarkably knowledgeable and progressive monks who had pioneered in vine-growing and wine-making. Moreover these monks were, so to speak, resident owners; they lived in, for, and with their vineyards and cellars. The nonclerical owners—and this included many nobles—were often absent from their estates for most of the year, returning only for vacation and the harvest. They did, however, hire skilled managers and cellarers, and those who had bought clerical vineyards usually maintained the old level of quality or even improved it. The Clos Vougeot is the most notable example of such continuity.

Just below this elite of the elite came another group of notables, who took a more direct and active role in the wine industry. They belonged to the same upper social category but were less wealthy, less inclined to view a great vineyard as a fine diamond or a handsome mistress acquired for one's adornment or ostentatious display. More rural than urban or more effectively combining the two worlds, they either lived on their estates or in a nearby town: Bordeaux, Libourne, Dijon, Mâcon, Beaune, to name only the most prominent. This group played a key role in the rising wine industry, often experimenting and innovating, were active in local agricultural societies, and their numbers steadily expanded during the century. It was they who saved the industry when it was threatened by powdery mildew in the 1850s and the phylloxera in the 1870s and 1880s. They were the best elements of non-Parisian France, a true gentry of old landed families, as well as a middle class of provincial lawyers, medical doctors, university professors, and a large number of wine wholesalers whose operations were limited to their regions. One salient characteristic of the century was the increasing role of merchants. They bought more vineyards and began to produce the wines they sold;

and with greater intensity than in the past they became *marchands-éle-veurs;* that is, they bought fresh musts or new wines from local growers, blended them to acquire a uniform taste, and then sold the product under their own labels. Most wine entering the market, while it was not fermented by them, was matured under their care and in their cellars.

Many large and medium land owners, especially those who lived on the land, were not friendly to urban merchants and developed a *mystique* intended to preserve their old viticultural traditions from the inroads of capitalists from the city. Their aim was to improve the processes of grape and wine production, to win a position of independence vis-à-vis the wholesalers and their local agents, and to keep the peasants on the land. Since they were traditionalists only in a social sense, not as regards technical innovation, they looked to Jules Guyot as their chief spokesman, or to his local advocates, such as A. Petit-Lafitte in the Bordelais. In Italy, gentlemen farmers and politicians such as Ricasoli lived by the same credo.

Their ideal society was strictly hierarchical, with a landowning class at the top, a dependent peasantry at the bottom, and no one but the parish priest in between. In the thinking of Jules Guyot, vines more than any other crop provided the basis for a return to an earlier age enjoying a more associative style of life. His desire, as far as we can discover, was not to restore the feudal system; rather he expressed a gnawing fear that peasants had become too independent of rural notables. Not only had they won the ballot in 1848, but new styles of life were made possible by the increase of urban jobs and easier transport away from their natal villages. That this disquietude was less keen in Italy undoubtedly resulted from two factors: the *Risorgimento* gave a common purpose to much of the population, and the lower classes did not get the vote until the eve of World War I.

An ideal society was associative in the sense that it functioned according to a division of labor. Guyot despised the idle rich as well as the idle poor. He was a leftover from the eighteenth-century physiocratic school in that he saw agriculture as the true and unique source of value and wealth; industry, trade, finance merely transformed that wealth. "It is human labor, applied to the soil, that makes all capital." [3] He therefore condemned city-dwelling landowners, who drained rural France for their own benefit, and urban bankers who possessed wealth without working and who loaned it to active agriculturists only at usurious rates. For Guyot work was the cornerstone of a civilized society and he anathematized all the idle. He was one of those odd characters who was in the forefront of viticultural technology, yet who was conservative to the point of paternalism as regards political and social institutions. For the same reason that he condemned the planting of good and bad vines in the same plot of land, he distrusted social relations of the sort that dissolved mutual bonds between large owners and small and between all owners and their workers. He made no effort to bridle his attacks upon absenteeism among owners or his condemnation of the inefficiency of untutored peasants and their backward viticulture. Rich owners who deplored the absence of field labor must share the blame for the fact that peasant wine, selling at low prices, barely sufficed to cover costs and therefore encouraged peasants to join the exodus from rural France. He vigorously insisted that progressive vine culture was the surest way to retain a large part of the peasant population on the land.

If we remember that his philosophy matured during the Golden Age of high prices and easy sales, his arguments hold much truth. Unfortunately he imagined that these good times, the true *Belle Epoque* of viniculture, would never end. The depression of the 1840s should have been a warning, but he ignored it and went about France preaching his doctrines, some of which were perfectly sound. To hold vignerons on the land, at least two conditions were necessary: first, vines should be planted only in places suitable to them, that is, on slopes, and especially in soil too rocky and poor for other crops. He saw in the vine a colonizer of areas not favored by naturally good soil. His views emphasized quality, but more plebeian in outlook than many owners, he did not belittle quantity—perhaps because large quantities of wine did not adversely affect prices during the Second Empire. His other condition was that the rural landowners seriously undertake to help their vignerons and to educate them in good viti-viniculture; they must seriously play the role of father of the people. These conditions would give the peasants ample reason for remaining on the land, for they would enjoy the concerned protection of the owner, a fairly rounded agricultural enterprise with vines an important but not exclusive crop, and ample revenue. Moreover the wine produced under these conditions would be pure and wholesome, a true *"boisson hygiénique."* Needless to say Guyot firmly approved of the crop-sharing system, the *vigneronnage.* By attaching the vigneron symbiotically to the owner, it made them partners, moreover it encouraged the peasant to produce a good crop because his own interests were involved. The wage system seemed to Guyot a bad one for agriculture, since it created antagonism between owners and workers and intensified class hostility because rural wages could never be high enough to satisfy workers. He insisted that the wage system was largely responsible for depopulation and that the Beaujolais was a good example of how crop-sharing would hold peasants.

Now Guyot and his disciples were by no means reactionaries. Part of what he wrote about the social consequences of the wage system was quite correct, and the rural exodus, a mere trickle in his time, became a torrent several decades later. Nor was he averse to the extension of an independent class of property-owning vignerons; on the contrary, he favored its growth, in conjunction with the extension of agricultural education. His major reservation was that small vignerons did not cultivate their vines or make their wine properly; often they were inadequately equipped, but they took out loans not to improve their viticulture but to buy more land, thereby inflating prices and distorting the channels of credit from improvement to purchase and speculation. Guyot placed his faith in enlightened landowners as the educators of peasants, as their natural leaders.

These ideals were preserved by rural idealists into the later nineteenth and twentieth centuries.[4] A kind of offshoot appearing round 1900 and after were rural conservatives who, unlike Guyot, showed a marked distrust and dislike of independent vignerons and who argued that the kind of tutelage he extolled was hardly possible in a wine district. These men were not critical because they were teetotalers, distrustful of alcohol and of people engaged in its manufacture. Teetotalers were anitalcohol crusaders outraged at the idea that anybody should make money from it; they were a special group which included the right and left in political and social opinions, and they did not condemn the vigneron as a social type. Quite different were Edmond Demolin and Paul Descamps, two publicists who were thinking more in terms of the social order than of physical health. The malady they feared was social change; they charged that viticulture exercised a pernicious influence on rural people, lending itself especially to the partition of land because an active vigneron could live if not thrive on one or two hectares. Vine culture inevitably "fractionalized" the land, and therefore society, into minute units, emphasized extreme individualism—a single family could easily cultivate a small vineyard—and undermind the unity required for social stability. Worse, vine-trimmers were excessively ambitious, indeed their ambitions easily outran their means as well as their expectations, which made them dangerous politically. They were levellers, egalitarians, petty, mean, and jealous.[5]

Viticulture on a small scale, they continued, also limited the size of families, causing depopulation, and set father against son, generation against generation. Although vines did tend to keep people on the land, the quality of these people left much to be desired. When prices were high, vignerons were spendthrift, ostentatious, noisy. They bought watches, lace, ribbons, all the trinkets of decadent urban society, and were indefatigable in mouthing their rights, while ignoring their duties to society. Lacking was any sense of devotion. They were not hard workers; unlike other peasants they exerted themsleves only for gain, not for the love of work. They engaged in viticulture because it involved no hard labor and left them much leisure to spend in cafes or traveling and picking up pernicious ideas.

These generalizations reveal the extent to which rural conservatives were upset by the small vineowners who had emerged as a more or less distinct type in certain parts of France. It is odd that nearly all of these general views had reference to the vine areas in the Loire Valley. We shall later show that the vignerons of France were not everywhere identical and even those in the Loire region were by no means all of a piece. Tradition, religion, family, and community remained sentiments strongly felt among many of them. Nonetheless the above generalizations do underscore the traits of a rising social group. Ostentation, individualism, love of gain, and ambition were the characteristics of *arrivistes* emerging from obscurity during the 1850s and 1860s. Vines and wines were a means of upward mobility and did help create a society fluid enough to menace the inherited power of an old ruling class.

In Italy landlord and peasant relations were sufficiently like those in France to engender similar problems. Yet the landowning classes there followed a somewhat different style of life, which impeded their becoming ideal or model leaders for the land workers. An elite of landowning viticulturists was concentrated in the Asti, Barolo, and Chianti districts. For Tuscany one thinks of the Georgofili of the Academy in Florence and particularly of Ricasoli; for Piedmont the name Cavour stands out. Both men, although they devoted most of their time to public life, were of a mind with Jules Guyot about the duties of landlords toward their peasants. Ricasoli acted on the principles of *noblesse oblige* and by all accounts contributed materially to the well-being of his peasants. He certainly was their educator. But apparently the examples of Cavour and Ricasoli were not widely followed. In the 1880s Francesco Meardi, deputy for the major wine areas of Turin, complained that the upper class in his district were mostly absentee landowners. His parliamentary report complained that they preferred city to country life and abandoned agriculture to "country folk, the most ignorant," who resisted innovation and science.[6] He quoted a letter of Cavour urging larger owners to live on the land in order to civilize their peasants.

Larger owners in the fine wine areas used the crop-sharing system, and they or their overseers did exercise some influence on the peasantry. But they were a small minority of their class. Those elsewhere, especially in the Center and South, did little if anything to educate their peasants; they preferred an ignorant lower class, obedient, poor, and dependent.

Since many French landlords shared this view, the lower classes without access to education and other means of self-improvement remained attached to the viti-viniculture of their ancestors and continued to turn out the gross beverages that were hardly likely to advance their fortunes.

Peasant Owners

The next rung down the social hierarchy of wine society consisted of landowning peasants who worked their holdings. The confiscation of church lands did not immediately benefit this social group, since the best lands in viticultural areas were sold at auction in large blocks, and only well-to-do buyers could acquire them. However speculators among this group subsequently divided their blocks into small holdings and sold them at inflated prices to the lower classes. French and Italian peasants had, of course, been buying vineyards long before 1789. They had acquired parcels when estates were divided by their owners, either because of bankruptcy or because the owner's absentee heirs needed cash or found a large estate unprofitable. Thanks to the Revolution and these age-old forces encouraging sales, French peasants were somewhat more aggressive about becoming owners than their Italian counterparts. In Italy the church and the nobles maintained their hold on real estate; there were no large-scale confiscations of church lands until after the *Risorgimento* achieved its goal in 1860. In both countries the vineyards were redistributed through purchase rather than seizure, as was true of other forms of land.

Vine culture was as likely as other forms of agriculture to offer a means of social and economic advancement; in some cases it was surer and quicker. However it was also more unstable and speculative, and, where practiced as a monoculture, just as likely to hurl the peasant down to the lower strata from which he had risen, and worse, to leave him burdened with debts.

The viticulture that made for instability in society was the new indus-
trialized type found in the areas of ordinary vines: in France, the vast
vineyard of the lower Southwest, the even larger one of the Mediterranean coast, the Rhône Valley; in Italy, the extreme Southeast centered
on Apulia. Vines in these areas were less expensive, yields were high,
costs moderate, and a family could eke out a living on two or three
hectares by doing all its own labor. Where large estates persisted or
emerged in these districts, they became veritable wine factories, producing cheap beverages for urban markets by using highly perfected equipment. They relied heavily on wage labor, especially in the two big
southern regions of France and Italy.

In the area of fine vines peasants were nearly but not entirely excluded
from purchasing land during the revolutionary era and also during most
of the nineteenth century. In upper Beaujolais and the districts around
Belleville and Beaujeu, middle-class city dwellers, members of the rural
bourgeois, and many nobles bought up the best churchlands and held
them. Since none of these persons cultivated vines, each established a
vine-trimmer on a *vigneronnage* and shared the crop with him. Large
holdings therefore were not worked as such; they were divided into small
plots, averaging between two and four hectares, that is, standing between small and medium property for vineyards. Independent small
owners did not even possess 10 percent of the land in upper Beaujolais, a
region of fine vines, and only held 30 percent in the lower Beaujolais,
where ordinaries predominated.[7] In the vineyard of Côte d'Or small
owners, who constituted about 80 percent of the population, managed to
acquire only 24 percent of the vines on the famous Golden Slope, but
they acquired up to 62 percent in the *arrière côte* (ordinary wine area).
Actually big and little growers possessed land side by side in all vineyards and were mutually dependent. Large owners needed highly skilled
laborers, and since they could not afford a large permanent labor force,
they hired small owners who needed extra cash part time. Many little
vignerons were thus both owners and wage workers, a practice that complicated the social structure of the wine population and strengthened the
symbiosis of large and small growers.

There was, it would seem, a certain sense of comradeship between
knowledgeable vine-owners and their skilled workers, and as we noted
already the first growers' congresses in the 1840s applied the term
"vigneron" to both the rich and the modest owner. Later in the century,
however, the large owners chose to call themselves "viticulturists," while
vigneron came to denote a simple peasant who trimmed vines regardless
of whether they belonged to him or to somebody else.

For the ruralists who looked upon the rise of an independent farming class as a civilizing progressive force in society, the Loire Valley was their utopia. Here the vigneron more often practiced a polyculture in which vines formed an important but not dominant part. The average holding in Touraine was between four and six hectares, on the border-line between small and medium property, and nearly everyone worked or managed his own land. In the famous wine canton of Vouvray in 1882 only six owners utilized a manager (*régisseur*); 1,764 farmed their own land full time, 586 were owner-workers, and there were only 178 landless laborers.[8] The Bordeaux area was also one of small vineyards directly cultivated by small owners. About 80 percent of the vignerons tilled a plot less than three hectares in size and their holdings made up about 40 percent of the total vineyard. Nearly all the great châteaux were quite large, thirty to eighty or more hectares, but they composed only about 12 percent of the vineyard area and produced only about 10 percent of its wine. Unlike other vineyards, the medium growers, with four to ten hectares, remained a major force, possessing nearly 33 percent of the vine acreage and producing over 40 percent of its wine. They managed to survive because the large number of small owners constituted the part-time labor force they required. Given this need for their services, small proprietors were to be found everywhere, but they were more prevalent in the area of ordinary wines on the east banks of the Gironde and Garonne rivers.[9]

If one can speak of an aristocracy of small owners, it must have existed in Champagne, a region of small property. In the earlier decades of the century most of them grew grapes and made their own still wine. Their chief market was limited to the champagne houses in Reims and Epernay and the numerous German companies that bought their wine, developed it in their homeland, then shipped it abroad in fancy bottles with even fancier labels suggesting French origins—which was perfectly true, at least as regards the wine. Save in terrible years, the rising demands of local and foreign champagne-makers kept the price of both grapes and still wine relatively high. Since the companies did not usually own extensive vineyards at this time, they had every interest in encouraging the numerous vignerons to produce both good grapes and wine. They paid high prices to keep them in business, with the happy result that these vignerons were probably the richest in Europe during the Golden Age when the average gross revenue went up to 5,600 francs. Furthermore the phylloxera did not attack their vines until the 1890s, which gave them twenty to twenty-five years of exceptionally high prices due to wine shortages everywhere else. Their costs were heavy, up to 3,000 francs per hectare, and the average vineyard was under two hectares, but prices could reach 725 francs per hectoliter, as in 1889. Averaging 44 hectoliters per hectare, a little grower could gross 30,800 francs and net 27,000. This was a princely income for a man with not even two hectares to his name. The years 1889 and 1892, however, were exceptional, and when prices thereafter fell drastically, this peasant aristocracy came to resemble the improverished barefoot *schlacta* of Poland. As we shall see, they resorted to action almost as suicidal as that of this Polish proletarian aristocracy.[10]

In Italy a small landowning peasantry also emerged, mainly in the North and the Southeast, particularly after midcentury when the new state took over many church lands and sold them to rich commoners who in turn divided them for sale to the peasant. In the North much of this land had not originally been planted in vines, because it was unsuitable. But from about 1860 to the late 1880s, when prices for wine rose precipitously, because of the phylloxera in France, many peasant sharecroppers bought land in the plains of the Po Valley, intermixed vines with other crops, and enjoyed considerable prosperity from their common wines. They also acquired much of the soil owned by communes, intending to convert it also. This prosperity, however, came to an abrupt end when the aphid invaded these northern vineyards around 1890. As regards quality this was a vinicultural blessing: vines planted in the plains produced a low-grade beverage that was becoming a drag on the market as the French restored their production. It did not even attain 10 degrees alcohol and pulled down prices even of good wine from the hills.[11]

A host of small owners in Apulia appeared for the same reasons as they had in the North of Italy and the South of France: the growth of an urban population demanding wine and improved transport. However since industrial urbanization and inland transport came slowly to Italy, the truly massive growth of the Apulian vineyards outreached national demand and could thrive only by expanding foreign sales. The thirsty French, deprived of their own wine, encouraged large numbers of Apulian peasants to buy land on credit. The price of good blending wine could reach 50 lire, but even when averaging 25 lire, net income rose to a minimum of 450 lire per hectare and could attain 1,000. Olive and almond trees, as well as cereals, were rooted up to make way for vines. Then, after 1888, prices fell to 10–12 lire, and net income to about 168.[12] Vines continued to offer a superior revenue to cereals, but not sufficient to live on. A minority of peasant owners, possessing the requisite skills, survived as landowners; most others, with minute plots, discovered that prices were too low to provide them a livelihood. In the communes of Conosa their net income came to a mere 43 lire annually, in Barletta only 29. Since house rents in this "frontier" area had shot up as a result of the inrush of population during the 1880s, these small owners, with one-third a hectare more or less, had to work for a wage in order to survive.[13] They were much closer to wage workers than to owners.

Workers

Full-time workers occupied the lowest rung in the hierarchy of any viti-cultural society. However even at the bottom level there were grada-tions. Indeed there was a group among them who, as regards income and status, were probably more fortunate than the petty owners whose mea-ger holdings forced them to hire out as wage workers. The fortunate were the crop-sharers of Burgundy, who received one half of the grape harvest, and the *prix faiteurs* of Bordeaux, who enjoyed a fixed wage for trimming a specified area of a large vineyard.

In the Beaujolais a large or medium owner divided his property into several sections called *vigneronnages*, each consisting of three to six hec-tares, sufficient for a family of five or six persons. At least two hectares contained vines, while the remainder served for food and fodder crops. The owner provided most or all of the heavy equipment, the chemicals, a house, and various other small structures; he also usually paid the land taxes, and on large estates he provided a press, vats, and other wine-making equipment. In return the vigneron provided his and his family's labor, most of the small equipment for trimming vines, and half of the barrels needed to store the vintage. He also contributed poultry, two or three cows, a pig, and his own household furnishing. Essentially the same system prevailed in the Mâconnais just to the north.

Under these conditions—which were centuries old—the vignerons constituted a distinct social class. Traditionally the *vigneronnage* passed from father to eldest son, and younger sons had to fend for themselves. They often worked as handymen or laborers (*domestiques*) attached to a vigneron until they could save money enough to buy the equipment needed to obtain a *vigneronnage* in their own right. This class, it is clear, was quite closed, self-perpetuating, and entry into it by outsiders almost impossible. The vigneron most often married locally and his wife's dowry in money, furniture, and clothing helped to set them up. The marriage usually took place in October and the newlyweds moved onto the land on 11 November, the day of Saint Martin, patron saint of many vinemen.

Usually their first child was conceived soon afterward and born in August or September of next year. It has been argued that this cycle was the result of careful economic and family planning. This was undoubtedly true, but it was hard on the wife, for she was expecting her first born at precisely the time of heaviest labor—for her and everyone else—the grape harvest. And undoubtedly she was expected to help out, for she was a partner of her husband, working in the vines, keeping house, and eventually, raising children.

Until the 1840s and 1850s being a crop-sharer had certain advantages. Believing in a paternalist relationship, his proprietor offered him various forms of protection in hard times, such as monetary advances, limited medical care, advice and counsel. On the other hand, the owner was more likely than not an autocrat expecting to be obeyed. He customarily collected a "gift" from each new crop-sharer upon arrival, as well as a tax called "basse cour," consisting of eggs, milk, chickens, or a sum of money that was quite heavy, sometimes 10 percent of gross revenue. Equally imposing was the landlord's privilege of buying his vigneron's wine, at below market prices, and of selling it himself. This custom deprived the lower classes of economic liberty, and what remained of their personal liberty was further restricted by debt, a customary feature of crop-sharing systems. Almost invariably landlords loaned their croppers money to tide them over bad years and to hire grape-pickers. After 1789 vine-trimmers were no longer serfs but they were not free men either, chained as they were by tradition, need, and debts.[14]

In the finer vineyards of the Côte d'Or and particularly in Côte de Beaune, the practice of *mi-fruits* prevailed. It resulted from the belief that these vastly expensive vineyards must never be turned over to unskilled workers. Owners, who were often absentees, preferred to entrust their vines to highly experienced trimmers; in return they gave them half the wine crop, a system similar to that of Beaujolais. Here, however, the vigneron often did not receive a house or fields or other forms of protection from the owner. In a sense he was more independent than his comrade in southern Burgundy, but he too was bound by debts until the 1850s. The owner, enjoying the right to sell both shares of wine, offered him a sum less than full price. And even this transaction did not bring the cropper any immediate cash, because the merchants who had purchased the wine did not pay their first installment until four to six months after they had put it on the market. The vigneron usually had to borrow from his master to live until he was paid; he rarely enjoyed an income sufficient to free him of debt, nor did he have legal recourse against dishonesty. The owner kept all the books and his word was accepted as concrete evidence in a law court, thanks to the Napoleonic Code. Th vigneron on shares did not earn enough to attain a necessary minimum standard of living during thirty out of the fifty-five years from 1800 to 1855.[15]

The golden age, however, brought marked changes in Burgundy. Most notable was an increase in revenues sufficient to free the vignerons of debt and even to put very small plots of common vines within their purchase power. Their rising expectations made them less and less subservient; they demanded improved conditions and got them. The old tax of "basse cour" disappeared, they won greater control over the sale of their share of wine, and with better education and a local press they acquired a knowledge of prices that put them in a better bargaining position vis-à-vis both masters and merchants. In their turn the masters, finding these new conditions intolerable, set out to abolish crop-sharing. Not only did they consider their vine-trimmers insubordinate, they could profit more from the high price of wine if they could pay wages rather than share and thus sell all the wine for their own gain. At precisely the time when crop-sharing began to benefit the workers, the owners sought to abolish it. In Côte d'Or many did so, but discovered that even high wages did not always retain workers on the land when the old bonds, however disadvantageous, were replaced by a cash nexus.

In upper Beaujolais, on the other hand, the old tenure system survived at least in the fine wine areas of Belleville and Beaujeu, where the entire population was more conservative and the owners lived either on the estate or in a nearby town. When the phylloxera struck and hard times followed, these vignerons who had remained faithful to the traditions of crop-sharing enjoyed the protection and aid that only large owners could offer. And most of them must have considered themselves wise for not having invested heavily in land and vines during the preceding two decades.

In the hierarchy of viticulture crop-sharers, especially those in Burgundy, blended in with small and even medium owners. Sometimes they enjoyed more security and higher economic benefits, and there is no indication that they were held in low esteem. Those who cultivated seven to ten hectares of land, with three or four planted in vines, were themselves employers of at least one full-time helper who lived in and of odd-job laborers who did not. What becomes increasingly evident is that during the 1860s the viticultural hierarchy tended to bunch up toward the middle and lower middle, forming not a true pyramid but rather a diamond-shaped structure. Many sharecroppers in the Loire Valley and the Southwest fell somewhat below the middle in this period because of lower incomes and wine prices there.

The lowest and not-too-enviable position was filled by another group of workers, the *prix faiteurs*. These trimmers, quite numerous in the Bordelais, contracted to cultivate about eight or nine *journaux* (2.5–3 hectares) of vines, in return for a fixed price (*prix fait*). In the 1830s the going rate for a skilled vigneron was 120 to 150 francs, plus lodging, a garden, firewood derived from one-half of the canes pruned from vines, flour for bread, and a few other benefits.[16] However during 1852 in the canton of Langon they were paid only 45 francs in cash and the equivalent of 380 francs in kind.[17] This hardly desirable situation was not confined to Langon. On the other hand, each *prix faiteur* performed only specified tasks, chiefly pruning, hoeing, and leafing, tasks occupying him and his family for about two-thirds of the year. For all the other jobs, chiefly winter work, harvesting, and layering, he received a daily wage that augmented his annual income. As the use of chemicals to protect vines from insects became general, the *prix faiteurs* also received an extra wage for spraying and dusting, unpleasant jobs to which he was not accustomed, and to which he consented out of economic necessity. Until the 1880s this form of labor contract—more often verbal, like that of the *vigneronnage*, rather than written—was used wherever there was large and medium property. Even in Côte d'Or there were families who worked fifty *ouvrées* (2.12 hectares) for a specified sum of money, a practice rather widespread in ordinary vineyards until the 1850s, when many owners, after they turned away from the *mi-fruit* method, adapted either *prix fait* or simple wages.

This tendency to abolish crop-sharing was more characteristic of France than of Italy. In the older wine areas of Italy there had existed for centuries crop-sharing systems similar to those in France. The most widely used system of land contract in the best vineyards was one referred to as *colonia parziaria* or *vignolante* in the Asti region. This was simply a form of *mezzadria*, resembling the *vigneronnage* of Beaujolais; it apparently worked well in providing a livelihood for peasants and in securing for them a respectable place or status in viticultural society. In Asti and Alessandria the *vignaioli* received one-third the grapes and one-half the grain and corn grown between the vine rows. Sometimes they retained all the produce grown between vines, but they had heavier costs to bear than their French counterparts. Up to the turn of the century relations remained mutually advantageous, even amicable and respectful, between owners and crop-sharers. As in Beaujolais, landowners acted to maintain the system because croppers were usually better workers than simple wage-earners and were less prone to emigrate.

Although petty property was widespread, the Italians preserved various crop-sharing systems on a wider basis as well as for a longer time than did the French. In France a mere 8 percent of vineyards were leased on a crop-sharing basis and 8 percent were rented, leaving about 84 percent worked by their owners either directly or by wage labor. Unfortunately exact data of this sort is lacking for Italy, but it is clear that far fewer owners worked their land directly, or that they supervised their croppers as closely and with as much skill as Ricasoli.

Traditional forms of social control enjoyed by landlords in Italy were similar to, but more extensive than, those of Burgundy. In central Italy the entire peasant family, not just its head, was attached to the landed estate; the owner or his agent took charge of their life in considerable detail, deciding upon the marriage of children and who among them would leave the land and who remain. The cropper, bound by debts and without the ballot that his French equivalent won in 1848, was not in a position to defend his person or to improve his economic standing. Furthermore he found it difficult to pay his debts because he had to make numerous "free" gifts to the owner and perform extra work for him. The Marquis Ridolfi, a Georgofilo in Tuscany, estimated that the average annual income in this wine-producing state was merely 87 lire in cash during the earlier nineteenth century.[18] The shares system, therefore, had to provide food and raw materials for clothing and shelter as well as grapes. It did not significantly encourage technological innovation, since too many absentee owners were not interested and the peasants resisted change. The small number of enlightened Georgofili did not influence viticultural society deeply enough, and they did not reach its lower strata at all. Different conditions existed for the peasants of the South who worked on the latifundia but lived in scattered villages. They too practiced shares, but enjoyed greater personal freedom than their comrades of the Center and North.

In both France and Italy workers who were entirely dependent on wages formed the majority at the bottom of our diamond-shaped society. Among those at the lowest point were the *domestiques*, employed by the year, housed and fed, and therefore paid little in money. Females could rarely move out of this condition unless they married a vigneron; males, as in Beaujolais, might be younger sons of vignerons who were doing an apprenticeship for a few years, saving desperately to buy equipment and

hoping to take over a vigneronnage. Since they were scions of vine families, however, they were on an equal social level with their employers,
dined with them and could solve their problems by marrying the boss's
daughter—a not infrequent occurrence. Their lowly status, therefore,
was provisional, the result of being second or third born, and was purely
economic, not social. Quite different was the fate of most *domestiques*,
who were unskilled immigrants from impoverished families in backward
mountain areas. They were hired at a low wage, 200 francs or so per
annum was the maximum, and their only way out, or rather up, was to
become wage-earning day laborers, a rise, of course, of barely one step.

At the lowest level were also those mountain immigrants who hired
themselves out to do hard labor: uprooting, digging the deep trenches
needed for planting, carrying back washed-down earth, and trenching
for drainage. They were temporary labor, migratory, following the job
market and rarely able to acquire the skills and tools needed to become
vine-dressers.

The top layer of wage workers were vignerons. They, like small
vineowners, were artisans in their trade; indeed, they blended into the
small-owner class, for many belonged to that intermediate group of owners who hired themselves out part time. These worker-owners were an
indispensable source of labor for large proprietors. Where big vineyards
existed, they were sometimes the predominant labor force, as on the
Mediterranean coast, in much of the Southwest, Bordeaux in France,
and Apulia in Italy. Even where they were not predominant, they were
important both in numbers and influence. In France, if the census data
of 1852 is more or less correct, their significance is quite evident. In the
quality wine canton of Pauillac (Médoc) there were 786 small owners,
1,222 owner-workers, and 910 full-time workers. In Pessac (Graves)
there were 1,142 small owners, 1,589 owner-workers, and 2,000 full-
time workers.[19]

This worker-owner category existed everywhere. Even Tuscany, a region of mixed agriculture with vines hung on trees, offered a similar
situation in the 1880s. Table 18 shows the numerical importance of small
owners, and alas, their financial impotence.

Since some part-time workers probably possessed more than one "very
small" plot, their number was less than 138,000, but it was undoubtedly
over 100,000. They had to take extra work for wages to supplement their
meager revenues, and most likely they left the cultivation of their own
crops to their wives and children. Their condition becomes starkly clear
if we compare ownership (A) with value and income (B):

TABLE 18: *Land Size and Income, Tuscany*

N of Plots	Net Income (lire)	Classification
138,000	Under 200	very small [owner-workers]
28,500	200–2,000	small [many owner-workers]
5,230	2,000–20,000	medium
270	over 20,000	large

Source: Giunta parl., III, 378

TABLE 19: *Types of Ownership and Property Values*

Types of owners	A. Percent of all owners	B. Percent of total value
Large	0.001	10
Medium	3	30
Small	16	45
Very small	80	15

In the province of Benevento a small owner and his family could earn, in a favorable year, about 500 lire from their own wine and 600 from wages, a total of 1,100 lire. Since they needed only 860 lire to live, they could save money for a bad year when they would not earn enough for bare necessities.[20] Two bad years in succession or closely following each other, however, could wipe them out as landowners, which is why many, perhaps most, small farmers preferred crop-sharing to ownership; the former offered less freedom but greater security.

It is more than possible that many of these very small owners were not part-time wage workers but crop-sharers or *mezzadri* cultivating a portion of a large estate as well as their own plots. This practice seems to have been more widespread in the South, where peasants did not live on the estate and therefore were able to combine the shares system with greater personal freedom than their counterparts elsewhere. They owned or rented their houses, bought or grew their food, and arranged their family affairs. Of course they enjoyed neither political freedom or power, as will be shown later.

If we consider the major wine areas of France and Italy, landless full-time wage workers were undoubtedly a minority. They were also an unstable group in the sense that many would move up into the small landed group for a period of time and then fall back again into the wage group as a result of poor management or one or more bad harvests in quick succession. Moreover many a laborer listed as full-time wage earner really owned a few vines worked by his wife and children. A true working class in the sense that this term is used for urban industrial laborers (a proletariat) was hardly present in the wine industry save in certain areas of lower Languedoc and Bordeaux where mass production devleoped. But even there the worker was often like a jack-in-the-box periodically jumping upward into landed status. Laborers who acquired enough land to become full-time owners during the Golden Age lost much of their property when the phylloxera took over, and when they managed to buy a few more plots of vines in the 1890s, the wine crisis of 1901–07 made them worthless. Such instability, rather than class alignment and consciousness, was the lot of the wage earner in vines.

Similar conditions existed in Apulia; first the prosperity of the 1880s and the later 1890s enabled many peasants to acquire small plots on which they planted vines. But when their foreign markets were closed by tariffs, most of them sank into what must have been a true proletariat. Crop-sharing practically disappeared and many of the surviving owners became rural enterpreneurs hiring labor. Table 20 makes this quite clear for post-1900 in the chief viticultural districts.

Concentration of ownership was an old phenomenon in Sicily, southern Italy, and other parts of the peninsula where crop-sharers were more prevalent than wage workers. France had more small property, but the tendency toward concentration, chiefly in the lower South and Southwest, skewed the curve.

Large and very large property constituted nearly 57 percent of the total vineyard area and if combined with medium property made up nearly 72 percent of the total, hence almost three-fourths of all vineyards required hired labor on a continuous basis. Since only about 16 percent of the national vineyard was dressed by crop-sharers and tenants, most work was performed directly by owners and by wage workers.

For a full-time wage worker to acquire property was as much a psychological as an economic need, but ownership did not always provide sufficient income, especially in the first half of the century. Small owners in Côte d'Or sometimes earned only a third of the revenue they required to buy the necessities of life. Wage workers were, perhaps, in worse condition. We cannot today determine with precision the level of their incomes and living conditions, since purely quantitative data is often missing, or too vague and incomplete. On the whole the picture is grim. Laurent's careful study emphasized that workers' conditions were more

TABLE 20: *Class Structure in Apulia, c. 1905–07*

District	Owners %	Renters %	Crop-Sharers %	Rural Laborers %
Foggia	11.37	2.6	1.25	64.46
Bari	18.04	4.87	1.39	60.88
Barletta	12.03	8.10	1.25	65.73
Brindisi	16.61	3.72	1.04	62.14
Lecce	13.89	11.77	5.86	57.37
San Severo	15.96	4.66	5.64	55.73
Gallipoli	18.60	4.95	5.65	58.37

Source: Min. Agri., *Inchiesta . . . merid . . . Puglia*, 276–77. Also see data in De Felice, 496 ff.

TABLE 21: *French Vineyards Classed by Size, 1892*

Size of holdings		Hectares	Percent of total
(hectares)			
Under 1	(very small)	136,200	7.6
1 to 5	(small)	370,100	20.6
5 to 10	(medium)	267,400	14.9
10 to 40	(large)	467,900	25.9
over 40	(very large)	558,900	31.0
Total		1,800,500	

Source: *Rev. Viti.*, VIII (4 Dec. 1897) 597–601

stable than depressed from 1809 to 1855, although the term depressed might be more accurate for the period 1832–55, over twenty years during which wages did not suffice for a minimum standard of living.[21] Compared to the thirty years of insufficiency among crop-sharers, wage workers were slightly better off. Of course full-time wage workers in Côte d'Or were a small minority in the quality vineyards, where owners preferred to use either *prix faiteurs* or crop-sharers who worked more responsibly and skillfully. But owners decided to hire more wage workers after midcentury, and it seems that they profited at the workers' expense, save for two decades. Considering wage levels in respect to the cost of wheat, workers found themselves at a disadvantage during about 50 of the 113 years from 1800 to 1914. The 1860s and 1870s were their happiest period, but this was followed by nearly three decades of low wages and high food costs. Happily, after 1857 there were no more years of near-famine conditions.

Quite clearly the wage worker before 1855 did not have much opportunity to become an owner. Although the value of vineyards had declined since 1808, and especailly since 1818–20, they remained expensive both to acquire and to maintain. Ironically, at precisely the moment when wages began to rise dramatically, after 1855, the price of vineyards also rose drastically, leaping beyond the means of many peasants. Indeed larger owners dropped crop-sharing precisely because profits from wine rose more sharply than did wages. Certainly workers began to buy a few small sections of vines after 1855, and they undoubtedly improved their lot in the 1860s and 1870s, yet the simple vigneron in Côte d'Or, whether cropper or employee, seems to have benefitted less during the golden age than his counterparts elsewhere in France.[22]

The trend of improving wages appeared in Beaujolais with maximum daily wages for adult males rising from 1.50 francs in the years from 1820 to 1845 to 2 francs in 1846–50, to 2.50 francs in the 1850s, and 3 francs from 1874 to 1880, a rise of 100 percent. Minimum or winter wages in 1821 were about 1 franc, in 1851 roughly 1.30 to 1.50 francs and in 1880 2.20 francs, a rise of 120 percent. Conditions were certainly improving for wage workers, and as elsewhere, their purchasing power rose during the golden age.[23] Wages reached their peak in the 1880s and achieved stability precisely when food prices began to decline. In the late 1890s, however, a period of industrial prosperity began, accompanied by rising prices for food and durable goods. The leveling-off of wages for vineyards workers show they suffered a decline of real income. When the crisis that began after 1900 in the wine industry made it difficult for owners to raise the workers' pay, they had little choice but to leave the land. The boom in industry was too enticing to be resisted.

In Gironde the *Statistique Agricole* for 1852 reflects the pessimism of midcentury observers upset by falling prices, food shortages, unemployment, and revolution. In canton after canton income did not cover the cost of living for a family of five (the model family in wine areas, where birth control was rigorously carried out). With an average wage of 1.50 or 2 francs per day, fathers of families could not cover expenses unless their wives and children earned supplementary incomes. A family of five required 695 francs to live for a year in Pessac canton, near Bordeaux. Here, the family bread bill rose to 390 francs, meat came to 50, wine to 40, and clothing to 110. These basic items totaled 590 francs, with bread taking up 66 percent. The fact that wine is included in this budget underscores the absolute dependence of these workers on wages; they did not even have family vineyards, and each father consumed while working the *piquette* he received as part of his earnings. The father worked 280 days for 1.50 francs plus the 52.50 francs he earned during the vendange, a total of, say, 472 francs. His wife labored 260 days at 60 centimes per day plus 25 francs earned for picking grapes. One child, active for 100 days at 60 centimes earned 60 francs, plus 25 for picking grapes. This would bring the total family income to 732 francs, allowing merely 37 for clothing, medicine, entertainment, and miscellaneous items. Clearly such a vigneron was not going to buy much land. The economic depression of the late 1840s and early 1850s made the improved conditions of the Second Empire seem all the more attractive, and at that time the purchase of small plots hastened the process of parcelization (*morcellement*) and upward mobility.[24]

During the phylloxera crisis there was no decline of wages because the owners who survived needed hands first to apply chemicals to suffering vines and then to replant. Wages even continued to rise in the lesser vineyards. In the Médoc, Sauterne, Loupiac, and Cadillac districts, they reached 3 francs for men and 1.25 for women on the eve of World War I, a 100 percent rise since midcentury.[25]

It is very difficult to obtain a clear understanding of the economic position of the *prix faiteurs* on the classed estates of Médoc. For Château Latour, a first-growth, there is some data available. Before 1819–20, when vignerons were paid a daily wage, each received 1.25 francs. Then, after the system of *prix fait* began, in the above years, the trimmers received a fixed sum, plus wages for extra jobs. Between 1820 and 1857–58, fixed remuneration rose from roughly 175 francs per *prix fait* to 219, and then in 1861–62 to 281, a 60 percent increase. Wages for extra work also went up 50–60 percent, so that in the mid-1860s, a vigneron earned about 973 francs, plus housing, medical services, and a small pension of 100 francs a year. There was also a "gratification" paid to all the personnel during exceptionally prosperous years, but this fell to nothing with the arrival of the phylloxera. The dread aphid caused wages to remain stationary between 1880 and 1913. Such stagnation was not limited to Latour and invariably produced a decline in real income after 1895, when the costs of living rapidly went up; so by 1911–12 trade unions were beginning to make headway in Médoc. To counter their influence, the large owners organized themselves into the Syndicat des Grands Crus Classés. But the smaller growers raised wages, bringing them to 2.50 francs a day for men and 1 franc for women, to which were added housing and some social services.[26]

It would seem, that despite rising wages workers were hardly better off on the eve of the war than they were in the heyday of the nineteenth century, for their wages barely kept up with the rising cost of living after 1895. Particularly deplorable was the income of women, who earned about half a man's wages, yet nearly always performed difficult tasks, sometimes the same tasks as men, or even more delicate ones, such as picking grapes and snipping the defective berries out of closely packed clusters. Public opinion accepted this differential, since in rural society all women were looked upon as part of a family, and their work, like their wages, was held to be supplementary to that of their husbands, their brothers, or their fathers. Since they were without an independent existence, no one recognized a claim for them to a higher status. What they earned was hidden carefully in the old woolen sock and ultimately put to use for purchasing land—that they could not own in their own name.

It would be absurd to imagine that an improvement of wages, even by 50 percent, allowed simple vignerons to acquire property planted with fine vines. Generally this was not their aim. In the few instances when they acquired such property, they rooted up each fine vine as it died in order to plant *gros productuers*, that is, vines giving mediocre quality but high yields and higher returns. In addition they bought land at relatively low prices that was not considered fit for vines and obstinately planted vines on it. In France as in Italy, rows of vines appeared in the flats and in heavy clay soils which had once held grass or cereals. Such rich soils doubled, even tripled, the yield, and millions of gallons of nondescript beverages went out to the burgeoning masses in the cities.

In the fine vineyards of Champagne wage workers, as distinct from small growers, seem to have held much the same economic position as their counterparts in other fine vineyards in France and Italy. Around the turn of the twentieth century wages climbed somewhat more rapidly than the cost of living, thanks to the exceptional prosperity of the large champagne houses. From about the 1880s on, these larger firms had begun buying land and hiring their own vignerons. Moët and Chandon alone employed about 800, and paid, in 1896, 3 francs per day for men and 2.25 for women in winter and from 3 to 5 francs in spring and summer. After 1900 spring-summer wages generally rose to about 5 francs per day in the Ay district, which put them slightly above the national average. This was offset perhaps by the higher costs of fuel incurred by everyone in this northerly province, save the employees of those large firms which provided supplements of fuel, as well as weather-proof housing.

All of these figures are merely suggestive as regards total remuneration, because conditions varied in agricultural labor. Rarely did men work more than 250 days in a year, and if rain or cold persisted, they were lucky to be hired for 200 days, a reduction seriously affecting their annual income. Another impediment to a precise measure of wages is that workers were often paid in kind, either food or wine or both. Where food was involved, it could amount to an important sum. Bread early in the morning, a cold breakfast at 8 A.M., lunch at noon (a soup with salt meat and bread), a "gouter" of bread at 4 P.M., and at 7 a dinner of soup, vegetables, perhaps meat and wine. Wine, ranging from one to three liters per day, accompanied all of these repasts and on some large estates was consumed by itself at hourly intervals morning and afternoon. The food and wine supplements came to roughly 1.50 francs per day. Some big owners complained that the total remuneration of labor came to 7 or 8 francs a day, a sum that is clearly exaggerated. But small owners, unable to match the high wages paid by the companies, complained of unfair competition.[27]

Slightly higher wages did not lead to a greater acquisition of land in Champagne; on the contrary, the number of workers went up as firms expanded their vine holdings. By 1912 there was a sizable agricultural proletariat in the Verzy district, where there were 859 owners, 408 owner-workers, and 729 laborers. In the Ay district owners and owner-workers were lumped together in the data and totaled 508 and laborers stood at 376; about the same proportions existed in Chatillon-sur-Marne, 713–470, while Cumières was the most proletarian commune with merely 164 owners compared to 530 laborers.[28] Probably the reason for the persistence of a rather large proletariat was the high price of vineyards and the equally elevated costs of growing vines. Even with higher wages, simple vignerons could not afford to purchase land suitable to fine vines, the type that was most profitable in Champagne. Therefore they followed the practice of peasants in other districts, bought land less suitable for vines, planted common stock, and sold their ordinary beverages to German firms and to lesser French firms in and out of Champagne.

As for the ambitious vignerons who became small owners, they were less inclined to serve as laborers after midcentury, provoking—unconsciously—a shortage of hired hands. This, in turn, pushed wages upward and consequently enabled full- and part-time workers to buy more land. Then as large and medium owners found it difficult to find help, they sold parts of their estates, increasing the vineyards on the market and whetting the desire of workers to acquire land. The cycle was complete, and in its upward spiral it carried with it some little vignerons to a higher socioeconomic status. Their fall, when it came with the phylloxera, seemed all the more horrendous. Land ownership, thought to be a cure-all for the ills and injustices in society, enabled a few peasant vinedressers to advance their status. But for a large number it was a deception; worse, it brought ruin and bitterness.

Wage workers in Italian vineyards also suffered from hard times but possibly less so than their Gallic counterparts. We have already noted that, except in the South, Italians rarely relied on vines exclusively, and their mixed farming gave them other resources to fall back on. In the Mezzogiorno, however, there was considerable suffering after the French closed their market in 1888 and the Austrians limited their purchases after 1900. In Apulia wages jumped from 80–90 centesimi in 1880 to 3 lire in 1887, and a wife and adolescent child could add 2 more lire per day.[29] After 1888 came a depression. For a while many workers had become the new rich, now they became the new poor, or rather, they returned to the low standard of living that had been their lot since time out of memory. Unlike the French, they could not push their wages up for a long period of time, in part because there was a surplus of labor and because rural wages were low generally in the peninsula. Around the turn of the century pay ranged from 1.20 to 1.25 lire per day in true vineyards (*vigneto speccializzato*) in the South.[30] In Tuscany a male worker already earned this rate by the 1880s, but a woman was paid 65 centesimi, often for the same type of work. If a man worked 200 days a year and his wife 100 days, they earned a mere 285 to 300 lire per year. Since this sum was not sufficient to live on, the couple had to find extra work, the man laboring on the roads, his wife doing household or garden tasks.[31] These were probably minimum wages, since no human being could have lived on less. In 1900–01, rates for general vine-trimming ranged from 1.20 to 1.40 lire for a six-hour day in winter and about 2 lire for a seven- to eight-hour day in summer. On an hourly basis summer work was barely more remunerative than winter work, 26 centesimi compared to 21.

By 1911, however, there had occurred a notable advance, almost rivaling the rates of the 1880s. Winter wages rose into the range of 2.20–2.50 lire and summer wages to 2.35–2.75. This 60 percent rise in the daily rate for winter work put Italians almost on a par with lesser paid Frenchmen. More important, however, was the 46 percent increase in the hourly basis of summer tasks, made possible by a slight increase of wages and a decline of hours from seven and a half to six and a half. Wages earned for sulfuring vines and picking grapes went up at about the same rate, attaining 3 lire, and helped to pull up the average income.[32]

In some areas the picture was slightly brighter. In Campania a family of six could make out. The father earned 2 lire per day for 250 days, totaling 500 lire; the wife worked 150 days for 1.10 lire; and two adolescents, working 200 days each at 1.30 or .90 lire, could add 456 lire, bringing the total family income to just over 1,100 lire, roughly the amount needed for a family of six.[33] This family earned enough for the necessities, and sometimes even a few superfluities, of life. The shorter hours that began after about 1905 made it possible for each member to take on additional work—if available—in order to achieve a slightly higher standard.

Shorter hours were a decided improvement for owner-workers, because they gained more time to tend their own plots. The other means of support necessary to workers in most wine areas did not always come from a small plot of land. Many peasants—and this was true in France also—practiced internal seasonal migration. Few left Italy for foreign areas, although a fair number went to Provence; rather they trod the roads to nearby communes to mow hay, harvest grain, pick grapes, and perform any other tasks that did not remove them from their vines at crucial moments. From hand to mouth they survived in good years and in bad.

Living Conditions

There is good reason to believe that vignerons in France enjoyed better living conditions than those in Italy. This difference was partly the result of the higher prices paid for French wine, not only in the international but also in the national market thanks to a higher standard of living throughout the nation. In the 1860s, after the unification movement achieved its initial successes in Italy, the per capita income in the new state was a mere 196 lire per annum; in France it was the equivalent of 650 lire. Vine-dressers, like all other farmers in Italy, suffered from the new nation's general poverty. They were heavily taxed, because the wars of unification had been costly and the new state willingly absorbed the huge debts of the deposed dynasties, estimated at 10.5 billion lire. To this burden must be added the costs of railroad-building, doggedly if somewhat sluggishly carried out, as a means of binding the provinces together. The new state "lifted" 17 percent of each Italian's income in the form of taxes, whereas a Frenchman paid only 12 percent of his income.[34] In at least one respect the two nationalities were alike: the lower classes carried the heaviest fiscal burden, for each administration derived about half of its income from those least able to pay, that is, from persons living just at or slightly above the level of subsistence.

In the earlier decades of the century most vignerons seem not to have differed notably from other peasants in their standards of living. They were all badly housed, partook of a monotonous diet, worked too hard, and died young. This list, summing up the negative side of human life, is certainly too limited in scope, however, we can begin with it.

Throughout the century vignerons lived in cramped housing. Whether they lodged in the huts provided on the larger estates, or lived in villages or country towns, entire families of four to five members squeezed into one or two rooms. This situation had not changed appreciably later in the century when Myard described how a typical family of five in the Beaujolais lived in one room that served as kitchen and bedroom.[35] Their house had few windows, little light, was humid, and stank. The domestic, hired by the year lived in a minute windowless room, an odd improvement over former times when he had lived in the stable and slept on loose straw crawling with vermin. Typical of peasant architecture, the stable was integral to the dwelling, and although there was rarely sufficient ventilation to remove the foul odors of animals and fermenting hay, a peasant family did not feel incommoded when it spent winter evenings there, basking in the warmth given off by a pig or two, a cow, an ox, or a horse. Generally there were three types of rural dwellings inhabited by vignerons (See figure 27). The house built at ground level with a vaulted cellar beneath it (II) was found chiefly in northern regions and limited to producers of fine wines who wanted to age them in wood. Vaulted below-ground storage guaranteed the vintage against changes of temperature and encouraged a slow constant maturation with the maximum development of aroma. The type constructed on an above-ground cellar (III) was most widespread in southern areas, where it protected the new wine from excessive atmospheric heat in the warm season and cold in the mild winter. It spread to the northeast, where growers used wood or coal stoves to protect their wine in the coldest months. Finally there was the type with the above-ground nonvaulted storage area which the French call a *cellier non voûté* (I) as distinct from the below-ground cellar (*cave*). Widespread in the southwest, this type was the easiest and cheapest to build, and in poorer dwellings it was simply a lean-to shed attached to one side of the house.[36] Although more frequently found in the West, it was also used by little growers everywhere who had no need to store wine over long months. Few wine-makers gave much attention to storage conditions, since nearly all of them sold either their musts or new wines as quickly as possible. Not even the great Bordeaux châteaux kept their wines but sent them off to merchant buyers who matured the new beverages in their own solid stone cellars. Only during bad years, when merchants bid too low or refused the new wine, did producers age their own juice, and then they complained of the costs of racking and bottling, and of the losses due to evaporation. Among small growers the cellar or press room was often but slightly partitioned from the stable and barn, with the result that their musts, fermenting in open vats, became more redolent of animals and hay than of grapes. So did the peasants.

The Bordelais, the reputation of its wines notwithstanding, offered little, if any, improvement. In 1849 the council on hygiene of the Gironde department issued a critical report. Peasants not only failed to wash themselves, they also neglected the most elementary rules of personal and public cleanliness. As in the Beaujolais they had few windows and kept these closed from fear of drafts, even in hot weather. Most of their houses had nearby open ditches into which the inhabitants, to obtain compost, abandoned garbage, manure, the remains of various vegetable and animal matter, even the cadavers of animals.[37]

To this bleak picture we must add the more cheerful coloring of prog-

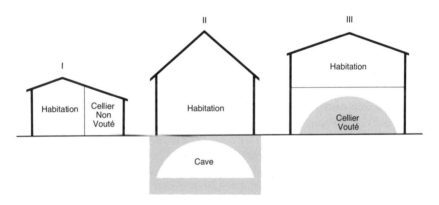

FIGURE 27: *Houses of Wine Growers*

Source: Parain, 299

ress. Somewhat before the golden age, and rapidly during its happy years, winemen began to ameliorate their conditions. Extra rooms were added to the old houses, roofs were repaired, furniture of a more comfortable nature appeared. There were even new-rich vignerons who acquired stuffed chairs and pianos for their daughters, which they put into newly built houses after abandoning their old cottages to their hired help. But, alas, when the phylloxera arrived, many of these luxuries were sold to pay debts. Even among well-established families hardship reappeared. However not even this economic setback forced growers and their families to return to the squalid existence of former times. After the 1830s in Beaujolais, wooden bowls had given way to tin or china plates, forks had replaced fingers, and the kitchen walls were hung with numerous household utensils. None of this disappeared entirely. Indeed, as we shall see, vignerons resorted to several forms of violence after 1900 to maintain the standards they and their forebears had acquired.

In Italy conditions were probably not different. Bad at first in the older areas of mixed vineyards, they showed improvement, at least during the era of active wine trade with France in the 1880s. According to the Jacini parliamentary committee to study living conditions, Tuscan peasants were cleanly and adequately lodged in solid houses, even with glass in the windows, and did not lack "la Latrina." [38] A great advance was the relocation of the manure pile far enough downwind so as not to pollute the air around the dwelling. Furniture, while simple, was solid, with beds made of metal and mattresses filled with corn husks.

The major exception was in the unstable frontier conditions of Apulia, where forms of jerry-built housing came into existence to lodge a too rapidly growing population. Since peasants newly arrived to plant vines were unreliable rent payers, landowners were not much inclined to provide them with houses; moreover rents were exorbitant, rising to 120 lire per year at the least. So peasants erected their own dwellings, and to economize on building costs they put the lower half of their one-storied structures underground. Stones rarely had mortar between them; the walls were sometimes plastered over and sometimes not, an incidental matter given the Mediterranean character of the weather. Whatever the sturdiness of the walls, interiors were clean; it was the streets that were filthy and as everywhere in the South, people spent more time out of doors than in. Wages and incomes were high in times of active trade, but so were costs, and improvements remained haphazard. There was a lack of clean drinking water, resulting from the use of cisterns rather than wells. Both typhoid and malaria were unrelenting, largely because of the scarcity of toilets, drains, and sewers, and the presence of stagnant water. In 1904 Apulia had the highest death rate in Italy: 26.68 per 1,000 as compared to 20.9 for the nation. Small wonder that southern peasants, malaria-ridden and undernourished, were hardly enterprising tillers of the sunbaked land.

Work in the vineyards was fatiguing and caused premature aging. Contemporaries often remarked on the physical deformity of the vigne-ron, especially his bent body. His persistent use of the short-handled hoe, required, he believed, by the stone-filled soils of vineyards, forced him to bend over for hours on end. So did vine pruning, staking, tying, and picking, because clusters were close to the ground. As noted earlier, the plow made slow progress at best among vine-trimmers; all labor was performed with hand tools until the phylloxera ended the old practice of planting *"en foules."* Hours were excessively long because so many vigne-rons held two jobs.

There was little in their diet to restore strength. Most striking was the near absence of fresh meat, an object of great luxury. Vignerons who were also general farmers raised some cattle, but chiefly as work animals, or, as with pigs and poultry, to sell in the local market. In Italy peasants made salami for home consumption, but they and their French counter-parts consumed meat almost exclusively on feast days. Game and wild fowl were fairly abundant in most wine areas, but hunting required a license that cost the equivalent of two or three weeks income. Hence the great extent of poaching and the endemic hostility between large owners of forested lands, or their forest guards, on the one hand, and peasants on the other. Peasants were also given to taking wood from private as well as from communal forests. During the golden ages in both nations, winemen had enough money to buy some meat, and the general lower-ing of tariffs after 1860 held meat prices at a reasonable level. But the return to protectionism in the late 1870s and 1880s sorely tried them. Although refrigerated ships were reducing the costs of transport, tariffs helped to raise the price of meat from the United States, Argentina, and Australia at precisely the time when the winemen were suffering reverses.

On what, then, did vignerons live? The answer is simple, bread and wine, but wine became abundant chiefly after mid century. These two commodities alone could provide a diet of three to four thousand calo-ries or more a day. Large quantities of both accompanied all meals, and of the two bread was by far the most expensive item. Families living on the vineyard or the large owner's estate or in small villages baked their own bread; however nearly all had to buy a part or all of the flour they used. But a large number of wine-makers living in towns, had to buy bread from local bakers, for they lacked baking facilities or found the cost of fuel prohibitive. As the century advanced the black bread habitual in peasant households gave way to white bread, formerly a luxury. But barley and oats by no means disappeared, especially in some isolated highland vineyards.

In the province of Alessandria southeast of Turin, vegetable soup and *polenta* (a mush made from maize or chestnut flour) were also consumed daily. In summer salads became popular: onions, garlic, cucumbers, lettuce, and green peppers were mixed with olive oil for the noon meal. Rice was also widely consumed in the Po Valley, where it was plentiful.[39] In the South boiled vegetables, fruit, and cheese were taken along with onions, garlic, and oil. Here in particular olive oil served to give taste to tasteless dishes such as bread and mush.

Before 1850 many vignerons did not drink wine with meals at home save on special occasions. They consumed it of course, in the field because it was part of their wage and also in cafés because cafés were cultural centers of tremendous importance where card-playing, dominoes, and other games took place, where local clubs or circles met, and where entire families gathered for festive evenings and to read newspapers. But many small and very small growers, especially in years of low prices, had to sell all their grapes and wine in order to make ends meet. Even in good years they consumed their *piquettes* rather then pure wine, which of course had a lower caloric value. In both France and Italy clever wine workers refused to exert themselves when pressing grape skins so that some of the remaining juice would lend added quality to their meagre drink. In the earlier decades of the century the poorest probably consumed little but *piquettes*, though this in considerable quantity, from one to three liters a day. Later in the century those working on large domains received a somewhat better wine as part of their wage, a practice that made them the envy of workers in general agriculture because of the calories it added to their diet. It is probable that the amount of homemade wine consumed by vignerons of all sorts rose steadily after midcentury. By the later decades treasury officials estimated home consumption at one-fourth to one-third of total production. With an output of 45 million hectoliters, and a viticultural population of 5 million, per capita intake in a year could total 2.25 hectoliters or .62 liters per day for male and female adults and older children. Such a rate could add roughly 300–400 calories to the daily diet. The phylloxera, which reduced this rate of consumption, was not only a financial setback, it was also a dietary hardship. These figures, based on the one-fourth estimate, are extremely rough approximations and assume an even distribution between sexes. In fact men consumed nearly all the wine, whether it was made at home or included as part of their wage.

Most was drunk while they worked in the vines, without any apparent ill effect, an indication that its alcoholic content must have been low and that much was eliminated as perspiration. Everyone in wine regions were convinced that wine was a health drink, a *"tonique"* beneficial for hard workers on the land. Alcoholism, they firmly believed, was hardly a malady among them, being rather a vice of urban dwellers who consumed distilled beverages of high alcoholic content. This was undoubtedly correct; moreover the simple wines vignerons imbibed so readily were less germ-infested than the water available to them. Hence the assertion of the great microbiologist Pasteur that wine was the healthiest of drinks, provided, of course, that it was not consumed in excess. For many growers three liters a day was not excessive, but rather "bracing." Equally bracing was a small glass of brandy early in the morning to "kill one's worms."

The privations accepted during the year came to an end with the commencement of the grape harvest. That is, unless the crop was so poor that privation gave way to lamentation. But in most years the months of September and October meant a combination of enormous labor and almost frenetic gaiety for vignerons and their families. For the small independent grower the *vendange* brought several weeks of intense work, involving grape picking, crushing, fermenting, and pressing. All the steps required for the primary fermentation were the equivalent of the birth of a child and as the midwife to the new vintage the vigneron rarely found time to sleep for several days on end. When the new wine was fermenting quietly in vats or in casks and the air was still heavily redolent with the sweet odors of fresh fruit and the pungency of carbon dioxide gas, then he and his family and the rest of the village came together for a celebration combining the awesome solemnity of Christian prayers, of church bells, of chants and hymns, of *Te Deums*, with the unleashed passions of their ancient inheritance, the gorging upon food, the swilling of wine, the ribald songs centuries old, and the abandon to joyous dancing sweeping up both young and old.

Perhaps the happiest of all were the grape pickers after their long hours of labor between the rows. Those of Catania in Sicily gathered after supper and the Rosary for their *baccanale*. The music came from cymbals, tambourines, bagpipes, and whistles of various sorts. The pickers danced, slowly at first but the tempo quickened and soon they were whirling, leaping, kicking without cessation for one or two hours until exhaustion overtook them. Then, in two files, one of women and one of men, they went off to sleep. In several other parts of Sicily the harvest began with an odd game of mutual insult, a kind of duel of invective between two contestants; the more imaginative and drawn out the expletives, the more ingenious the use of allusion and double meaning, the more there was applause and laughter bursting forth from the attending crowds.

In Apulia hoards of young girls went among the vines dressed in their Sunday best. Before picking, they removed their outer garments and began work dressed in their voluminous, varicolored petticoats and long-sleeved undershirts. They sang rhythmically as they moved down the vines, snipping bunches with their knives. After the harvest men and women gathered for a banquet of chicken, bread, and wine; then they marched into town in a cortege led by an ox-drawn cart surmounted by their landowner seated on a large barrel.[40]

France too, had its festivities. The most elaborate probably took place in Bordeaux where, after the harvest, estate workers chose the strongest among them to be their Bacchus, sat him, as in Apulia, atop a huge barrel on a vine-decorated wagon drawn by oxen and led him to the château where he toasted the lord, the lady, and numerous guests come from nearby Bordeaux and faraway Paris for the fun (see figure 28).

FIGURE 28: *Grape Harvest Festival*

At last, as vine leaves changed from green to bright red or yellow, life returned to normal and the merchants arrived to assess the new wine.

Wine Merchants

Not a great deal is known about wine merchants or the organization of their commerce, perhaps because their activities have lacked drama, have continued in war and peace over centuries of time, and because historians have been more concerned with the quantities and values of wine cargoes than with the lives of shippers. No information has emerged to suggest a commercial revolution in the trade or sudden modernization of its methods of distribution. On the contrary, until the 1860s the wholesale trade retained many of its guild characteristics. In the larger wine districts, such as those in the South and Southwest of France, much local buying and selling remained in the hands of brokers (*courtiers*), each of whom enjoyed a form of monopoly in the district where he was domiciled. Bordeaux brokers could trade only in Bordeaux; they were excluded from buying wine in the Médoc except through a broker from that district. Even if a large wholesaler (*négociant*) wished to make purchases in, say, Pauillac or Podensac, he was obliged to act through a broker in Bordeaux, who in turn contacted a broker in Pauillac. Only if there was no local *courtier* could the agent in Bordeaux handle the sale directly with the grower. This system, aimed at protecting the age-old interests and privileges of entrenched local and regional traders, increased the number of middle men and, it was widely believed, raised retail prices outrageously. Happily the law of July 1866 established freedom of trade.[41] Whatever its defect, laissez faire could at times cut away a great deal of deadwood in commerce.

Courtiers, however, did not disappear after losing their monopoly position. They survived because they were highly trained specialists who proved to be a desirable adjunct to large wholesalers unable to visit every area from which they required wine. Some *courtiers* specialized in lesser wines, others in fine wines; the two did not mix their specialties, since a taster of ordinaries was not considered qualified to judge the great growths.[42] For the large merchant the broker had to be able to assess the character of a young wine and to predict its future development. Above all he had to discover which of its qualities will be dominant and which weak, so that it could be blended with other wines displaying complementary qualities.

In the eyes of wine-growers, however, these commission agents were villains of a low order. A vociferous complaint in all wine areas singled them out, not as heroes of the fine palate, but as spies for wholesalers, sneaky fellows going around to discover unlucky vignerons with an excess of wine and a need of money who could be pressured to sell their produce at a low price for credit or cash. Large quality growers were just as hostile. Monsieur Lamothe, general manager of the illustrious Château Latour from 1807 to 1835 referred to the well-known wholesaler Pierre F. Guestier as "Pierre the Cruel," and he also was scathing in his comments about the brokers Lawton and Merman. Indeed he alluded to them all as "matadors" or "chartronais," as though the Quai des Chartrons, where most of their offices were located, was a den of iniquity. On the other hand, his predecessors had managed to maintain friendly relations with wholesalers, and, like so many growers and their managers, depended on them for loans until the first installments came in.[43] Yet relations by and large remained tense, the hostility that surfaced being part of that eternal conflict between producer, middleman, and consumer. Many peasant growers turned to vinicultural cooperatives in the hope of eliminating the merchants; but on the whole growers were slow to accept cooperatives, partly because they were almost fanatical individualists, partly because the honest *courtiers*—there were many— judged accurately the true value of their wine and stood as guarantors of its quality, and quality determined the range of prices for a given wine.

There is no doubt that middlemen raised prices for consumers. However in Bordeaux the wholesaler who purchased wine to ship within France received merely a three-franc commission per *tonneau* on wine selling under 150 francs, and 2 percent on wine selling higher. The Chamber of Commerce complained during midcentury that not only was the commission too low, but that the merchant had also to extend long-term credit to the grower.[44] Probably these were the prevailing national rates, and it was not everywhere customary for merchants to lend money. A practice that was universal, however, was for merchants to pay the growers four to six months after purchase, when the wine was distributed to retailers; the final payment might not arrive until a year later. When they did advance money, they charged an interest on it which growers had to include in their costs. In the Languedocian vineyard middlemen raised the cost of wine by about one-third. Between 1865 and 1879 the grower obtained an average price of 21 francs in the department of Aude, while the wholesaler received an average of 27 francs and the retailer 33. In Gard the mean sequence was 20, 29, and 30 francs, while in Hérault it was 18.6, 22.5, 29 francs.[45] In Burgundy the net profits of wholesalers came to about 20 percent of sales.[46]

Evidently the wine trade was sufficiently profitable to attract a large number of wholesalers. Unfortunately the data listing their numbers is probably not as accurate as one could hope. In 1826 there were, according to Bousquet, 28,036 *négociants*.[47] The total for 1869 came to 24,693; for 1889 to 27,777; for 1899 to 29,344 and for 1908 to 33,690.[48] These figures indicate a decline of 13.5 percent between 1826 and 1869 then a rise of 36 percent to 1908.

There was no comparable increase of wine production or of population to justify this expansion. There was, of course, a notable rise in the urban population, but this factor did not enhance demand; on the contrary, the number of wine drinkers leveled off in the last decade of the century and after 1900 the wine market became flooded, even though the quantity shipped out of the cellars was not significantly greater than during the golden age. There was not, it is clear, as marked a tendency toward concentration in trade as there was in production after 1900.

Interesting to note is the rather small size of most wholesale companies. At the turn of the century in the Paris region there were only 18 establishments with 21 to 50 employees, but 1,027 with merely 1 to 4, and 303 with 5 to 10. In the Gironde there were 16 companies with 21 to 50 employees, a number nearly equal to Paris and 4 with over 50 employees, thus surpassing Paris where there were merely 2. In Languedoc (Aude, Hérault, Gard) there were 15 wholesale houses employing 21 to 50 persons, but only 1 with more than 50. The vast majority of wholesalers, it is evident, hired fewer than 4 employees and the next largest employed 5 to 10.[49] Throughout most of France, therefore, the wine trade was controlled by companies of rather modest size who shared the market as best they could.

Many of the large firms have long and complex histories; some of the largest handling still wines appeared in Bordeaux during the eighteenth and nineteenth centuries, with more than half surviving and indeed thriving into the twentieth. Perhaps most remarkable was the extraordinary number of foreign merchants who settled in Bordeaux, or rather, just outside the city, in the Chartrons district, because in earlier times foreigners were prohibited from living within the city's bounds. Probably the earliest in modern times was J.-S. Beyerman, a Dutchman, who opened a firm in 1620 that still exists today. He was followed by two others from the Netherlands in the nineteenth century. The Irish were also active. Thomas Barton began in 1725 a partnership with M. Guestier that became in the following years the largest shipping firm then known. Barton and Guestier were also the first *négociants* to begin buying up classed estates and selling their own "home grown" wine.[50] In 1740

Abraham Lawton founded a firm that prospered and in 1830 took in M. Testet as a partner. William Johnston, of Scotch-Irish origins, set himself up soon after, in 1734. The Germans were and still are equally numerous: Schröder and Schÿler (1739), Clossman (1785), E. Kressmann (1871), and Sichel (1883). Even the Swiss were represented by the firm of D.G. Mestrezat (1814), and Schleswig-Holstein by Herman Cruse (1819). Although most of these men settled and founded families in Bordeaux and some of them became naturalized, they often specialized in trade with their native countries and were purveyors of wine to some of the reigning monarchs. The presence of such a large foreign contingent is clear evidence that the wine labeled "Bordeaux" enjoyed an extensive international trade and reputation.

Of course most of the wine from the Bordelais went to French markets, and there were numerous native firms also active in its shipment. Among the oldest were Beylot (1740), the Dubos brothers (1785), Leon Hanappier (1816), Louis Eschenauer (1821), Alfred de Luze (1820), Armond Lalande (1844), Alphonse Delor (1865), Octave Calvet (1870), and Fernand Ginestet (1899). By no means did they leave all foreign trade in the hands of other nationals; they too built up markets outside of France and acquired international reputations.

Champagne also encouraged the growth of large-scale commerce, particularly foreign commerce, since more of it was consumed outside than inside France. Like the Bordeaux trade, foreigners played a fairly active role as merchants and manufacturers. Names such as Bollinger, Vander-Veken, Heidsieck, Mumm, Roederer, Krug, Deutz, and Geldermann indicate the non-Gallic origins of some of the major firms, and it is clear that their founders came chiefly from the nearby Netherlands and the Germanies. England, although the largest market, sent only one representative, a Mr. Barnett, who traded under the French name of Périnet.[51]

As in Bordeaux, champagne merchants settled down and became naturalized either before or after founding their firms; and equally like the Bordelais they tended to marry within the local commercial circle, although there is not a great deal of information to support this generalization. Nonetheless, if there were few interlocking directorates, there were certainly many interlocking families, not only through marriage but even more through inheritance. Distinctions between the foreign and the native-born disappeared after two or more generations, for there were numerous French nationals in the business, and there were partnerships as well as marriages that united foreign and native names.

Again Champagne and Bordeaux resemble each other in the venerable age and stability of their great trading companies. The oldest in Champagne was Ruinart, founded by Nicholas Ruinart, a textile merchant of Reims. In 1729 he established the first firm to specialize in wine to the exclusion of other commodities. Prior to that it was considered too risky to narrow one's field of activity; besides there was little sparkling wine and the still beverage was not highly profitable. The house of Chanoine appeared in (1730), then Taittinger and Fourneaux (1734), Moët (1743), which in 1833 became Moët and Chandon, Vander Veken (1757), Dubois (1765), Clicquot (1783), Heidsieck (1785), and Jacqueson (1798). From 1795 to 1815, when French armies conquered Europe, champagne salesmen followed them, offering bottles to celebrate victories and creating new markets among rich nobles. Then unrelenting expansion during the nineteenth century encouraged more entrepreneurs to enter the field; among the best known in the Anglo-Saxon market were Mumm (1820), Pommery (1831), and Pol-Roger (1849). The list goes on, but it would be tedious to continue; suffice it to state that eighteen of them became known as "Les Grandes Marques," or, more awesomely, the "Crowned Heads of Champagne." [52]

Unlike most crowned heads little is known about the companies and considerably less about the men—and women—who founded and managed them. Their archives have either been destroyed during war, or remain closed, or, where opened, contain little information about managers, salesmen, and organization. The information available subsumes fact and fancy, legend, propaganda, and the memories of old men. For the Champagne area Patrick Forbes has gleaned enough information to provide us with some generalizations, a few of them self-evident.

The houses that succeeded and grew from modest beginnings enjoyed a combination of honest, skilled management, active salesmanship, and intense apprenticeship for younger family members. Sons, sons-in-law, nephews, and cousins entered either the family firm or another, and there learned the secrets of blending; they also traveled in foreign markets as salesmen. The Ruinarts are a good example of close family control and aggressive salesmanship. The grandson, great-grandson, and later heirs of the founder traveled in England, the United States, and Russia, where they made contacts with the rich and the powerful, obtained interviews with heads of state, and gave expensive receptions in order to make their sparkling wines known among the upper classes. The Ruinarts remained faithful to the Bourbon dynasty of France, acquired titles of nobility, and had extensive connections with the nobility of Europe, the class most given to drinking champagne. This fidelity was a great benefit to their business when the Bourbons were in power, but not a serious disadvantage when they were not. There were always nobles and rich persons to buy their sparkling beverages.

The Moëts became identified with the Bonaparte dynasty, but they were a well-established firm before the first Napoleon became ruler in 1800. The third generation of the family's wine-makers, with Jean-Rémy as head, already owned sizable cellars in Epernay, and the second generation could boast of having sold champagne to kings and their mistresses, including Madame de Pompadour, and of markets in Germany, Spain, Russia, America, Poland, and Bohemia. Napoleon appreciated Jean-Rémy's devotion, frequently visited him at Epernay when traveling eastward, and shortly before his abdication in 1814 pinned his own cross of the Legion of Honor on his host's chest, a dramatic but not uncommon gesture. The fall of Napoleon did not bring in its wake the fall of Moët; on the contrary adversity seemed to encourage him. There is a story that Russian officers, returning from their conquest of France, pillaged sizable amounts of champagne stored in Jean-Rémy's cellars, whereupon he is supposed to have said, "All these officers who are ruining me today . . . will make my fortune tomorrow. All those who drink my wine will become, on returning to their homeland, traveling salesmen praising my establishment." [53] On 31 December 1831 he ceded the company to his son Victor and his son-in-law Pierre-Gabriel Chandon de Briailles, after which the firm became Moët et Chandon. Its good fortune and excellent connections continued; in fact it acquired a near monopoly of sales to the rulers of Europe and to the American upper class. Policy called not only for expanding its business and the plant, but also the dimensions of its vineyards. By 1879 it possessed between 800 and 900 hectares of the finest vines and employed a personnel of 1,150 full time.[54] The record of sales explains more than words the company's growth: "In the 1820s Moët's average annual sales are believed to have been in the region of 20,000 bottles . . . ; by 1880 . . . nearly 2½ million." [55]

The firm that became Clicquot-Ponsardin displayed a different pattern of growth. When the son of its founder, François Clicquot, died while still a young man, his widow, who acquired fame as La Veuve Clicquot, decided to carry on in his place. Apparently she had not participated in the management before and had much to learn. At this point her ill luck in losing a husband was balanced by her good luck—and sound business sense—in acquiring truly exceptional assistance from her associates, both of whom were German. M. Bohne had been hired by her husband in 1806, and he opened the east European market, expecially Russia, so successfully that many Russians used the term Clicquot for champagne. Company correspondence makes clear the market conditions prevailing during and shortly after the French imperium. The British fleet controlled the northern seas, then the only passage feasible between Reims and the East, and both French and neutral ships were either destroyed or taken as prizes. Inland conditions were different for wherever French armies conquered, French merchants could move in. But champagne salesmen often found that the rich had fled or were burdened by Napoleon's fiscal exactions. Even in friendly lands, markets took time to become reestablished. In 1809 Bohne wrote from Hamburg:

> The port, closed with chains, is a pitiable sight. The lower classes beg and big business groans. Where am I in all this? I run from door to door. People speak to me of exchange rates, of war, of requisitions, of occupying troops, of losses incurred, . . . and when I lift my voice to cry my wares across all this lamentation, people laugh at me, deploring their unsold stock and blaming the politicians.[56]

In 1810 he lamented in a letter sent from Lübeck:

> Frightful stagnation in business. The decrees of our Emperor on colonial wares and English manufactured goods, have brought things to this point. English goods are burnt, there is no traffic by sea because of the English fleet and soon the sea will be blocked by ice. In Vienna the nobility cannot pay the merchants because they have three years' wheat harvest still unsold. The cost of living mounts terribly. After plague and famine, paper money is the most ghastly curse.[57]

Similar reports came in from other agents in Europe. After 1806 it would seem that the Widow was hardly earning enough to make both ends meet. In addition Bohne complained that the champagne she was sending him was inferior. So in the summer of 1810 she engaged a new cellar master, Antoine Muller, a truly ingenious blender. But her troubles were not over. Although 1811 was the "year of the comet," war broke out anew with Napoleon's invasion of Russia and business was bleak until 1814. Then the tide of pessimism ebbed. Bohne, in a prophetic vision, recognized that victorious Russians would want to celebrate their victory over the retreating French. With boldness to equal his vision he ordered 10,000 bottles, which he himself accompanied from Reims to Koenigsberg. From there his letter revealed the change of his spirits:

> I am adored here because my wines are adorable! . . . Oh! Honoured Friend, what a spectacle, and how I wish you were here to

enjoy it. You have two-thirds of the best society of Koenigsberg at your feet over your nectar. . . . Of all the good wines that have so far titillated northern heads, none has had the effect of Mme Clicquot's *cuvée* 1811 . . . I seek orders from no one, I just reveal the number of my hotel room and a queue forms outside it.[58]

Bohne sold most of his consignment in St. Petersburg for the fabulous price of twelve rubles a bottle; a second consignment sold as profitably. Despite the setbacks of the allied occupation of Reims, where Mme Clicquot hid her champagne more successfully than Moët, her salesmen took advantage of the long peace to expand their contacts and to organize their markets. In 1821 the demand for her champagne exceeded her supply by 100,000 bottles.

As Mme Clicquot aged she was confronted with the problem of succession. The Ruinarts, the Moëts, and other families had male heirs in abundance and their daughters often married men capable of carrying on the business. La Veuve, however, had only a daughter, and after Bohne's death, she had to rely on herself and a German named Kessler. He lacked prudence and nearly caused a bankruptcy when the bank that Mme Clicquot had taken over was on the verge of failure, but happily she was saved by Edouard Werlé, also of German origin, who led her back to concentrate on the wine business and who became her partner in 1831. A man of remarkable business acumen he was probably responsible for the tremendous growth of the firm. He inherited the business in 1866, for La Veuve had enough sense not to leave it to her son-in-law, the Count Louis de Chevigné, scion of an old aristocratic family, who preferred spending money to making it.

It is apparent from these brief family histories that entrepreneurship in the wine industry displayed its talents in management, quality control, and sales, but remarkable genius was no less present in advertising.

Before the mid-nineteenth century the scope of publicity was highly limited. There was no popular press, no glossy periodicals, no billboards, and of course no radio or television. There was little save personal contact. It is no exaggeration to state that cheap wines were simply sold by barmen in local taverns, and expensive wines were promoted by their producers. Everywhere aristocratic owners of fine vineyards sought to make their produce known to other nobles and to rich bourgeois. They served it during the large and sumptuous dinners they offered both at home and in the capital. Or they resorted to grand gestures. The Marquis di Barolo, so a story runs, sent fifteen wagons, each loaded with a cask of his wine and each from a different vineyard, to Carlo Alberto, ruler of Piedmont. News of this gift must have enhanced the fame of his wine.[59] Earlier, the Duke de Richelieu, governor of Guienne in 1755, sent some of his bordeaux to Versailles, where Louis XV served it, an act that certainly added to its fame. In fact bordeaux or claret was hardly known inside France because it was either consumed locally or sent to foreign markets. Until the eighteenth century it was a rather harsh beverage, sold in wood and still young when consumed.[60] Until growers came to understand the need to age it, so that it could compete with port and sherry, it could hardly have equaled the quality of red champagne or fine burgundy. Noble growers in these two areas competed for royal favor, especially that of Louis XIV, for their wines reached Paris more easily than bordeaux. Each side had friendly versifiers and epigrammists to glorify the virtues of their respective nectars, and the war of the poets ground out much wit and doggerel that was perhaps a shade or two higher in quality than present-day commercials. Fine wine producers and sellers have customarily sought to associate their beverages with royalty, to become official purveyors to reigning families, and to display this privilege on their labels. This form of snob appeal became the hallmark of their advertising.

Promotional activities also utilized the old medieval practice of organizing trade fairs. Wines dispatched to Paris in the 1850s, led to the classification of 1855. Wines appeared at international fairs, not only in Paris, but also in Philadelphia, London, and other major cities. Probably the first local fair of major proportions began in Bordeaux in 1909. This great Festival of Wine, devoted exclusively to Bacchus, has always drawn widespread attention. It has been especially useful as a means for the lesser growers to present their labels to a broader public always eager to discover untasted vintages and regional varieties.

When champagne firms became big business in the nineteenth century and large-scale *négociants* took over most bordeaux and burgundy sales, efforts to make wine known assumed gigantic, vastly expensive, proportions; on the whole they were also effective. Simply the names of these wines became household words, and producers in other countries, unable to match the French masters, adopted for their lesser vintages the names of France's most famous wine provinces. In the eyes of the French this was fraudulent, but diplomacy and court suits were never more than partially successful in preventing this abuse.

Champagne salesmen have always been resourceful. Sparkling wine has become known by the firm's name and the object of sellers has been to keep that name before the public. Merchants have induced—usually bribed—hotel keepers, restaurant and railroad personnel to push their labels when serving customers. Even the butlers of nobles were not immune to this tactic, for sellers felt it important to have the popular press report that the duke of this or the count of that had served their champagne and found it superlative. No one knows whether such tricks of the trade were really effective. From time to time champagne publicists made bigger news than the society columns. George Kessler, US agent of Moët and Chandon, in 1902 managed to substitute Moët for German sparkling at the launching of the German emperor's yacht *Meteor* in New York. Then he succeeded in having magnums of his company's wine served at a lunch attended by President Roosevelt and Prince Henry of Prussia. *Quel coup!* as the French would say; not even Jean-Rémy's second coming could have shown more resourcefulness—and the man who carried it out had a German name! The kaiser, it is said, was so infuriated that he recalled his ambassador. Kessler, however, was unperturbed and in 1906 dispatched an entire railway car of champagne to earthquake victims in San Francisco.[61]

Café frivolity, bubbling in its own right, was also a dimension of publicity. After the trade treaty of 1860 with England, music hall singers there took up champagne by the glassful and as a theme for their sprightly songs. In 1869 George Leybourne gained fame and the sobriquet of "Champagne Charlie" for his ditty *Moët and Shandon for me*. It was sung in Cockney of course: [62]

> Champagne Charlie was my name,
> Champagne drinking gain'd my fame.
> So as of old when on the spree,
> Moet and Shandon's the wine for me.

Perhaps we should put a *"hic"* rather than a *"sic"* after the Cockney spelling of "Shandon."

Not to be outdone, the Clicquot-Ponsardin firm turned to the Great Vance, who challenged Champagne Charlie to a singing-drinking (or vice versa) bout. With each man sitting on opposite sides of the stage, Leybourne sought to hold his own against Vance's

> Clicquot! Clicquot! That's the stuff to make you jolly,
> Clicquot! Clicquot! Soon will banish melancholy.
> Clicquot! Clicquot! Drinking other wine is folly.
> Clicquot! Clicquot! That's the drink for me.

And yet wine sales and promotional stunts were deeply distrusted by the public. Clearly sparkling wine drinkers had come a long way since the first decades of the century, when an old-fashioned connoisseur of still wines, Grimod de La Regnière, had warned his readers to drink champagne sparingly and rarely because "no other wine is less congenial to one's stomach and troubles more disagreeably one's digestion." [63] He was worried about the champagne sold in Paris at a time when the wine was shipped in wood, bottled inside the city, and sold with or without a label. No one knew its ingredients, but officials, more concerned with fiscal than public health, were little concerned. The *octrois* duties or municipal tolls, far heavier on bottled than on barreled wine, made it too costly to ship wine in glass—a condition later modified by the greater ease of smuggling bottles over the town walls. Wine in the barrel could never be guaranteed for purity by the grower or original shipper, quite simply because it passed through too many hands on its way to the consumer.

Courtiers were the object of the growers' distrust, but *négociants* often enjoyed no higher esteem among knowledgeable consumers. When ambassador to France in 1787, Thomas Jefferson warned a friend to avoid the merchants and to buy directly from the best growers, for "it is from them alone that genuine wine is to be got and not from any wine merchant whatever." [64] Champagne firms, of course, normally blended wines, and the house label was the mark of recognition and of quality. Nearly all other wholesalers—as well as some retailers—blended wines that they put on the market. The public might have been less skeptical had merchants explained why they blended and indicated the wines used, but blending remained the secret of each company. Partly they blended to maintain a constant character for each type of wine, partly to overcome weaknesses in the wines, but partly it was to fool the public. This last motive sometimes involved false labeling, i.e., selling wine as pure bordeaux when a large quantity of it came from elsewhere.

Merchants in Bordeaux almost always blended other wines into the claret they sent to foreign markets, especially to Britain, and in this practice they merely imitated native English merchants. To the classed growths they added varying amounts of wine from the Rhône, usually hermitage, a quality product offering greater body and intensity of color. To the lesser wines of Bordeaux they added about 10 percent of benicarlo, a rather low-grade Spanish wine of intense color and high alcohol content. Alicante and Languedocian wines served the same purpose before the arrival of Algerian wine later in the century.

Merchants served an important role in the industry. Quite apart from putting wine on the market, they matured most of it in their own cellars and prepared it to suit the taste of particular markets. In 1826 Jullien explained their role: "The wines of the first growths of Bordeaux as drunk in France do not resemble those sent to London; the latter, in which is put a certain quantity of Spanish and French Midi wine, undergo some preparations which give them a taste and quality, without which they would not be found good in England." [65] No wonder the 1842 edition of the *Encyclopaedia Britannica* lamented: "it is plain that few of those who imagine they are drinking the first growths of Bordeaux can even be drinking the second." [66] The wine consumed by the drinking public, therefore, was not the wine of the vigneron in a direct sense but that concocted by an alchemist denominated *négociant*. Dishonest ones sought to trick the public, honest ones sought to improve quality and prepare beverages suitable to the varying tastes of different markets. The significant growth of sales both within and without France attests to their success. And the repeated urgings of Italian enological journalists eventually prodded the merchants of that country into following the example of France. The role of the merchant grew in importance over the century and was reinforced by his purchase of important vineyards, thereby combining production and distribution in the same hands. Such concentration and rationalization revealed that the wine industry was in step with the general tendencies of Europe's economy as regards structure, organization, and distribution.

CHAPTER ELEVEN

The Commerce of Wine

The objective of this chapter is to point out the differences in the foreign wine trade of France and Italy and to explain their origins. In both countries wine was an important article of commerce, but the French were certainly the more successful in their efforts to expand sales, first, by turning out a product of sufficient quality to attract discriminating customers and second, by building up sales techniques and the capital investment required to expand in old and to conquer new markets. The Italians, on the other hand, suffered from factors that they could not easily overcome before 1860: political disunity and domination by foreign countries, first Spain and then Austria. Neither country found it expedient to encourage the Italian wine industry, a position quite distinct from that of the late medieval English conquerors of France who, despite their brief hold, played a major role in the growth of the Bordeaux and Atlantic vineyards. But then the Anglo-French Plantagenets had no vineyards of their own, while the Spanish and the Austrians had considerable vine acreage and hardly wished to buy or encourage the sale of competitive Italian beverages. But even after unification the Italian economy remained weak, especially as regards transport, investment capital, foreign connections, and the technological education of its viticultural population. Over a century ago the Italians could have made as much and as good wine as the French—they do so today, but only because they have finally learned to imitate the French. They have at last accepted the belief, widespread among winemen, that the incentive to conquer foreign markets urges growers to produce wines of superior quality. Probably the quality of vinicultural produce today is not quite as dependent on foreign sales as the above statement asserts—there seems at present to be a kind of reciprocal relationship between wine and commerce—but before the arrival of fast, cheap transport and scientific techniques for preserving fermented juices, the grower wishing to sell in profitable distant markets simply had to turn out a superior beverage, if only so that it could travel. The volume and value of trade, therefore, were closely connected with high-quality goods.

Volume and Value of Foreign Commerce in the Era of Tariff Protection (1800–1860)

FRANCE

Of the major wine-producing regions of Europe in the earlier nineteenth century, France held prime rank in every respect: quality and quantity, as well as shipments to foreign parts. Undoubtedly this high level of achievement was partly a function of the political unity and prestige that France enjoyed at this time. A sizable national state, she included three of the most prestigious viticultural regions in the world, Bordeaux, Burgundy, and Champagne, a strength that sales and prices reflected. Italy, on the other hand, was a melange of small, weak states economically disadvantaged by the confused condition of their politics. Until the 1840s no government there was politically motivated to expand foreign trade aggressively and merchants had no voice in economic policy. The great commercial exploits of the late medieval and renaissance city states were matters of history, not of contemporary public policy. Until 1860, then, comparing France and the Italian states is like comparing a giant and pigmies. The comparison would, perhaps, be more just if Burgundy were set beside Tuscany and Bordeaux beside Piedmont. But this method would also be unhistorical, since it would presuppose that a region highly integrated into a larger entity can be artificially detached for purposes of comparison with a region not so integrated. There were undoubtedly times when Bordeaux wine merchants wished that they could enjoy enough local freedom to ignore the tariff policies of the government in Paris. But no winemen showed sympathy for separatist movements and all the regional wine economies of France were strongly influenced by geographic, economic, and cultural ties to the nation. Wine-growers, although many depended on foreign markets, were as patriotic as other market-oriented groups. This was also the case in the Italian peninsula, where the *Risorgimento* enjoyed widespread support in viticultural areas, in large part because winemen hoped to strengthen their economic position through political unity and the end of internal tariff barriers.

French growers were undoubtedly at an advantage because the large geographic size of their homeland, a market fully open to them, strengthened their position in international trade. Most of their wine was sold "at home," and some profit acquired in domestic sales enabled the industry to improve the quality of the more costly wine destined for export. The limited quantities sent out are not indicative of the importance of foreign trade. In the first half of the century only 10 to 11 percent of total alcoholic beverages (brandy, cordials, wine, etc.) and only 5 percent of all wine entered foreign commerce.[1] Yet exports of alcoholic beverages constituted a major source of wealth. Wine shipments alone averaged 7 percent of France's total exports from 1827 to 1846. It is clear that only superior beverages crossed the frontiers, that is, the finest growths and the best ordinaries. The numerous common wines, bringing prices that nothing save extreme shortage could push upward, simply could not pay the costs of long voyages and more often than not turned sour after the rigors of travel.

Although the wines the French exported were of high quality, wine-growers and wholesalers after 1815 complained of the difficulty of selling their produce. They insisted that reversion to high tariffs everywhere in Europe, including France, had stifled exchange and therefore production. They claimed vineyard acreage had declined along with foreign sales, that producers and merchants were the victims of governmental policy biased in favor of protectionist cereal-growers and industrialists. High government officials, of course, did not agree with these estimates, ignoring the possibility that their own information might be erroneous, as it often was. Right or wrong, official figures indicated an increase of the land devoted to vines, as well as an increase of wine exports after 1787. If we use official trade figures, a comparison of the last three years of the Old Regime (1787–89) with the years 1826–28 reveals a rise of 15 percent in volume of exports. From 1828 to 1846 the increase was 22 percent.[2] Although officials were deeply impressed, their findings indicate a mere 37 percent rise over fifty-seven years or less than .7 percent a year.

Much of this increase, however, cannot be accounted for by authentic foreign trade but rather by the rise of markets in France's colonies, where consumption went up at the time when European states began erecting tariffs against incoming goods. In 1788 French colonies imported a mere 7,115 hectoliters; in 1846 they bought 628,000, 65 percent of which entered Algeria, invaded in 1829 by thirsty French soldiers. Bacchus merrily rode in astride military supply trains, and created sufficient demand to account for much of the increase of wine "exports" in the 1830s and 1840s. This geographic shift of trade from the centuries-old markets of the North to new ones in the South probably saved some growers from bankruptcy, but in the view of winemen this was not really foreign trade but simply "displaced internal consumption." [3] Frenchmen were drinking it in the colonies rather than at home, but they were using the national monetary supply to buy it. Moreover it was a very ordinary commodity, hardly worthy of the *gloire* the motherland's army was winning, and not particularly profitable, not the true product of foreign trade.

In truth, the growers' situation was less bleak than they claimed because the monetary value of their exports had improved. Percentages of rise in value were more impressive than those of volume. From 1827 to 1846 the increase came to 9.8 percent for wine in wood and 14.6 percent for that in bottle, about 1.2 percent per year. The increase in bottle exports reflected the growth of champagne shipments, now sent out almost exclusively in glass. These were significant gains in the two decades from the mid-twenties to the mid-forties, a time of stability in all the major studies of business cycles. Indeed growers and exporters benefited from a fairly stable, slightly rising market.

The worst years were 1822, 1824, 1830, and 1831, when the value of wine sent to foreign markets fell below 40 million francs. The best years were 1828, 1834, 1835, 1836, 1838, 1841, and 1845, when values rose to over 50 million. In a twenty-six-year span there were four bad and seven excellent years; the remainder registered exports in the mid and upper 40 millions.[4] Prior to 1848, however, no year was marked by the rise of great fortunes or a notable increase in prices. There were government officials, at least during the 1850s, who agreed with wholesalers that these were years of stagnation, that wine exports, although they had risen slightly in the late thirties and forties, had failed to keep pace with the rise in volume and value of other exports.

This news offered small consolation to Bordeaux merchants, who complained the loudest. Indeed they had reason for concern, even though they were unduly alarmist. The value of exports from Bordeaux seems not to have declined absolutely, but it did in relation to wines exported from other regions. The volume of wine shipped out as Bordeaux declined as part of all French wine exports, a decline which began with a drop from 69 percent of total exports in 1825 to 53 percent in 1830. Then for a while longer the great wine port held its own at 50 percent or more. Equally notable was the decline in value, as table 22 makes clear:

TABLE 22: *Bordeaux's Percent of Value of Exported Dry Still Wine, 1827–86*

Years	Wine in wood	Wine in bottle
1827–36	60	60
1837–46	54	47
1847–56	47	32
1857–66	45	41
1867–76	56	42
1877–86	64	24

These figures make clear that other vineyards of France enjoyed a marked rise in the value of their exports, at least until the phylloxera struck them in the 1870s. Bordeaux recovered by the mid-sixties for wine in barrels, but dropped precipitously for bottled wine, a result of the upsurge of burgundy and champagne, particularly the latter. Until 1875 sparkling wine had been classified with sweet wine (*vin de liqueur*), which accounts in part for bordeaux's strong place in table 22. By the 1880s champagne sales leapt ahead because northeastern France was not yet invaded by the phylloxera. In 1896 champagne moved ahead with 82 percent of the value of bottled exports, bordeaux ran quite behind at 10 percent, and the rest of France trailed at 7 percent. The line-up for the value of all wine shipped out in both wood and glass was champagne (38 percent), bordeaux (36.6 percent), rest of France (22.5 percent), and sweet wine (2.7 percent).

Bordeaux suffered particularly from the erection of tariff barriers in Prussia and other German states, as well as in those of southern Europe. Its produce had to compete with wines from the Rhine, where rising viticultural activity was encouraged by preferential tax treatment in states of the German Confederation. Even Britain ceased to be as active a market as formerly, because of high tariffs and a persistent preference for Spanish and Portuguese wines, such as sherry and port and the marsala of Sicily. These beverages, incidentally, English merchants transhipped to Germany, to the great disadvantage of all French alcoholic exports. France's colonial population, largely located in hot climates, preferred the light wines of Languedoc and Provence, which were often lower in alcohol as well as in price. Shipments to Algeria, in consequence, benefitted Marseilles rather than Bordeaux.

French viniculture was further disadvantaged by adverse fiscal policies and changing habits—the increasing consumption of coffee, tea, and other such hot drinks. These factors, of course, were often temporary and could change to the advantage of France as they did after 1860. Far more foreboding was the increasing vineyard acreage developing in southern Europe, especially in Italy; while it was not yet seriously competitive, it had marked future possibilities.

ITALY

Information on Italy's foreign and domestic wine trade in the first half of the nineteenth century is either absent, deficient, or unreliable. Until 1860–70 Italy was only a "geographic expression," a peninsula consisting of several small states, only four of which were in a position to carry out a truly independent commercial policy (Piedmont, Tuscany, Rome, and the Two Sicilies). Of these only two enjoyed the soil, climate, and know-how to produce wines capable of long voyages (Piedmont and Tuscany). However neither state was yet a major exporter of wine outside the peninsula, and most of the other Italian states suffered from an adverse balance of trade in the early years of the century. If the great Vincenzo Dandolo is correct, from 1807 through 1810 Italians imported wine valued at 26,626,000 lire and exported wine valued at a mere 5,411,000 lire.[5] They were, of course, under the thumb of their French conquerors and most of the wine they consumed, perhaps to toast the victories of French armies, they imported from France! This unfavorable balance continued until the 1830s when their imports of French wine fell to about two million lire.[6]

The chief exports of most Italian states consisted of olive oil, cereals, grains, and raw and semiworked silk. Villari's study of the Italian economy from 1815 to 1850 does not even mention wine (a more serious gap in his study than in the economy), and the Two Sicilies, producer of the largest volume of wine, was not considered an important exporter of it; rather the entire Mezzogiorno depended upon the sale of olive oil for much of its foreign income.[7] Nor does Graziani mention wine in his recent study. However Luigi de Rosa, while recognizing the faults of southern viniculture, valued Neapolitan wine exports for 1838 at 94,000 ducats and those of Sicily at 2,651,404 ducats. Wine accounted for about 1 percent of the value of total exports from the Kingdom of the Two Sicilies.[8]

In 1860 southern farmers produced about four million hectoliters of wine, yet exports declined.[9] This figure, though undoubtedly too low, indicates the large quantity of wine originating in the Mezzogiorno. In the past French and Swiss merchants had purchased some of this highly alcoholic brew to mix with weaker wines, but prices had fallen too low to be profitable for the growers. The Papal States, especially the Romans, were their chief foreign market prior to unification, with the result that the popes suffered an adverse balance of trade in wine during the 1850s.

The Piedmontese on the contrary consistently enjoyed a favorable balance of trade in wine until the 1850s.[10] It created a sizable amount of wealth, as table 23 shows:

TABLE 23: *Piedmont, Value of Wine Exports, 1819–60*

Years	Value of exports, means in lire	% of total exports
1819–24	3,403,551	4.94
1830–34	2,893,741	4.31
1840–44	3,029,281	4.67
1850–54	2,703,405	2.87
1856–60	11,597,594	5.14

The effects of powdery mildew are readily visible in the table for the earlier 1850s, but so is the remarkable comeback in the later years of the decade. Wine as a percentage of total exports also suffered a slump in the earlier 1850s, but though it recovered strongly, it did not match the more than fourfold increase in value. Cavour's free trade policies paid off as regards industrial development, exports of raw materials, and wine. But imported machines came from England and France and helped to empty Piedmont's pockets, while most imported wine came from Sardinia, a possession of the reigning House of Savoy, so that its trade amounted to shifting money from one pocket to another in the same pants.

Important to note is that usually over 90 percent of the profits from wine exports derived from sound common wines shipped in barrels (*botti*) at less than 20 lire per hectoliter. Shipments in bottles never amounted to much until the later 1850s. In 1835, for example, Piedmont exported over 129,400 hectoliters of commone wine, but only 19 of fine wine in wood, and merely 7,906 bottles. In 1857–60 the number of bottles rose to 197,503, thanks to the expansion of the vermouth industry. Clearly the natives consumed most of their own ordinaries, although they imported large quantities of it mainly from Sardinia, and they preferred their own finer beverages, although they continued to buy French fine wine both in wood and in glass. Unfortunately the data does not clearly distinguish French from other foreign wines until the 1850s, so exact quantities remain unknown.[11]

Judging from the volume of foreign trade, the powdery mildew struck Italian vines as severely as it did those of France. An adverse balance of trade in Piedmont began in 1852 and persisted, except for 1857–58, until Italy's unification in 1860. Despite this adverse balance Piedmont, unlike the Papal States, Tuscany, Lombardy, and Venetia, who suffered severe losses, increased her exports both in volume and value.[12] In 1850–51 her exports averaged 1,972,318 lire; in 1859–60 they amounted to 12,001,201 lire, a leap of 508 percent. Rise in volume of wine in wood came to only 51 percent, an indication that the increase of prices was as significant as in France, which in both countries helped viniculturists weather a near calamity. Domestic prices rose so drastically that merchants became fearful of losing Italian buyers, so in 1855 they began importing cheaper wine from France (93,311 hectoliters) and from Spain (105,257 hectoliters), bringing 1859 wine imports to over 6 percent of total imports, up from about 1 percent from the 1840s.

The years 1859–60 had different meanings in France and Italy. In France, they marked the end of the mildew era and the beginnings of a golden age. Prices, already rising, simply continued going up. In Italy there was no economic golden age as such. The victory over mildew was obscured by the victory over Austria. In both cases the French had helped win the battle.

Geography of Foreign Trade

ITALY

In the conquests of foreign markets Italy had to follow the advice of Mazzini; she had to go it alone. France, her chief rival after 1860, would not aid her, and Prussia, her ally in 1866 and 1879, never became a major buyer.

Long before unification the geographic pattern of international trade was fairly clear for most Italian wine-producing states. The Two Sicilies shipped their alcoholic beverages chiefly to Austria and the Austrian-held territories in the northern sector of the peninsula (Venetia and Lombardy) as well as to France, Switzerland, and the Papal States, her largest market. The range of distribution was quite limited. This was also true for Piedmont and Tuscany, whose cheaper wines went only to other

Italian states, to France, Spain, and Switzerland, and in considerable quantity to the Hapsburg territory of Lombardy. The city of Milan was an important market for both fine and common wines; on a much smaller scale it played a role similar to that of Paris for French wines.

The war against Austria and unification did not seriously effect this geographic distribution. What changed was rather the designation of "foreign" and "domestic." For example, Piedmont's sales to Austria in 1855 amounted to 4,376,665 lire, 80 percent of the value of her total wine exports. Two years later Austria accounted for 68 percent. In reality, most of this wine went to Lombardy and Venetia, but by 1865 exports to Germanic Austria, chiefly Vienna, amounted to merely 8 percent of total foreign wine trade. The Viennese, of course, continued to enjoy wine, as they enjoyed music, but now they looked eastward to Hungary, especially after 1867 when the Magyar state acquired near equality with Austria in the new Dual Monarchy.

As compensation, sales to Switzerland and Great Britain suddenly rose. In 1865 England bought 36 percent of Italy's exports in wood, and the Helvetian Republic absorbed 16 percent. Far more modest were Italy's exports to England in bottle, most of it marsala, vermouth, and probably chianti in straw-covered flasks. In 1865 Britain shipped in 37,166 bottles and paid 39,024 lire, just over one lira per bottle, a rather low price. Switzerland bought only 2,959 bottles and Austria a mere 1,600. These modest gains clearly indicate that Europe north of the Alps did not take Italian wine seriously.

Of note was Italy's failure seriously to penetrate the Anglo-Saxon market, where she sought to push aside the French. The consul at Liverpool complained that the wines arrived in a defective state, an indication that peninsula vintners still had much to learn. The wide round chianti bottle was difficult to cork without breaking, and although improved glassmaking overcame this,[13] the fiaschi could not be laid on their sides, so the corks dried out, letting air in. The Italians were equally unsuccessful in penetrating the United States. Ricasoli sent chianti in casks and bordeaux-type bottles, but Americans decided they were too expensive compared to French wines of equal quality. Not even Ricasoli's classic vintages could overcome Yankee distrust. According to consular reports, most of these wines arrived before they had been sufficiently clarified. Cloudiness probably resulted from bottling too early, often in the first spring, before the dregs had fully settled to the bottom of the casks. Wine in this condition tasted of dregs. In addition, the corks were frequently bad, allowing air to enter and wine to seep out, which occurred among the valpolicellas during the Philadelphia fair. At the Vienna Exposition corks had to be changed in order to avoid a similar embarrassment. Finally adulteration, the practice that turned Englishmen and Germans away in the eighteenth century, continued into the nineteenth.[14]

Quality was uneven. Italians had not yet mastered the art of blending different wines of several years in order to obtain a constant type of beverage. Their wines differed from year to year in color, aroma, density, and appearance. Italian merchants seemed unable or reluctant to invest time, patience, and money in building up a market. The sellers of Bordeaux, according to Italian consular reports, built up markets by selling their wines at a loss and by offering the best quality. Once they gained favor, however, these same sellers then raised prices and lowered quality.[15] Ricasoli also tried selling wine below cost in the hope of attracting buyers, but there is no reason to believe that he intended to lower quality later. He would eventually, like the French, have had to raise the price of each bottle merely to stay in business. Of course most French exporters of reputable wines did not lower the quality. The French were clever, and most certainly some of them were dishonest, but they did not build up the fame of their wines by despicable tricks. Their vinification procedures allowed them to make good wine of constant quality and they spent heavily to advertise it both in Britain and in the United States after the Civil War.

Italians were singularly unsuccessful in selling bottled wine on a large scale, except in two areas: South America, where the sale of vermouth in particular, but table wines also, rose spectacularly from 1861 to 1874, averaging 692,000 bottles yearly; and France, where the annual average came to 226,854 bottles. These were quality wines, chiefly from the Asti, Alba, and Tuscan regions. Since both South America and France were two major areas of Italian migration before the 1880s, undoubtedly taste in wine followed the flag.

Wholesalers in Britain and Switzerland bought large quantities of cheap Italian wine in wood, blended it with French produce, and then shipped it out with a French label. Thus Italian wine was really a raw material, rather than an article of direct consumption in these two countries. The height of irony came with the return of some of this wine to Italy, where its French label fetched a high price.

The relatively low quality of Italian export wine undoubtedly explains the limited income it produced. French wine consumed in foreign lands represented about 7 percent of the value of total exports just prior to the phylloxera blight in the 1870s and about 10–15 percent of all wine produced for sale. Between 1871 and 1877 Italian wine averaged only about

2 percent of total exports, and the value of exported wine came to not more than 2 percent of the total value of national wine production. Italy, therefore, enjoyed only a limited position in the world market, and yet her continuous adverse balance of trade in other goods meant that wine exports provided capital to pay some of her foreign debts. After unification the country continuously exported far more wine than she imported, and in the 1880s wine shipments went up markedly, accounting for 6.38 percent of her total exports, and 5.82 percent of the total value of her wine crops. Italy was beginning to rival France, a drastic change for which she had France to thank.

FRANCE

Since time immemorial France, like Italy, had traded with her immediate neighbors; her best customers were located on her northern and northeastern frontiers, lands above the zone of profitable grape-growing. Frost-bitten buyers eagerly drank the heavy wines fortified with alcohol that French and especially Bordeaux merchants had been sending them for centuries. Although tariff policies altered the volume of trade abroad after 1815, they did not appreciably change its compass direction. From 673,000 hectoliters in 1788, French exports to the north fell to 379,000 in the 1840s, a loss of 78 percent. Nonetheless Prussia, the German Confederation, and all of the Low Countries remained France's major market. A decline of serious magnitude, 57 percent, also occurred in the south European markets, chiefly Italy and Spain.

To compensate for these losses in the first half of the nineteenth century the French sought to broaden the geography of their trade, and they proved more aggressive than the Italians. Their sales in the United States rose from 2,900 hectoliters to 103,972, and in South America from zero to 54,524. Colonialism also paid, for wine sales leapt from 7,115 hectoliters to 627,686, or 8,722 percent. When one starts from zero or nearly zero, any gain is a profit, but this percentage leap was almost to heaven. These gains, combined with a successful penetration of the Swiss market by eastern growers (a rise of 159 percent) partly compensated for the declines in other European markets. But they did not, and we underscore this, bring wine exports into line with other exportable products, and they were compensatory, not a source of considerable new wealth.

During the golden age of the sixties and seventies the new geographic pattern of foreign trade did not change appreciably. The German Confederation and the Hanseatic towns on the Baltic coast (German Empire in 1871) rivaled Britain as the largest buyers of French wines. But the Germans, like the Belgians and Swiss, bought far more wine in wood than in glass and as much or more wine from eastern France as from Bordeaux. The English bought more claret, and about half of all wine shipped out in bottle. After the American Civil War (1861–65) the United States recovered its position, following Britain in its buying pattern. That is, the Anglo-Saxons, if not always the largest buyers, were the most discriminating. The majority of their imports came from Bordeaux, in the form of high-quality, bottled wine. The Germanic peoples took the mass of ordinaries, a pattern that Brazil, also an important consumer, followed, while the Argentinians favored claret shipped in casks. Exports in bottle went up for the Bordelais, from just under 63,000 hectoliters in 1860 to just over 100,000 in 1876, a rise of 59 percent. For the rest of France, chiefly Burgundy and Champagne, the increase came to 77 percent. Quite clearly this era of wealth and well-being encouraged the consumption of bottled wine, even though it was not necessarily better than wine shipped in wood. Bottled wine was, however, more likely to be authentic and undiluted. This buying pattern reflected national drinking habits. Unlike the English, continental Europeans of all classes were accustomed to obtaining their beverages "on tap," directly from the cask, whether ordering large or small quantities and whether for home consumption or in cabarets.

Far more than their Italian counterparts, French merchants were remarkably enterprising and successful not merely in finding new markets but also in shipping higher-quality and higher-priced table wines as distinct from sweet fortified beverages such as vermouth. The English, although less given to wine consumption (only 90 centiliters per person per year), spent heavily for their exotic beverages because wine in any way, shape, or form was the preferred drink of the upper classes. They imbibed considerable quantities of it before, during, and after dinner as well as in between meals, and much of their drink consisted of port and sherry, beverages considerably more alcoholic than the lighter ones carried over the Channel from Bordeaux. Like episcopal sees in the Anglican church, wine was a privileged drink of the privileged class, and its high position and price made it a profitable article of commerce, but its sales were limited by a middle- and lower-class preference for beer, ale, whiskey, and gin. Fine wine merchants throughout northern Europe faced the same widespread preference of the nonprivileged classes for beer, consumed with meals, and very alcoholic drinks such as schnapps and vodka, consumed at any time. The geography of refined taste shows the same frontiers as that of the wine trade.

Wine Trade and the Phylloxera in France

These preferences for lesser drinks notwithstanding, wine remained a kind of ideal beverage, a sign of social standing and wealth, or at least of pretension to high status, like a high hat compared to a worker's cap, or patent leather shoes contrasted to wooden clogs. The general increase of wealth and well-being that began in the 1850s amply proved this, for the consumption of wine went up, much to the delight of growers and sellers. The mid-1850s, the years of mildew and declining production, brought a serious drop in the amount of exports, but rising prices kept their value within a few percentage points of the forties.[16] Then in 1858–59 began an expansion of foreign shipments in volume and value that rose steadily until 1874, subsiding only gradually during the phylloxera decades. Along with the rise of volume came an even greater leap in value, pushed up at first by short supply in the 1850s and then by expanding demand after tariffs went down in the 1860s. In fact a veritable take-off occurred between 1847 and 1876. Wine in wood rose in value by 369 percent (averaging 12.7 percent a year) and in bottle by 354 percent (averaging 12.2 percent).

But then came the phylloxera, and volume fell off 64 percent by 1890 (averaging 4 percent a year). However prices held, so total values declined only 13 percent from 1867 to 1896. After such an auspicious take-off, this decline was more like a crash-landing than a simple plunge. Unfortunately wine did not go down alone; it followed the graph line of all French foreign trade. Given that wine exports were a major value in total exports, their slump naturally pulled down the total of trade. But another factor appeared about 1875 to keep the lines roughly parallel: while winemen suffered from the phylloxera, other exporters felt the effects of a worldwide depression that lasted until the midnineties. However general exports recovered by 1894, whereas wine experienced a setback because of renewed tariff wars.

But even as regards value alone wine steadily lost out to other exports. Table 24, if the data is more or less accurate (and it probably is), underscores this loss of leadership.

It is curious that wine's ranking, as distinct from its percentage of total exports, hardly changed, an indication that it retained its position as one of the major sources of revenue on the international market. This also shows that after midcentury Frenchmen began exporting a greater variety of goods, certainly more manufactured goods, than previously, but no single one was a source of high income, save textiles. It was rather

TABLE 24: *Place of Wine Among French Exports*

Years	Value of wine as percent of total exports	Rank among
1827–36	8	3d
1837–46	6	
1847–56	8	
1857–66	9	
1867–76	7	3d
1877–86	7	
1887–96	9	
1905–10	4	4th

Source: Min. Agri et Commerce, *Tableau.*

their combined value that adversely affected the percentage rating of wine after the economic recovery in 1896.

Another agent of decline was public opinion. Wine lost out somewhat to other beverages during the phylloxera decades, and then people began to distrust it because of frequent public scandals over the use of chemicals in its manufacture. Although not noxious unless used in excess, certain of these chemicals enabled winemen to preserve even low-grade ordinary wine, with the result that it too entered the list of items for foreign trade. In 1829 and still in 1869 wine shipments consisted chiefly of good ordinaries and very fine, expensive beverages, destined for the cellars and tables of upper-class connoisseurs or cabaret customers. However by the 1860s the amount of lower-quality wine increased; since it sold at lower prices it offered profitable returns only if exported in large quantities. With the near disappearance of authentic, undoctored wine during the phylloxera and widespread distrust of it afterward, the relative value of total wine exports naturally declined. Besides, wines of lesser breed had increasingly to face competition from Italian, Spanish, Hungarian, and Rhenish vineyards, especially with the arrival of free trade.

Era of Free Trade

Since the decline and fall of the ancient Roman Empire, both as a political state and as a vast free market covering the entire Mediterranean and its hinterlands, the wine trade, like trade in general, has been subject to all sorts of barriers. Until the formation of centralized dynastic states in the sixteenth and seventeenth centuries there existed numerous internal barriers in the form of tolls and fees to be paid when crossing from one province to another, when passing through a town or small principality, when fording rivers, crossing bridges, or traversing forests. These vexatious hindrances declined but did not disappear in France until the Revolution of 1789. The new state, a highly centralized administration, brooked no resistance to its power in the form of local rights involving tolls, fees, or payments on goods in transit. France, then, became a free market in 1790. For seventy more years, however, the various Italian states levied heavy tolls on the wine of their neighbors; they had no customs union comparable to that of north Germany. For Italian producers and merchants, therefore, the only solution was unification and the creation of a free market comparable to that of France. They had, obviously, more than purely emotional reasons for going to war against Austria.

Both French and Italian wine had once been regulated by mercantilism, a trade policy that was never fully consistent or systematic, but was nonetheless based on so-called state interests that did not always coincide with those of producers, sellers, or buyers. Producers and sellers of export wines generally desired a laissez faire policy. Of course prior to the midnineteenth century the only producers concerned were those near frontiers: Bordeaux for regions accessible by water: England, the Low Countries, northern Europe, and colonial islands; Burgundy and Champagne, for areas accessible by roads, canals, and rivers: the flat north of Europe and, to a lesser extent, Switzerland. Italian wine hardly had a market outside of the peninsula, until the French armies of Napoleon appeared, demanding—to accompany their victories—wine, women, and song, of which all three Italy had an abundant supply. Italy and the major inland producer-sellers of France enjoyed the vast market created by the first French empire and its client states of central Europe.

The Bordelais were more disadvantaged by Napoleon than the Italians. The British blockaded France's Atlantic coast, cutting Bordeaux off from foreign markets, especially England herself. Considerable suffering and numerous bankruptcies followed; vineyards fell into neglect. To buttress morale Napoleon came to Bordeaux in 1808 and promised loans at 2 percent with wine crops as collateral, but the emperor was no more faithful to these promises than he was to most. More practical was his policy of licensing trade with England, thereby establishing a form of semilegal contraband activity; by 1813 licenses to trade were so numerous and prices so high that some prosperity returned to the Atlantic port.[17] It was stimulated by the return of peace in 1814–15, and a brief period of free trade when the English bought up the magnificent vintages of 1802 and 1811 at fabulous prices and lesser vintages at proportionately high payments. But then came a combination of factors seriously detrimental to the wine trade: generalized hard times, a veritable depression in 1818–19, falling prices, and a return to tariff protection.

Tariff protection remained the bugbear of the postwar decades in every viticultural region of France. The Italians were less clear on protection, in part because their mixed agrarian economy divided their interests as regards foreign trade. Farmers growing both cereals and wines were protectionist regarding grains and either free traders or really indifferent regarding wine, since little of it entered foreign trade. Divided interest neutralized the rural population as a political force and mercantile interests were far weaker in the peninsula than in France. Nonetheless there was a growing desire for free trade within Italy, or at least within Piedmont, but the whole issue of tariffs was rather obscured by the overriding matter of unification.

French wine producers came out unanimously for free trade; in fact they were in the forefront of antiprotectionist movements during the 1830s and 1840s, modeled on the Anti-Corn Law League in Great Britain. One of them expressed their views succinctly when he asserted that high tariffs were to modern times what slavery was to antiquity, an outrage against morality. Free-trade economics received important backing from Frederic Bastiat and Léon Say, French disciples of Adam Smith, and from Cavour, his most enthusiastic Italian follower. The chambers of commerce of Bordeaux and Reims organized pressure groups which drew their support both from large merchants and the big champagne houses, as well as from producers active in agricultural and viticultural societies. Equally active were Bordeaux deputies Theodore Ducos, Pierre Guestier of the firm Barton and Guestier, and others.

The constitutional monarchies governing France from 1814 to 1848 and the various absolutist regimes of the Italian states—Piedmont somewhat more open-minded on this issue—were not impressed by free-trade liberals. Government tax revenues benefitted less from exported wine than from that sold within the realm. More important were the large number of rural notables and peasants who grew cereals and raised cattle and who were protectionist to the core. Almost as important were the growing number of industrialists who fiercely denounced all free traders as dupes of the English; everyone knew that "perfidious Albion" used free trade as a means of flooding the home market with cheap textiles and iron products. Curiously enough, wine and other interests with foreign markets benefitted more from authoritarian regimes that were in the process of reforming themselves than from old-line conservative or bourgeois republican regimes. With the Eden Treaty of 1786 the well-intentioned Bourbon king of France had opened the French market, which was subsequently closed by French revolutionaries and kept closed by succeeding monarchies. Under Napoleon III the Cobden-Chevalier treaty of 1860 reopened it, but conservative republicans cancelled the agreement a generation later.

When the terms of the 1860 treaty—reducing tariffs on French wines to a negligible amount in Britain—were extended to other nations, a brief era of open, or nearly open, commerce began. The extent to which France and especially Bordeaux profited is remarkable. British duties on French wine had gone down from 13 shillings 9 pence per gallon in 1819 to 5 shillings in 1849, which had encouraged imports to increase from 165,000 gallons in 1820 to 373,000 in 1851, a rise of 126 percent. This was an impressive increase of 4 percent a year, but from 1859 to 1868 there was an increase of 419 percent for all French wine sent to Britain, a jump of 46 percent annually. Over a longer period, from 1852–54 to 1892–94, the rise came to 610 percent.[18] Despite this promising result the treaty of 1860 might be looked on as a final, not a beginning step, in the free-trade movement up to 1939. As far as Franco-British trade was concerned, it brought the quickening of a process already underway. Lower duties did encourage the consumption of wine, especially claret, and Bordeaux benefitted most: between 1840–44 and 1865–69 its wine sent to Britain rose in volume by 862 percent, well above the national average.[19] Also encouraging was the fact that the value of bordeaux in bottles rose by 37 percent, and bordeaux in wood by 99 percent between 1837–46 and 1866–70. Expansion by volume exceeding expansion by price indicates that merchants were sending out lighter wine from regions other than Médoc and that the less affluent middle classes in Britain had taken to wining with their dining.[20] Happily the increase of price, even for lesser beverages, more than compensated for increasing production costs. Apparently it also compensated for increasing living costs in the Bordelais.

A similar phenomenon occurred in the champagne trade, where Britain outdistanced both Russia, whose gentry and noble class suffered an economic shock after the emancipation of the serfs in 1862, and the United States, caught in the throes of the Civil War. After the Civil War the US embarked on a protectionist policy that separated her from Europe and greatly reduced wine drinking. Between 1859 and 1876 exports to Americans fell by 110 percent, whereas between 1842 and 1859 they had risen by 321 percent. Gironde wine as well as champagne were severely affected by this drastic change of tariff policy and, presumably, of taste. Not until the later decades of the century did the situation improve, when newly acquired industrial and commercial wealth demanded fine, especially sparkling, wines and ostentatiously paid the high prices and higher tariffs. The industrial development of the United States more clearly stimulated champagne sales than did the development of continental Europe.

In compensation for North American losses, exports to France's neighbors improved. Belgium, already benefitting from trade agreements prior to 1860, increased her purchases of wine by 152 percent from 1842 to 1859. Parenthetically, this trade involved wine in casks, which meant that Belgian merchants added alcohol to the wine, bottled it themselves, and sold it at greater profit. A certain quantity of French wine, like the Italian, was a raw material, or rather a semifinished article, useful to a foreign economy. From 1859 to 1876, however, exports lost their earlier dynamism; they grew by only 29 percent, a truly mediocre achievement in this era of pulsating economic expansion resulting from liberal tariffs pushing prices down and gold rushes shoving them up. The Low Countries and Germany differed from Belgium. Like the British, they greatly augmented their purchases after 1859, the Dutch by 54 percent, the Germans by 98 percent, figures that reveal marked increases over the pre-free-trade era of 17 and 29 percent respectively.

Free trade, combined with such technological improvements in transport as steamships and locomotives, enormously benefitted the French wine industry, until the phylloxera struck. Then came Italy's turn. The special commercial treaty with France, lowering tariff duties on wine to a mere 2 francs per hectoliter, was a major factor. These special concessions to Italy were put through because wine merchants in southern France needed Sicilian and Apulian beverages. In return, French manufacturers obtained lower duties on their goods entering Italy and now competed successfully with industrialists in Turin and Milan.

Return to Tariff Protection

But in the midst of this new wealth winemen found themselves beset by a series of crises characterized by declining prices and losses in both domestic and foreign markets. These crises proceeded in part from "natural" phenomena, in part from the interaction of policies carried out by growers and politicians. These policies were not developed abstractly but were responses to concrete problems, the most important of which was the phylloxera. It was the true catalyst of all decision-making at this time. When the blight struck France, production of grapes dropped precipitately, and although a general European depression reduced the demand for wine somewhat, demand still remained well above the amount of wine on the market. After all the taste for it had grown during the Second Empire, and the men who were then in their twenties and thirties were now in their forties, fifties, and sixties and all the more bibulous. Lacking wine grapes, French growers (and nongrowers) began to make wine from everything available—fresh fruit, dried fruit, berries, chemicals. Rising prices sent men scurrying to their cellars, sheds, and laboratories to make a fast franc. Either to improve or supplement these false wines, merchants looked frantically about for foreign wines, which they could import cheaply, thanks to low tariffs. They found them in Spain and Italy, where the phylloxera was slow to arrive, and France turned from a major wine-exporting country to a major importer. Beginning in 1871 wine imports rose steadily, from 147,700 hectoliters to the peak of 12,282,400 in 1887. Thereafter came a gradual decline, save for 1891 when imports suddenly jumped to 12,278,000, but they fell to 9,400,000 the next year. From 1887 to 1896 imports averaged just over nine million hectoliters annually, exports just under two million.[21]

Costs of imports rose steadily with increasing volume. In the decade 1857–66 total French wine imports averaged 1,169,000 francs per year; in 1867–76 they averaged 76,464,000 francs; in 1877–86, 282,913,000 francs, and in 1887–96, 315,544,000 francs. This represented a leap of 1,816 percent after 1877. During this same time, exports fell in value by nearly 13 percent. Wine brought in from Spain and Italy ranked first among France's imports, and losses from the national revenue ran into millions of francs annually. The total bill from 1880 to 1896 came to 5,776,000,000 francs.[22] Although not all of these imports resulted from the phylloxera (over a million francs for foreign beverages was a normal item in the annual balance of trade), they were certainly without precedent for their magnitude.

Spain grabbed the lion's share of this trade, her exports rising from a mean of just over 8 million francs annually in 1857–66 to nearly 200 million annually in 1877–86, or 60 percent of France's total imports from Spain. From Italy French wine imports rose, for the same dates, from a mean of just over 1 million to 55 million francs annually or 12 percent of total imports from the peninsula. These, incidentally, are figures for general commerce; they include about 3 or 4 million francs annually of wine blended with native beverages, treated, and reexported—as French wine.

France's loss was the gain of Spain and Italy, whose wines suited their unfortunate neighbor's temporary needs perfectly, too perfectly for their own good in the long run. Their gains lasted only briefly, until France recovered from the blight, but while the situation lasted it brought considerable income to wine producers who consented to turn out the low-quality, high-alcohol beverages that French merchants demanded. Wine-growers, especially those in Apulia, were having a little golden age, but politicians in Rome concluded that northern industry needed protection and, raising tariffs, began a commercial war over industrial products. As rates shot up on all goods, shipments of wine from Italy fell to 821,360 hectoliters, then plummeted to 174,816 in 1889, and to a mere 23,409 in 1890, with only slight recovery in 1891.

The return to protectionism, combined with the recovery of France's vines, also frustrated another ambition of Italian growers: to penetrate several of France's important international markets. In 1874 they had sent merely 335 hectoliters of wine to Belgium, in 1890 it was 4,026, a leap of 1,100 percent. However 4,026 hectos is dwarfed beside Belgium's total wine imports for 1890, a mere 1.8 percent of 214,500.

Italy's penetration of the German market was far more profitable; from 8,773 in 1874 to 101,055 in 1890, a jump of 1,051 percent, and nearly 14 percent of Germany's total wine imports. Worth noting is the fact that Italy joined the Dual Alliance of Germany and Austria in 1882; her exports of wine to Germany rose accordingly.[23] Political alliances also undoubtedly helped her vinicultural trade with the Hapsburg Empire. When Franco-Italian trade relations broke down in 1888 and the tariff war commenced, south Italian wine producers suffered a severe setback, France having until then absorbed about two-thirds of their exports. The German Empire took some but only a fraction of South Italy's productive capacity. Italians hoped for additional purchases from Austria, but Hungary, an important producing state, had enough influence in the dual government to successfully resist Italian efforts to expand foreign sales there. Besides, Austria and Italy continued their long conflict over the last piece of territory claimed by Rome, the Trentino, and Italians referred to it passionately as *Italia irredenta*. Nationalist passions or not, *Italia vinicola* was desperate after 1888 for foreign markets. The total value of her exports of wine in wood had risen to 107,463,120 lire in 1887; in 1890 it had fallen to 34,364,426 lire, a drop of 213 percent! In 1886–87 wine in wood ranked second in value among Italy's exports, coming after raw silk; in 1890 it ranked fourth, running behind raw silk, olive oil, and citrus fruits. However luck still held, because when the phylloxera destroyed the vines of Hungary, opposition to imports disappeared. The Italian growers to benefit were those in Apulia, where the hungry aphid did not appear in large numbers until the turn of the century. In the trade treaty with Austria effective as of 1892 Italy received special tariff treatment. Her shipments immediately improved, but the data does not agree about the quantity. The increase had begun even before the agreement, however exports to Austria doubled from 1891 to 1892 and averaged over two million hectoliters annually until 1904 when the treaty expired and Hungary, having replanted her vineyards, successfully resisted its renewal.[24]

Once again Italian exports changed direction, for those headed to Austria-Hungary became almost negligible: an average of 8,040 hectoliters from 1909 to 1913, whereas shipments to France averaged 79,000 during these same years, and even rose to 229,000 in 1913. Unfortunately for Italy the French market remained a disappointment; the French had found another source of cheap, alcoholic wine in Algeria, conquered and settled by hordes of southern vignerons fleeing the phylloxera. Germany too proved a false hope, average exports there having fallen to a mere 87,720 hectoliters. The French had recovered part of that market, with an average of 330,240 hectoliters, and held on to the British market, with an average of 128,680, whereas Italy could not do better than 5,700. In fact the only important markets Italy enjoyed on the eve of World War I were Switzerland, Argentina, and Brazil (see table 25). That is, Italy, whose markets had existed chiefly in neighboring European states during the nineteenth century, found more lucrative markets in the New World, chiefly in South America, thanks to the large colonies of Italian emigrants there. The large Italian colony in the United States was apparently less faithful to the viniculture of the homeland. Clearly Italy's penetration of France's markets had been temporary; France recovered its European buyers, especially those in the North, with the result that 87 percent of her large exports went to the countries on her borders, chiefly her northern and northeastern ones. In contrast 40 percent of Italy's large exports went to the Americas and 50 percent to Switzerland. Italy had a military alliance with the Central Powers, but on the eve of the war, they brought more wine from France than from their partner in arms.

Table 25 also indicates that Italy, having become a major wine producer rivaling the French, had also become a major wine exporter. But Italy differed from France in that the bulk of her exports consisted of low-grade alcoholic wine from the Mezzogiorno, sold at cheap prices, for blending. Among her better, more expensive exports were marsala, sold chiefly in Argentina and Britain, and vermouth, sold extensively in Latin America and the United States. The USA was also the main market for chianti, marketed in the famous *fiaschi* and affectionately consumed by

TABLE 25: *Foreign Markets of France and Italy*

	Exporting country, mean 1909–1913	
Importing country	France	Italy
	(hectoliters)	(hectoliters)
Austria-Hungary	—	8,040
Belgium	222,040	1,400
Germany	330,240	87,720
Great Britain	128,680	5,700
Holland	71,880	—
Switzerland	205,820	535,580
USA	5,400	84,534
Argentina	102,260	180,560
Brazil	11,700	142,780
Uruguay	14,760	33,600
Total	1,092,780	1,079,914

Source: *Il Vino*, 48–51.

Italo-Americans. Unfortunately the superb wines of Piedmont saw little of the outside world, being consumed chiefly at home. Equally unfortunate was the reputation of Italian wine among the rising urban classes. What unscrupulous merchants sold as chianti had never seen the rolling hills of Siena and Florence; it was a sour, acid drink, that was thought to be typical of all Italian table wine. Italy's good reputation, therefore, rested on her higher-priced, sweet beverages. First-rate marsala and vermouth sold in the British market for an average price of 68 lire per hectoliter, the highest price of all Italian exported wine, well ahead of the 58.68 lire fetched in Argentina and the USA. Lowest in price was the blending wine sent to Switzerland (33.38 lire) and Germany (35.13 lire). In 1886 the total value of wine exported came to the high figure of 88,245,364 lire; average annual value from 1886 to 1890, a mixed period, came to 70,222,186. In 1910, a climatically terrible year, total value came to 86,480,613 lire, chiefly because the French crop was nearly zero and prices rose. But Italy did not recover her high position of 1886–87. There was the steady drop of prices, as table 26 shows, and after 1900 a fall of exports by volume.

As regards volume, the worst years were those immediately following the loss of an important market as a result of adverse commercial policy. From 1887 to 1890, when France closed her borders, the volume of exports fell by 285 percent! From 1903 to 1906, when Austria closed her

TABLE 26: *Value and Volume of Italian Wine Exports*

Year	Ordinary wine lire per hectoliter	Exports thousands of hectoliters
1876–80	35.19	938
1881–85	38.58	1,917
1886–90	42.73	2,032
1891–96	29.77	1,929
1896–1900	29.35	2,163
1901–05	27.98	1,417
1906–10	26.99	1,368

borders, volume fell by 166 percent. Recovery followed in 1907 and peaked in 1910, when rain and cold severely reduced France's grape harvest and prices went up somewhat, but 1911 and 1912 were weak vintages, bringing a fall in volume of 73 percent from 1910.

After 1905 southern growers were in a precarious position, and to make their situation worse the phylloxera had begun its irresistible invasion. Rome did not ignore or willfully neglect their interests; it contributed funds and expertise to fight the aphid. That less suitable lands were taken out of production helped in both the short and long run, since a lesser amount of wine would be easier to sell if the southerners improved its quality, which they did not. Nonetheless the government's commercial policy helped to deprive winemen of markets. Although never a total loss, France was an extremely limited market for Italy, whereas Spain, enjoying better commercial relations, continued to ship large quantities of wine across the Pyrenees after 1888 and even after 1900. The Austrian market was practically closed to Italian common wine in wood after 1904; it allowed in only an average of 8,040 hectoliters between 1909–13. France still did far better there with an average of 79,080, and Germany with 87,720. In Europe only Switzerland remained a truly important market for Italy.

There was also a distressingly steady drop in the volume of Italian exports relative to total annual production of wine. From 1881 to 1887 exports averaged 7.7 percent of production; from 1888 to 1895 the figure fell to 5.5 percent, and from 1904 to 1913 it dropped to a mere 3.2, only one percentage point above the nineteenth-century average. As far as exports were concerned, the end of the Austrian treaty in 1904 was as grave an event as was the end of the French treaty. This weakened position notwithstanding, graph 4 shows that wine exports, while falling

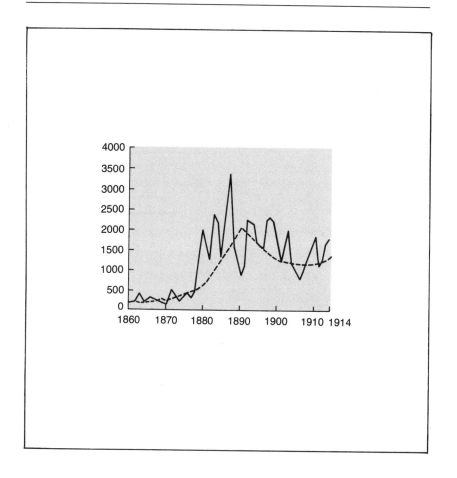

GRAPH 4: *Wine Exports, Italy (thousands of hectoliters)*

----- 10 year averages

Source: Capanna, graph 48.

TABLE 27: *Wine Exports*

Italy

	Total Exports (hectoliters)	Value in Lire (in thousands)	Price/hl.
1873	308,563	23,946	77.60
1875	362,995	20,310	55.95
1880	2,205,528	69,341	31.43
1885	1,480,828	59,062	39.88
Av. 1886–90	2,032,035	70,222	34.55
1891	1,179,192	40,481	34.33

from the high level of the 1880s, remained well above the level of the two decades after unification; indeed their volume had more than doubled. France enjoyed a similar expansion.

Although suffering from falling prices, overproduction, and inadequate markets after recovery from the phylloxera, France did not, like Italy, lose her foreign buyers. In a sense, Italy's difficulties arose because she depended on foreign markets for the huge sales her low-priced blending wines required. Italy was constantly at the mercy of foreign politicians, whose tariff policies reflected the desires of all the native cheap-wine producers who elected them. In France, meridional growers shared somewhat the same position, but they did not export much of their wine. Instead they shipped it northward to be blended or sold directly in the nonvinicultural areas of their homeland or in Belgium, Germany, and Switzerland. There retail merchants sold it directly out of the barrel or wholesale merchants blended it with strong Italian wine and either sold it as a purely French product or, preferably, kept silent about its origins. Frenchmen exported most of their better wines and made a great to-do about them, subtly suggesting in their advertising that *all* their exported wines were of the highest quality. The fine French wines, sent out as a finished product, enjoyed an exclusive clientele and suffered less from tariffs; the Italian beverage shipped out as a competing raw material. Table 27 shows this clearly as regards prices and values in relation to volume. The value of French wine aided, of course, by shortages, pushed up its price; the poor quality of much Italian wine, aided, of course, by plethora, depressed its prices.

The 1880s were Italy's golden years, but we should note the deterioration of prices there compared to the steady improvement of those in

| | France | |
Total Exports (hectoliters)	Value in Lire (in thousands)	Price/hl.
3,981,431	281,300	70.65
3,730,872	247,500	66.34
2,487,581	245,150	98.55
2,604,321	237,910	91.35
2,290,088	251,143	109.66
2,049,268	248,093	121.06

France up to 1891. Before 1860 Italy had suffered from an adverse balance of trade; after 1870 she corrected this but failed, despite huge sales, to acquire significant wealth from exports. In 1890 35 percent of her southern production consisted of blending wine. France, after the phylloxera struck, suffered from an adverse balance, but not a serious one, because the wine she imported was cheap and the wine she exported was expensive. A dark spot remained, nonetheless, since the prices for her wine declined after 1896, at precisely the time when the cost of production, not to mention the cost of living, rose precipitously. Compared to Italian wines, however, those of France remained rather costly. By Italian standards marsala and vermouth were high priced, selling in Britain for about 68 lire per hectoliter; a good medium castelli romani sold for about 40 lire. Common bordeaux in wood, on the other hand, fetched an average of 75 lire; even other French ordinaries in wood sold for 60 lire per hectoliter in world trade.[25] Italy was simply not in the same league, and this was as true of her effervescent as of her still wines.

Sparkling Wines

The champagne industry differed in many respects from the general wine industry, not only in its fabrication processes but also in its sales pattern. There hardly existed an ordinary champagne as regards price, all of it being expensive; some were more so than others, but all were above the price of ordinary and often even of fine still wine. Only the classed bordeaux and burgundy could match it. This expense was partly the result of the high production costs, but also a result of its association with the upper classes. It was a ceremonial drink, served even by the well-to-do chiefly for special celebrations; it was part of high living, part of the fun of life. As we have noted, it was a sweet drink until the second half of the century, even for the English, who consumed huge quantities of it, but chiefly on special occasions or, more often, as a dessert wine. For fun-loving foreigners it was the greatest invention to come out of France since the so-called "French kiss" and a sufficient quantity of it might induce the imbiber to practice that peculiar custom. It had the kick of the cancan, the frothiness of the Folies Bergères, and the mystery of Paris. Small wonder that foreigners were the most active buyers and often hardly considered it a serious product, a great work of art inherited from Dom Pérignon. Whether buyers wished to indulge a refined taste or put on a gaudy display—more likely some mixture of these two—the willingness to buy an inordinately expensive beverage clearly indicated that well-to-do persons recognized certain of its merits.

Some historians have believed that the remarkable growth of the industry, 5.33 percent per annum from 1844 to 1910 for foreign sales and 7.21 percent for domestic sales, was a result of the Industrial Revolution.[26] Undoubtedly the rise of factories, of commerce, of cities, and of personal wealth that eventually accompanied these phenomena, contributed to the consumption of both sparkling and superior still wine. Few persons drank any kind of wine until the rise of their incomes reduced its relative cost. However there is good reason to believe that the so-called Industrial Revolution was no more a major force in the rise of the sparkling wine industry than it was in the creation of the great sherry, port, bordeaux, and burgundian wine industries. Certainly the perfecting of these wines preceded the rise of factories and industrial capitalism, for along with barolo and chianti classico, they were seventeenth- and eighteenth-century creations. The champagne industry was well underway before France showed marked industrial growth, and the mechanization of champagne's production did not make serious headway until the late nineteenth century. Even its consumption was not yet clearly tied to industry. England, the leading industrial and commercial nation, became a prime market, but it seems likely that consumers were not the tight-fisted, sparse-living, pioneering entrepreneurs, but a large part of the old financial and commercial bourgeois families and the upper landed classes. Although too few in number to consume the huge numbers of bottles brought into their homeland, they none the less set the fashion, identified champagne-drinking with their active sporting and social life, and in various ways popularized it, as they did port, sherry, and claret. Certainly an expensive wine required a rich society for its successful sales, but often these riches did not come out of sprawling, ugly, noisy factories. Germany was also an important market, but before 1870 everyone looked upon its citizens as happy, backward, and rural, combining Prussian militarism and southern easy living, *Gemütlichkeit*. Even less inclined toward mechanized industry was Russia, where the gentry and nobles were enormous consumers of sparkling wine, sweet, alcoholic, and fizzy. Clearly the wherewithal to purchase champagne could as easily be derived from landed estates worked by slaves in the South of the United States, serfs and dependent peasants in European Russia, and free peasant laborers in France, as it could be derived from industrial capitalism.

But Forbes is certainly correct in his belief that sales of sparkling wine on a truly monumental scale accompanied the rise of wealth in the western world. Table 28 indicates the dramatic character of this rise:

TABLE 28: *Sales of Champagne*

	Mean number of bottles exported	Rate of change	Mean number of bottles sold in France	Rate of change
April 1844–April 1851	5,001,652		2,073,750	
April 1904–1911	22,604,170	+352%	11,938,280	+476%

Source: Chamber of Commerce, Reims, France.

It is noteworthy that sales inside France were only about 41 percent of sales in foreign lands during the 1840s. However the number of bottles sold inside France often dropped to less than a third of foreign shipments and even to a fourth or a mere fifth. Sales beyond the borders rose regularly from the 1840s on, despite a few brief setbacks, while domestic sales remained almost stationary until the 1880s. At that time they rose considerably, quintupling between 1888 and 1910. Authentic champagne-growers, however, continued to show more concern for non-French buyers, apparently because Frenchmen often purchased the less expensive "tisanes" (slightly sparkling) and the blends combining wines grown in regions outside of *Champagne viticole* (the delimited area), either in neighboring departments or even in the Midi.[27]

Despite these domestic drawbacks the champagne trade seems to have benefitted from a nicely balanced geographic spread of sales. When sales dropped in France, as happened during the upheavals of 1848–49, foreign sales held up fairly well, even though Russian aristocrats, fearful of the spread of revolution, cut their consumption. Russians and other central European states also curtailed purchases during the Crimean War of 1854–55, but then the domestic market held up well. The reports of the Chamber of Commerce of Reims, like those of Bordeaux, read like diplomatic reports, bringing out the close relation between world conditions and wine sales, especially luxury wine sales. The 1880s were years of hardship because of the tense Near Eastern question and the beginnings of a general economic malaise in Europe. Equally important was the return to protectionism, restricting some of the foreign markets. The result was that the graph of champagne exports followed fairly closely that of general exports, with a sharp rise after the mid-1840s, a decline in the mid-1880s, a rise to the high point of 1889, then a brief gradual fall, followed by a rapid ascent during the gay nineties and until the war.

Perhaps to a larger extent than the vineyard of Médoc, that of Champagne lived off foreign trade. The number of wholesalers and shippers steadily increased, and large amounts of capital poured into this rapidly growing enterprise. Champagne-making was big business, requiring a sizable investment in a short space of time. If the makers were to enjoy large returns, they had to purchase not only equipment, but also vast storage spaces both for aging and for accumulating a reserve of good wine to blend with the lesser ones that damp, cold vintages brought forth. They also needed sizable stocks to tide them over years of short harvests.

Big manufacturers and shippers did not consider themselves in a safe position unless they had a two- or three-year supply of wine, both in bottles and in casks. Along with their sales their reserve stocks went up, from more than 20 million bottles on 1 April 1844 to more than 110 million in 1910. Between these dates the most renowned companies had become sizable organizations, with hundreds of workers and office personnel. They had vastly enlarged their cellars—or rather their caverns, because they housed their bottles and casks in miles of tunnels deep under ground, where the temperature remained constant. Thanks to these supplies and expanding sales, which did not decline during the rather brief phylloxera invasion of Champagne in the 1890s, all or nearly all persons involved in the production and sale of sparkling wine were fairly safe from any serious economic setbacks resulting from a small harvest. Even the vignerons who sold either grapes or musts to the companies were paid a rather high price in order to keep them in business. This paternalism apparently did not extend to bottle-makers and coopers, for in years of low sales or poor harvests, the reports of the Chamber of Commerce warn that these groups will suffer either underemployment or unemployment.

Wine-making and sales were certainly among the most profitable activities in the towns of Reims and Epernay. The latter was primarily a viticultural center, so its very existence depended on the wine business, whereas Reims was much larger and woolen textiles held first place as a source of revenue. In 1858 the value of woolen goods came to 60 million francs, of which 20 million derived from foreign markets. The value of sparkling wine came to 15 million francs, with 12 million francs earned abroad and only 3 million inside France.[28] The average price per bottle was three francs at this time. If we apply this price, not only to the bottles sent out from Reims, but also to those shipped from Epernay and Chalons, that is, a total of 10,472,049 bottles, then gross income amounted to 31,416,147 francs. After 1900, when the average price per bottle came to about six francs, gross revenue in, say, 1910 amounted to 231,509,410 francs. These figures, of course, are rough estimates based on general information. They are useful chiefly as an indication of the considerable wealth derived from sparkling wine sales and the industry's growth over time. The figures indicate that from 1858 to 1910 gross revenue rose roughly by 637 percent, or an average of 27.7 percent each year. If only as indicators this information is useful, making it possible for us to understand certain social conditions in viticultural Champagne: the paternalistic policies of the bigger companies, relatively high income of small and medium vignerons, high wages for vineyard workers, and sizable fortunes for the handful of families directing production and sales. Champagne-selling was, for the most successful, an opening into the nobility.

Unfortunately our information about exports of *spumante* wine from Italy is almost nonexistent. Centered in the Asti region, it received little impetus from within Piedmont and even less from without until Italy was unified. Asti *spumante* simply never caught on prior to 1914; its highly sweet taste closed off the important English market without opening that of Russia, where French sweet sparkling dominated; its low alcoholic content did not give the desired kick, it was too much like soda pop; finally its price was too high for its lesser qualities. Exports, therefore, amounted to only about half a million bottles in 1913, with just under 50 percent going to Argentina, the remainder to France, Brazil, and a small amount to the United States.

Without any doubt, France dominated the world market for sparkling wine; the only competition which caught the attention of the Reims

Chamber of Commerce was "false champagne," that is, sparkling wine made chiefly in Germany or England and labeled as champagne.

The sparkling-wine towns were not the only ones dependent on the sale of wine. Bordeaux was the largest wine town in the world, a great port city whose wealth had once derived from the ocean commerce of sugar and slaves. In 1871 there was no longer a slave trade and sugar accounted for a mere 1 percent of the total value of its exports. Wine had become by far the most important single item, accounting for 33 percent of the value of exports, with silk textiles second in line, at 9 percent of the total. Exports from Bordeaux, like those from Reims, did not decline in value during the phylloxera period; quantities could go down, but the rise in price per bottle or cask amply compensated for these losses.[29] There was not even a serious decline in quantity in Bordeaux and Champagne, which suggests that vast amounts of common wine, well before the age of *appellation contrôlée*, were brought in from Spain and, to a lesser extent, Italy, blended with some local wine, and shipped out under various French labels. Perhaps not much of this blended beverage entered foreign trade, but certainly it was sold extensively in the domestic market.

Internal Commerce

The domestic commerce of wine followed roughly the same evolution as the international. Both aspects of trade participated in the expanding economy of western Europe and profited from the significant rise of personal income among the burgeoning urban classes, as well as from the technological changes that contributed to material progress at the lower levels of society. Ordinary beverages, as distinct from fine wine and champagne, were the chief beneficiaries of industrial expansion. Wine technology was a part of the growing mechanization of life, but mechanization affected wine far beyond the process of making it. The impact of machines markedly rearranged the geography of internal commerce.

Since time immemorial most wine was consumed by its makers and others nearby. Only superior wine could bear the cost of (and survive) long-distance transport. Before railroads, overland shipping costs stood at 18 percent of the price for ordinaries and 5 percent for fine wines. Since lesser beverages often turned sour during transport, trade of more than local scope was on a small scale. Well-to-do nobles and commoners, as well as a few prosperous artisans, were the chief consumers. The petty middle class and artisans, when they congregated in their cafés for conviviality, consumed the better ordinaries to which water and cheap alcohol had been added. Before midcentury the masses of rural dwellers, even in wine-producing regions, rarely tasted commercial wine. Such as they had of their own they reserved for Sundays and special occasions; they never bought wine in any significant quantity.[30]

The greatest obstacle to the democratization of wine consumption was obviously the difficulty and high cost of transport. In the first half of the nineteenth century there was relatively little change in the means of cartage on the continent. Overseas transport in sailing ships required that wine withstand the violent shaking of oceanic storms as well as changes of temperature and climate. Some wines, the superior ordinaries of the *palus* near Bordeaux, improved during such long voyages and served as ballast; others lost their finesse because tropical climates renewed fermentation or turned acid because of weak constitution; they simply became seasick, with no hope of recovery. Overland transport presented even more vexing problems, which explains why Bordeaux looked to the sea. Inland commercial vineyards, for obvious needs of transport, grew up near sizable rivers, the Loire, Rhône, Saône, and Marne. In the Southwest the Garonne and Dordogne were equally important factors in the creation of vineyards, and the Seine opened the huge Parisian market. In Italy rivers were important but perhaps less so because few vineyards were far from the coast. The Po opened an easy route eastward into Lombardy, Emilia, Venetia, and Austria for the wines of Piedmont, while the Arno did the same, but westward, for the chiantis of Florence and Siena. The Tiber connected the vineyards of Orvieto to Rome. These waterways were not always reliable, however, because of swift currents, shifting channels, and seasonal variations in water levels. In Italy canals were of no use, partly because the terrain was mountainous, partly because the coast was always so near and inland distances so short compared to France. In the seventeenth century the French therefore began to build canals, far more actively than the small Italian states could afford to do. These canals have been major supplements to the rivers, which partly explains why wines of France far outdistanced those of Italy. The wines of Burgundy-Beaujolais, Mâcon, and elsewhere were shipped along the Saône, then followed the Canal du Centre and the lateral canal along the Loire to the Seine and finally to Paris. Wines were also put on wagons for overland shipment, but roads were poor both in France and Italy and only the best of wine could stand such rough usage.

Voyages were long and hazardous whether on sea, river, or road. No stories have come down about highwaymen attacking wagons and making off with barrels of wine; their weight and bulk was its own safeguard. The thieves were the sailors and wagoners, who helped themselves, then filled the vacant space with river water. Long a major problem, this was resolved only by providing the haulers with one or two containers of wine for their own use during the trip. To further safeguard themselves, shippers tried to place seals on the bungs, but one seal could always be broken "by accident." They also sent samples ahead to the buyers, who could determine the authenticity of the wine upon its arrival, a more effective control, but how could one punish the shippers? [31] Sometimes the producer accompanied his wine. In 1971 I met a vigneron, over ninety years old, who still drove an open touring car of 1920 vintage and who recalled his pre-World War I trips to the Paris market. He and his companions told jokes, played cards, slept, and had such a good time that the two-week voyage seemed too short. "Quoi, on est déjà arrivé!" they exclaimed upon reaching their destination. These small producers then loaded their wine on wagons and went about Paris selling it themselves.

The application of steam to transport brought profound changes, albeit it did not do so all at once. Neither France nor Italy built and completed all the railway trunk lines and certainly not the secondary ones in a generation. Because roads were improved, canals maintained, and rivers deepened, traditional forms of transport held on into the twentieth century, aided in their fight for life by high railroad rates. Nonetheless sail gave way to steam for ocean and coastal transport, just as the horse and wagon found it increasingly difficult to compete with steam locomotives. Both France and Italy began laying down tracks in the 1840s, but the French moved more rapidly so that within about forty years, the major trunk lines were complete; the Italians made little progress until unification, when the new state took a more active part.

Railroads brought several changes of varying importance. Empty casks were returned more rapidly and in better condition; stealing of wine was reduced, although some winemen of the Midi accused transhippers in Lyon of taking from 20 to 50 liters from each barrel; and it was no longer necessary to provide extra wine for the carrier. Of far greater consequence were the definite reduction of shipping costs to 3 percent of value for ordinary and 1 percent for fine wine, and the greater rapidity of movement. These two factors made it possible for the low-grade southern wines to reach northern markets and caused the rapid expansion of hot-climate vineyards in both countries. Wines once thought unsuitable for consumption in their natural state and therefore distilled for their alcohol were now shipped to the growing industrial cities of northern France and Italy.

This shift adversely affected other areas producing common as well as good ordinary wine: the Beaujolais and Mâconnais in France, and the Chianti and Piedmont in Italy. They had formerly enjoyed secure markets both locally and throughout the North. All of these areas hoped to benefit from the railroads, and they did, but at the same time producers there were annoyed to discover their once secure markets were now flooded with cheap southern wine. Urban factory workers even began to drink southern wine with their meals. This was itself an innovation, that is, drinking wine with meals. In part it resulted from the discipline that factory production forced on workers. Self-employed or small-shop artisans had enjoyed greater freedom to repair to the local cafe during working hours for a quick drink and to take Monday off to recover from Sunday's inebriation, hence their "Saint Monday" holiday. But factory routine and terribly long hours of steady work left only mealtime for drinking and therefore encouraged the greater use of dry table wine among the proletariat, which explains its phenomenal rise of production. Railroad transport and the appearance of the tank car helped to democratize wine consumption (and liver ailments) by introducing it into the home where it took its place on the dinner table. Once there it became a "part of the meal, comparable to bread and meat." [32] And it began to appear more frequently on the table of dirt farmers whose forebears had been content with water. This democracy of consumption really transformed the structure and scope of the wine industry. Large estates, veritable wine factories, emerged precisely to turn out a low-grade beverage for the expanding urban market. This wine, formerly of purely local importance and made nearly everywhere, assumed national and international significance and became centered in regions more suited to its manufacture.

Of course the growers of common wines in the Center and North faced stiff competition. Their only hope lay in their ability to produce better wines at low prices in an appeal to highly skilled workers and the rapidly expanding lower-middle classes. The phylloxera hastened this evolution by clearing away the old vineyard and much of the old technology. In their conquest of the aphid, growers resorted to new techniques that expanded their productive capacity but that also aroused consumer distrust. Moreover the burgeoning of solid ordinaries capable of long travel came just when their exports began to decline. All of this added up to glutted markets and an economic panic in the industry.

PART THREE

Crisis & Renewal

CHAPTER TWELVE

Era of Crises

A startling paradox of the wine industry was its decline into a shattering depression at about the time that Europeans began enjoying their *Belle Epoque* or, if you prefer, Gay Nineties, although the gaiety continued beyond 1900. After the gray days of the two previous decades, nearly all classes found themselves with more disposable income and the will to indulge themselves in more food and more pleasure. It was a time of music halls, of *cafés concerts*, of ambulatory poets—the minstrels of the masses—of loose morals and, above all, of light-hearted drinking. For wine producers and merchants, for the numerous champagne houses, the new mores promised a second coming of the golden age, and for the growers of the South and Southwest, just recovering from their heroic struggle against the phylloxera, the streams of wine pouring down the throats of the rich and the masses must have seemed like a flood descending from heaven.

And yet before the *Belle Epoque* was half over, it proved a disappointment to winemen. For not even with the best of wills could the world of wine consumers absorb all the produce of the world of wine producers. The early gusto of the drinking man had been a glorious celebration to the end of the twenty-year depression, but gusto cannot last for long. Besides, a relative decline of wages among urban workers began around 1905 in industrial areas, thereby reducing somewhat the huge market for cheap *ordinaire* that had reached full tide at the turn of the century. The price of cheap wine plummetted; its growers drowned in unsold seas of it, made deeper by the rising volume of false and diluted wine entering the market.

Fraud

The crises that opened the new century in both France and Italy re-flected deep disturbances besetting these two industrializing societies.

Traditional ways of life came under attack from the leaders of new social and political movements. Stability and order were threatened by revolutionary socialism, anarchism, and right-wing nationalism. Violent strikes and rioting picked up their tempo in the cities as well as in the country. If one side of modernity was the Beautiful Age, the other was economic dislocation, class hatred, and a feeling of both material and emotional insecurity.

Among wine producers a sense of insecurity resulted largely from the enormous increase in false or fraudulent wine entering the market. Of course fraud was as old as vineyards, but it seems not to have been the cause of major crises in the past. What made it now a calamity was the magnitude of the wine industry by the end of the nineteenth century, the large scale on which fraudulent practices were carried out, and the increasing sales resistance of the public to a beverage containing possibly harmful chemical additives. The problem of adulterated wine came to the surface chiefly during periods of economic distress when both prices and sales fell drastically. At such times pamphlets would appear blaming the recession on an excess of wine debased by water to expand its volume and chemicals to disguise the water.

Throughout the nineteenth century honest wine producers were not legally equipped to suppress fraud. In France a law of 1787 prohibited the adulteration of both wine and cider, even under the pretext of improving them, and it provided horrendous penalties: up to three years in the dreaded galleys, a huge fine, and confiscation of the wine. However a law passed on the eve of the 1789 Revolution did not stand much chance of being enforced, for the leading revolutionaries, except for one brief period of a year or so, believed firmly in liberty and laissez faire, and in 1790 they dismantled most of the absolute monarchy's restrictive legislation. All of the regimes that followed, whether blatantly conservative like the Bourbon restoration or openly laissez faire like those succeeding, were not seriously moved by consumer mindedness. On the other hand there did exist legislation that penalized merchants deliberately bent on deceiving customers, chiefly as regards the place of origin of their produce. Unfortunately the laws were vague and difficult to interpret, leaving judges excessive leeway. Cabaret owners were even harder to control; after gaining egregious profits by watering wine, they might be fined merely six francs and sentenced to five days in jail, hardly a restraint. Even the use of poisonous chemicals brought only six days in jail.[1]

Politicians were not wholly unmindful of the public interest, but in an age that focussed on increasing production, the consumer had no voice in policy-making. Even political representatives from the fine-wine disticts sought to prevent fraud, not to defend the buyer, but to save the reputation of renowned vineyards. In 1819 the famous Clos de Chambertin produced 100 casks of excellent wine, but 3,000 casks were sold under its name.[2] The excellent chiantis once shipped to England lost their market there partly because dishonest merchants added water to them. Any beverage sent out in wood was easily tampered with, there apparently being no chastity belts suitable for barrels nor seals that could not be removed and replaced. Producers shipping in bottle began branding their corks as a guarantee of authenticity. Ministers, above all ministers of finance, were also concerned, for much fraudulent wine did not pay taxes. It was estimated that from 1829 to 1841 the national treasury lost over 15 million francs and that the city of Paris failed to collect over 20 million, due to the watering of wines within its walls.[3]

The addition of water was the most common form of adulteration because it was the easiest, most profitable for the practitioner to carry out, harmless to consumers, and the most certain way of avoiding taxes on the additional beverage thus "created." Let us say that an unscrupulous merchant buys 100 liters of pure wine. Shipping it to a large city such as Paris or Lyon or Marseille, he pays the tax on transport (circulation tax), then the *octrois* and the *droits d'entrée*, two imposts collected at the city gates, the former for the city, the latter for the state. Once his wine is inside the city, the merchant lodges it in his cellar. There—since our merchant is on the nether side of honesty—he adds water, and not always the purest. He can add 10 percent and increase his supply to 110 liters. Had he purchased 1,000 liters, he would now have a hundred extra liters for merely the cost of the water and his labor. And both the municipal and national governments were cheated of their taxes on a hundred liters of wine. Multiply these modest figures by the thousands of liters daily entering a large city and the amount of watered and untaxed wine becomes truly impressive. Besides, this brief statement presents only the wholesaler at work. There were several thousand retail distributors, cabaret and café owners, little shop merchants, and ambulatory criers of drinks with their small barrels slung to their backs and their metal cups swinging from hooks at their waists. To imagine that most did not dilute their wine is comparable to believing that the earth stands still. They, too, might add an additional 10 percent of water to the beverage.

Small wonder that knowledgeable drinkers referred to these shops as baptismal founts, or as *spas*. Since the well-to-do usually bought their wines directly from producers in large amounts, it was the lower classes

who were the victims of adulteration. These were the same people who
got sand in their sugar, base oils in their butter, and chalk water in their
milk.

Now wholesalers in particular recognized that only a drinker utterly
devoid of any sense of taste would not detect the weak savor of watered
wine. Therefore the wine they sent to retailers might be a special concoction of a watered *ordinaire* consisting of heavy black wines to retain
color and cheap Midi alcohol. These products added little to costs and
the urban masses consumed the mixture without complaint. In fact
drinkers hardly suffered, save in their pocketbooks, for whatever the
gastronomic failings of this wine, it was more hygienic than much of the
drinking water. No one was harmed, in a sense, except the wine growers
and the tax collector.

The grower, of course, had a few tricks up his barrel. He could not
add water, because the local broker readily detected its presence. But he
could guard against bad vintages. Perfectly honest wine-makers, as well
as some eminent enologists, considered the addition of sugar, especially
grape sugar, a sound vinicultural practice when that year's grapes were
low in sugar for want of heat and sun during the growing season. Legion
were the plans to safeguard the wine industry from unfavorable weather
conditions, and chaptalization, carried out by the producer rather than
the distributor, lay at their base. That is, enologists advocated the addition of sugar to raise the alcoholic content of weak wine to render it
salable in as pure a form as possible; they did not advocate sugaring
sound wine in order to maintain the alcohol level against the addition of
water. This sugared wine was neither pure nor false, it hung in a kind of
vinicultural limbo; it was frowned on, yet tolerated, and even the strict
law following the 1906–07 crisis provided for some doctoring in certain
years in order to save a vintage. The French administration enjoyed, and
still does, the power to exempt growers from certain legal restrictions
regarding "manipulation" of a must. The Italian government took up this
issue with less enthusiasm and put its trust in the honesty of native
producers and merchants—undoubtedly an error from which the reputation of Italian wine suffered. For there were harmful forms of adulteration that came into wide practice during the phylloxera crisis as a means
of saving faulty wines produced from faulty grapes.

Between the mid-1870s and about 1900 a great deal of French ordinary
wine tended to be defective. It was the product of vines either weakened
by phylloxera, or recently planted and immature, or overfertilized, or
attacked by rot. In all four cases the juice was thin, highly acid, and low
in sugar. To reduce acidity growers added a precipitate of chalk in the

form of calcium carbonate (*plâtre*); this was either spread over the grapes during the first crushing or put directly into the must. Both Chaptal and Fabbroni had suggested this method decades earlier, and it was known well before their time, but many medical experts harshly condemned it because it produced a permanent chemical change in the wine. It neutralized a certain amount of tartaric acid, thus removing the harsh taste; it also enhanced color and life and hence the value of the finished product. From the producers' and the sellers' point of view it had decided merits; from the consumers', however, it had serious drawbacks. The chemical change created sulphate of potassium in the wine which, apart from acting as a vigorous purgative, could also have a paralyzing effect on human muscles and provoke a heart attack in drinkers already suffering from a cardiac condition. In the 1870s Doctors D. Macogno in Italy and Michel Lévy in France, among many other hygienists, condemned the use of chalk in any amount as a violation of pure food laws already on the books. Certainly wine containing it should be labeled as such, as a warning to the public.[4] Of course numerous medical experts, as well as winemen, defended a moderate use of the chemical because only an excess of it had the above effects.

In Italy the Superior Council of Health decided that the use of chalk was not an adulteration, but a normal process of wine-making, and was not harmful. The council nonetheless urged the government to discourage its use lest the sale of Italian wine abroad be harmed; as a result the central power did not go beyond urging. The French government, although highly tolerant of false wine during the phylloxera crisis, acted somewhat more decisively, at least on the surface. When the Academy of Medicine warned that wine should not contain more than two grams of calcium per liter, the ministry issued a directive limiting it to that level. Since acid wine normally required three to four grams, winemen complained bitterly, and the Agricultural School of Montpellier issued its opinion that a dose of four grams was not harmful. The government refused to withdraw its prohibition; but it suspended its decree each year, leaving the wine made in France as unregulated as that made in Italy.[5] Some commentators believed that big wine merchants were the force influencing such vacillation on the part of politicians,[6] but one should not ignore the legion of small wine makers, armed with the vote and quite vociferous.

During the phylloxera crisis, French deputies, spending millions to aid viticulturists, were not likely to favor legislation adversely affecting the sale of anything labelled wine. And their Italian counterparts, happy with burgeoning wine sales in France and hoping to capture French markets elsewhere, did not want to weaken those sales by restriction. Perhaps, they reasoned, a little purging from chalk might do the French some good, along with a bleeding of their pocketbooks. After all purging combined with bleeding was an ancient cure-all. Besides, Apulian wines were normally quite alcoholic, full-bodied, and low in acidity, making chalk unnecessary.

In normal times the wines of southern France did not require chalk either, since they were low in acidity, but sugar was often insufficient because the high-yielding vines did not allow them to produce a sufficiency of it. Made aware of their plight during the phylloxera period, the French parliament voted the law of 29 July 1884, which permitted not only the sweetening of musts but also reduced taxes on sugar purchased for this purpose. This act not only relieved the wine industry, it brought unprecedented prosperity to the beet-sugar interests of northern France, as well as to the railroad companies carrying both wine and sugar. Viniculturists everywhere acclaimed this law and none were louder than those of the Mediterranean South. They were certainly the dominant economic group in the Midi and more numerous as a professional group there than their counterparts in other districts. Growers everywhere now purchased huge amounts of beet and cane sugar and used it to ameliorate their first wines. But then, as noted already, they went on to make second wines by adding sugar and water and acids to the pressed grapes. Next they added raisins from the Near East to their native grapes to make even more wine. And finally there appeared producers who used raisins exclusively to make "château" vintages—straight out of bathtubs in their city basements.

Since southerners were the first to reconstitute their vines, they were the earliest to lose some of their old enthusiasm for sugaring musts. As their new production grew, they came to see in false wines a serious rival to their own natural beverages. By 1890 they had reason to be apprehensive, if only because 1,886,000 hectoliters of second wines made with sugar and 3,178,515 hectoliters of wine made from raisins and sugar, a total of over 5 million, were put on the market. Produced cheaply, they competed successfully with wines made naturally from grapes.[7]

The wine lobby in Parliament now began to demand legislation to curb the use of sugar, although they did not want to eliminate it because many growers still required a sweetening agent to give the three or four degrees alcohol their wine often lacked. They also denounced the easy entry of southern Italian wine into the French market; in fact from ardent free traders, they became convinced protectionists! Most merchants, of course, disliked this shift immensely, insisting that wines of the Midi required adjustment either by sugaring or by blending with Apulian wine. The sugar interests of the North were also opposed to any laws weakening their sales, and they were a very powerful lobby. Huge profits were at stake, for in 1888 wine-growers bought 38,763,158 kilos of sugar.[8]

In the late 1880s, therefore, honest growers were less concerned about sugar than about false wines being sold as natural products. Their first step was to obtain a legal definition of fermented liquids which could be sold as "wine," thereby excluding false and debased beverages; this formed the substance of the Griffe bill, named after its sponsor, a senator of Hérault, which was passed into law during August 1889. Henceforth only liquids naturally fermented from unpreserved grapes could be legally sold as wine. Subsequently an amiable and complacent government passed a series of laws prohibiting the watering and, as noted above, the chemical adulteration of wine.[9]

It does not appear that this legislation was seriously enforced or that there was an outcry calling for the ministry of justice to be more vigilant. The market for natural wine picked up after 1893, a year of surplus production, and while prices declined, gross profits held their own and sales were satisfactory. Restored production of natural wine, rather than governmental action, helped to reduce false beverages in the market. Raisin wine, from its high level of 3,178,500 hectoliters in 1893, fell to 451,422 in 1897.

The *Mévente*

In 1900, however, the situation changed both drastically and suddenly; the huge crop of wine, over 67 million hectoliters, provoked a fall in prices and marked the opening of a difficult period for winemen. The term *mévente*, that is, a combination of surplus produce, low prices, and faltering sales, summed up their situation. The crisis was widespread in France, touching almost all producers of ordinary wines and even some of fine wines.

The causes remain difficult to discover. For the intransigent growers of common wine, the true culprit was the fraudulent and false wine that had flooded their markets since the phylloxera. They insisted that false beverages continued to flow in the normal channels of trade and that official data on its quantity were grossly below its true level. But worse, the justice department did not enforce the law drawn up precisely to keep illegal beverages out of the market. Since there was no accurate way to tell natural wine from its counterfeit, the public had simply stopped consuming both. This lament, particularly widespread in the Midi, had some truth behind it. Consumption of wine, especially table wine, had come under a massive barrage of hostile commentary during the 1890s, and a large number of people no longer believed that wine was a "health drink" (*boisson hygiénique*). Pasteur's old dictum no longer appeared valid about its purity. The belief spread that wine not only contained harmful additives but that alcohol itself was dangerous for human health. There were formidable antialcohol campaigns—not of the dimension of those in Anglo-Saxon countries, but serious enough. Water was no longer a major menace; mineral water now sold widely, became as much the fashion to taste as wine, and was widely touted by medical men. From the newly won colonial empire also came coffee, tea, and cocoa, three beverages that possibly turned the taste of some former wine drinkers.[10] There is really too little verifiable information to prove that wine consumption suffered a serious decline because of fears about additives or because of competition from other beverages, including cider and beer. The use of cider remained largely confined to the Northwest where it was made. Since its production doubled from 1890 to 1914 it undoubtedly replaced wine in its region of preference. On the other hand beer rarely competed with wine except in the North and Northeast and its expansion of sales was slight. Therefore wine seems not to have slipped in the market, and underconsumption hardly appears as the major cause of the *mévente*.[11] Probably many cut down or halted their consumption of it, but the rising standard of living that came after a long depression must have encouraged its faithful to increase their intake. According to Atger, the amount of wine that was taxed as it went on the market rose from 25 million hectoliters in 1860 to 43 million in 1900–05.[12] According to Chaffal these figures reveal a trend in contrast with that for average annual production: 53,700,000 hectoliters in 1861–75 and 43,700,000 in 1891–1905. Using this data, he argued that there was a dearth of wine after the phylloxera, not an excess. The crisis therefore was the result of the large quantity of false wine pushing down prices on the market.[13] Undoubtedly fraudulent wine did compete with natural wine, but no one knows its volume, precisely because it was illegal to sell it as "wine" after passage of the Griffe law. Chaffal's figures do not take all the data into account and Warner's table is more informative.[14]

Adding even the minimal estimates of sugar wine, plus watered wine, there does seem to have been a glutted market. The causes of it were due less to national production than to the decline of the amount distilled into alcohol and the enormous increase of imports, chiefly from Algeria.

TABLE 29: *Total Hectoliters of Wine Available in France, 1870–1907*

Period	Production	Exports	Imports	Distil-lation	Available on Domestic Market
1870–79	54,670,800	3,283,500	824,383	4,998,300	47,212,783
1900–07	55,179,200	2,053,750	5,299,750	2,252,900	56,172,300

TABLE 30: *Average National Price of Wine in France*

Years	Price per hectoliter in francs
1860–69	28
1870–79	29
1880–89	38
1890–94	29
1895–99	28
1900–07	19

Had the producers of ordinaries improved quality there would probably have been less need for Algerian wine, but they did not, and their negative attitude toward quality forced wholesalers to rely on North African imports for blending. The result was a steady deterioration of price levels.

It was above all the price of common wine that tumbled, from an average of 23–24 francs in 1871–75 to 10–11 francs in 1902–06. In the earlier period drinkers had become accustomed to paying high prices even when yield was up; in the phylloxera decades they also paid high prices because wine was scarce. By the 1890s and certainly by 1900 the market had returned to that natural state where prices fall as production rises; the days of anomalies being over, recession resulted.

The *mévente* was particularly severe among common-wine growers, because prices fell regardless of their rising costs. Falling prices nationwide did not greatly reduce gross income: 575 francs in 1891–1900 and 597 in 1901–07; suffering resulted, rather, from falling net profits. This was especailly true in the Midi where prices fell most drastically. The largest cost item was labor, which rose from 1.50 francs per day in 1848 to 3 or 4 in 1906. Since vineyards over two hectares usually required hired help, labor costs could rise to 75 percent of total costs on large

TABLE 31: *Rising Costs of Cultivating Vines*

Task	1856 (francs)	1893 (francs)
Trimming and tying	20	52.50
Turning earth	6	20
Fertilizer	18	162.50
Plowing	105	242
Sulphuring		78.50
Harvesting	30	185
General expenses and taxes	44	146
Rent	122.50	200
Total	375.50	1,026.50

Source: Atger, 18

estates, under 50 percent for smaller enterprises. In Languedoc a large strike broke out in 1904–05 among vine-trimmers and they had won notable gains as regards hours and pay. Their success resulted largely from the fact that full-time workers were going to the cities for work, so that those who remained were in short supply and more demanding. Although growers hiring labor had considerably improved their labor-saving technology since 1870, there remained numerous tasks that required skilled handwork, so labor costs steadily rose. On the estate of an efficient owner, Henri Marès, at Launac, the changes are typical; they are also striking.

Chemicals added enormously to expenses. Copper sulphate cost 65 francs in 1901 and 80 in 1906, sodium nitrate almost 20 francs in 1901, and 29 in 1906. Phosphate fertilizer doubled in price. The terrible rises were the result of monopoly control of certain chemicals. Nearly all the sulphur used in France came from Sicily, where a consortium, after buying all of it as well as the mines, fixed its price so as to attain maximum profits.[15] The independent vigneron was helpless against such price-gouging, for not even the wine lobby could force a rollback. The most it could suggest was the formation of cooperatives to purchase chemicals and sell them at cost, a scheme that required sizable financial backing and made little sense to peasants being evicted from their lands. Large growers, however, often used buying cooperatives profitably.

On the largest properties costs could be held to about 8–10 francs per hectoliter of wine; but on the vast number of smaller holdings cost rose to 16 francs if the peasant included his own labor and interest on capital, to 13 francs if he did not. In France the average price for all wines was about 19 francs per hectoliter from 1900 to 1907, resulting in an average profit of 6 francs by the latter calculation, or 3 by the former.[16]

In the lower South prices were even more depressed, with the result that revenue fell from an index figure of 89 for the 1893–99 period to 62 for 1900–1906. The worst years were 1904 (54), 1905 (47), and 1906 (37).[17] The huge vintage of those years left the average vigneron without enough casks for storage, so he had to sell off his wine; when he could not sell it to brokers, he offered it for one centime a pitcherful to anyone willing to take it. What remained he let flow into the streets, sometimes after he and his family had bathed in it.

This disastrous condition was not limited to the mass-production vine-yards of the Mediterranean; it appeared in nearly all large wine-produc-ing areas, affecting even the great growths of Burgundy and Bordeaux. The owners of Château Latour in Médoc suffered declines of income during the phylloxera period, and the 1890s were years of excessively high costs, with the result that they earned no dividend four years out of ten. But then came fiscal catastrophe from 1898 to 1907, when the rate of return on capital fell from 4.5 percent to 0.6 percent, and gloom was deep from 1900 to 1904 when there were no dividends at all. Moreover the estate was already heavily in debt to cover costs, estimated now at over 88 percent of gross income.[18] These losses resulted from the falling prices of the wines that had lost some of their former quality due to excessive yield and mildewed vines. Production rose because fertilizer was added to help infested vines and the use of water, needed to spread sulphocarbonate. Since water diluted grape juice, quality declined; so did value and reputation. In addition, growers were not prepared for the return of the mildew, which, infecting grapes, lent a foul taste to the wine made from them. Worse, about every third or fourth year the bever-age turned sour when it was bottled. Other fine growths, not all of which suffered as severely as Latour, were also disadvantaged, some seriously.

And yet growers in the more prestigious vineyards did not experience such a long period of falling net income as the southerners. In Beaujolais and the Côte d'Or the triennial 1901–03 marked the worst years, with declines from 1900 surpassing 50 percent in the Côte d'Or, 33 percent in Beaujolais.[19] But 1904 witnessed rapid upturns that held until the terri-ble year 1910. Although owners and their vignerons suffered a decline in purchasing power due to the rising cost of food and equipment, they were not hurt enough to turn to violent measures, as happened in the Midi.

Were it true that prices strongly influenced consumption, then the Mediterranean coastal producers should have sold all their wine right off. Professor Pech has discovered a high negative correlation between price and consumption: for 1893–1913 r=−.69 and for 1901–09 r=−.85. These coefficients are valid especially for Midi wines.[20] But prices do not seem to have affected sales beyond certain limits. High prices during the golden age and even higher prices during the phylloxera period did not turn drinkers away; in fact, there was even a slight rise of consumption, 8 percent, during the phylloxera despite the fact that a moderate general depression had set in. With the return of prosperity several factors combined to increase consumption, and it is possible that sales rose by 59 percent between 1901 and 1905. But ordinary Languedocian wine did not benefit greatly from this situation, because it did not sell generally throughout France and was not shipped overseas. It was the consolation of the rising masses, its market was the industrial cities of the North, Paris above all, where it competed with beer and grain alcohol. Politicians, to favor wine consumption in the capital, abolished the municipal tariff (*octrois*) in 1901. This act, combined with crumbling prices, did not lead at once to a notable rise of consumption from the 6,802,000 hectoliters in 1900; rather there was a slight decline to 6,623,000 in 1902.[21] Then came an increase as prices fell, but it leveled off in 1904. Apparently the great yawning gullet of Paris would not open wider under any conditions. No wonder the Mediterraneans were frustrated as prices continued downward, along with income.

Since midcentury they had created a vast wine-producing complex comparable to the textile and metallurgical complexes of the North, except that small and even tiny producers had either survived the tendency to concentration during the phylloxera or had come back into existence after its end. Family and marginal operators, these small producers lived a precarious existence. They were sufficiently numerous and individualistic to prevent the ordering and control of production and marketing. Heavily in debt from having borrowed to reconstitute or buy vineyards, they had no surplus to fall back on. They above all were at the mercy of *courtiers* and hated their guts. Living on credit, usually with their wine as collateral, they were not free to hold it off the market when prices fell. On the contrary, they had to sell it off quickly to obtain cash and in years of high yields they desperately rushed to sell it at any price. Their panic was a decisive factor pushing prices down. They were ignorant of market conditions, unaware of going prices in the national market and could not store more than a limited quantity anyway, so when their

TABLE 32: *Regional Concentration of Wine Production*

Region	1863–73	1875	1890–99
Northeast	14	23	10
Northwest	6	7	6
Center	10	14	10
West	32	32	16
South	38	24	58

Source: Bousquet, Chap. I

cooperage gave out and brokers bought no more, the remaining wine simply served for washing or was poured out into the dusty streets.

The true weakness of the southern vigneron resulted from his turn after the 1850s to the almost exclusive cultivation of vines and making wine. Even if he only produced grapes, he had to sell them to a local vintner, who could sometimes fix grape prices to his advantage. The little vigneron always thought he was free; changing market conditions dictated otherwise.

Once wine had been a national product, widely produced. Regional concentration went on apeace, however, between 1863 and 1900, as table 32 makes clear.

According to Pech, the four departments of Pyrénées-Orientales, Aude, Hérault, and Gard alone produced 29 percent of the national total in 1871–92, 42 percent in 1893–99, 35 percent in 1900–06, but achieved 50 percent in 1907–13.[22] It is important to note that between 1900 and 1906 their percentage fell, an indication that wine production in the rest of France had increased, thereby adding to the deluge of fermented juice.

The decision to practice monoculture was based on the belief that rising urban markets would endlessly absorb every drop of juice coming from the presses. Certainly Paris was a sponge, but once it became saturated, there were relatively few large cities capable of absorbing the increase of 1900 and after. Lyon bought much of its provision from the Rhône Valley and Beaujolais; the great port cities on the Atlantic absorbed the common beverages of the Southwest and the Charentes. Cider-drinking grew somewhat in the ports of the Northwest. Toulouse was divided between the Southwest and Roussillon-Languedoc. The industrial centers of the North and Northeast remained active, but beer was a serious competitor there. To enter the lists, Midi winemen demanded lower railroad rates and thundered against the rate advantages accorded wine from Algeria. In the 1860s Languedoc had exported its light cheap beverages to colonials in North Africa, but after 1900 Algeria—to which hordes of Midi vignerons had fled in the 1870s and 1880s—sent nearly 5 million hectoliters of wine duty-free into metropolitan France. Most of it was purchased by merchants who required its deep color and alcohol to strengthen weak southern and Bordeaux wines. It was their substitute for Apulian wine. Growers might call for a ban on North African produce; neither merchants nor politicians would listen because Algeria had become part of France. Algeria was not Apulia.

But politicians could be made to listen, or so the lower South believed. Viticulturists there numbered about 200,000; probably about an equal number of laborers were employed in the vineyards full-time or nearly full-time (we have no exact data on their number after 1900); and hordes of local bakers, butchers, and general merchants depended on the incomes of winemen. The total must have reached half a million at least. What was more important than an exact head count was their conviction that the only real cause of the *mévente* was fraud, for this conviction brought about a crisis of national importance.

The Midi Moves

Since the beginning of the crisis in 1901 southern vignerons had strongly supported the new coalition of left-of-center parties, the *Bloc de Gauches*, that ruled France. The *Bloc* was itself the consequence of a national political crisis that had begun with the Dreyfus case in 1898, which awakened among republican politicians the fear that right-wing forces might attempt to overthrow the Third Republic. They organized, therefore, into a defense league, bent upon reducing the powers of the proroyalist clergy, safeguarding the Republic, and initiating some social reform to win the masses away from socialism. Local agents of the central administration had assumed a friendly attitude toward vineyard workers during the 1904 strikes, at least the army and police did not try to intimidate them as was often the case during industrial disputes. Up to 1906 most of the vignerons of Roussillon and Languedoc were supporters of the Radical party, and those who were not supported the socialists, who favored the *Bloc* at this time.

Yet points of tension existed between vignerons and the leaders of the left; there was latent hostility arising from the government's persistent efforts to collect taxes and to expropriate the land of vine-owners who could not or would not pay up. When local fiscal agents were zealous, *jacqueries* (peasant uprisings) broke out, as in the Béziers district during 1901 (see map 5). At this early date several subprefects warned their superiors to moderate tax collections since there was serious and widespread despair stemming from the collapse of wine prices. The left-wing ministry was not insensitive; it was, however, concerned about income. To encourage wine consumption—to democratize that pleasure of life— it had a year earlier removed taxes on the transporting of wine, save the circulation tax of 1.50 francs per hectoliter. When the crisis grew worse in 1904, hard-pressed southerners wanted an end to land taxes, at least on small holdings. Radical deputies renewed their demands both for a soak-the-rich progressive income tax to replace the one on farmland, and new sterner legislation to keep sugared wine off the market. Local socialists agreed.

But it was neither a socialist nor a Radical who rose to leadership among southern growers, it was a simple vigneron and café owner named Marcelin Albert, sometimes called the "Redeemer" by the excited crowds he harangued. His little town, Argeliers, stood just northeast of Narbonne in that vast jungle of vines where grape-growing was about the only profession, if not the oldest. Albert and his fellow Argeliens were moderate republican, that is, *progressiste*, in their politics, and none of their workers went on strike in 1904. Nearly all of them were small and medium landowners or owner-workers threatened with extinction. For his followers, as for the mass of peasants like them, Albert came to symbolize the sense of grievance so widespread in the lower Midi when Georges Clemenceau became premier.

By October 1906, after harvests were in, the situation was on the point of eruption, especially in and around Narbonne, but also farther inland where bad weather ruined the cereal crop. The grape crop had been abundant and small vignerons were selling it at a terrible loss or dumping it in the gutters. There had also been a growing antinorthern feeling ever since the defeat of a bill presented by southern deputies to prohibit the sale of northern beet sugar to vintners. The sugar lobby proved so much stronger than the wine lobby that all efforts to further strengthen legal prohibitions against fraud also failed. Local leaders and peasant masses now turned to large-scale demonstrations as a way to pressure the politicians. The first of these had already taken place in the late spring of 1906 at Narbonne, where Albert and his fellow leaders, known as the committee of Argeliers or, more affectionately, the *comité des gueux* (the beggars), were steadily expanding their influence. Their cause received a boost when the socialist mayor of Narbonne, Ernest Ferroul, joined them. By now there were numerous viticultural defense

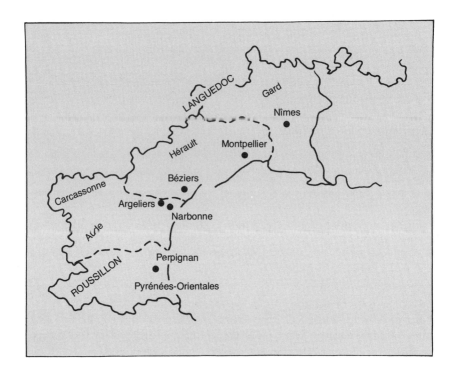

MAP 5: *Lower Languedoc and Roussillon*

committees recruited from small owners and owner-workers. These latter and the landless workers now turned away from strike activities in order to concentrate on political action.[23]

Pressure of this sort was precisely what Clemenceau distrusted. He was, of course, sympathetic toward the South. He had represented the department of Var from 1885 to 1893 and had been elected senator there in 1902. Moreover his cabinet was heavily southern in its composition. He therefore curtailed expropriations for nonpayment of taxes, made money available to aid local credit institutions, and created a parliamentary committee to find a solution to the wine crisis. Vignerons were not appeased. The solution? They knew it already. The committee proceeded with the usual slowness of such investigative bodies. Clemenceau himself did not act with dispatch. A nervous man, impatient of others, he had begun as a politician in the Radical opposition group. After 1900 he came to distrust the newly organized Unified Socialist party (SFIO) as well as the General Confederation of Labor (CGT) and its revolutionary syndicalist ideology. He reacted with outrage when postmen and teachers, who are nearly all civil servants in France, began joining the CGT. In his younger days he had proclaimed that there were no enemies to his left; now all his enemies seemed to stand there, including most of the Mediterranean Radicals. Even Albert Sarraut, representing the area around Narbonne, felt compelled to resign from the cabinet, if only to save his political future.

Clemenceau's intentions were honest. Unfortunately he displayed more hesitancy than decision; even though the prefects on the scene and southern Radical deputies warned him that the situation was extremely dangerous, he insisted that the Midi must be patient and its problems would be solved.

But the vignerons of Languedoc were no longer patient. In 1907, almost a year after the Narbonne demonstration, came another, this time at Béziers. Over 100,000 persons massed in the streets, and this time calm gave way to violence and property damage. By now the crisis that had been purely an economic and human tragedy had become a political issue, with Radicals accusing royalists of provoking violence and the royalists replying in turn. Fearful, local Radicals urged Clemenceau to push through a bill putting a surtax on sugar, hoping that this gesture would appease the winemen. But the premier, still smarting from the postal workers' strike and the CGT's violent diatribes against him, hesitated. Perhaps, given Clemenceau's former medical practice, he was trying to sweat out the fever. Perhaps he believed that it would relive the symptoms if he offered no opposition to the mass meeting. He even allowed local officials to provide free railway transport to them! In May and June 1907 the highways and byways in the valleys and hills of the South were covered, each Sunday, with people walking or riding in every conceivable kind of vehicle, and the railway stations became like Bedlam as country folk poured into Perpignan (172,000 people), Carcassonne, where violence again erupted (200,000), Nîmes (150,000) and Montpellier (500,000). Everywhere there were marching demonstrators, drums and bugles and flags at their head, and down the columns, floating above the berets of vignerons, the derbys of the viticulturists, and the sunbonnets of the vigneronnes were placards, bobbing like buoys, reading "Down with fraud," or offering uncomplimentary remarks about merchants, Clemenceau, and tax collectors. No one paid taxes any more and no fiscal agent dared try to collect them for fear of lynching. Everywhere Marcelin Albert was cheered as a savior. Certainly in the southern heat of June there was ample sweating, and there was laughter and merriment as well as unrelenting determination.

Then emerged a tactic once advocated during the brief 1893 wine crisis: a call came for the mass resignations of local elected officials, from mayors to dog catchers, in order to bring all public life to a halt. Clemenceau, refusing to accept their resignations, decided to arrest the committee of Argeliers, as well as Ferroul, for he rightly concluded that the mayor of Narbonne had acquired more effective leadership over the protest movement than Albert. Ferroul, like Clemenceau, was a medical doctor as well as a testy politician, extremely popular in his city, and Clemenceau made a dreadful error when he ordered his incarceration. He turned a popular leader into a martyr, and it took an army unit to carry out the arrest. On 19–20 June the city was bordering on rebellion. Men, perfectly respectable and calm in their daily lives became bestial and cruel when swept up by mob frenzy. Perhaps Gustave Le Bon was right, the crowd that becomes a mob is less rational and more cruel than the individuals composing it.[24] In two unpublished studies J. Harvey Smith has conclusively proven that townsmen committed the acts of violence, not vignerons. The mob sought to hang the subprefect and two generals, attacked the town hall, and set part of it on fire. Not since its brief experience with a communard insurrection in 1871 had this ancient city been the scene of so much violence. The tragic climax came when nervous troops fired on a crowd angrily pursuing two plainclothesmen; several persons were killed and others wounded.[25] By this time nearly all southern deputies and senators had broken with Clemenceau, denouncing his tactics, especially his absurd decision to use the Seventeenth Line

Regiment to quell disorder. Most of these soldiers were Languedocian and they mutinied rather than use force against relatives and friends. They were subsequently punished with duty in North Africa.

Meanwhile the law of 29 June placed a limit of twenty-five kilograms on the amount of sugar that each grower could use for making wine without a special permit. Other hastily passed measures provided the government with more controls over the grape crop as well as information about the quantity of wine owned by buyers of sugar. Calm reappeared, arrested leaders were released from jail, public life revived. Ferroul remained a hero, but Marcelin Albert disappointed his followers when it became known that he had traveled secretly to Paris where he not only surrendered to Clemenceau but assumed an abject posture before him. With train fare given him by the premier he returned to Argeliers a defeated and despised man. Formerly intransigent vintners, now fearful of how far they had gone toward open rebellion, turned to passive resistance and their vines. Recovery of the wine market in 1908 banished their cause for grievance. From 6 francs per hectoliter in 1906 prices rose to 9 francs in late 1907 and to 12 the next year. In 1910, a disastrous year, prices lept to 37 francs, merely 2 below the national average, and although there was little wine to sell, gross income rose significantly in the Midi as in all the wine regions of France. In fact from 1911 to 1913 there was a little golden age, as harvests went up in volume and prices climbed to heights not seen since the phylloxera years.[26]

The Mezzogiorno

The south Italian wine growers were as heavily dependent on the wine market as their French *confrères*, or, more appropriately, their *nonfrères*, since the two areas competed for the same cheap-wine markets. Many went bankrupt after 1888, when they either turned to other crops or drifted away. Some went to other parts of Italy, some to Provence to labor in vineyards, others went to North and South America. Only a few, chiefly in Apulia, had been briefly lifted out of their traditional proverty, so they were somewhat less likely to resort to the pattern of violence practiced in France. The Languedocians were fairly well organized; they produced leaders capable of moving and inspiring huge masses of people, of giving the movement emotional overtones as well as a rational basis in economic terms, and of singling out a common enemy, the *fraudeur*. Not only the masses, but a large number of local elected officials had acted in concert to achieve specific ends. The great demonstrations in the Midi were a modern mass phenomena, with an old-style *jacquerie* breaking out only in Narbonne.

In the Mezzogiorno, on the other hand, the peasant population was emotionally bound by tradition, unorganized, without influence, and without sympathetic leadership. Unlike their Gallic counterparts, who had a long tradition of left-wing political action, in addition to the right to vote, an aggressive sense of southerness, and a revolutionary background, the southern Italian, including the Pugliese, had conservative leaders and a long experience of submission and poverty. They had neither the ballot nor a truly revolutionary tradition. When the Italians did act, they united into rather small bands or *fasci* and initiated *jacqueries* with limited goals rather than broad movements of reform. During the early 1890s there were several peasant and worker uprisings, some in the wine-growing districts of Apulia and Sicily; however, they were not clearly related to viticultural issues. Rather they were the violent expressions of desperate men whose incomes and living conditions periodically became intolerable. It was a condition not unknown to winemen, who indeed might have responded in greater numbers except that the Austrian market at this time gave them new hopes.

Hope, however, was dashed in 1903–04 when that market closed again. During the ten years of fairly active trade with Austria, the north Italian market had also grown, and wine interests everywhere were somewhat more experienced in organization. There were several viticultural journals, and some influential enologists and growers emerged who were politically oriented and who urged their followers during the 1890s and afterward to imitate the French in seeking to control production. And why not? Many Italians during the phylloxera had already begun copying the French by making false wine that now competed with southern wines, especially after the closing of the Austrian market. Identical problems called for identical solutions.

In July 1904 the government in Rome promulgated a law identical to the Griffe law of France (1889), which prohibited the making, and also the labeling as wine, of any beverage not derived from the fermentation of fresh grapes. It also provided rather stiff penalties: 100 lire plus 5 lire for each hectoliter of false wine put on sale; for a second offense the fine rose to 1,000 lire, to be followed by revocation of the offender's license to sell. This law had two objectives: to improve the reputation of Italian wine with foreign buyers and to aid the Mezzogiorno growers. It was above all aimed against sugared beverages. Since southerners had little reason to add sugar, except in bad years, they were less likely to sell adulterated or false wine. Another law in 1897 offered them additional advantages, for it prohibited adding sugar to any must, and consequently northern growers thereafter had to buy strong southern wine to blend with those vintages lacking natural sugar.

Northerners complained about the 1897 law so effectively that a 1905 revision of the legislation gave them considerable latitude to adjust their vintages. They could add sugar, tartaric and tannic acid, postassium sulphate, and pure alcohol, in fact, anything considered a "natural ingre-dient" of wine, including chalk, provided its contents did not exceed the limits demanded by public health.[27] Authorities, however, were not clear about these limits and chalk was hardly a natural ingredient.

The mere existence of these laws apparently satisfied winemen. A few of them recognized that local and national enforcement agencies were lax, perhaps corrupt, and, like Arnoldo Strucchi, set up vigilante organi-zations on the French model to fight fraud.[28] Quite evidently, however, they were not prepared to use violence in imitation of the French.

Champagne

The protest movement that took place in Champagne had different goals: growers in the Northeast sought above all to safeguard not the "purity" of the commonest beverages, but the quality of their types of vintages. They were harshly critical of southern growers for flooding the markets with cheap drink; for them, adulteration consisted less in the use of sugar and water than in the addition of cheap southern wine to their own superior products. Their chief enemy was the merchant who performed this blending operation and labeled its end product champagne. Now here was a situation different from that of a Vouvray vintner using the term champagne for wine that had never left the Loire Valley. At least the several firms located in and around Reims that were mixing varying amounts of native wine with "exotic" beverages included some authentic champagne in the end product. This was not illegal; it was a means for lowering the cost—and the quality—of sparkling wine and marketing it to persons unable to pay the high price of the authentic drink. This, too, was an old practice, dating from the lowering of the costs of transporting lesser wines to Champagne. Wholesale merchants in Bordeaux, Bur-gundy, and Beaujolais were doing the same thing, as were their equiva-lents in Piedmont and Tuscany. How else could the growers of chianti have made in one year more than the region could have turned out in several? It was to be expected that native vignerons in the above regions would become as angered by this practice as those of Champagne, yet only the Champenois followed the Languedocian example. Why was this?

Various theories explaining the origin of violent behavior are not appropriate, since many vignerons, although suffering serious economic reverses after 1900, did not all resort to violence. Those in Languedoc did so because a majority of them had become entirely dependent on wine for their income. Confronted with absolute ruin and convinced that fraud was the enemy, they expected immediate solutions from the government on which they had become so dependent since the phylloxera crisis. Their ruin during the 1880s, their slow recovery during the 1890s, and their ruin again after 1900 too seriously upset their lives; it unnerved them and gave to their conviction the stuff of fanaticism. The transition from an old-style viticulture to a new style was too upsetting, too crisis-filled, with the consequence that violence became the only way to express their anguish; and it provoked a normally peaceful population of small growers, highly independent and individualistic in their attitudes and style of life, into becoming supporters of a collectivist solution to their problem. Undoubtedly the marked increase in the number of large estates and the appearance of veritable wine factories brought about a certain proletarianization of the southern grape-trimmers. There came into being a larger number of wage-laborers and worker-owners than was the case in most other vine areas and an extraordinarily large number of vignerons did nothing but grow grapes which they sold to large capitalistic winemakers. In short, a sizable majority of the viticultural population not only depended on wine for a livelihood, they were utterly at the mercy of the vintners and merchants who bought their grapes. But though they were economically dependent, they were not yet dependent in their minds and hearts. Theirs was a tradition of individualism and personal freedom based on land ownership. The gap between reality and their ideal left only a void of violence, into which they fell.

Grape-growers in Champagne found themselves in a similar situation as a result of the post-1900 crisis and the terrible year of 1910. Their attitude was conditioned by their relation to the large companies that made and sold champagne, and it is in this relation that one must look for understanding.

The companies did not merely distribute an item of daily consumption; they created a luxury article and most enforced rigid quality controls. To sell their creation the Moëts, the Mumms, the Clicquots, etc., spent considerable sums of money to convince the public that champagne was a unique achievement, a work of art, and as necessary to the gaiety of life as silk stockings, white tie, and tails. Their success had been proven by the persistent efforts among sparkling wine-makers either to appropriate the word "champagne" for their wines of lesser breed, or to associate their products with the area (hence the inferior concoctions that went under the labels "Champagnole," "Champenois," Champanisé" and so on).

In their efforts to prevent the use of the champagne label for wines made elsewhere, the big firms were not well armed legally. In 1824 the government passed a law prohibiting the seller from deceiving the buyer as to the geographic origins of his product. Had the law been rigorously applied, all cheese sold as Roquefort would have had to come from that small area in southern France, all Dijon mustard from the capital of Burgundy, and all champagne from grapes of that old, picturesque province. Since the law was vague and subsequent governments reluctant to apply it, the big companies had to unite and do battle themselves. In the 1840s they took on the winemen of Vouvray who made sparkling wine and labeled it "Champagne." After a lengthy court battle they were successful in 1844, which apparently settled the issue until the Third Republic. By 1870 the companies had organized into the Syndicat de Commerce des Vins de Champagne. This organization continued the struggle against the Loire Valley winemen, who persistently tried to place the word champagne in the public domain, to indicate, at worse, any bubbling wine, at best, a sparkling wine produced by the same technique as in Champagne but from grapes grown outside of that area. In the 1880s and 1890s suits were almost constantly coming before the lower and higher courts in Tours and Angers and were generally successful.[29]

Since sellers in foreign countries also put "champagne" on their sparkling wine, the Syndicat urged the French government to persuade foreign powers to suppress this form of fraud. In 1891 France, Great Britain, Spain, Switzerland, Portugal, Tunisia, Brazil, and Guatemala met in Madrid and issued a convention prohibiting "false indications of origin" of any product. Curiously, Italy refused to attend, as did the United States, Sweden, Norway, and the Netherlands.[30] Germany and Russia also did not recognize the convention and German wine-makers regularly bought peasant wines in Champagne, blended them with their native vintages, and sold the results as "French" champagne.

There the issue stood in the Gay Nineties, when champagne sold widely, and vignerons were so remarkably well off that even the appearance of the phylloxera did not upset them unduly. The big companies prospered and paid almost unheard of prices for the grapes they used. In this respect, incidentally, the Champenois were considerably luckier than the Languedocians, for their golden age went on for well over thirty years.

Perhaps it was the sudden ending of this propserity and the serious economic letdown following it that provoked the vignerons to violence: their rising expectations were so suddenly frustrated. This pattern of events fits the causal model developed by several students of revolution However it is really too simple in itself. Economic disappointment undoubtedly was a force inducing men to riot both in Languedoc in 1907 and in Champagne in 1911. But the same sequence appeared in other vineyards and violence did not result. There was something special about these two areas where it did break out. And indeed the wine industry in Champagne bears similarities to that in Languedoc, particularly the relations between the large wine-making firms and the vignerons.

Far more than those in the Midi, small growers in Champagne had become conscious of marked changes in their status. In earlier decades they had enjoyed a somewhat tenuous independence from the big companies because they not only grew grapes, they made wine, which they often sold. It the price of grapes was too low, they made their wine and held it until they observed a rise of prices. Of course only vignerons with sufficient cooperage and other equipment enjoyed this privileged position. However by the later nineteenth century an increasing number of grape-growers abandoned wine-making with its heavy expenses and sought to make a living by selling their grapes alone. This decision reduced their costs but increased their dependence on the companies, their only buyers. Moreover they had to sell quickly, before the grapes rotted, and so lost much control over prices. Many of them who owned valuable vineyards in the best sites were able to contract with the companies for the regular purchase of their grapes; they obtained security, but lost their former freedom. On the whole they were well treated by reputable merchants, who were committed to making fine champagne and who saw their own interests involved in the growing of quality grapes. But what all of the vignerons wanted was a setup whereby the companies would have to buy *their* grapes to make champagne and not the grapes or wines of growers outside of the district. That is, if the local vignerons were to be dependent on the companies, the companies would also have to become dependent on the local vignerons. This goal was possible, but only if wine marketed as champagne was made exclusively from grapes grown in that specific area so denominated. The Syndicat de Commerce des Vins de Champagne, representing the reputable firms that most actively opposed the adulteration of wine, was fully behind this objective. Indeed, there would be little purpose in the struggle against false labeling if the wine itself lost its reputation as a fine product.

The wine lobby in Paris, aided by extensive pressure and violence from the southern growers, pushed through several laws between August 1905 and June 1907, giving the government extensive powers to suppress fraud. At this point deputies and senators representing areas of quality wines came forward with proposals that had little to do with the South and its ordinaries. Their chief proposal sought to safeguard not merely purity but also quality, and to identify both purity and quality with the geographic name of the area of grape-growing and wine production, an issue of little concern to Mediterranean growers inasmuch as few sold any juice to champagne firms. Guided by the wine lobby, the ministry took the first steps in August 1908 toward creating areas delimited as the source of specified wines; it decreed that only wines originating in these areas and made according to "local usage" and custom were entitled to bear the area's name on their labels.

Having advanced this far, the cabinet had to take another step, far more difficult and complex: it had to draw the boundaries. Most vignerons in Marne department wanted an area excluding all of the old province of Champagne except sections of the three small *arrondissements* of Reims, Epernay, and Châlon. Growers in other parts of Champagne, especially those in the department of Aube, were furious. All of Champagne, they insisted, must be included, for they too, had a right to its title. Had not Troyes, their present capital, been the ancient capital of the province before 1789 (see map 6)

The government created a local commission, loaded with deputies from Marne, and accepted its conclusions.[31] Although it included eighty-two communes in Aisne department to the north, it totally rejected the claims of the Aubois, pointing out that the vine species, the methods of trimming them, and their yield were not representative of a "typical vineyard" in the now delimited area called "Champagne viticole." With the approval of the Council of State, a consultative body of legal-administrative experts, the cabinet accepted the decision of the local commission, and on 17 December 1908 it issued the first decree law establishing a regional delimitation. Similar procedures were used for delimiting Cognac, Armagnac, Banyuls, Clairette de Die, and Bordeaux, where a few "incidents' occurred, but nothing comparable to the riots of Champagne.[32]

That rioting occurred there was probably inevitable. Unlike other wine areas, especially the lower South, the Northeast suffered a series of

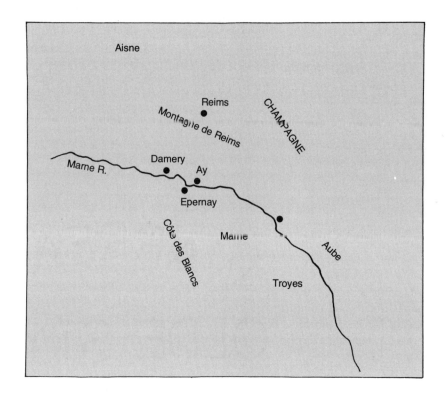

MAP 6: *Champagne viticole*

low yields. The average annual crop from 1864 to 1908 had been 420,000 hectoliters. From 1908 to 1911 it averaged 136,000.[33] The phylloxera, late to arrive, was partly responsible, but so was bad weather; and frosts combined with heavy rains nearly wiped out the crop of 1910. Normally prices rose in scarce years, and this began to occur and was encouraged by fairly good quality. Long before this point, however, some merchants turned from the high-priced grapes of Marne and began the regular and large-scale buying of lesser grapes and wine in Aube. Wine sold for 60 francs in Marne, but only 30 in Aube. The maneuver infuriated Marne vignerons; then came 1910, *l'année terrible*, when most vignerons had neither grapes nor wine in cask to sell at suddenly inflated prices. From the richest of growers they had fallen to the lower depths. They were burdened with debts, three-fourths had mortgaged their lands to get cash, and their costs of production had risen sharply. Had 1910 been a vintage of average abundance, perhaps they could have pulled through. The loss of income that year, however, set them off, and they came to believe that all their troubles were the result of fraud. Like the Southerners, they too found the perpetrators.

Unfortunately Champagne had become the headquarters of a group of promoters, new men tempted by the continued rise of sales and the prosperity of the big companies. Seeking to get rich quickly, they bought the lesser wines produced in several areas of Champagne, blended them with even cheaper wines brought in from the Midi, then sold the finished product as natural champagne. This defied the spirit of the 1908 delimitation law, but not always its wording, at least not for these merchants who simply added other wines in limited quantities to local ones. Perhaps this was why the authorities hesitated to prosecute them. But the Ministry of Justice was also slow to take action against out-and-out frauds who sold nonlocal wine as champagne.

Angered in the extreme, thousands of vignerons decided to take the law—or lack of it—into their own hands. On 16 October 1910, distressed by the lack of grapes to sell, several thousand (10,000 affirm some witnesses) went to Epernay and demanded that adulterators be forced to abide by the law of 1908.[34] The vignerons no longer acted in isolation: many of them had joined the Fédération des Syndicats de la Champagne, set up in 1904 to defend their interests. But their enthusiasm for action went well beyond what the legal-minded heads of the Federation sanctioned, if only because the authorities in Paris, although amply informed of the crisis by departmental officials, sat on their hands. Imitating the Languedocians, some municipal councils dominated by growers began to resign; at the same time vignerons started a campaign against paying taxes. More decisive action did not come until 8 November, when those at Damery discovered that "foreign" wine had just entered the local railway cargo depot. They massed there and forced the owner of the wine to ship it back south. During the night four barrels were staved in. In the chill of December came several small manifestations, and on the day after Christmas 2,400 liters of southern wine flowed into the streets of Epernay.

The onset of winter made conditions worse. Quite clearly professional agitators now began to stir up the crowds, and red flags appeared on poles atop town halls. On 17 January 1911, a crowd at Damery emptied over 2,000 bottles of wine into the Marne River, while another crowd sacked the cellars of a nearby merchant, pouring some 76 hectoliters of wine and 200 liters of liqueur into the street. Three days later similar occurrences took place at Hautvillers. Fearful for their stocks, most merchants agreed not to bring in Midi wine.

By now Paris belatedly became aware of the gravity of the situation. The Chamber of Deputies and the Senate voted to reinforce their measures against fraud. Until now numerous merchants had contined to buy wine in Aube to blend with that of Marne, but these new measures sought to cut off this supply by reaffirming the obligation of merchants bringing in wine from the Midi or Aube to keep it in a separate cellar.

Now the Aubois grew angry once more. After 1908 merchants had continued to buy their wine, so they acquiesced in that year's delimitation, but now they saw themselves seriously threatened and their representatives sought to reverse the delimitation with massive demonstrations and political action. Their cause was furthered by some national-minded deputies and senators who believed that delimitations divided the country, created local animosities, and weakened national sentiment. In April they actually won a sizable majority in the Senate for a bill that would abolish delimitations throughout the country.

Hardly had the Senate recorded its vote, and the news been made known in Marne than local growers rang the tocsin bells at Damery, shot off their *paragrêle* cannons, and sounded their horns. On 12 April masses of vignerons armed with picks, hoes, and clubs came running to the town. Had the interior minister alerted the prefect in time, this official might have sent soldiers earlier, but Paris still seemed unaware of how intensely vignerons hated merchants whom they believed engaged in fraud. It took only a short time to sack the firm of Delouvin: wagons were demolished, casks and bottles were thrown into the street, and they would have burned the building had not the straw they used for tinder been soaked by spilled wine. They then invaded five more cellars and a veritable river of wine flowed in the unpaved streets, creating a slush several inches deep and an intoxicating stench.[35] When two squadrons of dragoons finally arrived, they took two hours to get inside the town because of the barricades thrown up and the resistance of local women. According to the best witnesses, vigneronnes played a major role in these riots, urging on their men and even entering the front ranks.[36]

Another crowd had, in the meantime, moved on the town of Dizy, and there sacked the cellars of Raymond de Castelane. This time they found dry tinder and burned the buildings and all their contents. In Ay, near the Marne River, devastation and burning literally destroyed several firms, unfortunately including Ayala and Bissinger, both of which were honest in their dealings. This terrible mistake indicates that some in the crowd, members of which carried red flags and sang radical songs, were motivated by class hatred for all big merchants, not simply by viticultural concerns. The Moreau brothers, Lucien and Emile, may have led this left-wing faction, but they were later acquitted of instigating violence. Quite different was Emile Michel Lecacheur, vice-president of the Federation, a huge man of stentorian voice, who although acquitted later, played a dubious role as agitator and pacifier. He was dumbfounded when he learned of the destruction at Ayala. As an ardent nationalist, member of Paul Déroulède's veteran organization, and an officer in the reserves, he had no intention of leading a revolt in favor of socialist goals. A well-to-do viticulturist, he belonged more to the forces of order than of disorder, which probably inspired his efforts to limit the destructive penchant of the crowd once it was unleashed.[37] In fact several socialists and extremist unionists accused him of weakness, and the Federation did not follow a clear-cut policy during the troubles.[38]

In contrast the riots and their perpetrators seem to have had a perfectly clear aim: the punishment and banishment of fraudulant merchants. Save for a few extremists, they did not display any sense of themselves as belonging to a mass movement seeking profound social and economic change; they certainly were not revolutionaries bent on overthrowing the power of the capitalist merchants. The big firms of Epernay and Reims were not molested, suffering neither damage nor reputation. There is even less indication of class struggle. The participants were local people, chiefly small and medium vine-owners and some of their hired workers. The enemy was not capitalism but fraud, and in this respect the vignerons of Champagne and Aube were similar to those of Languedoc and Roussillon. But they differed in that the former were not politically touched by these events, so neither political tradition nor social structure were upset by the events of 1911.

Only the Aubois continued to manifest their discontent. Simultaneously with the Marnois, but for different reasons, they began a noisy, but undestructive, campaign of demonstrations and protests against their exclusion in 1908 and the reinforcement of it in February 1911.[39] Finally in June 1911, after a further inquiry by the Council of State, the cabinet issued a new decree that delimited the viticultural cantons of Aube as "Champagne *deuxième zone*," or second zone Champagne. For them it was the equivalent of a twilight zone and not acceptable. But there the matter stood when World War I broke out.

CHAPTER THIRTEEN

Wine & Politics

France

The profound crises affecting the wine industry after the 1880s inevitably heightened the relations between winemen and the government. In this respect wine did not differ fundamentally from other products, for as economic activity expanded everywhere, so did the regulatory powers of state officials. However, the connection between politics and wine assumed a special intensity that distinguished it from other industries. The ideal of laissez faire, raised to the level of a natural law in the eighteenth century and proclaimed as a natural right by the Revolution, strongly influenced all French governments after 1789. Even the Second Empire (1852–70), with its Saint-Simonian penchant for intervention in economic affairs, sought merely to stimulate industry and trade; indeed it was more consistently free trade in its policies when it abandoned the tariff protection of its predecessors. Most politicians preferred to leave business alone, including the wine business. That the realization of this ideal proved impossible resulted from two factors: the governments' fiscal policies and the impact of wine crises on large numbers of voters, who, having won some objectives by rioting, decided the ballot was more effective.

But long before the vigneron won the vote, he and the merchants who sold his wine had to pay taxes on it. Now winemen were not opposed to taxes as such, at any rate not more opposed than other people. They complained rather against discriminatory taxes, against a fiscal system that weighed heavier on wine than on other products. The politics of winemen, therefore, was usually a defensive strategy, one seeking to safeguard the beverage from undue taxes that eager ministers and politicians sought to impose on what they perceived as a bottomless well of wealth.

Wine had always been heavily taxed, but then so was every article of trade, even necessities such as salt for animals in France and flour for bread in the Italian states. Old regimes were as inequitable in their fiscal as in their social arrangements. The French in 1789 set out to abolish the old and patently unjust fiscal system. However since no state could exist without an income, the revolutionaries, seeking not at all to abolish the state but rather to modernize it, put forward schemes to create men equal in the eyes of the tax collector. The most radical called for a tax, perhaps progressive, on income. But almost every person who owned a square meter of property and had more than one pair of shoes objected to income taxes, so the new fiscal system, as it finally emerged first under the Directory (1795–99), then under Napoleon between 1804 and 1808, resembled that of the Old Regime, just as Napoleon's other policies began to resemble those of Louis XIV as he undertook the very costly process of becoming the super sun king. The new fiscal setup combined much of the old and a little of the new. And the Italian states, when they united in 1860–61, laid out a system quite similar to it. Essentially regressive systems, they relied heavily on indirect taxation and played down, without entirely ignoring, differences in the quality of goods in the interest of uniformity and simplicity; in consequence they placed greater tax burdens on the lower classes than on the wealthy. Until the later nineteenth century most wine-growers and merchants, as property owners, saw nothing wrong with this; by no means did they advocate progressive income taxes. They simply believed that wine was taxed more heavily than other articles of commerce. Ferociously inegalitarian in their social views, they were fairly democratic regarding fiscal matters; they thought that all articles of trade, like all men, should be equal before the law, including the state's budget law. What they wanted throughout most of the century were lighter taxes on wine, not a different fiscal system; they wanted relief, not revolution.

The fiscal system of France, although reformed during the Revolution, was the creation of Napoleon, and all succeeding regimes (five in number) preserved it until the first World War.[1] Regarding wine as a commercial product the emperor levied a tax on shipments by wholesalers, the *droit de circulation*, a form of transport tax levied on quantities exceeding 25 liters. In 1816 it varied from 1.50 francs to 1 franc depending on the alcoholic content of the liquid; this rate held remarkably stable until 1871, when the governement raised it to help defray the costs of the unsuccessful 1870–71 war against Germany. Then in 1880 it fell to a range between 2.50 francs and 1 franc. The retail tax, *droit de détail*, hit shipments under 25 liters and was more definitely a consumers' tax, affecting wine sold by small local merchants and in cabarets. Its rate varied between 10 and 18 percent of value, with value determined partly by alcoholic content. The entrance tax, *droit d'entrée*, fell on all wine entering towns over 4,000, and later over 4,500, inhabitants. The amount of the tax, which varied according to the size of the town and its estimated wealth, ranged from 60 centimes to 4.80 francs per hectoliter. Not until 1880, and then as a result of the phylloxera, did the range go down to 40 centimes and 3 francs. In addition all owners paid a land tax, and vineyards were usually valued higher than pasture or plowland. Finally there was a municipal tax, the *octrois*. Its amount was determined by each municipal government, but its rate was not to exceed the national entry tax. However as towns grew into cities and became expensive to run, the *octrois* went up; eventually it was double the entry tax.[2]

It has been estimated that all these taxes raised the price of wine by 100 percent or more. According to one source in 1829, three million hectoliters of fine bordeaux paid 15 million francs in taxes, and 12,500,000 hectoliters of ordinary wine, valued at 7 francs per hectoliter, paid 105 million. Since the total value of these ordinary wines came to 87,500,000 francs, they were taxed at 120 percent of their value. Petitions from the Moselle district affirmed that wine there paid a tax equal to 200 percent of value; other petitions from Toulouse, the Lot, Burgundy, and the Pyrenees deplored similar fiscal excesses and serious loss of income by wine producers.[3] A widespread pamphlet campaign in the late 1820s, incidentally, indicates that winemen achieved some coordination in their efforts to influence the Bourbon rulers of France, acting undoubtedly through their local agricultural societies.

The restored Bourbon king had been received by wine districts according to their condition under Napoleon. Bordeaux was delighted, since his return meant the breakdown of the so-called Continental System, designed to destroy England by cutting her off from continental markets. This had seriously hurt the wine trade of all port cities, especcially those on the Atlantic. On the other hand, the empire's expansionist policy had opened markets hitherto closed to Burgundy and Champagne, so they preserved their Bonapartist traditions, especially some of the rich Champagne families. Since all these areas had a goodly admixture of legitimists among their notables and vinegrowers, none of them worked toward the overthrow of the Bourbons in 1830. That was the work of Paris.

The revolution of July 1830 put Louis-Philippe on the throne. As head of the Orleanist dynasty and embarrassed when the masses of Paris, who had really wanted a republic, elevated him, Louis-Philippe set out to win friends and influence people—chiefly rich people—and the rural population. Since his officials believed that some two million persons were engaged in viticulture, he was not unmindful of their grievances. In fact many growers and small merchants had taken advantage of the turmoil in Paris to forcefully resist the entry tax by burning the offices and records of tax officials; Bordeaux had become the center of this resistance movement. In December 1830 the king decided to end the entry tax in certain towns and he lowered nearly all wine and alcohol taxes by one-third, a reduction of some 30 million francs. Since income from these taxes had averaged about 88 millions from 1820 to 1830, his decision made a considerable gap in his finances. Detaxing helped most the wine sold in cabarets, so it was facetiously observed that the 1830 law created the civil list of cabaret owners.[4]

Amicable relations between the crown and the vineyard did not last; the tax reduction of 1830, unboubtedly a fair effort to correct the excessive impositions of previous decades, did not suffice to relieve growers during the harsh years beginning in 1835. In 1829 taxes on all alcoholic drinks had risen to 93,600,000 francs from 58,690,000 in 1816. In 1831 the tax bill of all alcoholic beverages fell to 56,584,000 francs; then rose to 69,799,000 francs in 1835; 78,412,000 in 1840; to nearly 80 million in 1842 and 96 million in the next year. If one deducts from these sums about 12 to 15 millions for beer, cider, and vinegar, these tax returns were quite high, and to them must be added the *octrois*.[5] It alone accounted for 50 percent of the price of wine in Lyon.[6] It was probably not quite that high in Paris, where its rates had fallen from 27–30 francs per hectoliter in 1815–28, to 20.35 francs in 1830, but after that the Paris *octrois* on wine alone could not be reduced further because it accounted for one-third of the city's total income from all drink taxes. Paris was already the biggest single market for both fine and common wines, but taxes pushed retail prices up and limited sales.

Wine producers complained that the decline of tax rates might help the merchants, but they did not keep pace with the decline of prices paid the producers for their new wine, and the wine industry was in a depression. More wine entered all markets, but net income and rates of return had fallen to abysmal lows. The state had recovered the former level of its income because wine sales had risen, and tax rates, based on alcoholic content, did not take falling prices into account. Admittedly falling prices were partly responsible for the malaise, and the governement could not change that; but it could reduce exactions on alcoholic beverages, which were still overly taxed.

The July Monarchy, skeptical of criticism and distrustful of reform, simply did not believe these laments. The king displayed the same indifference to them that he did toward movements for parliamentary reform and extension of the suffrage. And yet the 1840s were indeed years of notable depression, and a general economic malaise, which reached its peak in 1846–48, had a disheartening effect on wine sales. During the 1840s the larger vine owners began to organize, chiefly to disseminate information about professional developments, but also to discover the needs of the industry and to inform the government of them. They met annually, drew up petitions, and, on one occasion, a delegation presented their grievances to the king—who politely informed them that his government was not in a position to make additional fiscal sacrifices.

However serious their grievances, winemen were not prepared for revolution. It was urban, not rural, France that built barricades and overturned crowns; and to preserve its skill, it did so once again in February 1848. From this exercise, there finally emerged a new government, called the Second Republic. Its leaders, too, hoped to win over both wine producers and drinkers, so on the eve of elections in May 1849 it proclaimed the abolition of drink taxes as of 1 January 1850. By this time universal male suffrage had been established and small growers could more effectively make themselves heard in the chambers. Viticultural regions, however, did not line up behind a particular group of politicians or party, although some left-wing candidates promised to abolish tariffs and to shift the burdens of taxation from the lower to the richer classes by means of progressive income taxes. The candidates stood on the proposition that once taxes were removed from wine it would, as a *boisson hygiénique*, become truly the drink of the masses; under their leadership, they proclaimed, both politics and wine consumption would become democratic.

This cry was not without an echo. In the Mediterranean vineyard, in those of the Rhône and Saône valleys, as well as in much of the Loire Valley, many peasants, vignerons, artisans, and some members of the middle classes chose candidates of the extreme left, who carried the title of socialist-democrats.[7] It is not likely that many little vignerons really believed in socialism, in the substitution of collective for private property. Rather they thrilled to the denunciation of taxes and to the promise of cheap credit precisely so they could buy more land for their private use. By no means, however, did all vignerons in the coast and valleys rally to the left. In the fine-wine cantons of the Beaujolais the owners of vigneronnages favored conservative candidates and enjoyed enough control over their crop-sharers to induce them to vote accordingly. Their task was difficult because eastern France was inclined toward republican sentiments. Peasants had been buying land for decades, were more self-sufficient and independent-minded, especially in Côte d'Or.[8]

On the other hand, western France remained staunchly conservative, Catholic, and devoted to its *seigneurs*. From the lower Loire Valley through the Bordelais, and especially in the latter, conservatives won their victories precisely where viticulture tended to dominate. It was here that right-wing leaders took the initiative in the free-trade movement, and the committees created in 1842 and 1846 to abolish tariffs were the same as those set up so successfully for the elections of 1849. Many rich owners lived close to their vine workers and assumed leading roles in every movement to further the cause of wine; in consequence their agents and propagandists were listened to in viticultural communes.[9] There was a curious contradiction here of which the newly enfranchised masses were apparently unaware. All the Gironde was ruled by an oligarchy of monied wine producers, merchants, brokers, ship-fitters, and shippers, many connected by family ties and all Orleanist to the core.[10] They were also hostile to tariffs. Yet the Orleanism they supported in France was dominated by bankers, merchants, industrialists, and rentiers, most of whom were staunchly protectionist and opposed to fiscal reforms threatening their high incomes and extensive property holdings. Torn between two opposites, local notables opted for political authority against economic freedom, a decision that facilitated their rally to the formerly hated Bonapartist line in 1850.

Champagne, however far removed geographically from the Bordelais, joined it politically. Conservatism was as deeply rooted in the wine areas as the vines. The city of Reims had a majority of republican elements, but in the vineyards the peasant population, attached to the big firms, voted for conservatives.[11]

All winemen could agree on the need to lower taxes and tariffs, but no government after 1800 (Bonapartist, legitimist, Orleanist, republican) provided the extensive relief from taxes they demanded along with stability and the safeguard of property rights. Indeed the Second Republic proved the most unacceptable, for when dominated by Orleanist conservatives voted back into power in May 1849, it reestablished the drink taxes ended just before the elections!

Curiously, relief came from a government that none anticipated, and probably none wanted, save the Champenois. When Louis Napoleon seized power in December 1851, his illegal act was approved by most vignerons and certainly by most owners, save those in the Mediterranean vineyard. Unlike his uncle Napoleon I, he enhanced his popularity among vintners when he cut the entry tax by half and the retail sales tax by 15 percent. These measures became law just as the oïdium crisis began, and while his Second Empire did nothing to end that malady, certain of his measures contributed to the growth of wealth and well-being during the golden age.

By a curious twist of fate Louis Napoleon consciously sought to win over the Bordelais, whose overseas commerce had been so severely hurt by his uncle. Distinguishing himself from the ardent protectionist rulers of the previous regimes he initiated the first in a series of treaties drastically lowering British tariffs on wine and French duties on British manufactured articles. The Bordelais were wildly jubilant; at last it seemed that the government was taking their side against industrialists and cereal growers, both of whom fumed against the treaty as a sellout to the Anglo-Saxons. For decades the winemen had considered themselves downtrodden contestants in a political struggle among vested interests. Before 1860 they often bitterly denounced the industrialists for having the ear of the ministry. And they were not wrong. Top administrators rebutted their plea for lower tariffs by insisting that protection of France's industry was really in the interest of wine growers themselves. If industry were harmed and workers laid off, who would buy wine? The great urban markets, on which viniculturists had become so dependent, would decline and everyone would be ruined.[12]

Winemen had responded that their interests should receive special consideration. Wine was a "tonic" that workers required to bear up under the hardships of labor in factories where life was harsh, exhausting, destructive of a whole generation of France's youth. Viticulture, on the other hand, was healthful, providing work out-of-doors, with sunshine and fresh air. When in prosperity growers could pay adequate wages, provide decent housing, and encourage high moral standards fostered by the old rural traditions preserved among landowners. Agriculture of all kinds also made for a stable, obedient population. It was certainly not vignerons who built barricades and overturned rulers.[13]

Napoleon's sympathy to this point of view seems borne out by his commissioning the travel and studies of Dr. Jules Guyot. But however deep his commitment to agriculture and wine, he also greatly admired the English for their economic progress. He was probably more concerned about forcing French industrialists to modernize their plants to make them competitive in world markets than about agriculture, for he granted sizable loans to accomplish this end, while the amounts of capital made available to rural growers remained exiguous. Indeed, it sometimes even ended in the pockets of urban speculators rather than in the credit accounts of dirt farmers.

In many respects he resembled Cavour, the prime minister of Piedmont-Sardinia, who also sought to modernize both agriculture and industry. And it was Napoleon who sent his armies in 1859–60 to help the Piedmontese liberate northern Italy from Austrian domination. None of this activity had any direct or indirect connection with wine, save that France received in recompense the provinces of Savoy, whose sparse vineyards produced a pleasant white wine, and Nice, where there were few vines but many drinkers. More important for our subject was the extension of trade treaties with other European states; these benefitted the other wine regions of France, whose produce began to penetrate more abundantly the markets of the Low Countries, Germany, Switzerland, and Italy.

The Second Empire disappeared in 1870 for the same reason as the first, military defeat. However both general prosperity and that of wine continued into the 1870s and the founding of the Third Republic. All taxes were raised slightly to pay war debts, but in 1880 the triumphant republicans, responsive to their constitutents' distress in the Midi, cut the entry, retail, and transport taxes by one-third and ended a surtax that had been levied on wine in bottles. With the phylloxera invasion, the government found it necessary not only to lower taxes but even to detax the land of vignerons who simply had no income because they had no wine to sell. Reversing centuries of fiscal tradition, the state now began to subsidize winemen in their struggle against the aphid. Left-wing deputies, as they won wider favor in the country, began to call for a serious revision of the entire fiscal structure; they advocated the lowering of sales taxes in order to shift the burden to incomes and to business activity, the *patentes* or license fees. This project did not get far, in fact, little reform came about until the turn of the century, and most winemen outside of the lower South simply did not vote for these left-wing candidates, known as the Radicals.

Growers were not alone in their distress. Both the national and municipal administrations found themselves in difficulties resulting from a general depression beginning in the 1880s and the loss of tax revenue because of the phylloxera. In the 1870s national taxes on wine returned an annual average of 156,745,200 francs, with the octrois adding 73,252,000, bringing the total to 229,997,200. In the 1880s all these taxes produced an annual average of merely 213 million. Only in the mid-1890s, with replanting, did tax returns begin to match those of the

1870s.[14] If we take into account only the indirect taxes levied by the
state, wine paid approximately 12 to 13 percent of the total collected in
the mid-1890s. Since all income derived from wine sales, an unknown
figure, certainly did not approach this percentage of the national income,
there was a growing recognition that the indirect taxes on wine and other
articles of common consumption were unjust. In 1895 Senator Léon
Bourgeois of the Marne tried to push through an income tax law, but his
measure died in the upper house. However a majority in both houses
rallied round several proposals to lower taxes on wine and between 1897
and 1900 effected a small fiscal revolution. A law of 1897 allowed communes to abolish the *octrois,* and that of Paris fell from 10.20 francs to a
maximum of 4 francs per hectoliter and subsequently continued downward. In these years national and local fiscal charges together fell from
about 20 to 3.75 francs per hectoliter. As a result wine consumption
rose, according to Barailhé, by more or less 40 million hectoliters. This
figure is of doubtful value, even for the Gargantuan drinkers of the *Belle
Epoque.*[15]

Not all wine areas profited equally from these changes. Undoubtedly
Midi producers gained the most, because their wines, the cheapest,
flooded all parts of France, especially Paris and the northern industrial
cities. Common wines from other areas, such as Burgundy, profited less,
because now, more than ever, they had to compete against the tidal wave
coming from the South. It was ironic that the Côte d'Or, with its excellent gamays that had been less disadvantaged than cheap Midi wine by
high taxes, should now suffer from the surge of the southern beverages.[16] Northern alcohol producers and brandy distillers of the Char-
ents, Cognac, and Armagnac were the most ill at ease; in fact they were
furious because the law of 1900 that finally and drastically reduced taxes
on wine, beer, and cider raised as drastically the impost on brandies and
on alcohol made from beet sugar. Since the 1880s deputies from wine
districts had sought to shift the burden of taxes from *boissons hygiéniques* to
highly alcoholic beverages such as brandy, arguing that high taxes on
table wine encouraged hard-working lower-class people to ruin their
health by consuming excessive amounts of cheap brandy. The old fiscal
balance was detrimental to public health and to the future manpower
and military resources of the nation. Wine was not only a tonic, it was a
patriotic drink!

The Bordelais were also somewhat upset about various aspects of governmental fiscal policy. They were naturally delighted with lower taxes,
for even their finest wines in bottle paid per unit the same amount to the
treasury as the cheapest southern drinks. But, like the Burgundians,

their common wines suffered from southern competition, and worse, foreign duties on exported wine had risen in retaliation for the protectionist French tariff law of 1892.

The most striking aspect of these tax reforms was their failure to improve growers' incomes after 1900. Despite a notable increase of consumption, the industry entered a period of crisis, and producers, to their great distress, discovered that taxes had not been the only or even the primary factor influencing wine sales. Now, looking for another whipping boy, they turned upon the politicians.

Considering the wine industry in its relation to politics one paradox after another emerges. Several social scientists have singled out wine production as a factor encouraging democracy. If this generalization is accurate, and we shall test it shortly, it is truly strange, because neither the vine nor its wine thrive under a fraternal regimen; few plants are less adapted to mixed agriculture than wine vines, and between the finest and the most common of wines there exists a distinction that precludes even the mention of liberty, equality, and fraternity. As we have noted earlier, the vocabulary of viti-viniculture was associated with the rigid hierarchy of prerevolutionary society. There were noble and there were common grapes; there were bourgeois and peasant *crus*; and the respective price levels constituted as rigid a hierarchy as any status-minded sociologists could imagine.

And yet at certain historic moments and under certain conditions, viticulture was definitely an agent of left-wing politics. As Armand Perrin wrote, "The puissant growth of the vine in France in the first half of the nineteenth century is a democratic factor." [17] Peasants became landowners, taking over and transforming pastures and forests into vineyards, he asserted, and in doing so, they invaded noble land with the same vigor they had used to destroy the feudal system. Now Perrin's generalization has elements of truth, but it is not valid for all the wine areas of France, and certainly not of Italy. Let us try to refine it by looking at the electoral results of various regions, chiefly after 1870, when many peasants were living off the land they had purchased during the golden age.

Long before the rise of democracy the Bordeaux area had a liberal, though not a democratic, tradition, its chief formulator having been one of its viniculturists, the Baron de Montesquieu. During the French Revolution the deputies from the Gironde area, known as the Girondins, became a focal point for the political "left" when liberals sought to replace the absolute monarchy with a constitutional one and to erect a secular state on the ruins of the former clerical regime. Like the big landowners, wholesale merchants, and ship-fitters who held power in much of the Southwest, they were soon eliminated by a more decidedly left-wing and truly democratic Jacobin movement, whose source of power lay chiefly in Paris and a few other cities. The Girondins believed that society, as well as vineyards and wine cellars, had a natural hierarchy, however they favored a fairly fluid society, one that allowed an intelligent man born at the bottom to rise to the top. More consistent were the authentic blue bloods, the true proponents of nobility, who believed that men of varying social ranks were, like different varieties of vines, fundamentally distinct. A peasant could not become a true nobleman for the same reason that an Aramon grape could not become a Cabernet: the distinction was created by divine will and rightfully perpetuated by breeding. Now the Jacobin accepted none of this. A firm egalitarian, he asserted that all men were born equal, more or less, and that the pursuit of equality demanded that the land be given over to those who worked it, the peasants. If the peasants wanted to uproot Cabernets and replace them with Aramons, then they should do so. Uprooting Cabernets was, after all, not far different from beheading nobles, and both were necessary at the time as a precondition for founding a truly egalitarian society. At the same time there were Jacobins who wanted to engender equality by planting the best species everywhere, and then every man would be king.

Now we readily admit that the above sketches are caricatures, but caricatures usually resemble the real model closely enough to contain much truth. What our sketches suggest is that where men, like the Girondins, emphasized freedom and diversity, considerations of quality (both of men and vines) rather than of equality remained strong, and politics tended to be liberal, emphasizing individual excellence rather than mass homogeneity. This was as true of the Côte d'Or and Champagne as it was of Bordeaux, of the Astigiano and the Chianti areas. And liberals during most of the nineteenth century favored a parliamentary monarchy. In times of crisis, as during the Terror of 1793–94 and during 1848–49, they could and did find it convenient to ally with conservatives out of fear for their lives, freedom, and property. Hence the conservative victory in the May 1849 elections in France. But reactionary conservatism, preaching rigid hierarchy, clericalism, and absolute authority, did not find widespread support in vine-grower regions.

We cannot fully test a region's political inclination until the establishment of universal male suffrage, that is, until the Second Republic in France (1848–49) and the elections of 1910–13 in Italy. The right to vote

had previously been confined to a small fraction of the total adult population, from 2 to 5 percent, and only a slightly larger fraction of the adult
male population. Women did not receive the ballot in either country
until after World War II. Politics, like wine, belongd to the world of
men, despite the fact that women paid taxes and worked hard in the
vineyards. Inasmuch as Frenchmen received the ballot long before the
Italians, they occupy a larger place in this study, if only because their
longer history of democracy offers more documentary evidence and
greater precision in measuring results. On the other hand, it is necessary
to accept the fact that political elections do not always provide the re-
searcher with an exact measure of opinion, precisely because in France
and especially in Italy, he cannot always pinpoint the votes of people so
dependent on wine that its production and sales would clearly influence
their political leanings. We shall concentrate therefore on the regions
where viti-viniculture was truly a determining factor.

When French wine-producers first received the vote in 1848, they
were by no means of one mind. In fact their political choices tended to
follow those of the broader geographic area to which they belonged: the
West was conservative, the East and South republican, with the Mediterranean coast verging toward the extreme left. These tendencies were
the result of many factors: the ability of a conservative ruling class to
persevere during times of crisis when its existence was challenged; the
survival of traditional values enjoying the acceptance of several classes,
or their replacement by new values resulting from the emergence of new
men in positions of power; the outbreak of economic crises serious
enough to have an adverse impact on local interests.

In the mid-nineteenth century winemen were adversely affected by
falling prices and diminishing sales. Economic crises of this dimension—
and the entire economy of Europe suffered a similar fate—often provoke
political change. In the Mediterranean vineyard, republicans profited
from these setbacks to win widespread support among the mass of small
growers. From an area formerly dominated by Catholic monarchists, the
lower South took an important step toward republican and even radical
goals, and when the phylloxera struck, this left-wing orientation was
reaffirmed. In an area so dominated by wine interests, we can assert that
the needs of winemen played a leading role in politics; especially left-
wing parties, and latter-day Jacobins won power because they identified
with those interests, and believed that the democratic state could solve
the problems of its citizens. Southern growers, confronted by the problems arising from mass production for an undetermined market, looked
to the government for the kinds of laws and financial support that would

balance production and demand and offer them a safeguard against cata-strophic monetary losses. In this area viticulture was definitely a democ-ratizing force, creating the true ingredients of the Jacobin or Radical left: a mass of small owners and an extensive rural labor force living in large villages and towns in an area of easy communication and organization.

Areas with similar conditions—extensive small property and ease of communications—showed similar political tendencies in midcentury and after. The Rhône, Saône, and Loire valleys fit this description; however political opinion was far more complex than the above generalization leads one to believe. Unlike the deep South, where vines stretched from horizon to horizon, valley vineyards were spotted here and there, did not require many wage workers, and often were simply a part of general agriculture. Therefore viticulture, even where it covered many hectares, was often not a determining force in politics, and we must focus on the limited areas where it was. In the lower Rhône, wine predominated in the triangle formed by the towns of Avignon, Carpentras, and Orange. This area was part of the Vaucluse department, that was royalist and moderate republican during the Second Republic, but became predomi-nantly Radical during the 1870s. The populations growing ordinary wines followed the lower Midi and moved leftward, especially after the election of 1885. Distinct however was the fine wine district of Château-neuf-du-Pape, where conservative Catholic forces remained entrenched, at least until the 1890s, when they rallied to the Third Republic.[18]

The evolution toward the left can be explained partly by social struc-ture, and undoubtedly the phylloxera, which first appeared in Vaucluse in the 1860s, had an effect there similar to its effect in the rest of the Midi. The politics of crisis tended to favor the extreme left. But this was less true in areas of fine wines, where many owners acted promptly, had sufficient capital for replanting, and hired workers to carry it out. Châ-teauneuf-du-Pape fits this category.

In the Saône Valley, the Beaujolais vineyard tended to resemble Châ-teauneuf-du-Pape during the Second Republic. Medium and large land-owners, conservative in politics, kept firm control over their vignerons.[19] This social control waned, however, after 1870. Under the Third Re-public, owners more willingly rallied to the new government, supporting the moderate republicans, the Opportunists, who posed no threat to private property and acquired positions. Winemen, therefore, favored at first the right, then the center or, preferably, the center right, which was republican by the 1890s when it assumed the label "Progressiste." Not even the *mévente* of 1906–07 turned them from moderation in politics.[20]

Just to the north, in the Mâconnais and Chalonnais, politics followed a more decidedly leftward path. Perhaps wine production had little to do with this tendency, save that by encouraging a commercial economy it opened certain rural areas to outside influences. Where conservative traditions were already weak, it helped to create an independent peasantry and undermine traditional religious influence. The peasant without the priest could easily swing to the left and this was what happened in the Midi and much of the Rhône and Saône valleys.

In the Mâconnais and Chalonnais, vignerons were far less dominated by landowners than their counterparts in the Beaujolais, in part because the bond of religious belief was far weaker. The local vignerons, land hungry for centuries, had been frustrated by the great abbeys of Cluny and Tournus and by the religious chapters of Mâcon, that had held the best land for their own benefit. Peasant hostility went back to the tenth century but flared up only rarely until 1789 and after.[21] Equally important was the geography of river valleys, especially in eastern France, where new ideas spread from Paris, passed by Dijon, Beaune, Chalons, Mâcon, Lyon, and on to Marseilles in Provence and to the major wine centers of Languedoc: Béziers, Narbonne, and Perpignan. Ideology tended to follow the routes of the wine trade. And it is interesting to note that new ideas encountered resistance almost exclusively in the areas of fine wines. There monarchist, Catholic owners resisted them at first and only came to accept a very moderate form of republic, the Third Republic, when it became dominated by a combination of socially conservative landowners, industrialists, merchants, and financiers on the one hand and rising members of the petty bourgeoisie, mostly lawyers and professional politicians on the other. What was extraordinary about the Mâconnais was its swing to the extreme or Radical left.[22] In this respect it went beyond both the Beaujolais and the Côte d'Or, although they all had similar social and authority structures. Perhaps its major difference was a larger number of independent peasant growers, who showed greater eagerness to oppose those structures, or to find a higher place in them.

The Côte d'Or, viticulturally, comprises only two cantons: Beaune and Nuits, and both were republican by the mid-nineteenth century. Nuits, closer to the urban center of Dijon, held to its moderate politics. The peasants of the arrière côte, having acquired their small vineyards, did not need left-wing forces to satisfy their goals. Those of Beaune voted for politicians who labeled themselves Radicals, but who in practice were not unlike the moderates. Large owners, conservative and clerical, quite clearly did not lose much of their influence, not even when they abandoned the *prix fait* and shares system after 1850, precisely when these systems promised decided improvements for workers. A strong basis for moderation, however, was the extreme individualism of the small vignerons, who resisted both the egalitarian ideal and the income tax proposals of the extreme left. To them both smacked of collectivism.[23] It is also possible that the many producers of common wines associated the Radicals with the southerners, so that their dislike of Midi wine extended to the party. This dislike was particularly intense because Burgundian vignerons considered their wine superior to that of the Midi and were rather snooty about it.

The Loire Valley presented conditions similar to those of the Rhône and Saône. Wine production was concentrated chiefly around the cities of Blois, Tours, and Angers. In the first area most was ordinary wine, grown by small peasants working their vines along with other crops. In the Tours area the district of Vouvray and Bourgueil produced high-class ordinaries and a limited amount of fine wine, and revealed a more clear-cut tendency toward monoculture than did Blois. Yet voting was similar in both places and followed the political pattern of the Loire eastward toward its source. Republicans of a moderate cast enjoyed considerable backing, particularly in the Blois area, where they won their first victories under the Second Republic.[24]

Although the phylloxera crisis did help Radicals to make a strong showing in wine towns during the 1885 election, they remained decidely weaker than their Opportunist rivals. But each party taken separately was weaker than authentic conservatives in and out of wine areas. The left openly appealed to small vignerons, the right to large cereal growers, and the right proved stronger in an area where cereals were more extensively planted than vines. In the 1880s even several wine cantons (Contres, Montrichard, St. Aignon, Selles-sur-Cher, Montoire, Vendôme, etc.) gave sizable majorities to conservative candidates. Subsequently moderate republicans came to dominate over both the left and right.

The Touraine vineyard more definitely evolved from right (1848) to left (1890s). Orleanists and Bonapartists won majorities in 1849 and moderates in the 1870s and 1880s.[25] Perhaps the phylloxera crisis accounted for the popularity of Boulangists in 1889; but by 1893 the vine-trimmers turned to Radicals, albeit of a fairly moderate nature. This shift to the left was not limited to the vineyards; it was a general phenomenon, characteristic of almost the entire department of Indre-et-Loire after 1900. In fact in 1910 a revolutionary socialist won easily in the wine cantons of Amboise and Vouvray, perhaps a result of the wine crisis of the preceding years.[26]

As the Loire flowed westward, it entered the land of counterrevolution. The old province of Anjou formed a kind of frontier between the France that accepted the Revolution and the extreme west that resisted it. In the 1790s the wine-producers in the short Layon Valley sided with the forces making the revolution and refused to join in the counterrevolutionary insurrection centered in the Vendée.[27] In this context they were progressive, liberal. But in the context of the Third Republic, when most of France had finally accepted republicanism as a fact of life, they emerged as a conservative force, at one with the ferocious Vendéans. Most of them owned their vines and were far more independent-minded than their peasant neighbors. Yet in 1876 as in 1906, they gave over 73 percent of their votes to conservatives, that is, to men who detested the anticlerical policies of the Republic. According to Joël Le Theule, they did not necessarily vote for an aristocrat as such, but for the local notable, whether a true noble or a wealthy bourgeois, a person they knew, a resident of the nearby château. They voted to support the Catholic church against the attacks of both moderate and left-wing republicans.[28]

In the Saumur area (Saumurois), the only other significant vineyard in the valley before the river enters the sea, the same kind of conservatism prevailed, as well as the same attachment to the individual candidate. Party labels seem not to have been of great importance; the Saumurois remained fundamentally attached to traditional values. Although living in a flat landscape that was easily penetrated by new ideas, they barely evolved; and although they came to accept republicanism, they absorbed only its most conservative form. They distrusted the left until the Radicals had shifted toward the political center after 1900. The liberal influence of Angers undoubtedly led them away from their earlier attachments, but not far, and the timeless mass of the conservative western bloc held them like an anchor against the storms of anticlericalism, Radicalism, and socialism.[29]

Bordeaux was also enclosed in the western conservative bastion. Here was the center of the movement for free trade, a policy aimed directly against that of the July Monarchy. And here the legitimists, the extreme monarchist right, took the lead in organizing the movement against tariffs during 1842 and 1846. These same men, as we noted already, organized their party's election in 1849 and enjoyed remarkable success; in fact the right won its victories precisely where vineyards were most extensive—the exact opposite result of the electoral geography of south-

ern France. These royalists were rich landowners and the leading defenders of wine interests; they had agents and propagandists in the viticultural communes where small owners, like those in the estuary of the
Loire River, voted for their local notables.[30]

This conservative stronghold persisted through the 1870s and 1880s
with this modification: abandoning legitimist sympathies, the right came
to identify itself more decidedly with Bonapartism.[31] Possibly this explains its gradual demise after 1890, except in Médoc, an isolated peninsula where new ideas penetrated very slowly, and the Blaye vineyards.
Where little vignerons had bought land extensively, as in the Libourne
district, and had established themselves as independent owners, republicans made headway by vigorously defending their interests. Médoc,
much like Beaujolais, was peopled by numerous vignerons who depended on large owners for employment and voted accordingly. However the coming of the phylloxera and the general economic depression
that began in the early 1880s enabled the right to reactivate its party by
criticizing the moderate republicans for moving toward protective tariffs
and spending money on colonial wars in Indochina rather than for replanting vineyards in France. Winemen, they argued, paid heavy taxes
to conquer the Orient, but no one there drank wine. The right, therefore, profited in western France by using the same tactics the Radicals
employed in the South. There was one difference, however. The Bordelais wanted to continue the free trade policies of Napoleon III; the southerners shifted to advocate tariff protection from Italian wine.

There was one oddity worthy of mention. In 1889 the Médoc actually
elected a moderate republican, Perier de Larson, a native landowner
whose program included a proposal to protect French wine—now in
short supply—against foreign wine. His victory as a native son, combined with the left-wing influence of the city of Bordeaux on the upper
Médoc, brought that once reactionary bastion into the republican camp,
albeit a very moderate republican camp.

The election of 1893 brought everywhere a major victory for the moderate republicans; the old royalist and Bonapartist movements lost their
force, even after they coalesced. In fact the conservative noble, Pierre de
Lur Saluces, owner of Château Yquem, lost out in his stronghold, although he won a sizable majority in the Sauternes district.[32] When Blaye
followed in the same path, all the deputies of Gironde were moderates,
and they stood by the center right that passed the Méline tariff of 1892,
marking a nearly complete repudiation of free trade. Only the crises
affecting the smaller growers can explain this about-face, certainly their

opposition to the massive imports of Spanish wine. Large producers, with markets chiefly outside of France, were not carried away by protectionism, but they could no longer control their dependents as in the past.

In reality the traditional forces of the right, formerly in favor of free trade, became attracted by conflicting ideals around the time of the Dreyfus Affair. To a man they hated Dreyfus and were openly anti-Semitic; this new right, to which the reactionaries gave their undivided loyalty, was a nationalistic force, French-firsters, if you will, and far more favorable to tariff protection just because they were superpatriots and undauntingly royalist. Ideological imperatives overcame economic interests. In this situation moderate republicanism was able to strengthen its following precisely because it had become nationalistic and protectionist in the 1890s (when it assumed the title "Progressiste") and now attracted conservatives who could no longer believe that royalty would ever be restored. Even Pierre de Lur Saluces, scion of an old royalist family, ran as a "Progressiste" in 1902, but he lost.[33] This defeat encouraged some members of the viticultural aristocracy to abandon its pretense at republicanism and to turn openly toward the new nationalist, antiparliamentary right; they became fervent promoters of the newly founded *Action Française*. Count Eugene de Lur Saluces became local head of the *Action Française*, which had roots, some shallow to be sure, in the vineyards east of Bordeaux, and in the noble and lower-middle classes.[34] On the other hand, the Porgressiste republicans won over nearly all of the upper middle class of both landowners and international merchants, the Blanchys, the Guestiers, and Johnstons, and remained faithful to the parliamentary regime. Political action, therefore, assumed the trappings of class war, but it was closer to that of the eighteenth than of twentieth-century France.

The Champagne growers were somewhat similar to those of Bordeaux. In mid-nineteenth century they were conservative; they imitated the owners of the large companies, who had revealed a strong Bonapartist tendency ever since Napoleon I pinned the Legion of Honor on Jean Moët. The small growers, however, were more flexible, tending to follow the same pattern as most of eastern France: they were Bonapartist under the Second Empire, then gradually shifted to moderate republicanism in the 1880s and 1890s, and then turned to the Radicals during the time of troubles following 1900. The earliest to turn left were peasants in the Chalonnais, where vines covered a quite small area. They were probably influenced by textile and artisan workers in Reims and Epernay. After 1906, and especially after 1910, the angry vignerons made a more definite move to the Radical left, but we must remember that by this time the Radical party had shifted toward the political center. Champagne, like most of France, became Radical when Radicals were no longer faithful to their former programs, when they were simply no longer radical. Only the southern vignerons recognized this, and they had already turned to socialism, but they were only followed by a fraction of the viticultural population in other regions.[35]

The Champenois clearly did not follow them; most were small or medium property owners, hiring far fewer workers than the southerners and heavily dependent on the large firms that bought either their grapes or their wines. Moreover, in their struggle for the appellation the large firms were on their side. Their riots, however much they might seem like a defiance of the law, resembled more the lynchings of law violators whom the authorities would not prosecute. Their aim was too narrow to involve them in a critical evaluation of either the political or economic system influencing their destinies. Apart from organizing a professional union, most of them did not even dream of changing their relations with the large firms, much less their loyalties toward the government.

After this rather lengthy description of the political leanings of the major wine areas, several generalizations can be made. Winemen spread themselves over the entire party spectrum, extending to the extremes of both left and right. They were not, therefore, naturally more progressive than other sectors of the rural population. Rather they were inclined to follow the general tendencies of the broader populations and regions to which they belonged. Outside of the South there was no particular reason for them to follow the left, for politicians of this persuasion more often appealed to the urban masses than to peasants, and often they were ignorant of the needs of rural folk. The deputies who, after the 1870s, came together to form a pressure group for wine interests in the Chamber of Deputies, stretched from the right to the left, with moderates predominating, but with a strong Radical contingent representing the lower South.[36]

Certainly most vignerons came to accept the Third Republic during or just after the 1880s, but so did most Frenchmen. And looking closely at communal electoral returns, it becomes clear that viticultural communes rarely set themselves apart from nonviticultural ones. It would be significant if villages with, say, 25 to 35 percent of their lands planted in vines voted differently from villages with none or under 20 percent in vines. But such a consistent pattern exists only where there was considerable interest in wine, such as the South, Bordeaux, Beaujolais, Côte d'Or, and Champagne. And, as we noted, the South was left-wing, Bordeaux and Beaujolais conservative, the Côte d'Or moderate republican, while

Champagne combined Bonapartist and republican traditions. About the only generalization we can draw from this is that the massive production of common wines opened the door to Radicals, while producers of quality wines tended to be conservative or moderate in their politics. This would be a nice distinction—if Bordeaux and Burgundy produced no common wines. But of course fully 70 to 80 percent of their production was about as common as the better wines of the Midi—and it did not induce them to vote for the left. Besides, the growers of the commonest of common wines, the Italians of Apulia, did not follow the politics of their Gallic counterparts at all.

Italy

It is particularly difficult to perceive a clear correlation between vine growers and politics in most of Italy, or to make a comparison with France, for the Italian experience was quite different. The major impulse of her most dynamic political force was nationalism, the goal was unification, and the controlling groups in the *Risorgimento* were an elite of nobles and upper-class commoners. When they, with the help of various republican groups led by Mazzini and Garibaldi, achieved unity, they did not establish a system of government that permitted the lower classes to express their particular interests. They showed at best only lukewarm desire to integrate the masses into the public life of the new nation. The *Risorgimento* did achieve administrative and political unity, but it failed to create a sense of national identity. Italy in 1870, when Rome was finally absorbed, had nearly attained the degree of unity that France had attained by 1789. In the formation of Italians, as distinct from an Italian state, Italy was fully half a century behind France.

The great majority of Italians were separated from public life by a severely restricted suffrage. To vote one had to own a sizable amount of taxable property and pass a literacy test. In 1870 barely 2 percent of the population enjoyed the right to vote, about the same situation that had prevailed in France before the revolution of 1848 established universal male suffrage. However short-lived, the Second Republic reinforced the republican tradition in France. Nothing comparable happened in Italy until after 1900, despite the existence of communal republics in Rome and Venice in 1848–49. The Italian masses, especially the rural masses, whose poverty and illiteracy were nearly insuperable obstacles to their political activity, never acquired the tradition of independence that most French voters enjoyed under the Third Republic.

Another point of difference was the persistent use of mixed farming everywhere save in the Barolo district and the lower South. It is impossible, therefore, to discover a prevailing "interest" among the growers that could condition their political attitudes and behavior. For example, in the vineyards of Piedmont the peasants usually acquired one-half the cereal crop, but only one-third the grapes, a shares system that undoubtedly put them among the grain rather than the grape interests. Again, the persistence of the cropper system gave larger landowners considerable influence over the peasants who worked their lands, which tended to obscure the croppers' true interest, not to mention their opinion that dared not express itself too openly.

Vignaioli were on the whole a conservative or moderate group. From the 1870s to World War I the vineyard areas of Piedmont, Tuscany, Apulia, and Sicily, to mention the most identifiable, supported conservative or center politicians. They firmly endorsed the parties that favored a constitutional monarchy, the defense of property, and the continued dominant role enjoyed by the wealthy. While industrial and commercial workers in Turin, Milan, and Florence turned to the left and supported socialists after 1900, the rural population persevered in its backing of Constitutionalists, that is, liberal monarchists in the tradition of Cavour, the equivalent of French Opportunists in the 1880s and Progressistes after 1890.

There was really no tradition in the North urging wine producers to organize into pressure groups: when the Subalpine Agrarian Association was reorganized in 1867, it showed little interest in viticulture save on the theoretical level. And as was made clear in the struggle over viticultural research and teaching, most small and medium growers remained aloof from innovative efforts even when undertaken to urge the new state to help organize the inefficient wine industry. Northerners wanted no laws in respect to sugaring, watering, or adding alcohol and chemicals.[37] *Appellation controllée* did not interest them. Regarding tariffs, they had no general opinion, except that they regretted the loss of their French outlets in 1888 and asked the government to desist from disturbing the wine market. Yet they repeatedly elected the same deputies, who supported the liberal Crispi and Giolitti cabinets, both strongly protectionist. Growers simply believed that the aid afforded their grains offset the disadvantages burdening their wine. Except for the few who prepared beverages for export, foreign wine markets did not interest them. As Italian cities grew, encouraged by constitutionalist policies, they found new markets among urban dwellers in Turin, Milan, Genoa, Leghorn, Florence, Venice, and Bologna. Their main competitor now was cheap

Apulian wine, which perhaps reinforced their antisouthern bias. In this respect they were not unlike their French counterparts in the Loire and Saône vineyards.

The Asti and Alessandria regions resemble the Beaujolais in their social relations. *Mezzadria* or crop-sharing was widespread, and many owners were absentees because they preferred to live in towns where the liberal professions afforded them additional income, status, and entry into public life. But since most of them lived in nearby towns, their relations with their croppers generally remained cordial. The peasants, for their part, were less submissive, faithful, and obedient than formerly, and considerably more demanding of material improvements. Yet they stood closer to their owners in politics and outlook than did the casual workers. When they received the suffrage in 1912, they cast their ballots for moderates, not for the left.[38] Their politics resembled the right-of-center tendency of the Beaujolais, Angevin, and Bordelais peasants rather than the nonsocialist left that characterized the Saône and middle Loire.

The major difference between the two countries appears in a comparison of the two southern mass-production vineyards. Languedoc-Roussillon became a major center of left-wing politics; Apulia remained firmly conservative or moderate. In fact the entire South and Sicily became almost the preserve of the various ministerial parties, the monarchist right before 1876 and the ministerial or constitutional center afterward. Politics in the South remained in the hands of a small group of well-to-do landowners, both noble and roturian, whose property was planted chiefly in cereals. Supporting them were their "clients" or followers, who filled local administrative posts (including dog-catching and street-sweeping) and lent the prestige of their numbers and the support of their relations, always in return for favors and protection. Southern notables enjoying this kind of backing early struck a bargain with northern proindustrial politicians whereby they offered their patronage in return for guarantees of subsidies and control over the lower classes. Since illiteracy and poverty were far more widespread in the Mezzogiorno and Sicily than in the Center and North, the right to vote was more restricted there; this facilitated the social control which enabled a small political group to safeguard their large and middle-size estates, their real and minilatifundia.

Wine production in the South, therefore, did not stimulate political opposition. Although vineyards were separately planted and quite extensive, there did not emerge a class of freethinking vignaioli comparable to that of Languedoc. The results created a paradox: as the South became the biggest vineyard of Italy, the tariff policies of the Roman government were more favorable to industry and also to grain, a culture that declined in the South by nearly one-half between 1870–74 and 1890–94, whereas wine production rose by nearly two-thirds.[39] But a truly independent-minded peasantry did not appear. They remained economically dependent on well-to-do owners and this dependency was reinforced by the Catholic church and its support of conservatism. Anticlericalism, so widespread in France and a stimulant to democracy, hardly existed outside of cities in the South. Among the peasants hostility toward the clergy consisted of telling dirty jokes about the local priest or of ridiculing him in the ubiquitous graffiti, but had no serious political implications. Given their need for foreign markets, the southern growers were highly dependent on the government to open such by means of trade treaties. Although more mindful of protecting industry and cereals, the central government did seek wine markets, but after 1904, when the Austrians limited their purchases to protect Hungarian wines, the central power in Rome could not find a replacement. Southern growers, already in the throes of the phylloxera, entered a period of crisis as intense as that of their French counterparts. But there were no riots. In the 1890s some peasants had organized leagues that could and did resort to violence and some Sicilian and Apulian vignaioli joined them after the loss of French buyers. But this action seems not to have carried over into politics when peasants finally won the vote. There was, however, a stronger left-wing tradition in Apulia and eastern Sicily than in other southern areas, and vine-trimmers there lent greater support to opposition politicians than peasants elsewhere. But theirs was not a truly regional manifestation. The average of all left-wing parties in the Mezzogiorno during 1913 was a mere 13 percent of ballots; in Apulia it was 20 percent, with most of that support going to socialist and syndicalist candidates.[40] Socialism by 1913 had a large element in its ranks favoring small property and calling for the division and distribution of latifundia among peasant cooperatives.[41] Socialists in France had taken the same line, and when the phylloxera finally invaded Apulia after 1900, economic conditions there began to resemble those of France. Yet socialism, even left-wing democracy comparable to French Radicalism, could not win over the peasant majority. They remained submissive and were more dependent than ever on large owners because the rate of foreclosures on their tiny plots was higher than in other parts of Italy. They continued to support political parties dominated by the rich and without programs to aid them. Servile and impotent, they voted as the local magnate and the parish priest told them to. They lived in a world far removed from their ebullient French cousins. They were not even prepared to participate in the reorganization of the wine industry.

CHAPTER FOURTEEN

Reorganization of the Wine Industry:

BEGINNINGS, C. 1890-1914

The general crisis of the early twentieth century made dramatically clear to hordes of grape-growers and wine-makers that their respective industries were in serious need of reorganization. It also made clear that the conditions of life in vineyards had been undergoing changes that should have been obvious, but were not easily perceived by the growers themselves. The steady trend toward centralization in both viticulture and viniculture had a marked effect on the multitudes involved. As wine-making establishments became larger, the fully and semiindependent vignerons found their status changing for the worse after 1900. Like many petty merchants and artisan shopowners, they found it increasingly difficult to compete with their larger, more efficient neighbors, and falling wine prices drove them either to or over the brink of bankruptcy. What saved many of them was the government's inability to collect taxes in the face of peasant resistance and its own unwillingness to confiscate their land. Undoubtedly some were pushed down into the rural proletariat; however others managed to hold on to their property, even if they could not hold on to their status in society.

In this latter respect they were unwilling victims of another tendency. While they retained their land, they, as small entrepreneurs, could at best own and use only the simplest of hand-operated equipment. It seemed that technological progress was against them. To be sure, some innovations did prove beneficial—newly invented small, portable presses and crushing machines liberated them from dependence on large owners and merchant viniculturists who owned and rented the large presses. However the new, complicated scientific processes and equipment needed by up-to-date enology put the half-educated peasants truly in a quandary. The devices to measure acidity, to control alcoholic content (as required by recent complicated legislation), the expensive material to pasteurize wine, all put the small peasant grower almost *hors de combat*. The result was that an increasing number gave up wine-making. They restricted themselves to growing grapes which they sold to professional winemakers, usually merchants, who in turn hired enologists for the vinicultural process. This meant, of course, they could no longer keep their product off the market, if only for a few months, in the hope of better prices. When prices declined, they now felt themselves to be the victims of the merchants and of a new breed of wine-maker, the enterprising enologist. In the past their limited storage capacity and their need of cash or credit had deprived them of much control, but as independent, unorganized grape-growers they enjoyed practically none at all. Wine-making was becoming a truly specialized capitalist enterprise involving considerable investment of money and skills of organization and technology beyond the little grower's ability, indeed, beyond his dreams.[1]

Simply stated, a division of labor appeared that put the mere grape-grower at a disadvantage, at least until the coming of *appellation controlée*, which gave him some direct control over grape production and some indirect control over wine-making. But except in the finest vineyards, the appellation did not appear before 1914. And long before then the small growers feared for the independence they had once enjoyed or believed that they had once enjoyed.

The problem was felt particularly among small growers in areas of mass production, such as southern France and to a lesser extent the Mezzogiorno. Southern Italians, although faced with the same problems, were far less knowledgeable about possible remedies, and in hard times they chose to emigrate. They did not learn how to use politics or other methods to defend their interests. On the other hand the French small growers were politically active, turned to collective violence when they felt it useful and sought to acquire control of the grape and wine market by more subtle means, particularly by the use of cooperatives.

France

Developing more rapidly in France than in Italy because there were more French peasant landowners, cooperation offered several advantages to the small grower that other forms of organization could not provide. Early in the century growers of all sizes in France had organized syndicates, that is, local societies offering several services to their members. Before these syndicates were given specific standing in law in the 1880s, they were usually disguised as mutual aid societies. Each member paid an entrance fee and periodic dues; in return he obtained help during illness or his family received money if he died. Other members even looked after his vines during a sickness. Such assistance, however, remained insufficient because small growers either would or could not pay fees and dues large enough to build up a sizable treasury. More helpful were the syndicates that purchased chemicals and fertilizers for their members, taking advantage of lower prices for bulk sales and also guaranteeing purer material. In time these syndicates became important local organs expressing the needs and aims of growers, and they influenced those politicians who formed the wine pressure group in the national government.

These syndicates acquired legal status in the 1880s, and in 1888 a large owner from Gard, Jules Cazelles, set up a national Syndicat des Viticulteurs to centralize the disparate local organs. However differences of goals between quality and mass producers led to its transformation into the Société des Viticulteurs de France, a really new organization dominated by large owners concerned chiefly with quality wine and the tracking down of fraud. It encouraged the formation of the Société du Levant, a merchandising association located next to Les Halles, the huge food market in Paris, for the purpose of selling its members' wines.[2] This association could handle up to 200,000 hectoliters, but since it specialized in superior beverages it was useful chiefly to larger growers, not the mass of small men who produced millions of hectoliters of common stock and were ignorant of market conditions. Of course it was not at all useful to the rising mass of simple grape-growers.

Smaller winemen, especially the legions in the Midi, demanded a more drastic reorganization of the industry. Their anger was directed not only against those who committed fraud, but against the merchant as well—in their eyes these two were often one and the same person. Even if the merchant were trustworthy as regards quality, he bore the taint of dishonesty since he earned outrageous profits by underpaying the producer and overcharging the consumer.

Without doubt, vignerons were grossly oversimplifying the problems of the wine trade, but they were correct in their concern over the high market price of the finished product. Wine for which a vigneron received 10 francs per hectoliter sold for 50 francs wholesale and 60 or more retail.[3] The fees of brokers, wholesalers, and retailers constituted perhaps 10 to 15 percent of the total costs, but only the brokers' fee of about 2 percent on cheaper wines was clearly visible and easy to calculate. Operations of the wholesaler fused into his own costs. If he bought grapes or new musts, he paid for fermentation, storage, losses due to racking and evaporation, and barreling. In addition he was responsible for the expenses of local and national transport, warehousing, credit, and final marketing; the retailer had the costs of his shop and services to cover in the prices he charged.

Overhead charges were so heavy because most sales outlets were unbelievably small. Wholesalers and retailers combined made up about one-fourth, more or less, of the persons engaged directly and primarily in the wine industry. This is a rough estimate because some distributors handled other produce as well. If the estimate is fairly accurate, it meant that every three producers had to support one seller. This burden was somewhat lightened by concentration at the wholesale level, but at the retail level the costs of distribution remained exorbitant in both France and Italy. A minute neighborhood grocery store would have a large barrel in the rear from which the owner dispensed the wine, usually into the customer's own bottles or jugs. There was no guarantee that the liquid coming out the spigot was pure and natural. Until 1901 taxes also burdened the industry, but while they fell sharply after this date all other distribution costs followed a general inflationary trend.

The growers slowly came to the conclusion that production cooperatives selling directly to consumers, could provide their members with a larger share of profits. Merchants, as might be expected, denounced such schemes as subversive of private property, as wild-eyed socialism. They accurately recognized a growing movement against capitalism; their fears for their property, however, proved to be unjustified.

The cooperative movement in Europe began in the early nineteenth century as a form of socialism, but even during the revolutionary troubles of 1848 nonsocialist thinkers came to favor cooperation among workers as a means of avoiding the worst features of capitalistic industry. Their concern was limited to the industrial laborers of the cities, the true fomenters of collective violence during the century. As regards peasant associations, however, few thinkers or activists believed them possible or even desirable, given the deep-rooted individualism of soil tillers.

Despite the failure of socialism to win many converts in rural areas, there grew up in the South of France during the 1880s a strong left-wing frame of mind and some of the earliest viticultural experimental cooperatives to arise there were definitely socialistic. By this we mean that collective ownership replaced private ownership in all the means of production; to our knowledge the first such effort came at the turn of the century with the founding of the Free Vignerons of Maraussan in lower Languedoc. The force behind it was Elie Cathala, an active left-wing organizer. The vignerons of this small hillside town pooled their vineyards and equipment, made the sweet dessert wine for which the district was famous, and then shared equally the net proceeds. It was an entirely successful venture, surviving both the 1907 crisis and the World War.[4] It was exceptional, however, not only in its success, but in its completely collectivist base.

The vast majority of southern vignerons, their leftward proclivities notwithstanding, could not so readily abandon their individualism. They preferred the type of cooperative that combined private and communal ownership. Under this system the vigneron members purchased stock in a society that used this capital to obtain a cellar and vinicultural equipment. The members tended their own vines on their privately owned land, but after harvest they carried their grapes to the cooperative for crushing, pressing, and fermenting. The cooperative employed its own personnel to make the wine. When the final product was ready for marketing, the cooperative either restored it on a *pro rata* basis to each vigneron, who was then free to sell his share as he wished, or, far more frequently, it marketed the wine under its own label and distributed the net profits among its members on a *pro rata* basis. This system did not make for full equality, since not all the members produced equal amounts of fruit. Moreover each member was not required to turn over all of his grapes to the cooperative, only a minimum amount or weight. Therefore incomes varied, but probably not very much, given the fact that chiefly small growers were drawn to the system.[5] There were some growers, more likely with medium-size harvests, who allowed their cooperatives merely to blend their wines and to market the finished product. In this instance, the cooperative was essentially a marketing organization, replacing the middleman as best it could, but only rarely with notable success. Hence their limited number. For one of the major advantages of having the cooperative make, rather than blend, the wine was improved finished product, the result of expertise and the use of clean, up-to-date equipment. Peasant wine, even when produced on sizable holdings, was often defective, and to blend the bad with the good wine of the membership simply reduced the quality of all the wine. Unlike large wholesalers, these small cooperatives did not have a large variety of beverages to blend and therefore could not maintain the character of the finished product year in, year out. Moreover internal conflicts often led to the dissolution, or reorganization of such cooperatives.

Dissension could occur in the more typical cooperative too. Not all the vignerons in a commune were equally skilled or hard-working or honest. For this reason the elected administrators of successful associations had to insist that members bring in only healthy grapes capable of making salable wines. It is not difficult to imagine the wrangling and acrimony when grape evaluators announced to a proud, self-willed peasant that part or all of his fruit was unacceptable. The democratic, egalitarian spirit behind these cooperatives must often have run counter to the demand for good quality. And yet their numbers, membership, and sales grew, a clear indication that their wines attained a desirable level of quality. In fact cooperation and socialism grew up together in the South.

However not all advocates of cooperation were socialists. In fact many, perhaps most, small growers before 1914 refused to join cooperatives partly because the growers were extremely individualistic partly because they connected cooperatives with revolutionary collectivism. On the other hand, a growing number, especially after 1906–07, saw in cooperatives an acceptable, noncollectivist form of socialism. To them their associations performed a special mission, the salvation of small property, which was in truth more threatened by capitalist investors and middlemen than by bomb-in-the-pocket social reformers. The small owner displayed a certain class consciousness; he was hostile to big business without being friendly to landless workers, who, of course, could not join the cooperative. Because of this special mission the small owners demanded legal privileges for their formations, such as exemption from the expensive license to carry on business (*patente*). The friends of private enterprise rejected this proposal as a threat to fair competition. However when the petty bourgeois Radicals came to power, they pushed through a bill in December 1908 exempting cooperatives that made wine from the grapes of members, but excluding those that sold or blended homemade wines. Then a finance law in April 1910 included even the latter group. This law also gave fiscal exemption to dividends and interests paid by cooperatives to shareholders and other investors.[6] That politicians, most of whom were hostile to collective ownership, offered not only fiscal privileges but even considerable subsidies to initiate wine cooperatives clearly indicates one of two phenomena: either everybody had become socialist or cooperation had won support precisely because it did preserve small propertied growers—all of whom had the vote. The little and medium peasants owning land had become the *enfants chéris* of the Republic; indeed after 1900 many socialist deputies also claimed to be their saviors, and profited in the South as a result. It seems clear that not everyone had become socialist, not even the socialists.

Needless to say merchants predicted that the end of the world was at hand. But in time many came to cooperate with the cooperative managers, who, as it turned out, were more reliable than individual peasants and provided them with inexpensive, well-made wine in large quantities, saving them the expense of elaborate equipment and cellars, as well as brokerage fees. Heads of producer associations turned to merchants because they had little success selling to consumer cooperatives located in cities.[7] These consumer cooperatives were often small in size and preferred for the sake of convenience to place their orders with a local merchant. The dream of a great cooperative commonwealth of producers and consumers therefore did not emerge. Rather such associations, especially those of producers, became special interest groups, and time proved that they could be as indifferent as capitalist merchants to the public interest.

Outside of the South, there were practically no producers' associations for wine. The first to appear in Côte d'Or came only in 1909, at Vosne-Romanée; its object was the making of fine wines and by 1914 its membership had risen from thirty-four to forty-four.[8] For Gironde I found no trace of vinicultural cooperatives in the departmental archives [9] and apparently the first appeared only in 1932.[10] In Champagne the "Pur Champagne" appeared in about 1893, founded by R. Lamarre at Damery, but the small growers there were among the most individualistic in France and organized mainly to force the big companies to buy their grapes rather than to make champagne together.

Italy

Italy turned to cooperative organization chiefly during the long period of depression following her trade rupture with her Gallic neighbor. In both countries, therefore, newer forms of organization aroused interest mostly as a result of bad times, of economic pressures. And in both countries the principal factor retarding economic growth was the weakness or absence of rural credit institutions, a condition that also impeded the founding of cooperatives. The first wine cooperatives in France obtained a part of their funds by selling stock to their membership, but peasant growers rarely had sufficient savings to provide their cooperatives with the substantial capital they required merely to purchase equipment. Since credit was decidedly less available in Italy, sympathetic governing bodies, such as communal councils, often granted a subsidy to organized groups out of local tax income. Had Italian villages been wealthier, this practice would have solved many problems, but since they were not, communal grants had to be supplemented by a regional banker; however many Italian banks failed in the crisis of the 1880s and 1890s, with the result that peasants usually had to rely on village usurers to get cash for sheer survival. Happily cooperative banks, as well as straight agricultural credit outlets, began to appear around the turn of the century. Their funds, however, were limited and wine cooperatives did not appear until a national law of July 1904 provided a subsidy of one million lire to encourage the growth of *cantine sociali,* or producer associations along cooperative lines. Three hundred thousand lire of this sum were destined exclusively to purchase wooden casks for small growers' organizations.[11]

Undoubtedly the law, passed just after the trade treaty with Austria-Hungary ended, sought to relieve small growers by offering them the means to improve the quality and sales appeal of their wine, and doubtless it was partially aimed at the mass of vignerons in Apulia. However of the thirty-six associations founded, nearly all were in the North, with a few in Sicily and in Lazia. By 1906 there were fifty-five *cantine* receiving governmental aid, thirty-four in the North, twelve in the Center, three in the South, and three in Sicily.[12] Time did not change this imbalance. It was the direct opposite of France, where most of the vinicultural associations were in the Mediterranean South.

The South of Italy was quite different from that of France. First it was too heavily dependent on foreign markets, whereas its counterpart sold chiefly in the domestic market, and apparently this difference influenced the history of the cooperative movement. The Italians were too heavily dependent on private merchants with foreign outlets to set up for themselves. Moreover they lacked political sophistication and did not bring sufficient pressure on Rome; nor did they find the skilled leadership required to change their age-old economic structure. Giuliano Pisacane had argued convincingly that Apulia could save itself after 1888 only by turning to cooperation, but to no avail.[13]

Not all of these *cantine sociali* were true cooperatives, for some were set up by wealthy producers and membership excluded peasants. There is a point to note here: many of these organizations, since they were set up chiefly in fine-wine areas, emphasized quality and charged high prices. They also sought markets in Europe, the United States, and Latin America, rather than in the nearby industrial centers. In this respect the Italian cooperative movement differed markedly from that of France, for the major French markets were industrial cities and the lower classes.

This difference is not easy to explain. Certainly an important factor, as regards the two Souths, was the independence of the lower rural classes in France and the near feudal conditions of the *mezzadri* in Italy. In the southern Adriatic provinces there was no serious tradition of social organization outside of inherited customs and religion, both of which enclosed the individual in his family and village community, leaving insufficient latitude for new ways of thought and action. The southern Frenchmen, on the other hand, had thrown off the conservative mantle of the Church or, as a Protestant, had rebelled against it. Even the rural laborers stood up against medium and large landowners. As wage earners, not as crop-sharers, they were among the first to organize unions, and in 1903–05 they went out on strike and won most of their demands in Languedoc and Roussillon. They naturally joined the numerous small owners during the riots of 1907 and voted socialist before and after. Besides, more than half of them were part owners and therefore eligible to join a local cooperative.

Before World War I producer associations of wine, milk, cheese, etc. were still in their infancy; their big surge ahead would come in the 1930s when the world depression threatened the small, independent grower with extinction. But in the wine industry there continued to exist in good times and bad the true artisan, the man who persisted in the belief that the good life is a creative life and that good wine is a creation so personal and intimate that it cannot be made by the indifferent technique of mass production, that standardization is the enemy of quality viniculture precisely because it removes the adventure and the art of creativity. The problem for these small and medium growers was to find the consumers who shared this Bacchic *mystique*.

Syndicates

For the vintners, and they were the great majority, who saw neither in politics nor in cooperation the solution to the problem of selling wine, there remained the possibility of direct sales between producer and consumer as a means of getting around the middlemen. Producers of good *ordinaires* and fine beverages tried on several occasions to organize wine fairs; perhaps the first essay at this arrangement occurred in Côte d'Or during 1862.[14] Generally the procedure was simple. They sent bottled samples of their products for display in special stalls or exhibits and also for tasting by prospective customers. More often the grower carried his samples himself and served them, along with a short, chatty sales talk, to anyone willing to taste—local bums excluded. Most of these fairs remained small, limited to a region or even to one large town. Nearly all were initiated by the local syndicate or trade organization, not to be confused with cooperatives, and, according to contemporary literature, none were really successful, at least not successful enough to become annual events.[15] Small growers, for whom the fairs were intended, simply did not possess the salesmanship and capital to enter with success the commercial side of the industry. From the local drinker's point of view there was little incentive to purchase a years' supply at a fair; he rarely had sufficient storage space and enough ready money. Moreover the costs of this kind of petty commerce pushed up prices because the producer sought to recover his normal profit plus that of the merchant. In consequence these fairs never seriously threatened private merchants, which, incidentally, is still true. The well-to-do, who did buy large quantities for home consumption, usually went directly to the maker rather than to a fair. But their number was limited.

All in all, neither in France nor in Italy did the efforts of producers to reorganize wine commerce lead to notable success prior to 1914. Beginnings were made, but the process would be slow until peasant individualism gave way before the exigencies of the age of mass production.

The slow weakening of traditional outlooks came about less from an effort to reorganize the industry than from an attempt by small vignerons and more well-to-do viticulturists to act collectively to defend their interests. Their first effective reaction to the crisis after 1900 was to remove abuses in the existing system, not to change it. Viticultural interests had traditionally been the concern of larger growers, and only slowly became separated from the general interests of agriculture. In the earlier nineteenth century nearly every department in France had an agricultural society of some sort, often combined with commercial, scientific, and cultural groups, which explains why the names of these associations are so infernally long. In 1867 when these local organs set up the Société des Agriculteurs de France, viticulture was still merely another facet of general farming. The first real distinction came in 1880 when republican politicians, opposed to the political conservatism of the parent group, set up the Société Nationale d'Encouragement à l'Agriculture to spread both farming knowledge and republican ideas among the rural folk.[16] Not until eight years later did the nonsectarian Société des Viticulteurs de France make its appearance, with the aim of influencing public opinion in favor of French wine. After 1890 it became an important contact between many local wine organizations and the wine group within parliament. It was an important source of the technical information needed to enact laws, especially against fraudulent wine.[17] In 1900 the old practice of periodical congresses was reestablished. The first had been held in the 1840s but were discontinued after the 1848 revolution.

Following the riots of 1907, winemen, southern ones above all, really went on the warpath. The mayor of Narbonne, Ferroul, and some of the viticulturists in the Midi founded the Confédération Générale des Vignerons, CGV, a title imitative of the militant labor organization, the CGT, and equally sectarian, since the enemy of both was the premier, Clemenceau. The Midi branch covered Languedoc and Roussillon; the Southeast branch, set up in 1909, included most of Provence as well as the department of Gard.[18]

The CGV had a rather stormy beginning. It became a political weapon under the headship of Ferroul and figured in his fight against southern Radicals, especially his local arch opponent, Maurice Sarraut. Although a socialist, Ferroul allied with conservative landowners to achieve his political goals—but the Sarraut clan was powerful enough to defend itself. The result was that the mass of vignerons in the Narbonnais gave more attention to politics than to cooperation, with the result that far fewer coops existed in Aude than in the other major southern wine departments.

On the other hand, the CGV became the wineman's bulldog in the fight against fraud. It won governmental recognition as a quasi-police agency, with powers to inspect private cellars and to prosecute anyone accused of illegal vinicultural practices. In 1907–08 the Midi branch employed twelve special agents, a number that rose to thirty-nine in 1913–14, in addition to twelve temporary agents to survey wine imports from Algeria and Spain. The Southeast branch hired seven regular and five temporary agents in 1913. Without doubt the CGV was well endowed financially, collecting dues chiefly from departmental and local wine syndicates. Considering its energy and successes it was perhaps more effective in furthering wine interests than the CGT was in advancing labor's cause. In 1907–08 the Midi branch took 876 samples of wine in various cellars, initiated 142 prosecutions for fraud, and won 67 convictions. Its high point came in 1911–12 when it took 3,042 samples, initiated 777 prosecutions, and won 601 convictions. In the same year the Southeast branch initiated 963 suits and won 263.[19]

The CGV played a role similar to that of the big syndicate of champagne makers. A major victory came when the higher courts of France decided to permit the CGV to sue for and collect damages from those convicted of fraud, an action that recognized fraud as prima facie evidence of injury to wine-producing members and arranged a process for their compensation. Such victories were not won cheaply. Between 1907 and 1914 the Midi branch of the CGV, by far the most active, spent 1,600,000 francs for inspection and prosecutions. In 1913 its budget came to 412,000 francs, an enormous sum considering that the national government budgeted a mere one million francs for all its inspection work including food, medicines, and mineral water. For every ten cases involving wine fraud, the public prosecutor initiated two, the CGV of the Midi eight! Some of the pecuniary weight was taken over by the Syndicat National de Défense de la Viticulture (SNDV), which represented wine syndicates outside of the Midi, but its work barely matched that of the CGV, nor was it as influential politically.

The SNDV was probably less effective than the CGV because it sought to represent producers of fine as well as of ordinary wines, and it also attempted, in the interest of all, to overcome the strong regional identity of wine growers. But there were regional and qualitative differences too deeply engrained to be overcome. In the Bordelais the fine growers set up the Syndicat des Crus Classés in August 1901. Its objective was to encourage sales abroad and to combat the merchants in foreign lands selling false bordeaux. Unlike the CGV, however, it was not a vigorous organization and rarely brought court suits in England, Belgium, or Germany, where falsification was widely practiced. Its task was more difficult; foreign laws were not clear as regards false origins and courts were hardly willing to convict their own nationals. The merchants, more keenly aware that false and inferior wines sold as fine growths ruined the reputation of the latter, acted with more vigor. They organized into the Union Syndical des Négociants en Vins de Bordeaux, which brought suits with greater regularity, at least in England, and won convictions. Unfortunately the Bordeaux wine interests were divided, growers favoring a strict appellation of origins, excluding upland wines entirely, the wholesalers advocating a far broader appellation which would allow them to blend external beverages with the native.[20]

The companies making champagne organized into the Comité Interprofessionel, which was easily as active as the CGV in suppressing fraud. Indeed in Champagne even the grape-growers were well in advance of those in other fine wine regions in their ability to organize.

By 1914 grape-growers and wine-makers in France had achieved notable progress in furthering their interests, bringing pressure on politicians, and influencing opinion. In Italy, where the roots of provincialism were as deep as those of aged vines, there was practically no headway made. Perhaps failure here resulted from the near absence or weak position of viticultural interests in a land of mixed farming and retarded technology. It was difficult for peasants to conceive of themselves as belonging to this or to that pressure group, since they did not specialize. Moreover most of them lacked the right to vote until shortly before the World War, so they had no way of pressuring the government even if they managed to identify their interest. When they finally did receive the ballot—as a gift they had not fought for—they were too naive politically to know how to use it.

Conclusion

The wine industry, like most other industries, went through notable changes during the nineteenth century. If these changes were of a magnitude to warrant the adjective "revolutionary," then the growing of grapes and wine formed part of the dramatic and often traumatic industrial and agricultural revolutions. However we must bear in mind that viti- and viniculture before World War I had only completed the initial stage of a major technological and organizational change. A true revolution in nineteenth-century industry was limited to textiles and metallurgy and in agriculture to cereals, cattle, and pasturage. In both cases rates of production and productivity registered rapid and enormous increases. Numerous other industrial and rural enterprises were considerably slower to achieve comparable rates, especially on the continent, and the cultivation of vines and the making of wine would be more legitimately compared to horticulture or legumes on the one hand and to construction or clothing on the other. Like them, the wine industry expanded its operations, became more orderly, more productive, and required higher levels of capital investment. It was, in short, revolutionary, provided we use this adjective in its figurative sense to mean change that was unprecedented rather than sudden and complete.

There were too many inhibiting forces for the wine industry to achieve the miracles of production and technology that marked the truly innovative sectors of the European economy before 1914.

First, despite increasing centralization and rationalization, most wine growers remained highly individualistic, with enterprises moderate in scale. They were either too small in their operations and limited financially or devoted to achieving high quality and therefore skeptical of techniques to increase productivity. Although the amount of wine produced by small growers declined in relation to total production, they survived as an economic and social category. In fact they survived, because they were perfectly capable, without elaborate and costly equipment, of achieving and even surpassing the levels of productivity attained by huge wine factories.

Second, the most enterprising growers were limited in their ability to transform production, even in the making of ordinary beverages. They encountered two insurmountable bottlenecks—the nature of grapes themselves and distribution. One striking characteristic of wine-making was its increasing tendency toward capitalist organization, such as concentration and a resulting increase in the size of producing units, without a comparable increase in the mechanization of grape production. Several activities in vineyards were not susceptible to mechanization. Even in the huge vineyards of Mediterranean France, as Rémy Pech has pointed out, the dressing and pruning of vines and the harvesting of grapes did not lend themselves to the application of machines.[1] The result was that labor costs remained high, the human element continued to predominate, and productivity remained stable after the 1890s. The only way to increase productivity was to enhance yields, but unlike cereals, enhanced yields reached a point of no return, because quality declined in an almost geometric ratio. In consequence, a true "take-off" in productive capacity was checked by the very nature of producing grapes. In addition, there was the bottleneck of retail distribution. Wine continued to be sold in small stores where costs and therefore prices remained high. Undoubtedly the coming of *appellation controlée* curtailed grape output in the interest of quality; but it cannot account for the limited production of the entire industry. From 1913 on the amount of controlled production was less than 5 percent of total production; it may be compared to other luxury articles, such as high-grade textiles and stainless steel, which also enjoyed secure but limited markets. But even ordinary wine, unlike ordinary textiles and metals, did not enjoy an unlimited market; nor did it command a solid price structure, often the result of monopoly formation.

A third retardative factor was precisely the limited market for fermented beverages. Save for the golden age and the Gay Nineties, consumption was like a sponge; and when it was saturated, severe crises and economic setbacks resulted. As wine-making and selling became big business creating undreamed of wealth, the growers of ordinaries discovered that they had periodically to destroy much of that wealth if only to curtail supply and avoid surpluses. With glad hearts and a sense of divine mission growers created their ruby and golden liquids, with a sense of tragedy and foreboding evil they emptied them into the gutters, unable to comprehend why men would not or could not consume them with Gargantuan thirst. In their thinking wine was a food, just as bread was, and contemporary social theory argued that all men should eat to

TABLE 33: *Growth of French and Italian Wine Industries*
Mid-century to 1910–14

France	1861–70	1901–10	Percentage Rate of Change
Average production (millions of hectoliters)	51.7	51.8	0
Average consumption (millions of hectoliters)	*1855–64* 46.4	*1905–14* 58.3	25.6
Average consumption per head (liter/year)	1.31	1.62	23.6
Population (millions)	*1850* 36.5	*1910* 41.5	13.6

Italy	1861–70	1901–10	Percentage Rate of Change
Average production (millions of hectoliters)	23.5	44.1	87.4
Average consumption (millions of hectoliters)	*1855–64* 22.7	*1905–14* 42.1	85
Average consumption per head (liter/year)	.97	.93	−4.3
Population (millions)	*1850* 23.9	*1910* 36.2	51.5

the level of their hunger and drink to that of their thirst. Whether all men satisfied their thirst is a matter for conjecture; but the limits of either their thirst or their incomes put a ceiling on the expansive tendencies of the industry and on technological innovation.

The truth is that the technology available before the phylloxera was perfectly capable of meeting market demands. Table 33 makes clear that French production first peaked in the golden age, when manufacturing methods were more traditional then innovative, and that in Italy the application of techniques discovered in France allowed a steady but moderate growth up to 1914.

Italian production and consumption after unification expanded considerably, averaging about 1.7 percent a year. A rising standard of living and an expanding population probably were greater incentives to production than technology; indeed, population growth surpassed wine production, with the result that consumption per head fell slightly. On the other hand French production reached its first peak during the golden age, fell, and then reached a similar peak after 1900. Since population growth achieved relative stability shortly after midcentury, the recovery of production was perhaps less a result of improved techniques than of rising consumption per capita, which paralleled the rise of average consumption.

Production was also limited by deep-rooted vinicultural traditions emphasizing quality. The rather slow introduction of new technology in areas of renowned beverages clearly indicated that old ways of vinification were considered the best. In fact this desire to avoid making second-rate wines led to another major trend of the century, the steady growth of state control over the industry first in the name of quality control, then of public health. In this tendency, too, the Italians followed the French.

Now royal governments in the past had not been indifferent to the safeguarding of quality. Centuries earlier the kings of France had sought to prevent the "commoner," the Gamay grape, from invading lands planted with the "noble" Pinot, but royal ability to enforce its decrees rarely matched its pretentions to power. On the other hand, the Third Republic could muster a vast array of administrative manpower to enforce its laws. And growers of fine and common vines now called upon it to prevent fraud, to make and enforce laws respecting controlled appellation, to enjoin railroad companies to desist from unfair rate schedules, to erect tariffs against foreign wines, to provide technical training in grape- and wine-growing, and so on, and to lower taxes on wine at the same time. All of these things the government attempted to do, since winemen constituted a most powerful pressure group both in Paris and eventually in Rome. Thanks to this expanding government role, wine consumers in France and Italy after 1900 probably enjoyed beverages that were somewhat less drugged and watered and that were more honestly labeled. In fact the politicizing of the wine industry was in some ways more drastic—revolutionary if you will—than the introduction of new technology, for it affected both fine and common beverages.

As for the producers, especially the mass of small and marginal vignerons, they seem to have won a slightly higher standard of living. But generalization here is hazardous because periodic crises set them back with unrelenting regularity. Neither the government nor all the government's men could save them from their own follies: overplanting, overproduction, and plummeting prices. The crises that beset the mass-production industries of nondescript wines, which worsened after 1904 in both countries, were not a culmination but only a beginning. Capitalist investment made possible advanced technology, wider markets, and increased production. But it did not bring stability. Rather, the continued recurrence of crises forced winemen to turn to the government as a savior, and all it became was a regulator, which did not save them even from themselves. The freedom and individualism that had formerly characterized the wine industry steadily disappeared, giving way to ever tightening controls and to a corporative way of life that combined cooperative wineries and integrated political action.

The wine grower of 1800, who was capable of quenching the thirst of a European world already at war, would have marvelled at the wine factories of southern France and Italy, of Champagne and Tuscany; but he would have felt himself in a truly alien world when confronted with the growing array of laws, regulations, controls, and political pressure groups that characterized the industry about to enter the age of total war in 1914.

Appendix

Quality of Vintages by Decades

Numbers without parenthesis indicate the number of vintages attaining a particular value; numbers in parenthesis give the score. Thus 2 vintages rated 7 equal a score of (14). All decimals have been rounded out.

Values	7	6	5	4	3	2	1	Score. Total of row
Côte d'Or								
1820s	2(14)	0	0	1(4)	4(12)	2(4)	1(1)	(35)
1830s	1(7)	0	1(5)	5(20)	1(3)	2(4)	0	(39)
1840s	2(14)	1(6)	2(10)	3(12)	0	1(2)	1(1)	(45)
1850s	2(14)	1(6)	1(5)	1(4)	3(9)	2(4)	0	(42)
1860s	2(14)	3(18)	1(5)	2(8)	0	0	2(2)	(47)
1870s	0	3(18)	2(10)	1(4)	1(3)	2(4)	1(1)	(40)
1880s	0	1(6)	3(15)	2(8)	3(9)	1(2)	0	(40)
1890s	0	1(6)	5(25)	2(8)	0	2(4)	0	(43)
1900s	3(21)	1(6)	2(10)	3(12)	1(3)	0	0	(52)
Total of Column	12	11	17	20	13	12	5	42 mean
% of total of row	13	12	18	22	14	13	5	
			66			33		

Values	7	6	5	4	3	2	1	Score. Total of row
Beaujolais								
1820s	0	2(12)	1(5)	1(4)	0	6(12)	0	(33)
1830s	0	3(18)	4(20)	2(8)	0	1(2)	0	(48)
1840s	0	4(24)	3(15)	1(4)	0	2(4)	0	(47)
1850s	0	3(18)	2(10)	1(4)	0	4(8)	0	(40)
1860s	0	3(18)	4(20)	0	0	3(6)	0	(44)
1870s	0	2(12)	4(20)	2(8)	0	2(4)	0	(44)
1880s	0	2(12)	5(25)	2(8)	0	1(2)	0	(47)
1890s	0	2(12)	3(15)	1(4)	0	4(8)	0	(39)
1900s	0	0	3(15)	4(16)	0	3(6)	0	(37)
Total of Column		21	29	14		26		42 mean
% of total of row		23	32	15		28		
			70			28		

Values	7	6	5	4	3	2	1	Score
Bordeaux								
1820s	0	2(12)	1(5)	1(4)	1(3)	4(8)	1(1)	(33)
1830s	0	2(12)	1(5)	2(8)	4(12)	1(2)	0	(39)
1840s	0	3(18)	4(20)	0	1(3)	1(2)	1(1)	(44)
1850s	0	1(6)	5(25)	2(8)	1(3)	0	1(1)	(43)
1860s	1(7)	2(12)	4(20)	0	2(6)	0	1(1)	(46)
1870s	0	4(24)	0	4(16)	2(6)	0	0	(46)
1880s	0	1(6)	2(10)	4(16)	2(6)	1(2)	0	(40)
1890s	1(7)	1(6)	2(10)	5(20)	0	0	1(1)	(44)
1900s	1(7)	2(12)	4(20)	2(8)	1(3)	0	0	(50)
Total of Column	3	18	23	20	14	7	5	43 mean
% of total of row	.03	20	25	22	15	7	5	
			70			29		

Values	7	6	5	4	3	2	1	Score
Champagne								
1820s	2(14)	1(6)	1(5)	2(8)	2(6)	1(2)	1(1)	(42)
1830s	1(7)	3(18)	3(15)	2(8)	1(3)	0	0	(51)
1840s	2(14)	2(12)	2(10)	1(4)	3(9)	0	0	(49)
1850s	1(7)	2(12)	0	1(4)	3(9)	2(4)	1(1)	(37)
1860s	3(21)	2(12)	2(10)	0	1(3)	0	2(2)	(48)
1870s	2(14)	1(6)	1(5)	1(4)	2(6)	2(4)	1(1)	(40)
1880s	2(14)	1(6)	0	2(8)	2(6)	2(4)	1(1)	(39)
1890s	3(21)	2(12)	2(10)	0	1(3)	1(2)	0	(48)
1900s	3(21)	1(6)	2(10)	3(12)	1(3)	0	0	(52)
Total of Column	19	15	13	12	16	8	6	45 mean
% of total of row	21	17	14	13	17	8	6	
		65				34		

Notes

List of Abbreviations

A.D.	Archives départementales
A.N.	Archives Nationales
A.C.H.S.	*Annales cisalpines d'histoire sociale*
A.E.U.I.	*Archivio economico dell'unificazione italiana*
C.A.S.I.	*Cinquanta anni di storia italiana*
M.A.C.	Ministère de l'Agriculture et du Commerce
M.A.I.C.	Ministero di Agricoltura, Industria e Commercio
M.F.	Ministero delle Finanze
N.Q.S.R.	*Nuove questioni di storia del Risorgimento e dell'unità d'Italia*
R.V.	*Revue de viticulture*

Chapter One

1. Henri Guilhem, *La Blanquette de Limoux* (Paris, 1951), p. 37.
2. Jules Guyot, *Etude des vignobles de France* (Paris, 1868), I, p. 63.
3. James Busby, *Journal of a Recent Visit to the Vineyards of Spain and France*, 3rd ed. (London, 1840), pp. 66–70, 84–85; M. Cavoleau, *Oenologie française* (Paris, 1827), pp. 26–30, 97 ff.; Victor Rendu, *Ampelographie française*, 2nd ed. (Paris, 1857), pp. 37 ff., 486 ff.

Chapter Two

1. Cavoleau, *Oenologie*, pp. 13, 82, 282–83; Rendu, *Ampelographie*, pp. 99–142; Guyot, *Etude*, I, pp. 203–13, II, pp. 90–96, 236–41, 264–65, III, pp. 6–9; Alfred Giry, *Etudes économiques et sociales du département de Vaucluse* (n.p., 1952), p. 136; Yves Lavesque, "L'Agronomie du Vaucluse dans la première partie du XIXe siècle," (Diplôme d'Etudes Supérieures, Université d'Aix-en-Provence, 1970); A.D. Vaucluse 6M 52–53; A.D. Drôme 58M 1; Jean Reiller, *Transformations de l'agriculture vauclusienne* (Avignon, 1945).
2. *Revue de viticulture* 4 (1895):251.

3. Gilbert Garrier, *Paysans du Beaujolais et du Lyonnais, 1800–1970* (Grenoble, 1973) I, chaps. 1–3; André Jullien, *The Topographie of All Known Vineyards* (London, 1824), pp. 80–154; F. Myard, *Le Vigneronnage en Beaujolais* (Lyon, 1907), pp. 254–60; V. Vermorel and R. Danguy, *Les Vins du Beaujolais, Mâconnais et Chalonnais* (Dijon, 1893), pp. 22–23, 140–41.

4. Robert Laurent, *Les Vignerons de la Côte d'Or au XIXe siècle* (Paris, 1958) I, chaps. 1–5.

5 *Ibid.,* 27; M. R. Danguy and C. Aubertin, *Les Grands vins de Bourgogne* (Dijon, 1892), pp. xv–xvi.

6. Cavoleau, *Oenologie*, p. 61.

7. J. Lavalle and J. Garnier. *Histoire et statistique de la vigne et des grands vins de la Côte d'Or* (Dijon, 1855), pp. 73–114.

8. Laurent, *Vignerons*, I, pp. 176–81.

9. Cavoleau, *Oenologie*, pp. 340–41.

10. Rendu, *Ampelographie*, pp. 276–83; Guyot, *Etude*, III, pp. 286–319; Paul Leuillot, *L'Alsace au début du XIXe siècle* (Paris 1959–60), I, pp. 120–38; Lucien Sittler, *La Viticulture et le vin de Colmar à travers les siècles* (Paris, 1956), pp. 125–55.

11. René Gandilhon, *Naissance du champagne: Dom Pierre Pérignon* (Paris, 1968), pp. 131–33, 244.

12. *Ibid.*, p. 102.

13. Patrick Forbes, *Champagne, the Wine, the Land and the People* (London, 1967), pp. 161–63.

14. *Ibid.*, chaps. 7–13; Emile Chantriot, *La Champagne* (Paris, 1905), p. 7 ff.; M. Holland, *Connaissance du champagne* (Paris, 1952), pp. 26–33; C. Moreau-Berillon, *Au Pays du champagne* (Reims, 1922), pp. 108–27, 449; E. J. Maumené, *Indications théoriques et pratiques sur le travail des vins* (Paris, 1858), pp. 411–74; André Simon, *The History of Champagne* (London, 1962), pp. 80–137; C. Tovey, *Champagne, Its History, Manufacture, Properties* (London, 1870), pp. 56–58; Rendu, *Ampelographie*, pp. 319–35.

15. Guyot, *Etude*, II, p. 664.

16. *Ibid.*, II, p. 183 ff., 637; Rendu, *Ampelographie*, p. 375; Cavoleau, *Oenologie*, pp. 189–92; A. D. Indre-et-Loire, 10M 5; R. Dion, *Val de la Loire* (Tours, 1934), p. 621 ff.; A. Chauvigne, *Monographie de la commune de Vouvray et de son vignoble* (Tours, 1909), pp. 2–33; Charles Vavasseur, *La Touraine et ses vins* (Poitiers, 1933), p. 86 ff.; Joel Le Theule, "Deux monographies du vignoble français," *Annales, économies, sociétés, civilisations,* 9 (1954):37–39, 62; P.-C. Guillory, *Les Vins blancs d'Anjou et de Maine-et-Loire* (Angers, 1874), pp. 47–106.

Chapter Three

1. Louis Ravaz, *Le Pays du Cognac* (Angoulême, 1900), pp. 239–54.

2. *Etude*, I, p. 507–13.

3. P. Fénelon, "Le Vignoble de Monbazillac," *Revue géographique des Pyrénées et de Sud-ouest,* 16 (1945–46):27–29.

4. Rendu, *Ampelographie*, p. 461.

5. Cavoleau, *Oenologie*, p. 179.

6. J.-A.Delpon, *Statistique du département du Lot* (Paris, 1831), II, pp. 270–72.
7. Rendu, *Ampelographie*, p. 472.
8. Guyot, *Etude*, I, pp. 352, 472.
9. A. D. Gironde 7M 131.
10. W. Franck, *Traité sur les vins du Médoc* (Bordeaux, 1824), pp. 58–64.
11. Edmund Penning-Rowsell, *The Wines of Bordeaux* (New York, 1970), pp. 247–48.
12. A.-M. Moquet, *Tableau analytique et synoptique des prix des vins . . . de la Gironde* (Bordeaux, n.d.).
13. Robert Forster, "The Noble Wine Producers of the Bordelais in the 18th Century," *Economic History Review*, 2d s., 14 (August 1961):18–33; Charles Higounet, ed., *La Seigneurie et le vignoble de Château Latour* (Bordeaux, 1974) I, pp. 316–17.
14. A. Charles, *La Révolution de 1848 et la seconde république à Bordeaux et dans le département de la Gironde* (Bordeaux, 1945), pp. 20–21.

Chapter Four

1. Dina Rebaudengo, *I Vini del Piemonte* (Turin, 1966), p. 37.
2. *Ibid.*, p. 119.
3. *Guida vinicola per la provincia di Cuneo* (Cuneo, 1903), pp. 4–8; Renato Ratti, *Della Vigna e del vino nell'albese* (Turin, 1971), chaps. 1–10.
4. G.-B. Croce, *Della Eccellenza e diversità dei vini che nella montagna di Torino si fanno* (Turin, 1606), p. 8 ff.; Giulio di Cassato, *Note statistiche, circondario d'Asti* (Asti, 1897), pp. 212–16; P. L. Ghisleni, *Le Coltivazioni e la tecnica agricola in Piemonte dal 1831 al 1861* (Turin, 1961), pp. 8–21.
5. G. Bracco, "Produzione e commercio dei vini piemontesi nei secoli XVIII e XIX," *A.C.H.S.*, s.1, no. 3 (1972):164–70; Luigi Bulferetti and R.Luraghi, *Agricoltura, industria e commercio in Piemonte dal 1814 al 1848* (Turin, 1966) I, p. 67 ff., II, p. 18.
6. Mario Romani, "Produzione e commercio dei vini in Lombardia nei secoli XVIII e XIX," *A.C.H.S.*, s.1, no. 3 (1972):147 ff.; *L'Agricoltura in Lombardia dal periodo delle Riforme al 1859* (Milan, 1957), *passim*.
7. Francesco De-Bosis, *La Esposizione ampelografica marchigiana-abruzzese* (Ancona, 1873), pp. 99–137; Ministero di Agricoltura, Industria e Commercio, *I vini italiani, Piemonte* (Rome, 1914), pp. 3–75; M. Pellegrini, *Le Condizioni economiche, sociali, culturali e politiche di Jesi dal 1849 al 1859* (Jesi, 1957), pp. 21–85; P. Spaggiari, *L'Agricoltura negli stati parmensi dal 1750 al 1859* (Milan, 1966), p. 180; S. Mondini, *Produzione e commercio del vino in Italia* (Milan, 1899), pp. 105–10.

Chapter Five

1. Mondini, *Produzione*, p. 27.
2. B. Farolfi, *Strumenti e pratiche agrarie in Toscana dall'età napoleonica all'unità* (Milan, 1969), p. 136.

3. Ildebrando Imberciadori, *Economia toscana nel primo ottocento . . . 1815–61* (Florence, 1961), pp. 21–79; Arturo Marescalchi and J. Dalmasso, *Storia della vite e del vino in Italia* (Milan, 1932–37), III, p. 562 ff.; F.Melis, "Produzione e commercio dei vini italiani . . . nei secoli XIII–XVIII," *A.C.H.S.* s.1, no.3 (1972):107–33; Lamberto Paronetto, *Chianti: The Story of Florence and Its Wines* (London, 1970), *passim;* R.Villari, "L'Economia degli stati italiani dal 1815 al 1848" in *N.Q.S.R.*, (Milan, 1961) I, pp. 628–30.

4. B.Ricasoli, *Bettino Ricasoli, agricoltore* (Florence, 1950), p. 105 ff.

5. Paronetto, *Chianti*, p. 108.

6. G. Friz, "Produzione e commercio dei vini del Lazio nei secoli XVIII e XIX," *A.C.H.S.*, s.1, no. 3 (1972):207, 213–17.

7. C. Mancini, *Il Lazio viticolo e vinicolo* (Città di Castello, 1888), *passim.*

8. Ministero di Agricoltura, *I Vini italiani, Campania* (Rome, 1914), p. 1–11.

9. O. Forcadi, *La Produzione, i prezzi ed il commercio dei vini in Italia nel quinquennio 1888–1892* (Rome, 1893), p. 5.

10. C. de Cesare, *Delle Condizioni economiche e morali delle classi agricole nelle tre province di Puglia* (Naples, 1859), pp. 41–78; L. de Rosa, "Produzione e commercio dei vini nel meridione nei secoli XVIII e XIX," *A.C.H.S.*, s.1, no.3 (1972):197.

11. F.-J. Piétri, *La Question des vins en Italie et l'antagonisme du Nord et du Sud* (Paris, 1906), pp. 1–40.

12. G. Frojo, *Il Presente e l'avvenire dei vini d'Italia* (Naples, 1876), p. 47 ff.

13. De Rosa, "Produzione," pp. 198–201.

14. Marescalchi and Dalmasso, *Storia delle vite*, III, p. 665; S. Mondini, *L'Industria dei vini marsala in Sicilia* (Riposto, 1896); S. Romano, ed., *Storia siciliana post-unificazione*, 3 vols, (Palermo, 1958).

Chapter Six

1. A.Berget, *Les Vins de France, Histoire, géographie, et statistique du vignoble français* (Paris, 1900), pp. 171–80.

2. *Moniteur viticole*, 29 October 1856; Rémy Pech, *Entreprise viticole et capitalisme* (Toulouse, 1975), p. 38.

3. George Ordish, *The Great Wine Blight* (London, 1972), p. 16.

4. R. Pijassou in Charles Higounet, ed., *La Seigneurie et le vignoble de Château Latour* (Bordeaux, 1974), II, p. 380.

5. F. Convert, *La Vigne et le vin depuis 1600* (Paris, 1901), pp. 14–15.

6. Berget, *Vins de France*, pp. 161–70.

7. A. Perrin, *La Civilisation de la vigne* (Paris, 1938), p. 112 ff.

8. A. du Breuil, *Culture perfectionnée et moins coûteuse du vignoble* (Paris, 1863), pp. 219–20.

9. P.-C. Guillory, *Les Congrès des vignerons français* (Paris, 1860), p. 294.

10. *Ibid.*, pp. 301–2; Busby, *Journal*, pp. 109–19; Du Breuil, *Culture perfectionnée*, pp. 228–29.

11. M. Berengo, *L'Agricoltura veneta dal Risorgimento all'unità* (Milan, 1963), pp. 292–95.

12. Villari, "L'Economia" in *N.Q.S.R.*, I, pp. 628–30, 767.

13. *Della vigna*, p. 125.
14. Pijassou in Higounet, ed., *Seigneurie*, I, p. 273 ff.
15. Busby, *Journal*, p. 120.
16. Jean-Antoine Gervais, *Opuscule sur la vinification* (Montpellier, 1820); G. Rossi, *Memoria diretta a variare sisteme sulla fattura dei vini* (Pisa, 1831).
17. Guillory, *Congrès*, p. 123.
18. Franz Malvezin, *Bordeaux: histoire de la vigne et du vin en Aquitaine depuis ses origines jusqu'à nos jours* (Bordeaux, 1919), pp. 158–59.
19. *R.V.* 2 (1894):619–22.
20. G. Bord, *Essai sur les variations de l'encepagement* (n.p., n.d.), pp. 18–19.
21. Edmund Penning-Rowsell, *The Wines of Bordeaux* (New York, 1970), pp. 192–93.
22. Marescalchi and Dalmasso, *Storia*, III, p. 562.
23. René Gandilhon, *Naissance du champagne: Dom Pierre Pérignon* (Paris, 1968), pp. 172–73.
24. *Ibid.*, pp. 131–33.
25. *Ibid.*, p. 187; Patrick Forbes, *Champagne, the Wine, the Land, and the People* (London, 1967), p. 119 ff.
26. H. Vizetelly, *History of Champagne* (London, 1882), p. 139; data from A. Simon, *History of Champagne*, p. 89.
27. Rendu, *Ampelographie*, p. 151.
28. *Ibid.*, p. 323.
29. *History of Champagne*, pp. 136–37.
30. Vizetelly, *History of Champagne*, p. 161, note.
31. *Ibid.*, p. 161.
32. Moreau-Bérillon, *Au pays du champagne*, pp. 122–24.
33. *Bulletin* du *Laboratoire Expérimental de Viticulture et d'Oenologie*, 1, 15 (July 1901):287; Emile Manceau, *Théorie des vins mousseux* (Epernay, 1905), pp. 18–23.
34. See his major work *Indications théoriques et pratiques sur le travail des vins mousseux* (1858).
35. Moreau-Bérillon, *Au Pays de champagne*, p. 124.

Chapter Seven

1. J.-C. Toutain, *Le Produit de l'agriculture francaise de 1700 à 1958: La croissance* (Paris, 1961), p. 154.
2. Enjalbert in Higounet, ed., *Seigneurie*, I, pp. 1–56.
3. See C. Cocks and E. Féret, *Bordeaux et ses vins*, 6th ed. (Bordeaux, 1893).
4. P. Butel and P. Roudié, "La Production et la commercialisation des vins du Libournais au début du XIXème siècle," *Annales du Midi*, 81 (1969): 385.
5. Moquet, *Tableau analytique*; W. Franck, *Traité sur les vins de Médoc* (Bordeaux, 1824), pp. 5–6; Chambre de Commerce, Bordeaux, *Tableau relatif aux récoltes des vins du Médoc depuis 1795*, Séance du 3 mai 1882.
6. Pijassou in Higounet, ed., *Seigneurie*, I, pp. 315–16.
7. Butel and Roudié, "La Production . . .," pp. 386–87
8. Germain Lafforgue, *Le Vignoble girondin* (Paris, 1947), pp. 313–14.

9. Chambre de Commerce, Bordeaux, *Réponse aux questions relatives au régime des boissons* (Bordeaux, 1850).
10. F. Jouannet, *Statistique du département de la Gironde* (Paris, 1837–43) 2 vols.; Franck, *Traité*.
11. Franck, *Traité*, 1824 edition, p. 111.
12. Jouannet, *Statistique*, I, pp. 380–82.
13. Pijassou in Higounet, ed., *Seigneurie*, I, pp. 219, 316, II, pp. 334, 433.
14. *Ibid.*, II, p. 346.
15. R. Laurent, *Les Vignerons de la Côte d'Or au XIXe siècle* (Paris, 1958) II, pp. 193–97.
16. *Ibid.*, II, pp. 207–9; Pierre Goujon, "Le Vignoble de Saône-et-Loire au XIXe siècle, 1815–70" (Thèse de Doctorat de 3e cycle, Univ. de Lyon, n. d.) Annex IV; *Annuaire statistique*.
17. Alfred Angot, "Etude sur les vendanges en France," *Annales* du Bureau Central Météorologique, 1 (1883): b-33.
18. Garrier, *Paysans du Beaujolais*, II, p. 94.
19. *Ibid.*, II, p. 208; Goujon, "Vignoble de Saône-et-Loire," annexes III–IV; Laurent, *Vignerons de la Côte d'Or*, II, pp. 182, 208.
20. Goujon, "Vignoble de Saône-et-Loire," pp. 176–77.
21. Garrier, *Paysans du Beaujolais*, II, p. 97.
22. Giunta Parlamentare per la Inchiesta Agraria, *Atti* (Rome, 1881–86), VIII, pp. 284–306.
23. *Ibid.*, III, p. 290.
24. *Ibid.*, p. 291.
25. *Ibid.*, p. 292.
26. *Ibid.*, p. 366.
27. M.A.I.C., *Inchiesta parlamentare sulle condizioni dei contadini nelle province meridionali e nella Sicilia* (Rome, 1909), pp. 108–9.

Chapter Eight

1. George Ordish, *The Great Wine Blight* (London, 1972), chaps. 1–3.
2. *Ibid.*, pp. 5–7.
3. Berget, *Vins de France*, p. 8.
4. Ordish, *Great Wine Blight*, pp. 35–47.
5. L. Lheureux, *Les Syndicats dans la viticulture champenoise* (Paris, 1905), pp. 50–52; *R.V.* 1 (1894): 247–48.
6. *Journal d'agriculture pratique* 2 (July–December 1876): 762–65.
7. Ordish, *Great Wine Blight*, p. 83.
8. Dr. Crolas, *Phylloxera et sulfure de carbone* (Lyon, 1888), defends the sulphurists' point of view.
9. *R.V.*, 1 (1894): 600–1.
10. Berget, *Vins de France*, p. 67.
11. Jean A. Barral, *La Lutte contre le phylloxéra* (Paris, 1883), pp. 67–80.
12. Laurent, *Vignerons*, II, p. 172; Pijassou in Higounet, ed., *Seigneurie*, II, pp. 467–74.
13. Laurent, *Vignerons de la Côte d'Or*, I, p. 343.
14. Henri Sempé, *Régime économique du vin* (Bordeaux, 1898), appendices.

15. Laurent, *Vignerons de la Côte d'Or*, II, pp. 208–9.
16. Barral, *La Lutte*, p. 157.
17. Ministère des Finances, *Lois sur le budget général des recettes et des dépenses, 1878–1909.*
18. *R. V.*, 2 (1895), 580.
19. Marescalchi and Dalmasso, *Storia*, III, p. 558.
20. *Ibid.*, III, p. 588; Rebaudengo, *Vini del Piemonte*, p. 85.
21. Naples, Archivio Nazionale, Ministero di Agricoltura, fascescoli, 31, 132–33.
22. F. Paulsen, "Histoire de l'invasion phylloxérique et de la reconstitution du vignoble en Italie," *R. V.*, 78 (1933): nos. 2010 to 2018.
23. M.A.I.C., *Annali di agricoltura*, 43 (1882): 1–28.
24. Ordish, *Great Wine Blight*, p. 172; Mondini, *Produzione*, pp. 36–38; Andrea Caizzi, *Terra, vigneto e uomini nelle colline novaresi durante l'ultimo secolo* (Turin, 1969), pp. 45–49.
25. *Ibid.*, pp. 49–50.
26. Piétri, *La Question des vins en Italie*, pp. 243–45.
27. C. de Cesare, *Delle condizioni economiche e morali delle classi agricole nelle tre province di Puglia* (Naples, 1859), p. 89.
28. G. Pisacane, *La Crisi vinicola delle Puglie* (Milan, 1892), pp. 9–10.

Chapter IX

1. M. Augé-Laribé, *Le Problème agraire du socialisme* (Paris, 1907).
2. J. Guyot, *Etude des vignobles*, III, p. 54.
3. Raoul Chandon de Briailles, "Le Vigneron champenois," *R. V.*, 9 (1898): nos. 158, 168, 201, 210, 226, 230.
4. Edoardo Ottavi, *Gli Spari contro grandine in Stiria* (Casale, 1899), p. 19 ff.
5. Caizzi, *Terra, vigneto e uomini*, p. 90.
6. L. Descours, *Pasteur et son temps* (Paris, 1907), p. 165.
7. R. Vallery-Radot, *Life of Pasteur* (N.Y., n.d.), pp. 113, 158.
8. Ulysse Gayon, "Etude sur les appareils de pasteurisation," *R. V.*, 3 (1895): nos. 78–80.
9. G. Barbut, "Le Vignoble de l'Aude, monographie du Domaine de Jouarres," *R. V.*, 9 (1898): 541–45, 566–71, 595–600, 684–89, 709–14.
10. Primo Congresso Enologico, Turin, *Atti*, pp. 1–43.
11. *Giornale vinicolo italiano*, 23 (11 April 1897), pp. 169–71; *Rivista di viticoltura*, 1 (1877): 66 ff.; G. Frojo, *Il Presente e l'avvenire dei vini d'Italia* (Naples, 1876), pp. 8–20; A. Guffanti, *L'Avvenire viticolo ed enologico d'Italia* (Milan, 1877), pp. 43, 95–97; A. Strucchi, *Dei Mezzi atti a dare maggior sviluppo all'industria dei vini in Italia* (Turin, 1893), pp. 8–9.

Chapter Ten

1. *Annuaire statistique;* Berget, *Vins de France*, p. 173.
2. P. Degrully, *Essai historique et économique sur la production et le marché des vins en France* (Paris, 1910), p. 232.

3. Guyot, *Etude*, II, p. 730.
4. Pierre Barral, *Agrariens français de Méline à Pisani* (Paris, 1968).
5. Demolin, *Les Français d'aujourd'hui* (Paris, 1898); Descamps, *Les Populations viticoles* (Paris, 1907); see also O. Dutailly, *Les Vignerons de Salvignac* (Nantes, 1887); Henri de Laguérenne, *Etude sur les vignerons d'Ossoudun Saint Amand (Cher)* (Paris, 1902).
6. Giunta parlamentare, *Atti*, VIII, p. 535.
7. Garrier, *Paysans du Beaujolais*, I, pp. 115–73.
8. A. D. Indre-et-Loire 10M 19 10M 5; Chauvigne, *Monographie de la commune de Vouvray*, p. 20.
9. A. D. Gironde 7M 131[1].
10. A. D. Marne 158M 13, 172M 3; Lheureux, *Syndicats dans la viticulture champenoise*, pp. 6–22.
11. Giunta parlamentare, *Atti*, IV, pp. 303–5, VIII, 442–44; Berengo, *Agricoltura veneta*, pp. 88–104; Caizzi, *Terra, vigneto e uomini*, p. 32; R. Zangheri, ed., *Le Campagne emiliane nell'epoca moderna* (Milan, 1957), p. 140.
12. Fiorese, *Storia della crisi*, pp. 34, 46.
13. Giunta parlamentare, *Atti*, VIII, pp. 535–70; M.A.I.C., *Inchiesta . . . meridionali, Puglia*, p. 406.
14. Garrier, *Paysans du Beaujolais*; Myard, *Vigneronnage en Beaujolais*; Billiard, *Vigneronnage et vignerons* for the Beaujolais; Goujon, "Vignoble de Saône-et-Loire" for the Mâconnais.
15. Laurent, *Vignerons de la Côte d'Or*, I, pp. 277–80, II, p. 215.
16. Franck, *Traité sur les vins*, 225; Jouannet, *Statistique . . . Gironde*, II, p. 224.
17. A. D. Gironde 6M 1361.
18. Emilio Sereni, *Il Capitalismo nelle campagne, 1860–1900* (Turin, 1947), pp. 209–15.
19. A. D. Gironde 6M 1360–61.
20. M.A.C., *Inchiestas . . . meridionali, Campania*, pp. 410–12.
21. Laurent, *Vignerons de la Côte d'Or*, I, p. 280, II, p. 215.
22. *Ibid.*, II, p. 194.
23. Garrier, *Paysans du Beaujolais*, II, pp. 98, 113.
24. A. D. Gironde 6M 1360–61.
25. J. Boyreau, *Profits et salaires dans la viticulture de la Gironde* (Bordeaux, 1921), pp. 82–84.
26. Pijassou in Higounet, ed., *Seigneurie*, I, pp. 243–45, II, pp. 399, 519, 569–72.
27. E. Chantriot, *La Champagne* (Paris, 1905), *passim*; Lheureux, *Syndicats dans la viticulture*, pp. 25–27; A. D. Marne 172M 3; Rendu, *Ampelographie française*, p. 314.
28. A. D. Marne 155M 12.
29. Fiorese, *Storia della crisi*, pp. 66–67.
30. Mondini, *Produzione e commercio del vino*, p. 109.
31. Giunta parlamentare, *Atti*, III, pp. 473–80.
32. M.A.I.C., Ufficio del Lavoro, *Materiali per lo studio delle relazioni tra le classi agrarie in Romagna, 1905–10* (Rome, 1910), pp. 162–63; M.A.I.C., *Inchiesta . . . merid., Puglia*, p. 202.

33. *Ibid.*, *Campania*, p. 408.
34. Luraghi in *N.Q.S.R.*, II, p. 390.
35. Myard, *Vigneronnage en Beaujolais*, pp. 327–30.
36. C. Parain, "La Maison vigneronne en France," *Arts et traditions populaires* 4 (1955):299.
37. A. Charles, *La Révolution de 1848 et la seconde république à Bordeaux* (Bordeaux, 1945), p. 308. There are also descriptions in the novel of Jean Vignaud, *Terre ensorcelée* (Paris, 1906).
38. Giunta parlamentare, *Atti*, III, p. 499 ff.
39. *Ibid.*, VIII, p. 649.
40. Marescalchi and Dalmasso, *Storia della vite*, III, pp. 106–10.
41. F. Malvezin, *Histoire du commerce de Bordeaux* (Bordeaux, 1892), IV, pp. 118–19; A. D. Gironde 8M 51.
42. Paguierre, courtier en vin, *Classification et description des vins de Bordeaux* (Bordeaux, 1829), pp. 24–25.
43. Pijassou in Higounet, ed., *Seigneurie*, I, pp. 239–43; Penning-Rowsell, *Wines of Bordeaux*, p. 91.
44. Chambre de Commerce, Bordeaux, *Réponse aux questions*, p. 16.
45. Degrully, *Essai historique et économique*, p. 311.
46. Jean Richard, "Production et commerce du vin en Bourgogne aux XVIIIe et XIXe siècles," *A.C.H.S.*, s.1, no. 3 (1972):45.
47. A. Bousquet, *Le Régime économique du vin* (Paris, 1904), p. 93.
48. Degrully, *Essai historique et économique*, p. 232.
49. Direction du Travail, *Négociants en vin* (n.p., n.d.).
50. Penning-Rowsell, *Wines of Bordeaux*, chap. 7, is my main source for Bordeaux.
51. Vizetelly, *History of Champagne*, p. 184; M. Holland, *Connaissance du Champagne* (Paris, 1952), *passim*.
52. Forbes, *Champagne*, p. 45.
53. R. Bonnedame, *Notice sur la maison Moët et Chandon d'Epernay* (Epernay, 1894), p. 22.
54. [Turgon], *Etablissement Moët et Chandon* (Epernay, n.d.), p. 63.
55. Forbes, *Champagne*, p. 422.
56. J. de Chimay, *Life and Times of Madame Veuve Clicquot-Ponsardin* (Reims, 1961), p. 13.
57. *Ibid.*, p. 14.
58. Forbes, *Champagne*, p. 439.
59. Rebaudengo, *Vini del piemonte*, pp. 134–35.
60. H. Enjalbert, "Comment naissent les grands crus: Bordeaux, Porto, Cognac," *Annales, économies, sociétés, civilisations*, 8 (July–September 1953): 315–28, (October–December 1953):457–74; A. Petit-Lafitte, *Le Vignoble bordelais en 1875* (Bordeaux, 1875), pp. 36–37.
61. Forbes, *Champagne*, p. 157.
62. *Ibid.*, pp. 159–60.
63. A. Grimod de la Reynière, *Manuel des Amphitryons* (Paris, 1808), p. 298.
64. Quoted in Penning-Rowsell, *Wines of Bordeaux*, p. 91.
65. *Ibid.*, p. 93.
66. *Ibid.*

Chapter Eleven

1. M.A.C., Direction Général des Douanes, *Tableau général du commerce extérieur*, years 1827–66. Henceforth cited as *Tableau général*.
2. A.N.F.[12] 2525.
3. *Ibid.*
4. Ibid., and F[20]744; *Tableau général*.
5. V. Dandolo, *Enologia ovvero l'arte di fare conservare e far viaggiare i vini del regno* (Milan, 1812), II, pp. 194–95.
6. L. Serristori, ed., *Statistica dell'Italia* (Florence, 1839), pp. 3–6.
7. R. Villari, "L'Economia degli stati italiani dal 1815 al 1848," *Nuove questioni di storia del Risorgimento*, I, pp. 610, 637.
8. De Rosa, "Produzione e commercio dei vini . . ." p. 195.
9. D. Demarco, *Il Tramonto dello stato pontifico* (Turin, 1949), p. 769.
10. F. Bonelli, "Il Commercio estero dello stato pontifico nel secolo XIX," *A.E.U.I.*, s.1, 9 (1961):242–43. Hereafter cited as *A.E.U.I.*
11. Archivio di Stato, Turin. Azienda generale delle regie gabelle, *Stato generale della bilancia di commercio;* G. Bracco, "Produzione e commercio dei vini piemontesi nei secoli XVIII e XIX," *A.C.H.S.*, s.1, no. 3 (1972):171–74.
12. Ira Glazier, "Il Commercio estero del regno lombardo-veneto dal 1815 al 1865," *A.E.U.I.*, s.1, 15 (1966):161; G. Parenti, "Il Commercio estero del Granducato di Toscana dal 1851 al 1859," *A.E.U.I.*, s.1, 8 (1958):59.
13. Paronetto, *Chianti*, p. 214.
14. *Il Vino, undeci conferenze* (Turin, 1880), pp. 197–98.
15. *Annali di viticoltura* (1872): pp. 62–86.
16. A.N.F.[12]2525; Degrully, *Essai historique et économique*, p. 335.
17. F. Crouzet, "Les Importations d'eau de vie et de vin français en Grande Bretagne pendant le blocus continental." *Annales du Midi*, 65 (1953):91–106; Malvezin, *Hist. commerce Bordeaux*, IV, pp. 24–35.
18. Ralph Davis, "The English Wine Trade in the 18th and 19th Centuries," *A.C.H.S.*, s.1, no. 3 (1972):104–5; A. L. Dunham, *The Anglo-French Treaty of Commerce of 1860* (Ann Arbor, Mich., 1930), pp. 286–87.
19. Chambre de Commerce, Bordeaux, *Procès-verbaux* (1870):449.
20. Davis, "English Wine Trade," pp. 101–2.
21. *Annuaire statistique*, 17 (1897):295.
22. Sempé, *Régime économique du vin*, p. 184.
23. M.A.I.C. *Notizie e studi sull'agricoltura* (1891) p. 1ix.
24. M.A.I.C. Direzione Generale della Statistica, *Annuario statistico italiano* (1905–07):501; *Il Vino*, pp. 44–45. See also *Giornale vinicolo italiano*, no. 47 (22 November 1903):553–55.
25. *R.V.* 7 (1897): 132–33.
26. Forbes, *Champagne*.
27. A. D. Marne 172M 2–3, reports of Chamber of Commerce, Reims.
28. A. D. Marne 172M 3.
29. Malvezin, *Histoire du commerce*, pp. 56–57, 336–37.
30. Laurent, *Vignerons de la Côte d'Or*, I, pp. 198, 217; Eugen Weber, *Peasants into Frenchmen* (Stanford, Calif., 1976), pp. 144–45, 146, 216–17; Jean Vidalenc,

La Société française de 1815 à 1848: Le Peuple des campagnes (Paris, 1970) and *Le Peuple des villes et des bourgs* (Paris, 1973), *passim*.

31. *Moniteur vinicole,* 24 September 1856, p. 3; Goujon, "Vignoble de Saône-et-Loire," p. 153; Butel and Roudié, "La Production et commercialisation des vins," pp. 404–05.

32. M.A.C., *Enquête agricole,* 1866, ser. 2 vol. 14, p. 295.

Chapter Twelve

1. A.N.F.[12]2525; *Le Globe* (Paris) 10–14 January 1844.
2. Laurent, *Vignerons de la Côte d'Or,* I, p. 211.
3. *Le Globe,* 10 January 1844.
4. *Annali di viticoltura,* 1 (1877):217–23; *Il vino,* pp. 56–65.
5. A. Bouffard, *Etude comparée de quelques procédés de vinification* (Montpellier, 1889), p. 6.
6. *Annali di viti.* 1 (1877):218.
7. *Bulletin de statistique et de législation comparée* (1890).
8. *Ibid.,* (1888).
9. Leo Loubère, *Radicalism in Mediterranean France* (Albany, N.Y., 1974), p. 185.
10. G. Chaffal, *Les Crises viticoles modernes* (Lyon, 1908), pp. 74–77.
11. Rémy Pech, *Entreprise viticole et capitalisme* (Toulouse, 1975), pp. 124–25.
12. F. Atger, *La Crise viticole et la viticulture méridionale, 1900–1907* (Paris, 1907), p. 47.
13. Chaffal, *Les Crises viticoles modernes,* pp. 74–84.
14. Charles Warner, *The Winegrowers of France and the Government since 1875* (New York, 1960), p. 37.
15. Atger, *La Crise viticole,* p. 18; Chaffal, *Les Crises viticoles modernes,* pp. 122–23.
16. Degrully, *Essai historique et économique,* pp. 297–318.
17. Pech, *Entreprise viticole,* p. 137.
18. Pijassou in Higounet, ed., *Seigneurie,* II, pp. 553–58.
19. Laurent, *Vignerons de la Côte d'Or,* II, pp. 193–95; Garrier, *Paysans de Beaujolais,* II, p. 121.
20. Pech, *Entreprise viticole,* pp. 99–100.
21. Atger, *La Crise viticole,* p. 41.
22. Pech, *Entreprise viticole,* p. 109.
23. J. Harvey Smith, "Village revolution: Agricultural Workers of Cruzy (Hérault)," (Ph.D. thesis, University of Wisconsin, 1972), p. 252 ff.
24. *The Crowd: A Study of the Popular Mind* (London, 1909).
25. P. Carbonel, *Histoire de Narbonne* (Narbonne, 1954), pp. 472–92; F. Napo, *1907: La Révolte des vignerons* (Toulouse, 1971), *passim*.
26. Warner, *Winegrowers of France,* p. 48.
27. A. Marescalchi, *Le Leggi sui vini* (Casale Monferrato, 1908), pp. 1–27.
28. *Giornale vinicolo italiano,* 29 November 1903, pp. 565–67.
29. A. Legrand, *Vin de champagne,* p. 49 ff.
30. Lheureux, *Syndicats dans la viticulture champenoise,* p. 127.
31. A. D. Marne 155M 3.

32. E. Clémentel, *Un Drame économique, les délimitations* (Paris, 1914), pp. 87–150.
33. P. Vernier, *De l'Evolution du commerce des vins de Champagne* (Paris, 1923), pp. 21–23.
34. J. Nollevalle, "1911, l' agitation dans le vignoble champenois," *La Champagne viticole* (January 1961): 6–30.
35. *Journal des débats*, 13 April 1911.
36. A. D. Marne 155M 9–12.
37. Nollevalle, "1911" pp. 20–21.
38. J. Saillet, "Les Mouvements vignerons de Champagne," *Le Mouvement social* 67 (April-June 1969): 86–89.
39. P. Gabriel, *La Viticulture dans le département de l'Aube* (Paris, 1913), *passim*.

Chapter Thirteen

1. R. Schnerb, *Deux siècles de fiscalité française, XIXe-XXe siècle* (Paris, 1973), pp. 55–227.
2. P. Barailhé, *Eléments de législation viti-vinicole* (Bordeaux, 1955), pp. 109–10; Degrully, *Essai historique et économique*, p. 164; G. Rousseau, *Les Impôts intérieurs d'état sur les vins* (Bordeaux, 1903), pp. 64–78.
3. The Library of the Chamber of Commerce in Bordeaux has large numbers of these pamphlets and petitions.
4. Chambre de Commerce, Bordeaux, *Réponses*, 14.
5. A.N. F¹²2525.
6. Garrier, *Paysans du Beaujolais*, I, p. 242.
7. Loubère, *Radicalism in Mediterranean France*, chap. II.
8. Laurent, *Vignerons de la Côte d'Or*, I, pp. 491–98; Garrier, *Paysans du Beaujolais*, I, pp. 310–23.
9. J. C. Drouin, in *Vignobles et vins d'Aquitaine* (Bordeaux, 1970), pp. 315–23.
10. Charles, *Révolution de 1848*, pp. 62–89, 153–83.
11. A. D. Marne 7M 28.
12. A. N. F¹²2525.
13. Chambre de Commerce, Bordeaux, *Réponse*, pp. 24–37.
14. *Bulletin de statistique et de législation comparée*, yearly.
15. Barailhé, *Eléments*, p. 110; Berget, *Vins de France*, p. 197; Rousseau, *Impôts intérieurs*, pp. 78–80.
16. Laurent, *Vignerons de la Côte d'Or*, I, p. 384.
17. A. Perrin, *La Civilisation de la vigne* (Paris, 1938), p. 178.
18. G. Nemoz, "Les élections législatives des 8 et 22 mai 1898 dans les départements de Vaucluse, des Alpes-Maritimes, du Var, des Bouches-du-Rhône," (Diplôme d'Etudes Supérieures, Université de Paris, 1969–70), pp. 5–30.
19. Garrier, *Paysans du Beaujolais*, I, pp. 310–23.
20. Goujon, "Vignoble de Saône-et-Loire," pp. 134–35, 197–251, 268; A. D. Rhône, unclassified electoral results; *Courrier de Lyon*, 21 August 1881; *Journal de Villefranche*, 8 May 1906; Municipal Library of Lyon, A 498347, packet of press clippings.
21. Goujon, "Vignoble de Saône-et-Loire, pp. 134–35.
22. A. D. Saône-et-Loire, unclassified electoral results.

23. R. Long, *Les Elections législatives en Côte d'Or* (Paris, 1958), pp. 171–256.
24. G. Dupeux, *Aspects de l'histoire politique du Loir-et-Cher, 1848–1914* (Paris, 1962), pp. 662, 956; A. D. Loir-et-Cher, unclassified electoral results.
25. M. Laurencin, "L'opinion publique en Indre-et-Loire dans les élections législatives de 1869 . . ." (Diplôme d'Etudes Supérieures, Université de Tours, 1966), pp. 71, 183 ff., 265–89.
26. A. D. Indre-et-Loire, unclassified.
27. Charles Tilly, *The Vendée* (Cambridge, Mass., 1964), pp. 31–42, 213–14.
28. J. Le Theule, "Le Vignoble du Layon," (Diplôme d'Etudes Supérieures, Université de Caen, 1951), pp. 218–21.
29. G. Bodinier, *Les Elections et les représentants de Maine-et-Loire depuis 1789* (Angers, 1888), p. 249; *Union de l'Ouest*, October 1885, September 1889, August 1893; A. D. Maine-et-Loire 8M 73, 108; *Journal de Maine-et-Loire*, April 1906, April 1910.
30. Drouin, in *Vignobles et vins d'Aquitaine*, pp. 315–23; Charles, *Révol. 1848 Bordeaux, passim.*
31. M. Goasquen, "L'Opinion médocaine," *Actes* du XVIe congrès de la Fédération Historique du Sud-Ouest (1963):177–91.
32. A. D. Gironde 3M 214.
33. *Ibid.*, 3M 222.
34. R. Boudon, "Débuts de l'Action Française en Gironde," (Diplôme d'Etudes Supérieures, Université de Bordeaux, s.d.), pp. 10–18.
35. For electoral results, see *Département de la Marne et la Révolution de 1848* (Reims, 1948), pp. 64–77; A. D. Marne 7M 28, 57, 59, 63, 67, 68; G. Boussinesq, *Histoire de Reims* (Reims, 1933) II, pp. 614–15, 791–92.
36. See their names in *R.V.*, 3 (1895): 225–26.
37. Caizzi, *Terra, vigneto e uomini*, pp. 39–40.
38. Giunta Parlamentare per la Inchiesta Agraria, *Atti* (Rome, 1881–86) Vol. VIII, fasc.ii, pp. 535–845; Ministero di Agricoltura, *Statistica delle elezioni generali politiche* (Rome, 1876–), *passim*; G. Schepis, *Le Consultazioni popolari in Italia dal 1848 al 1957* (Empoli, 1958), p. 46 ff.
39. Sereni, *Capitalismo nelle campagne*, p. 244.
40. A. Schiavi, *Come hanno votato gli elettori italiani* (Milan, 1914), pp. 96–97.
41. G. Salvemini, *Opere* (Milan, 1961–), Tome IV, vol. i, pp. 22, 234–43.

Chapter Fourteen

1. Laurent, *Vignerons de la Côte d'Or*, I, pp. 187, 375–77; Berget, *Vins de France*, pp. 182–87.
2. *R.V.*, 1 (1894):46–48.
3. *Ibid.*
4. M. Moureau, *De l'Isolement au groupement chez les vignerons du Narbonnais. La Coopérative de Lézignan* (Paris, 1911), pp. 19–20.
5. *Ibid.*, pp. 20–50; Henri Gervais, *La Rémunération du travail dans la viticulture méridionale* (Paris, 1908), p. 156.
6. René Worms, *Les Associations agricoles* (Paris, 1914), pp. 140–54.
7. Edouard Castelnau, *Des Associations de vente du vin dans le Midi de la France* (Paris, 1907), p. 22.

8. Laurent, *V ignerons de la Côte d'Or*, I, pp. 376–77.

9. A. D. Gironde 10M 12, 44–49.

10. J.-R Guyon, *Au Service du vin de Bordeaux* (Bordeaux, 1956), p. 71.

11. M.A.I.C., *Annali di agricoltura*, No. 255 (1908).

12. G.Nicosia, *Cantine sociali e cooperazione viti-vinicole*, 2d ed. (Rome, 1935), p. 31; R. Felice, *Aspetti e momenti della vita economica di Roma e del Lazio* (Rome, 1965), pp. 178–79 gives slightly different figures.

13. Pisacane, *La Crisi vinicola delle Puglie* (Milan, 1892), p. 43.

14. Laurent, *Vignerons de la Côte d'Or*, I, 237.

15. Castelnau, *Des Associations*, p. 44.

16. Michel Augé-Laribé, *Syndicats et cooperatives agricoles* (Paris, 1926), p. 76.

17. *R.V.*, 3 (1897):47–49.

18. S. B. Ross, "The Development of Governmental Protection and Regulation of the French Wine Industry," (Ph.D. thesis, University of Pittsburgh, 1931), p. 62 ff.

19. *Ibid.*, pp. 91–95.

20. Pijassou in Higounet, ed., *Seigneurie*, II, pp. 565–64.

Conclusion

1. Pech, *Entreprise viticole*, pp. 420–61.

Bibliography

Documents in Archives

Archives Nationales F^{12} 2525
Archives Départementales
      Drôme 12M 1–11; 51M 35–40; 58M 1–8; 135M 8
      Gironde 3M 214, 222; 6M 1360–61; 7M 131^1; 10M 12, 44–49
      Indre-et-Loire 8M 18, 67, 69, 73, 88, 108; 10M 5–8, 18–19
      Loir-et-Cher unclassified electoral lists, and data on agriculture
      Marne 7M 28; 155M 3; 172M 2–3; 54M 7–12
      Maine-et-Loire 8M 73, 108; 59M 2–6
      Saône-et-Loire unclassified electoral lists, and property evaluations
      Vaucluse 6M 52–53; 7M 122, 128–129
Naples, Archivio Nazionale, fascescoli 31, 132–33
Turin, Archivio di Stato, Azienda Generale delle Regie Gabelle, *Stato generale della bilancia di commercio*

Periodicals

Annali di viticoltura ed enologia italiana
Bulletin de statistique et de législation comparée
Courrier vinicole
La Feuille vinicole
Giornale vinicolo italiano
La Gironde vinicole
Journal d'agriculture pratique
L'Oenophile, revue mensuelle de viticulture, d'oenologie et d'oenotechnie
Revue de viticulture
Rivista di viticoltura

Books and Articles

FRANCE

Allen, Herbert W., *The Wines of France*. New York, 1924.
Andrieu, Pierre, *Petite histoire de Bordeaux et de son vignoble*. Montpellier, 1955.

Angot, Alfred. "Etude sur les vendanges en France." *Annales* du Bureau Central Météorologique 1 (1883); B29–B120.

Atger, Frédéric. *La Crise viticole et la viticulture méridionale 1900–1907*. Paris, 1907.

Auffray, Jacques. *Etude de la législation relative aux fraudes et falsifications des vins*. Paris, 1911.

Augé-Laribé, Michel. *Le Problème agraire du socialisme*. Paris, 1907.

———— *Répertoire bibliographique d'économie rurale*. Montpellier, 1953.

———— *Syndicats et coopératives agricoles*. Paris, 1926.

Barallhé, Paul. *Eléments de législation vini-vinicole*. Bordeaux, 1955.

Barbut, G. "Le Vignoble de l'Aude: monographie du Domaine de Jouarres." *Revue de viticulture*, 9 (1898):541–45, 566–71, 595–600, 684–89, 709–14.

Barral, Jean-Augustin. *La Lutte contre le phylloxéra*. Paris, 1883.

Barral, Pierre. *Agrariens français de Méline à Pisani*. Paris, 1968.

Beauregard, J.-F. de. *Statistique du département de Maine-et-Loire*. Angers, 1850.

Berget, Adrien, *Les Vins de France. Histoire, géographie et statistique du vignoble français*. Paris, 1900.

———— *La Viticulture nouvelle: la reconstitution des vignobles, étude, plantation et culture des vignes franco-américaines*. Paris, 1896.

Bernard, A. "La Vigne et le vin en Mâconnais septentrional pendant plus d'un siècle, 1800–1921." *Bulletin de la Société des Amis des Arts et des Sciences de Tournus*, 33 (1933):148–214.

Bertall, Charles. *La Vigne*. Paris, 1878.

Beucher, René. *Du Bail à complant dans le département de Maine-et-Loire*. Paris, 1899.

Billiard, Raymond. *Vigneronnage et vignerons Beaujolais, notice historique, juridique et sociale*. Mâcon, 1938.

Bodinier, Guillaume. *Les élections et les représentants de Maine-et-Loire depuis 1789*. Angers, 1888.

Bonnedame, Raphael. *Notice sur la maison Moët et Chandon d'Epernay*. Epernay, 1894.

Bord, G. *Essai sur les variations de l'encepagement*. n.p. n.d.

Bouchard, A. *Essai sur l'histoire de la culture de la vigne dans le département de Maine-et-Loire*. Angers, 1876.

Boudon, R. "Débuts de l'Action Française en Gironde." Diplôme d'Etudes Supérieures, Université de Bordeaux, s.d.

Bouffard, A. *Etude comparée de quelques procédés de vinification*. Montpellier, 1889.

Bousquet, Adrien. *Le Régime économique du vin. Le marché des vins*. Paris, 1904.

Boussinesq, Georges. *Histoire de Reims depuis les origines*. Reims, 1933. 2 vols.

Boyreau, Jean. *Profits et salaires dans la viticulture de la Gironde*. Bordeaux, 1921.

Bréjoux, Pierre. *Les Vins de Loire*. Paris, 1956.

Breuil, A. du. *Culture perfectionnée et moins coûteuse du vignoble*. Paris, 1863.

Busby, James. *Journal of a Recent Visit to the Vineyards of Spain and France: forming a guide to the profitable culture of the vine in New South Wales*. 3d ed. London, 1840.

Butel, P. et Roudié, Ph. "La Production et la commercialisation des vins du Libournais au début du XIXème sieècle." *Annales du Midi*, 81 (1969): 379–408.

Carbonel, Paul. *Histoire de Narbonne*, Narbonne, 1954.

Castelnau, Edouard. *Des Associations de vente du vin dans le Midi de la France. Coopératives et trusts.* Paris, 1907.

Cavoleau, M. *Oenologie française, ou statistiques de tous les vignobles et de toutes les boissons vineuses.* Paris, 1827.

Cazalet, Jean-Louis. *Cette et son commerce des vins de 1660 à 1920.* Montpellier, 1920.

Chaffal, Georges. *Les Crises viticoles modernes et la dépréciation actuelle du vignoble.* Lyon, 1908.

Chambre de Commerce, Bordeaux. See Moquet.

Chambre de Commerce, Bordeaux. *Réponse aux questions relatives au régime des boissons.* Bordeaux, 1850.

Chambre de Commerce, Bordeaux. *Tableau relatif aux récoltes des Vins du Médoc depuis 1795.* Séance du 3 mai, 1882.

Chambre de Commerce de Reims. *Commerce des vins mousseux de Champagne, 1905–1914.* Reims, n.d.

Chandon de Briailles, Raoul. "Le Vigneron champenois." *Revue de viticulture,* 9 (14 May 1898). Nos. 158, 168, 201, 210, 226, 230.

Chantriot, Emile. *La Champagne: étude de géographie régionale.* Paris, 1905.

Chappaz, Georges, et Rousseau, Eugène, *Étude sur le vignoble de Chablis.* Nancy, 1904.

Chappaz, Georges. *Le Vignoble et le vin de Champagne.* Paris, n.d.

Chaptal de Chanteloup, Jean Antoine Claude. *Traité théorique et pratique sur la culture de la vigne, avec l'art de faire le vin, . . .* Paris, 1801. 2 vols.

Charles, Albert. *La Révolution de 1848 et la seconde république à Bordeaux et dans le département de la Gironde.* Bordeaux, 1945.

Charles, A. "La Viticulture en Gironde et le commerce des vins de Bordeaux sous le Second Empire." *Revue historique de Bordeaux et du département de la Gironde* 11 (1962):193–220.

Chauvigne, A. *Monographie de la commune de Vouvray et de son vignoble.* Tours, 1909.

———— *Le Vignoble de Touraine.* Paris, 1913.

Chevreul, Théodule. *Etude sur les vins d'Anjou.* Angers, 1892.

Chimay, J. de. *Life and Times of Madame Veuve Clicquot-Ponsardin.* Reims, 1961.

Clause, Georges. *Note sur la viticulture et le vignoble champenois au debut du XIXe siècle.* Châlons-sur-Marne, 1965.

Clementel, E. *Un Drame économique; les délimitations.* Paris, 1914.

Cocks, Charles and Féret, E. *Bordeaux and Its Wines, Classed by Order of Merit.* 2ed. English edition. Paris, 1883.

Convert, F. *La Vigne et le vin depuis 1600.* Paris, 1901.

Crolas, Dr. *Phylloxéra et sulfure de carbone.* Lyon, 1888.

Crouzet, François. "Les Importations d'eau de vie et de vin français en Grande Bretagne pendant le blocus continental." *Annales du Midi,* 65 (1953):91–106.

Cuny, Hilaire. *Louis Pasteur.* New York; 1966.

Danguy, M. R. and Aubertin, C. *Les Grands vins de Bourgogne.* Dijon, 1892.

David, T. and Foillard, L. *Vins de Beaujolais.* N.p.,n.d.

Davis, Ralph. "The English Wine Trade in the 18th and 19th Centuries." *A.C.H.S.* s.1, no. 3 (1972):87–106.

De Breuil, Alphonse. *Vineyard Culture Improved and Cheapened.* Cincinnati, 1867.
Degrully, Paul. *Essai historique et économique sur la production et le marché des vins en France.* Paris, 1910.
Delpon, J.-A. *Statistique du département du Lot.* Paris, 1831. 2 vols.
Demeure-Despinoy, A. *Contribution à l'étude du Jura viticole.* Besonçon, 1923.
Demolins, Edmond. *Les Français d'aujourd'hui.* Paris, 1898.
Département de la Marne et la Révolution de 1848. Reims, 1948
Descamps, Paul. *Les Populations viticoles.* Paris, 1907.
Descours, L. *Pasteur et son oeuvre.* Paris, 1921.
Dion, Roger. *Histoire de la vigne et du vin en France.* Paris, 1959.
———— *Val de la Loire.* Tours, 1934.
Direction du Travail. *Négociants en vins.* N.p., n. d.
Douarche, Léon. *Le Vin et la vigne dans l'économie nationale française.* Paris, 1943.
Drouin, J. C. See *Vignobles et vins . . .*
Duhamel, L. *Les Représentants de Vaucluse.* Avignon, 1893.
Dunham, Arthur L. *The Anglo-French Treaty of Commerce of 1860.* Ann Arbor, Mich., 1930.
Dupeux, Georges. *Aspects de l'histoire politique du Loir-et-Cher, 1848–1914.* Paris, 1962.
Dutailly, O. *Les Vignerons de Salvignac.* Nantes, 1887.
Emion, Victor. *Le Régime des boissons.* Paris, 1878.
Enjalbert, Henri. "Comment naissent les grandes crus: Bordeaux, Porto, Cognac." *Annales, économies, sociétés, civilisations.* 8 (July-Sept., 1953): 315–28; (Oct.-Dec., 1953):457–74.
Faure, Hippolyte. *Coup d'oeil rétrospectif sur la question vinicole.* 2d ed. Narbonne, 1891.
Faye, Henri (pseud. H. Langeron). *Les Représentants du département d'Indre-et-Loire depuis 1789.* Tours, 1885.
Fénelon, P. "Le Vignoble de Monbazillac." *Revue géographique des Pyrénées et de Sud-ouest* 16 (1945–46):5–35.
Féret, E. (See Cocks, C.)
Forbes, Patrick. *Champagne, the Wine, the Land and the People.* London, 1967.
Forster, Robert. "The Noble Wine Producers of the Bordelais in the 18th Century." *Economic History Review* 2d s. 14 (Aug. 1961):18–33.
Franck, W. *Traité sur les vins du Médoc.* Bordeaux, 1824.
Gabriel, Pierre. *La Viticulture dans le département de l'Aube.* Paris, 1913.
Gadille, Rolande. *Le Vignoble de la côte bourguignonne.* Paris, 1967.
Galtier, Gaston. *Le Vignoble du Languedoc méditerranéen et du Roussillon.* Montpellier, 1958. 3 vols.
Gandilhon, René. *Naissance du champagne: Dom Pierre Pérignon,* Paris, 1968.
Gandon, Yves. *Champagne.* Neuchatel, 1958.
Garrier, Gilbert. *Paysans du Beaujolais et du Lyonnais, 1800–1970.* Grenoble, 1973. 2 vols.
———— "Les Enquêtes agricoles du XIXe siècle: une source contestée." *Cahiers d'histoire* 12 (1967):105–13.
Gayon, Ulysse. "Etude sur les appareils de pasteurisation." *R.V.* 3, nos. 78–80 (1895).
Genieys, Pierre. *La Crise viticole méridionale.* Toulouse, 1905.

Gervais, Henri. *La Rémuneration du travail dans la viticulture méridionale*. Paris, 1908.

Gervais, Jean-Antoine. *Opuscule sur la vinification*. Montpellier, 1820.

Gervais, Misael. *La Coopération en viticulture*. Paris, 1915.

Gervais, Prosper. *Le Reconstruction du vignoble: quantité ou qualité*. Paris, 1902.

Girard, Abbé. *La Vigne et les vignerons en Sancerrois à travers les siècles*. Sancerre, 1941.

Girault, Jacques. "Le Rôle du socialisme dans la révolte des vignerons de l'Aube," *Le Mouvement social* No. 67 (April-June 1969):89–109.

Giry, Alfred. *Etudes économiques et sociales du département de Vaucluse*. N. p., 1952.

Goasquen, M. "L'Opinion médocaine." *Actes* du XVIe Congrés de la Fédération Historique du Sud-Ouest (1963):177–91.

Goujon, Pierre. *Le Vignoble de Saône-et-Loire au XIXe siècle, 1815–70*. Thèse de Doctorat de 3e Cycle, Université de Lyon, n.d.

Grand, Roger. *Le Contrat de complant depuis les origines jusqu'à nos jours*. Paris, 1917.

Grimod de la Reynière, Alexandre. *Manuel des Amphitryons*. Paris, 1808.

Guilhem, Henri. *La Blanquette de Limoux*. Paris, 1951.

Guillory, P.-C. *Les Congrès des vignerons français*. Paris, 1860.

———— *Les Vins blancs d'Anjou et de Maine-et-Loire*. Angers, 1874.

Guyon, Jean-Raymond. *Au Service du vin de Bordeaux*. Bordeaux, 1956.

Guyot, Jules. *Etude des vignobles de France*. Paris, 1868. 3 vols.

Higounet, Charles, ed. *La Seigneurie et le vignoble de Château Latour*. Bordeaux, 1974. 2 vols.

Holland, Maurice. *Connaissance du champagne*. Paris, 1952.

Jamain, Paul, et al. *Atlas vinicole de la France et de ses colonies*. Paris, 1901.

Jamain, Paul. *La Vigne et le vin*. Paris, 1901.

Jouannet, François. *Statistique du département de la Gironde*. Paris, 1837–43. 2 vols.

Jullien, André. *The Topographie of All Known Vineyards*. London, 1824.

Kerdéland, Jean de. *Histoire des vins de France*. Paris, 1964.

Lacomme, Léon. *Les Elections et les représentants de Saône-et-Loire depuis 1789*. Paris, 1885.

Ladrey, Claude. *L'Art de faire le vin*. 4th ed. Paris, 1881.

Lafon, André. *La Maison sur la rive*. Paris, 1914.

Legrand, A. *Vin de champagne*. Reims, n. d.

Laguérenne, Henry de. *Etude sur les vignerons d'Issoudun, Saint Amand (Cher)*. Paris, 1902

Lallemand, Georges. "Edouard Werlé, négociant en vins de champagne, . . ." *Champagne économique* 9 (1954):3–12.

Langeron, see Faye, Henri.

Laurencin, Michel. "L'Opinion publique en Indre-et-Loire dans les élections législatives de 1869 . . ." Diplôme d'Etudes Supérieures, Université de Tours, 1966.

Laurent, Robert. *Les Vignerons de la Côte d'Or au XIXe siècle*. Paris, 1958. 2 vols.

Lavalle, J. and Garnier, J. *Histoire et statistique de la vigne et des grands vins de la Côte d'Or*. Dijon, 1855.

Lavesque, Yves. "L'Agronomie du Vaucluse dans la première partie du XIXe siècle." Diplôme d'Etudes Supérieures, Université d'Aix-en-Provence, 1970.

Legras, Charles. *Vigne aux bras ouverts*. Paris, 1928.

Leroy, Réné. *La Chambre syndicale du commerce en gros des vins et spiritueux de Paris . . . 1840–1902*. Paris, 1903.

Le Theule, Joel. "Le Vignoble du Layon." Diplôme d'Etudes Supérieures, Université de Caen, 1951.

Le Theule, Joel. See Wagret, Paul.

Leuillot, Paul. *L'Alsace au début du XIXe siècle*. Paris, 1959–60. 3 vols.

Levadoux, L. "Contribution à l'étude du vignoble auvergnat." *Annales* de l'Ecole Nationale d'Agriculture de Montpellier 25 (1939):353–436.

Levasseur, Emile. *L'Histoire du commerce de la France*. Paris, 1911–12. 2 vols.

Lheureux, Lucien. *Les Syndicats dans la viticulture champenoise*. Paris, 1905.

Long, R. *Les Elections législatives en Côte d'Or*. Paris, 1958.

Loubère, Leo. *Radicalism in Southern France*. Albany, 1974.

Maisonneuve, P. *L'Anjou, ses vignes et ses vins*. Angers, 1925–26. 2 vols.

Malvezin, Frantz. *Bordeaux: histoire de la vigne et du vin en Aquitaine depuis ses origines jusqu'à nos jours*. Bordeaux, 1919.

——— *Histoire du commerce de Bordeaux*. Bordeaux, 1892. 4 vols.

Manceau, Emile. *Théorie des vins mousseux*. Epernay, 1905.

Marre, E. *Monographie des vignobles de l'Aveyron*. Paris. 1894.

Marres, Paul. *La Vigne et le vin en France*. Paris, 1950.

Maumené, Edme J. *Indications théoriques et pratiques sur le travail des vins et en particulier sur celui des vins mousseux*. Paris, 1858.

Mauron, Paul. *La Vigne et le vin en Berry du Cher*. Bourges, 1947.

Michel, Francisque. *Histoire du commerce et de la navigation à Bordeaux*. Bordeaux, 1870.

Milhau, Jules. *Etude économetrique du prix du vin en France*. Montpellier, 1935.

M. A. C. Administrations des Douanes. *Tableau décennal du Commerce de la France avec ses colonies et les puissances étrangères*. Paris, 1838–.

——— *Tableau général du commerce extérieur*. Paris, 1880–.

M. F. Lois sur le budget général des recettes et des dépenses de l'exercice . . . Paris, 1878–.

Moquet, A.-M. *Tableau analytique et synoptique des prix des vins . . . de la Gironde depuis 1808 jusqu'au mois d'avril 1850*. Bordeaux, n. d.

Moreau-Bérillon, C. *Au pays du champagne, le vignoble et le vin*. Reims, 1922.

Moureau, Marceau. *De l'isolement au groupement chez les vignerons du Narbonnais. La Coopérative de Lézignan*. Paris, 1911.

Mouton, Régine. "Les élections législatives dans le département de Vaucluse en 1910." Diplôme d'Etudes Supérieures, Faculté des Lettres de l'Université d'Aix, 1970.

Mugnier, Marcel. *Essai sur l'exportation des vins fins de Bourgogne*. Dijon, 1909.

Myard, François. *Le Vigneronnage en Beaujolais*. Lyon, 1907.

Napo, Félix. *1907, La Révolte des vignerons*. Toulouse, 1971.

Nemoz, Georgette. "Les Elections législatives des 8 et 22 mai, 1898, dans les départements de Vaucluse, des Alpes-Maritimes, du Var, des Bouches-du-Rhône." Diplôme d'Etudes Supérieures, Université de Paris, 1969–70.

Nollevalle, J. "1911: l'agitation dans le vignoble champenois." *La Champagne viticole*, 43 (Jan. 1961):2–32.

Ordish, George. *The Great Wine Blight*. London, 1972.

Orizet, Louis. *Les Vins de France*. Paris, 1964.

Paguierre, courtier en vin. *Classification et description des vins de Bordeaux.* Bordeaux, 1829.

Parain, Charles. "La Maison vigneronne en France." *Arts et traditions populaires* 4 (1955):290–331.

Pech, Rémy. *Entreprise viticole et capitalisme.* Toulouse, 1975.

Pech de Laclause, Jacques. *La Vigne dans les Basses-Corbières depuis le XVIIIe siècle.* Toulouse, n. d.

Penning-Rowsell, Edmund. *The Wines of Bordeaux.* New York, 1970.

Perrin, Armand. *La Civilisation de la vigne.* Paris, 1938.

Petit-Lafitte, A. *Le Vignoble bordelais en 1875.* Bordeaux, 1875.

Petrie, Sir Charles. "Politics and Wine." *Quarterly Review* 291, no. 598 (1953):445–56.

Pic, Paul and Godart, Justin, eds. *Le Mouvement économique et social dans la région lyonnaise.* Lyon, 1902–3. 2 vols.

Pijassou, R. "Un Château du Médoc: Palmer." *Revue d'histoire de Bordeaux* 13 (1964):183–203.

Pris, Claude. "Répertoire des monographies des maisons françaises à incidence vigneronne." *Arts et traditions populaires* 4 (1955):334–49.

Proffit, A. and Bureau, G. *La Vallée de la Loire et ses vins: Orléanais, Sologne, Touraine, Saumurois et Anjou.* Orléans, 1910.

"Rapports Cazeau Cazalet sur la situation critique de la viticulture à la Chambre des Députés" Rapport No. 1023, à la session de 1907; Rapport No. 2512, à la session de 1909.

Ravaz, Louis. *Le Pays de Cognac.* Angoulême, 1900.

Ray, Cyril. *Lafite.* New York, 1969.

――――― *Bollinger. The Story of a Champagne.* London, 1971.

Raynal, Paul. *Le Vignoble français et l'Afrique du Nord.* Paris, 1912.

Reiller, Jean. *Les Transformations de l'agriculture vauclusienne depuis le début du XIXe siècle et l'action des pouvoirs publics.* Avignon, 1945.

Rendu, Victor. *Ampelographie française, comprenant la statistique, la description des meilleurs cépages, l'analyse chimique du sol, et les procédés de culture et de vinification des principaux vignobles de la France.* 2d ed. Paris, 1857.

Riol, J.-L. *Le Vignoble de Gaillac depuis ses origines jusqu'à nos jours.* 2d ed. Paris, 1913.

Robert, J. "Les Vins du Mâconnais." *Les Etudes rhodaniennes* 11 (1935):13–38.

Rodier, Camille. *Le Clos de Vougeot.* Dijon, 1931.

Ross, Samuel B. "The Development of Governmental Protection and Regulation of the French Wine Industry." Ph.D. thesis, University of Pittsburgh, 1931.

Rouille-Courbe, négociant. *15 Oct. 1852. Réception de S.A.I. le Prince Président dans la ville de Tours.* Tours, n. d.

Rousseau, G. *Les Impôts intérieurs d'Etat sur les vins.* Bordeaux, 1903.

Rousseaux, R. "Le Vin à Véron (Yonne) de 1790 à 1851." *Annales, Economies, Sociétés, Civilisation* 9 (1954):150–75.

Saillet, J. "Les Mouvements vignerons de Champagne," *Le Mouvement social,* No. 67 (April-June 1969):79–88.

Sempé, Henri. *Régime économique du vin.* Bordeaux, 1898.

Simon, André L. *The History of Champagne.* London, 1962.

Sittler, Lucien. *La Viticulture et le vin de Colmar à travers les siècles.* Paris, 1956.

Smith, J. Harvey. "Village Revolution: Agricultural Workers of Cruzy (Hérault), Ph.D. thesis, University of Wisconsin, 1972.

―――― "Work Routine and Social Structure in a French Village: Cruzy (Hérault) in the 19th Century," *Journal of Interdisciplinary History* 5 (1975):357–82.

Société des Viticulteurs de France et d'Ampelographie. Congrès international de viticulture, 13–17 juin, 1900, Paris. *Compte rendu* . . . Paris, 1900

Sutaine, Max. *Essai sur l'histoire des vins de la Champagne.* Reims, 1845.

Syndicat Agricole et Viticole de Mâcon. Congrès national viticole de Macon. *Compte rendu in extenso des travaux du congrès, 20–23 octobre, 1887.* Paris et Mâcon, 1888.

Syndicat du commerce des vins de champagne. *Compte rendu des travaux de la chambre syndicale, pendant l'exercice annuel.* Reims, 1899–1913.

Thiébaut de Berneaud, Arsène. *The Vine Dresser's Theoretical and Practical Manuel.* 2d ed. New York, 1829.

Thuillier, G. *Aspects de l'économie nivernaise au XIXe siècle.* Paris, 1966.

Tilly, Charles. *The Vendée.* Cambridge, Mass., 1964.

Toutain, J.-C. *Le Produit de l'agriculture française de 1700 à 1958: La croissance.* Paris, 1961.

Tovey, Charles. *Champagne, Its History, Manufacture, Properties.* London, 1870.

[Turgon]. *Etablissement Moët et Chandon.* Epernay. n. d.

Turpin, E. *Les Vignes et les vins du Berry.* Paris, 1907.

Vallery-Radot, René. *Life of Pasteur.* Garden City, N. Y., n. d.

Vavasseur, Charles. *La Touraine et ses vins.* Poitiers, 1933.

Vergnette-Lamotte, A. de. *Le Vin.* Paris, 1867.

Vermorel, Victor. *Traité général de viticulture.* Paris, 1901–10. 7 vols.

Vermorel, V. and Danguy, R. *Les Vins du Beaujolais, Mâconnais et Chalonnais.* Dijon, 1893.

Vernier, Pierre. *De l'Evolution du commerce des vins de Champagne.* Paris, 1923.

Viala, Pierre. *Les Maladies de la vigne.* 3d ed. Montpellier, 1893.

Vidalenc, Jean. "Notes sur la vigne en France de 1789 à la fin de la Restauration." *Annales de la Faculté des lettres d'Aix* 29 (1955):139–76.

Vignobles et vins d'Aquitaine. Bordeaux, 1970.

Vignaud, Jean. *Terre ensorcelée.* Paris, 1906.

Vizetelly, Henry. *History of Champagne.* London, 1882.

Wagret, P. and Le Theule, J. "Deux monographies du vignoble français: Le Vin à Véron de 1790 à 1851; le vin du Layon." *Annales, économies, sociétés, civilisations* 9 (1954):166–88.

Warner, Charles K. *The Winegrowers of France and the government since 1875.* New York, 1960.

Worms, René. *Les Associations agricoles.* Paris, 1914.

Yoxall, H. W. *The Wines of Burgundy.* New York, 1970.

ITALY

Albertoni, P. and Novi, I. *Sul bilancio rustico del contadino italiano.* Bologna, 1893.

Arcari, Paolo. "Le Variazioni dei salari agricoli in Italia dalla fondazione del regno al 1933." *Annali di statistica* s. 6, 36 (1936).

Archivio Centrale dello Stato, Roma. *L'Inchiesta sulle condizioni sociali della Sicilia, 1875–76.* Bologna, 1968–69. 2 vols.

Bachi, Riccardo. *L'Italia economica nell'anno 1909.* Turin, 1910.

Bagiotti, Tullio. *Storia economica della Valtellina e Valchiavenna.* Sondrio, 1955.

Bassi, Agostino. *Memoria sui nuovi metodi di vinificazione.* Lodi, 1823.

―――― *Nuova maniera di fabbricare il vino a tino coperto senza l'uso di alcuna macchina.* Lodi, 1824.

Berengo, Marino. *L'Agricoltura veneta dal Risorgimento all' unità.* Milan, 1963.

Beretta, Giuseppe. *Della coltivazione delle viti e dell' arte da fare il vino.* Verona, 1841.

Bizzarri, A. *Sull' operazione che in Toscano appellarsi governo dei vini.* Milan, 1877.

―――― *Del vino da pasto toscano.* Florence, 1858.

Bocchio, G. *Gli Spari contro la grandine.* Brescia, 1900.

Bodrero, P. *Sulla Statistica italiana del commercio con l'estero.* Rome, 1914.

Bonelli, F. "Il Commercio estero dello stato pontifico nel secolo XIX." *A. E. U. I.,* s. 1, 9 (1961):190–243.

Boschiero, Giovani. *Relazione sulla industria dei vini.* Alessandria, 1873.

Bracco, G. "Produzione e commercio dei vini piemontesi nei secoli XVIII e XIX." *A. C. H. S.* s. 1, 3 (1972):163–80.

Brancato, F. *La Sicilia nel primo ventennio del Regno d'Italia.* Bologna, 1956.

Bulferetti, Luigi and Luraghi, R. *Agricoltura, industria e commercio in Piemonte dal 1814 al 1848.* Turin, 1966. 2 vols.

Caballo, Ernesto. *Storia della Cinzano,* Turin, 1957.

Caizzi, Andrea. *Terra, vigneto e uomini nelle colline novaresi durante l'ultimo secolo.* Turin, 1969.

Candeloro, Giorgio. *Storia dell'Italia moderna.* Milan, 1960–.

Cantamessa, Filippo. *Sulle condizioni presenti della produzione vinicola italiana: conferenza.* Rome, 1892.

Capanna, Alberto and Messeri, R. *Gli Scambi commerciali dell' Italia con l'estero.* Rome, 1940.

Capilupi, A. *I Vini mantovani dell'anno 1887.* Mantua, 1888.

Caracciolo, A. *L'Inchiesta agraria Jacini.* Turin, 1958.

Carocci, G. *Agostino Depretis e la politica interna italiana dal 1876 al 1887.* Turin, 1956.

Carolis, Carlo de. *La Cooperazione agraria in Italia.* Rome, 1927.

Cerletti, Giovanni B. *Produzione, consumo e commercio del vino in Italia.* Milan, 1876.

―――― *Notes sur l'industrie et le commerce du vin en Italie.* Rome, 1889.

Cinelli, Origene. *Quanto costa l'uva ed il vino? Studi di economia rurale.* Rome, 1882.

Cinquanta anni di vita italiana, 1896–1946. Naples, 1950. 2 vols.

Coletti, Francesco. *La Popolazione rurale in Italia.* Piacenza, 1925.

Congresso (Primo) enologico italiano. Turin, 1875. *Atti.* Turin, 1875.

Croce, G. B. *Della eccellenza e diversità dei vini che nella montagna di Torino si fanno.* Turin, 1606.

D'Adda, Egidio. *Vino e suoi effetti: Conferenza d'igiene.* Piacenza, 1891.

Dalmasso, Giovanni. *La Cooperazione enologica in Piemonte.* Turin, 1966.

Dandolo, Vincenzo. *Enologia ovvero l'arte di fare conservare e far viaggiare i vini del regno.* Milan, 1812. 2 vols.

Da Schio, Giulio. *Enologia e viticoltura della provincia di Vicenza.* Vicenza, 1925.

De-Bosis, Francesco. *La Esposizione ampelografica marchigiana-abruzzese.* Ancona, 1873.

De Cesare, Carlo. *Delle Condizioni economiche e morali delle classi agricole nelle tre province di Puglia.* Naples, 1859.

De Felice, F. *L'Agricoltura in Terra di Bari dal 1880 al 1914.* Milan, 1971.

Demarco, D. *Il Tramonto dello stato pontifico. Il Papato di Gregorio XVI.* Turin, 1949.

De Rosa, Luigi. "Produzione e commercio dei vini nel meridione nei secoli XVIII e XIX." *A.C.H.S.*, s. 1, 3 (1972):181–206.

Devincenzi, Giuseppe. *Della Società dei viticoltori italiani e della richezza nazionale.* Rome, 1885.

De Viti de Marco, A. *Un Trentennio di lotte politiche, 1894–1922.* Rome, 1930.

Di Cossato, Giulio. *Note statistiche, circondario d'Asti.* Asti, 1897.

Di Nola, Carlo. *Politica economica e agricoltura in Toscana nei secoli XV–XIX.* Rome, 1948.

Direzione Generale dell'Agricoltura. *Notizie e studi sull'agricoltura.* Rome, 1892.

L'Economia italiana dal 1861 al 1961. Milan, 1961.

Fabbroni, Adamo. *Dell'Arte di fare il vino ragionamente.* Florence, 1790.

Farolfi, B. *Strumenti e pratiche agrarie in Toscana dall'età napoleonica all'unità.* Milan, 1969.

Felice, Renzo. *Aspetti e momenti della vita economica di Roma e del Lazio nei secoli XVIII e XIX.* Rome, 1965.

Felloni, G. "I Prezzi sul mercato di Torino dal 1815 al 1890." *A. E. U. I.* 5 (1957):1–34.

Fiorese, Sabino. *Storia della crisi economica in Puglia dal 1887 al 1897.* Trani, 1900.

Focardi, Orazio. *I Partiti politici alle elezioni generale dell' 1895.* Rome, 1895.

———— *La Produzione, i prezzi ed il commercio dei vini in Italia nel quinquennio 1888–1892.* Rome, 1893.

Fortuna, A. *Sul Congresso enologico di Firenze nel settembre 1877.* Rome, 1878.

Franchetti, L. *Condizioni economiche ed amministrative delle province napoletane, abruzzi e molise, calabrie e basilicata.* Florence, 1875.

Friz, G. "Produzione e commercio dei vini del Lazio nei secoli XVIII e XIX," *A.C.H.S.*, s.1, 3 (1972):207–228.

Frojo, G. *Il Presente e l'avvenire dei vini d'Italia.* Naples, 1876.

———— *Sul Miglior modo di coltivare la vite in Italia.* Genoa, 1871.

Fuà, G. ed. *Lo Sviluppo economico in Italia.* 2d ed. Milan, 1975.

Gagliardo, G. B. *Del Vino, mode di fabbricarlo e conservarlo.* 3d ed. Naples, 1822.

Garoglio, P. G. "Pasteur e Fabbroni." *Italia agricola* 100 (1963):729–38.

Gerini, Carlo. *Monografia della viticoltura in Valtellina.* Rome, 1883.

Ghiglia, F. *La Viticoltura italiana e i suoi bisogni.* Acqui, 1878.

Ghisleni, P. L. *Le Coltivazioni e la tecnica agricola in Piemonte dal 1831 al 1861.* Turin, 1961.

Gianoli, Carlo. *Il Vino di Ghemme e le sue qualità igieniche.* Varallo, 1904.

Giunta Parlamentare per la Inchiesta Agraria. *Atti.* Rome, 1881–86.

Glazier, Ira. "Il Commercio estero del regno lombardo-veneto dal 1815 al 1865." *A. E. U. I.* s. 1, 15 (1966):1–314.

Glazier, Ira A., V. N. Bandera, and R. B. Berner, "Terms of Trade between Italy and the United Kingdom, 1815–1913," *The Journal of European Economic History* 4 (Spring 1975):5–48.

Glazier, Ira A. and Vladimir N. Bandera, "Terms of Trade between South Italy and the United Kingdom, 1817–1869," *The Journal of European Economic History* 1 (Spring 1972):7–36.

Graziani, A. "Il Commercio estero del regno delle Due Sicilie dal 1832 al 1858," *A. E. U. I.*, s. 1, 10 (1960):1–88.

Guffanti, Angelo. *L'Avvenire viticolo ed enologico d'Italia.* Milan, 1877.

Guida vinicola per la provincia di Cuneo. Cuneo, 1903.

Huber, Vincenzo. *Saggio di enologia pratica.* Milan, 1824.

Imberciadori, Ildebrando. *Economia toscana nel primo ottocento, . . . 1815–61.* Florence, 1961.

Istituto Centrale di Statistica. *Sommario di statistiche storiche italiane, 1861–1955.* Rome, 1958.

Izzo, Luigi. *Storia delle relazioni commerciali tra l'Italia e la Francia dal 1860 al 1875.* Naples, 1965.

Lavizzari, Adele. "La Coltivazione della vite e la produzione e commercio del vino . . . Valtellinesi." Tesi di Laurea, Università di Milano, 1953–54.

Lémonon, E. *L'Italie économique et sociale, 1861–1912.* Paris, 1913.

Lissone, Sebastiano. *Condizioni sociali e economiche della gente di campagna.* Rome, 1905.

———— *I Vini d'Italia.* Turin, 1907.

Luraghi, Raimondo. "Problemi economici dell'Italia unita, 1861–1918," *N. Q. S. R.* 2:389–428.

Maddalena, Aldo. "I Prezzi dei generi commestibili e dei prodotti agricoli sul mercato di Milano dal 1800 al 1890," *A. E. U. I* s. 1, 5 (1957):1–35.

Maestri, Peitro. *L'Italie économique en 1867.* Florence, 1868.

Maggioni, Nereo. *L'Enotecnia nel Veronese.* Lagnago, 1903.

Malenotti, Ignazio. *Manuale del vignaiolo toscano.* Florence, 1831.

Mancini, Camillo. *Il Lazio viticolo e vinicolo.* Citta di Castello, 1888.

Manzi, Arcangelo. *Il Vino: urgente bisogno di un credito industriale e vinicolo in Italia.* Naples, 1893.

Marescalchi, Arturo. *G. A. Ottavi e i 50 anni del "Coltivatore."* Casale Monferrato, 1904.

———— *Le Leggi sui vini spiegate popolarmente.* Casale Monferrato, 1908.

———— and Dalmasso, J. *Storia della vite e del vino in Italia.* Milan, 1932–37. 3 vols.

Melis, F. "Produzione e commercio dei vini italiani (con particolare riferimento alla Toscane) nei secoli XIII–XVIII," *A. C. H. S.*, s. 1, 3 (1972):107–33

Mengarini, Flavio. *La Viticoltura e l'enologia nel Lazio.* Rome, 1888.

M. F. Direzione generale del demanio e delle tasse sugli affari. *Bollettino di statistica e di legislazione comparativa.* Rome, 1901–.

———— Direzione generale delle gabelle. *Movimento commerciale del Regno d'Italia.* Turin, 1860–.

M. A. I. C. *Inchiesta parlamentare sulle condizioni dei contadini nelle provincie meridionali e nella Sicilia.* Rome, 1909. 8 vols.

———— Direzione generale dell'agricoltura. *Cantine sociali ed associazioni di produttori di vino.* Rome, 1908.

———— *I Vini italiani, Piemonte.* Rome, 1914.

———— Direzione generale della statistica. *Annuario statistico italiano.* Turin and Rome, 1863–.

———— *Statistica delle elezioni generali politiche.* Rome, 1876–.

———— Istituto centrale di statistica. *Annuario statistico italiano.* Rome, 1878–.

———— Ufficio del lavoro. *Materiali per lo studio delle relazioni tra le classi agrarie in Romagna, 1905–10.* Rome, 1910.

Mondini, S. *L'Industria dei vini Marsala in Sicilia.* Riposto, 1896.

———— *Produzione e commercio del vino in Italia.* Milan, 1899.

Monteregale, Giovanni. "Sul Commercio dei vini del Piemonte." *Repertorio d'agricoltura e di scienze economiche ed industriali del medico Rocco Ragazzoni.* Turin, 1835.

Morandi, Carlo. *I Partiti politici nella storia d'Italia.* Florence, 1963.

Moscati, Ruggero. *Il Mezzogiorno d'Italia nel Risorgimento.* Florence, 1953.

Necco, Achille. *La Curva dei prezzi delle merci in Italia negli anni 1881–1909.* Turin, 1910.

Nicosia, Giuseppe. *Cantine sociali e cooperazione viti-vinicola.* 2d ed. Rome, 1935.

Onorati, Nicola. *Memoria sul miglioramento di vini napoletani.* Naples, 1808.

Ottavi, Edoardo. *Vino ed olio nei trattati di commercio colle potenze centrali.* Casale, 1901.

———— *Gli Spari contro grandine in Stiria.* Casale, 1899.

Ottavi, E. and Marescalchi, A. *Guida vinicola della Toscana.* Casale, 1902.

Ottavi, Giuseppe. *Eureka! Eureka! Nuovo metodo per fare fruttificare abbondamente le viti.* Casale, 1878.

Ottavi, Ottavio and Strucchi, A. *Enologia: Precetti ad uso degli enologi italiani.* 5th ed. Milan, 1904.

Parenti, G. "Il Commercio estero del Granducato di Toscana dal 1851 al 1859." *A. E. U. I.* s. 1, 8 (1958):1–71.

Paronetto, Lamberto. *Chianti: The Story of Florence and Its Wines.* London, 1970.

Paulsen, Frederico. "Histoire de l'invasion phylloxérique et de la reconstitution du vignoble en Italie." *R. V.* 78, nos. 2010–2018 (1933).

Pellegrini, M. *Le condizioni economiche, sociali, culturali e politiche di Jesi dal 1849 al 1859.* Jesi, 1957.

Petino, Antonio. "I prezzi di alcuni prodotti agricoli sui mercati di Palermo e di Catania dal 1801 al 1890." *A. E. U. I.* s. 1, 8 (1959):1–22.

Piétri, F.-J. *La Question des vins en Italie et l'antagonisme du Nord et du Sud.* Paris, 1906.

Pisacane, Giuliano. *La Crisi vinicola delle Puglie.* Milan, 1892.

Plebano, Achille. *Storia della finanza italiana nei primi quarant' anni dell'unificazione.* Padua, 1960.

Raffiotta, Giovanni. *La Sicilia nel primo ventennio del secolo XX.* Palermo, 1959.

Ramazzini, Enrico. *Brevi parole sulle viti, uve, mosti e vino del modenese.* Modena, 1884.

Ratti, Ranato. *Della Vigna e del vino nell'albese.* Turin, 1971.

Rebaudengo, Dina. *I Vini del Piemonte.* Turin, 1966.

Ricaldone, Giuseppe Aldo. *Barbera, storia e nobiltà di un vino.* Asti, 1971.

Ricasoli, Bettino. *Bettino Ricasoli, agricoltore.* Florence, 1950.

Rodolico, Niccolo. *Il Popolo agli inizi del Risorgimento nell' Italia meridionale, 1789–1801.* Florence, 1925.

Romani, Mario. *L'Agricoltura in Lombardia dal periodo delle Riforme al 1859.* Milan, 1957.

———— *Un Secolo di vita agricola in Lombardia, 1861–1961.* Milan, 1963.

—— "Produzione e commercio dei vini in Lombardia nei secoli XVIII e XIX," *A.C.H.S.* s. 1., 3(1972):135–64.

Romano, Salvatore. *Le Classi sociali in Italia dal medioevo all'età contemporanea.* Turin, 1965.

—— *L'Italia del novecento.* Rome, 1968.

—— *La Sicilia nell'ultimo ventennio del secolo XIX.* Palermo, 1958.

—— *Storia dei fasci siciliani.* Bari, 1959.

Rossi, G. *Vera causa per cui i vini toscani vanno sempre più deprezzando.* Pisa, 1841.

—— *Memoria diretta a variare sistema sulla fattura dei vini.* Pisa, 1831.

Rovasenda, G. *Saggio di una ampelografa universale.* Turin, 1877.

Salvemini, Gaetano. *Opere.* Milan, 1961–.

Sannino, F. *Lezioni di legislazione enologica.* Alba, 1920.

Santangelo-Spoto, I. *La Questione enologica in Sicilia.* Palermo, 1888.

Scala, E. *Storia della vite e del vino.* Turin, 1925.

Schepis, Giovanni, *Le Consultazioni popolari in Italia dal 1848 al 1957. Profilo storico-statistico.* Empoli, 1958.

Schiavi, Alessandro. *Come hanno votato gli elettori italiani.* Milan, 1914.

Sereni, Emilio. *Il Capitalismo nelle campagne, 1860–1900.* Turin, 1947.

Serristori, L., ed. *Statistica dell'Italia.* Florence, 1839.

Sindacato vinicolo Piemontese, Alba. *Congresso nazionale per la tutela delle denominazioni di origine dei vini tipici italiani.* Alba, 1909.

Società Generale dei Viticoltori Italiana. *Carta vinicola d'Italia.* Rome, 1887.

Sommario . . . See Istituto Centrale di Statistica.

Sormani, G. *Catalogo ragionato delle opere di viticoltura ed enologiche,* Milan, 1883.

Spaggiari, P. L. *L'Agricoltura negli stati parmensi dal 1750 al 1859.* Milan, 1966.

—— "I Prezzi dei generi di maggior consumo sul mercato di Parma dal 1821 al 1890." A. E. U. I. s. 1, 8 (1959):1–24.

Stringher, B. "Gli Scambi con l'estero e la politica commerciale italiana dal 1860 al 1910." *C. A. S. I.* vol. 3.

Strucchi, Arnaldo. *Biografia di insigni agronomi Piemontesi.* Turin, 1885.

—— *Dei Mezzi atti a dare magior sviluppo all'industria dei vini in Italia.* Turin, 1893.

—— *L'Enologia piemontese.* 2d ed. Alba, 1904.

—— *L'Industria dei vini spumanti in Italia.* 3d ed. Turin, 1891.

—— *Il Vermouth di Torino.* Casale Monferrato, 1907.

Ufficio di Statistica Agraria. *La Produzione dell'uva e del vino in Italia . . . 1909–1920.* Rome, 1921.

—— *Il Vino in Italia.* Rome, 1914.

Valeri, Nino, ed. *La Lotta politica in Italia, dall'unità al 1925.* 4th ed. Florence, 1966.

Verri, Carlo. *Saggio di agricoltura pratica sulla coltivazione dei gelsi e delle viti.* Brescia, 1803.

Vianello, A. and Carpenè, A. *La Vite ed il vino nella provincia di Treviso.* Turin, 1874.

Villari, Rosario. "L'Economia degli stati italiani dal 1815 al 1848." *N. Q. S. R.* 1:607–48.

—— *Mezzogiorno e contadini nell'età moderna.* Bari, 1962.

Villifranchi, Cosimo. *Oenologia toscana.* Florence, 1773.

Il Vino, undici conferenze. Turin, 1880.

La Vite ed il vino nella provincia di Alessandria: Guida vinicola. Casale, 1911.
Voglino, Pietro. *La Fillossera in Italia.* Casale Monferrato, 1899.
Zangheri, R. ed. *Le Campagne emiliane nell'epoca moderna.* Milan, 1957.
Zuccagni Orlandini, Attilio. *Ricerche statistiche sul Granducato di Toscana.* Florence, 1848–58. 5 vols.

Index